Tobacco Control in China

Gonghuan Yang

Editor

Tobacco Control in China

 Springer

Editor
Gonghuan Yang
Department of Epidemiology and Biostatistics
Institute of Basic Medical Sciences
Chinese Academy of Medical Sciences
Beijing
China

ISBN 978-981-10-8314-3   ISBN 978-981-10-8315-0   (eBook)
https://doi.org/10.1007/978-981-10-8315-0

Library of Congress Control Number: 2018940525

Printed on acid-free paper

This Springer imprint is published by the registered company Springer Nature Singapore Pte Ltd. part of Springer Nature
The registered company address is: 152 Beach Road, #21-01/04 Gateway East, Singapore 189721, Singapore

Foreword

About 6 years ago, I prefaced the *Tobacco Control and China's Future: Chinese and Foreign Expertise Joint Assessment Report on Tobacco Use and Control in China* compiled by Professors Yang GH and Hu AG to promote tobacco control in China. The Joint Assessment Report suggested that "Government leaders and officials to take the lead in banning smoking in indoor public places as the exemplary role." As a result, the General Office of the Central Committee of the Communist Party of China (CPC) and the General Office of the State Council issued a joint document on promoting smoke-free public places, requiring government leaders and officials to take the lead in banning smoking in all public places in December 2013. The policy also directed government officials to take the lead in abiding by the existing smoke-free laws, to promote awareness about the harms of smoking and the importance of tobacco control, and to ban smoking and tobacco products from all government functions and events. In May 2015, China's Ministry of Finance announced an increase in tobacco taxation. China has also recently adopted stronger restrictions on tobacco advertising in the National Advertising Law, which came into effect on September 1, 2015. All these show that China has made some progress on tobacco control over the past few years. However, tobacco control in China is still far behind compared to most countries in the world. The efforts on tobacco control are far from enough to control the severe epidemic of tobacco use in China.

By telling either successful or failed stories, *Tobacco Control in China* by Professor Yang GH reviews the history of tobacco control in the past 30 years in the country. This book provides an important perspective of understanding tobacco control for sustainable development when the Chinese economy comes to a new normal. In the meanwhile, it emphasizes the importance of system building when the shadow of pure profits pursuing tobacco industry stands in the way. The five key conclusions and eight recommendations provided in the book are crucial.

In my view, the final goal of our work is to improve the whole environment of public health when the economy is under the transformation of development models. Thanks to the experts group headed by Professor Yang GH and the team's hard work, this book has been completed with academic excellence. It is certainly a contribution for recording the history of tobacco control in China as an important part of public health in China.

Qide Han, M.D.
Peking University Health Science Center
Beijing, China

Chinese Medical Association
Beijing, China

Foreword

Tobacco Control Is Good for Building a Healthy and Prosperous China

Documenting the history and current situation of tobacco control in China is a necessary but major undertaking. One in every three cigarettes smoked in the world is smoked in China, and if the global tobacco epidemic is to be reduced, reducing the number of smokers in China is central to any success.

Tobacco control in China, the world's largest producer and consumer of tobacco, has a long history—it began in the 1980s with the first national prevalence survey and a conference on tobacco held in Tianjin. Since then, there have been dozens of research papers, partial restrictions on smoking and tobacco advertising, public education campaigns, and the ratification of the World Health Organization Framework Convention on Tobacco Control, but progress has been slow. As is pointed out in this book, the state-owned tobacco industry remains a major obstacle to tobacco control. Other obstacles include misperceptions about the economic importance of tobacco to China. Studies in China have clearly shown that when farmers switch to other crops, they earn far more than from growing tobacco. There are other major financial debits from tobacco, ranging from the cost of fires caused by careless smoking, the huge amount of litter that must be collected and disposed of every day, the use of land that could grow food, as well as the economic impact on smokers and their families with income diverted to buy cigarettes that could be used for family food, health, education, greater sickness, time off work, and premature death; and the economic impact of secondhand smoke on smokers' families and coworkers.

In the last few years, tobacco control efforts have accelerated. The Chinese Central Party School, the ideological think tank of the Communist Party, published a tome on tobacco in 2013. This was followed by a spate of activity: directives to government officials; regulations issued by the Ministry of Education, the People's Liberation Army, and the Healthy City Standards; tobacco clauses in national advertising and philanthropy laws; the creation of a smoke-free Beijing, Shanghai, and

Shenzhen; an increase in tobacco taxation; and a national smoke-free law currently (and for a long time) in draft.

There is a crucial need for China to build upon these recent developments in accepting the economic research evidence of the debit of tobacco to the Chinese economy; in implementing robust, comprehensive legislation; in increasing cigarette price through taxation; and, most challenging of all, in tackling the power and influence of the state tobacco monopoly over tobacco control.

I would like to congratulate Professor Yang Gonghuan and the chapter authors on compiling such a comprehensive history of tobacco control in China. Let us hope its main effect will be a wake-up call to implement ever stronger tobacco control policies. The health and economic knowledge is here; this book is a call to action.

Judith Mackay
Asian Consultancy on Tobacco Control
Hong Kong, SAR China

Vital Strategies, New York
NY, USA

World Health Organization
Geneva, Switzerland

Foreword

I first met Professor Yang Gonghuan and learned about the enormity of China's tobacco epidemic in 1995 when I made my first visit to China. Although long involved in tobacco control in the United States, my work outside of the United States had been quite limited. My visit was at the request of fellow Johns Hopkins faculty member Dr. Carl Taylor, a giant in global health who had been the UNICEF representative to China in the 1980s. Several of his Chinese colleagues from that time were involved with initiating the Chinese Association on Smoking and Health or CASH (now the Chinese Association on Tobacco Control or CATCH) and one was the Minister of Health—Chen Minzhang. China was to be the host for the 1997 World Conference on Tobacco, and with anticipation of that conference, CASH and Minister Chen hoped to showcase national activities in tobacco control and to present findings from a new national survey on smoking, the last being carried out in 1984. Professor Yang was charged with leading these efforts but had extraordinarily limited resources to do so.

While great progress was being made in tobacco control in the United States in the 1990s, the scale of the tobacco epidemic in China was obvious and comparable to the situation in the United States in the 1950s, and China-wide tobacco control efforts had not yet been initiated. In China, at the time of my first visit, the majority of men were daily smokers of cigarettes, although only a few percent of women were smoking; clean indoor air laws were lacking; and cigarettes were engrained in the social environment as a positive. Cigarettes were given as gifts and offered to visitors; being naïve to China, I was shocked when the Deputy Director of the Chinese Academy of Preventive Medicine offered me a cigarette when we first met.

From this visit, Professor Yang and I forged a collaborative bond based around our passion for tobacco control and the mutual anticipation that our work could help reduce tobacco consumption in China. Earlier, Judith Mackay and Richard Peto had repeatedly called attention to the dangerous, emerging epidemic of tobacco use in China and the need for government action to avoid the inevitable wave of cancer and other smoking-caused diseases. Since 1995, the partnership between Professor Yang and her colleagues at Peking Union Medical Center and the China CDC, and my colleagues at the Johns Hopkins Bloomberg School of Public Health and myself, has flourished, resulting in surveys of active and passive smoking, assessment of cotinine (the nicotine biomarker) in Chinese smokers, measurements of airborne nicotine in indoor spaces, and population-level tobacco control interventions. Together, we received funding from the Fogarty International Center of the US National Institutes of Health, the Bloomberg Philanthropies, and other funders.

Professor Yang has been insistent on looking for opportunities to affect policy through research findings. Early on, we thought that sufficient insights had been gained into patterns of smoking in China and the health consequences of smoking to develop a national plan for action. Such a plan was an outcome of a meeting held in 2000 that was developed collaboratively with CASH, the Ministry of Health, and the World Health Organization. While the plan was reasonable, action did not follow.

This book, *Tobacco Control in China*, explains why the plan did not lead to action. It sets out the complexities of tobacco control in China that have too often stymied evidence-based actions to control cigarette smoking. The government, through the State Tobacco Monopoly Association, *is the tobacco industry*, generating still substantial revenues from the sale of tobacco products. The existence of state monopoly is a fundamental barrier to tobacco control and an unavoidable consideration in developing national strategies. Nonetheless, progress has been made, China long ago signed and ratified the WHO Framework Convention on Tobacco Control (WHO FCTC). China has moved forward on its commitments through the WHO FCTC, and tobacco control capacity has greatly expanded since 1995 when national capacity comprised Professor Yang and a few junior colleagues. The prevalence of smoking among males has dropped from about 65% to just over 50%, and smoking has not risen among women. Some cities are now smoke-free, including Beijing and Shanghai, and smoke-free laws are being followed, unlike the past when smokers were noncompliant.

Looking forward there is still much to be done, and the full armamentarium of tobacco control measures has not yet been used, in part because the China National Tobacco Corporation is a national monopoly. *Tobacco Control in China* addresses key issues related to continuing to advance tobacco control in China. In describing the scope of the tobacco epidemic and its consequences, it leaves no doubt as to the necessity of moving forward aggressively to curb tobacco use. It sets out a blueprint for action, based around the FCTC, that should be followed. The reach of the book should be broad and it should be read not only by the tobacco control and public health communities, but also by the policymakers within the government who need to understand that profits are being made at a high cost to public health.

Looking back, one of the greatest legacies of the collaboration with Professor Yang has been the capacity-building efforts funded by the Fogarty International Center and then Bloomberg Philanthropies. I am delighted to see some of the trainees from these efforts among the contributors to this book. I congratulate the tobacco control community in China, long led by Professor Yang, for its persistence and its successes. There is still work to be done and this book, *Tobacco Control in China*, will be an invaluable resource for the future in continuing to push for an end to epidemic tobacco use in China.

Jonathan M. Samet
Colorado School of Public Health
Denver, CO, USA

Foreword

When China ratified and brought into force the WHO Framework Convention on Tobacco Control (FCTC) in January 2006, the vision of a tobacco-free world could be finally visualized.

After all, China, with 1.3 billion people, is the world's largest producer, consumer, and manufacturer of tobacco, accounting for 40% of global production or 2.5 trillion cigarettes annually. More than 50% of Chinese adult men are smokers. China has more than 300 million smokers and 740 million nonsmokers exposed to secondhand smoke. In China, tobacco is arguably the biggest driver of the huge burden of noncommunicable diseases. Tobacco is estimated to cause more than one million premature deaths, projected to reach two million by 2030 and three million by 2050.

In this volume, Professor Yang Gonghuan and her colleagues mobilize the highest quality scientific evidence to describe the tobacco story in China. Driven by a quiet passion, the authors tell thestory of how China's tobacco control movement is struggling to protect and advance the health of the Chinese people. In 14 chapters, they comprehensively examine the evidence of tobacco control in contemporary China. Many forces, some very powerful, will have to be overcome. The gap is not lack of awareness, nor is scientific evidence lacking. Instead, the authors analyze the "deep factors" of institutional, economic, cultural, and political systems that influence tobacco in China.

Pro-tobacco interest groups, as in all countries, push back against tobacco control. In China, tobacco is a profit-making government monopoly. In 2015, the tobacco industry contributed Rmb1.1 trillion to the central government, constituting 6.5% of state revenues. At every turn, the responsible governmental units have pushed back against protection from secondhand smoke; helping quitting; cigarette package warnings; product regulations; banning of advertising, promotion, and sponsorship; and raising the tobacco tax. This is why there has hardly been progress during the first 5 years of FCTC. China, it is estimated, stood at the bottom 20% of nations implementing WHO FCTC. After 2015, some positive policies have been developed, especially in expanding smoke-free public places.

To build upon recent successes, the authors draw some major conclusions and recommendations. Most important is political commitment from national leaders. A promising start was the 2016 pledge by President Xi at the National Health Conference of "health in all policies," which led to the Central Communist Party and the State Council to expand smoke-free public places. China must transition from a "health-hazard economy" to a "health-friendly economy." China should vigorously comply with the WHO FCTC. While some progress may be observed, big gaps remain. Priorities are smoke-free laws for all indoor public and working places; a national plan of tobacco control 2016–2020; strengthening public education; educating doctors and medical professionals; and regularly monitoring and evaluating progress.

Most important is to moderate the pro-tobacco interest groups, which includes a combination of government and enterprise. Compliance with the WHO FCTC is all-too-often "games" between health department and tobacco industry. The Steering Committee of the State Tobacco Monopoly Agency should adjust its membership to dampen very influential pro-tobacco forces. To win the war against tobacco, political and financial resources for tobacco control will have to be harnessed. Coalition building and diverse actor groups will have to be mobilized. Especially important are the press/media, civil society organizations, and international reinforcement from the WHO and philanthropy.

Tobacco Control in China is an essential "must-read" for anyone interested in tobacco control, either in China or worldwide. The China tobacco story indeed is the centerpiece of global efforts at tobacco control. The editor, who is a Chinese public health leader, has devoted 25 years to tobacco control. She deserves much applause, along with a dozen contributors, all Chinese from Chinese institutions, for telling China's compelling tobacco story.

Lincoln C. Chen, M.D.
China Medical Board
Beijing, China

Foreword

A Few Words on Tobacco Control

Congratulations to Dr. Yang Gonghuan on the book *Tobacco Control in China* published under her general editorship.

This book records and evaluates tobacco control efforts in China in the last 30 years, especially after the WHO Framework Convention on Tobacco Control (WHO FCTC) came into force in 2005. The book describes major actions to fulfill the FCTC and control tobacco, analyzes difficulties, assesses effectiveness, and gives insights into the future in China, as one of the parties earlier ratifying FCTC. All the achievements and failures are vividly presented to the readers.

Dr. Yang is one of the major investigators as well as a leading promoter and activist of tobacco control in China. She actively took part in developing the WHO FCTC and every stage of its implementation in China. This book is also written by public health, legal, and media experts who study and actually promote tobacco control in China. Therefore, under her general editorship, this book includes both in-depth theoretic analysis and abundant practice and evidence. It plays a crucial part in understanding tobacco control in China, as well as further reducing tobacco use and improving public health.

China is the largest tobacco producer and consumer around the world. The population of current smokers is up to 315 million and comprises 27.7% of all the adult Chinese over 15 years old in 2015. Tobacco use caused about one million (840,000 male; 130,000 female) deaths in China in 2010. This clearly shows the tremendous harm of tobacco use.

All the tobacco control efforts are described in detail in this book, of which I am simply a reader. The reason that Dr. Yang invited me to write a few words for this book may be that I was a smoker once and had successfully quit smoking later. Due to experience from these two aspects, I have my own understanding of the harm of smoking and benefit of quitting.

Currently, there is a tendency to use long history to justify everything, and it seems that the longer the history is, the more justifiable a thing is. This also applies to tobacco use. Both tobacco sellers and smokers often mention this. According to them, long history means it has ever been like this, so it should be taken for granted. This reminds me of Lu Xun's *Madman's Diary*, in which the madman says, "Is it right because it has always been like that?" Besides, the history of smoking is not so long after all. Chinese did not smoke in the past and no tobacco grew in China. In order to prove the history of tobacco, China tobacco industry spent a lot of money and hired many people in the last years to find evidence of long history of tobacco cultivation and use in China. None of these projects are successful, and their money was spent for nothing. Eventually, long history of tobacco is just nonsense. Nevertheless, what difference does a long history make? Tobacco was originally from America and Indians were the first tobacco users. However, despite long smoking history, tobacco control has gathered great momentum in these countries.

Tobacco was imported into China in the mid-late Ming dynasty, and its history is only 3–400 years. Cigarettes were not introduced until the early republic period (i.e., early twentieth century) and gradually became popular. Unexpectedly, in just 100 years, cigarettes are everywhere, China became the world's largest tobacco producer and consumer, and the hazard brought by smoking in China is most severe around the world. Dr. Yang has provided solid evidence in this book. Most Chinese, including senior leaders, do not understand the hazards of tobacco. In the 1950s, when Marshal Kliment Voroshilov of the former Soviet Union visited China, he advised Marshal Chen Yi to quit smoking, but Chen answered, "My smoking is an act of patriotism." This story was widely told once. Recalling this several decades later, although foreign and domestic cigarettes may be different from an economic point of view, the harm of smoking does not differ on the basis of place of origin and country. Back then, the severity of harm from smoking was less understood than today. Eventually, Chen left his beloved country prematurely due to disease related to smoking. Alas!

I started smoking 60 years ago when I was in college. Because everything should "leap forward" and junior students should also work as "scientific research satellites," we had courses in the daytime, while in the night, we read in the library and made cards until we became extremely tired. A tutor in the library stayed with us every night. When he saw me napping on the desk, he walked towards me and knocked on the desk, saying "Chen Siyi, lacking energy?" After seeing my tired face, he offered me a cigarette, saying "Refresh yourself." My first taste of cigarette made me snotty and tearful, but in the meantime painfully refreshed. After the first try, I never said no to others' cigarettes. However, it happened only occasionally, and I was not addicted. I had not been addicted to smoking until the so-called Three Years of Great Chinese Famine. At that time, resources were scarce, and everything required vouchers and was limited. Other than grains, oil, cloth, sugar, etc., a pastry voucher was needed to buy dessert, and of course the same goes to cigarette. Back then, smokers in Shanghai may have one class A cigarette voucher, three class B cigarette vouchers, and six class C cigarette vouchers every month. Class A includes Mudan, Shanghai, Fenghuang, etc.; class B includes Daqianmen, Qingdao, Guangrong, etc.; and class C includes Dalianzhu, Dashengchan, etc. Due to limited quantity, it was rare to share cigarettes, even among friends. However, many occasional smokers also got cigarette vouchers. Although they seldom smoked, vouchers were a good gift. Soon occasional smokers like me became real smokers in the process of sharing cigarettes and because of unwilling to "waste" cigarette vouchers.

The smoking habit is always accompanied by diseases, including catching cold endlessly, constant coughing, emaciating day by day, and recurring lung diseases. However, habits like these are hard to give up; therefore, smokers always delude themselves with "the harm may be exaggerated" and sometimes delude others, too.

I am a literature student, and I know there are many smokers among the literati. For example, many pictures and description by his contemporary friends recorded Lu Xun as a smoker. I used to admire his elegant smoking posture. At that time, the transliteration of inspiration was "烟是笔里春," which means smoking inspires writers. Later on, some said literary works are forged by burning cigarettes. However, I know that I smoke mainly because I am bored when I find difficult to write on. If I were really inspired, there is no time to smoke. Later by scrutinizing Lu Xun's writing, I knew that he was actually deeply troubled by smoking.

"In fact, I am not sick. In the last days, my doctor have done loads of tests from blood to urine, and finally decided that the culprit is too much drinking and smoking but too less sleeping." (Lu Xun 1925, A letter to Xu Qinwen)

"Today I noticed that my hand was shaking slightly, which is caused by heavy smoking. Recently I smoke over 30 cigarettes every day, and I have to reduce it from now on." (Lu Xun 1926, A letter to Xu Guangping)

Such records are plenty and proved that he knew the harm of smoking. However, tobacco is something addictive and hard to abstain once you are addicted. Even a great man like Lu Xun is troubled by smoking. This is the hateful side of tobacco. One major cause of Lu Xun's premature death is heavy smoking, which is supported by scientific assessment by doctors. Until now, China tobacco industry has still been encouraging people to smoke using great men like Lu Xun. This is ridiculous and extremely cruel.

Among literati who smoke, many came to understand the risk of smoking, such as Mr. Liang Shih-chiu. When he attempted to quit, he wrote, "I have been smoking for decades, and finally switched to free fresh air. If someone is smoking in public or even shooting out toxic smog directly to myself, I immediately go away as far as I can, and dismiss himself 'I used to be such a nuisance'." I really hope more people learn from Liang.

I also quitted smoking because of my doctor's advice and my suffering from diseases. After quitting, I regained my strength and vigor, and my lung trouble, which relapsed twice, was also gone with the cigarette.

The WHO Framework Convention on Tobacco Control entered into force in February 2005. The implementation of the Convention will save millions of lives. Chinese government approved to join WHO FCTC, with an intention of saving lives. Of course, ratification was just the beginning, while fulfillment is the actual redemptive. On the one hand, there are hundreds of millions of victims of smoking; on the other hand, interest and tax from tobacco nearly trillion RBM. For Chinese government and top policy makers, how to decide? how to weigh test their wisdom and conscience. Addictiveness of tobacco use means that tobacco control is a long process, while the serious health hazards of tobacco use leave no room for stagnating. Dr. Yang's book objectively evaluates achievements and failures of tobacco control in China. This academic work will definitely draw the attention of the academic community. Moreover, I hope that both leaders and relevant authorities could also pay more attention to this book, because such a public health issue concerning health and lives of billions of Chinese requires not only study and appeal by the academic community, but also real promotion from wise policy decision and forceful action from the government.

As a Buddha quote goes, saving a life exceeds building a seven-storied pagoda. Tobacco control saves not just one life, but also millions of lives. Such merits and virtues would be too great so that the people's government should be duty bound.

Chen Siyi
A retired Senior
editor of Outlook Newsweek

Preface

In October 2015, I received an invitation from Springer to write or compile a book about tobacco control in China. I, as a Chinese public health expert, have been engaged in tobacco control for more than 25 years. The longer I was engaged, the more confused I became. Why can't China make a difference to tobacco control as based on the requirements of the WHO FCTC, like other countries? I decided to review the history of tobacco control in China so as to seek out some answers on why this should be. So, I was very pleased to accept the invitation and compiled this book entitled *Tobacco Control in China.*

Is there a lack of awareness of tobacco control in China? No. The famous experts of China's medical community headed by the Minister of Health, Professor Chen MZ, initiated tobacco control in the early 1990s to set up the Chinese Association of Smoking or Health. China has ratified the WHO Framework Convention on Tobacco Control (FCTC), and it came into force in China on January 8, 2006. Some action has already been taken, and it is not too late for effective tobacco control in China to be implemented.

Is there a lack of evidence on the health hazards of tobacco use in China? No. Since the 1980s, China has initiated several studies on the health hazards of smoking. The findings from several large-scale national case–control or cohort study (research articles published in peer-reviewed international journals) have repeatedly proved that over one million premature deaths annually are induced by tobacco use. This will grow to two million annually by 2030 and three million annually by 2050 unless decisive and immediate action is taken to drastically reduce smoking rates. Tobacco use is a major driver in the rapid increase of noncommunicable diseases, the biggest public health problem and health security issue in China.

Tobacco control in China needs to be appreciated from a broader perspective. For the past 30 years, China has had the largest tobacco industry (Chinese National Tobacco Company)in the world, with over 40% of global tobacco production (2.5 trillion cigarettes). Such a powerful tobacco industry, especially as it is a government department, has the support of the government; thus, the State Tobacco Monopoly Agency has become the major barrier to tobacco control. China's tobacco control would still face a great challenge if the Chinese government does not change its development ideology to align with the WHO FCTC statement that the "Parties to this Convention [are] determined to give priority to their right to protect public health."

Experts and scholars engaged in tobacco control in China were invited to contribute to this book, including scholars from Peking Union Medical College, the University of International Business and Economics, Fudan University, and Chinese Academy of Social Science; experts from China CDC and US CDC; and international and national nongovernment organizations, such as the International Union Against Tuberculosis and Lung Disease and the Think-Tank Health Development Center. They have both theoretical and policy knowledge, as well as in-depth experience in particular areas of tobacco control.

The detailed evidence of the book shows that China's tobacco control has made progress in recent years, but the gap between the Convention and the Convention is still very large and has been lagging behind in the global tobacco control process. The reasons are as follows: (1) Tobacco industry grabbed the partial leading power on tobacco control in China. (2) The development ideology of GDP first restricted the Chinese governor's understanding of the significance of tobacco control and action. (3) Evaluating the performance of Government officials based on GDP made weakness of tobacco control in most governors of China. (4) Political and financial resources restricted the momentum of tobacco control campaign in China. Tobacco control is closely related to national development and people's health and welfare. It needs to carry out eight actions as soon as possible, including the whole society, especially the top leaders, to understand tobacco control from the perspective of China's future development, and strengthen the implementation of the WHO FCTC into the government performance assessment; to adjust the Steering Committee, removing the obstruction of tobacco control; to adopt a strong, comprehensive national smoke-free law urgently to ensure 100% smoke-free in indoor public and working places; to regularly issue the national plan of tobacco control; and so on.

We expect comments from international and domestic experts, advocators, governors, and volunteers concerned with tobacco control, public health, and people's health in China.

Finally, the book *Tobacco Control in China* as a part of study and dissemination of Disease Burden in China has been completed thanks to the support of the China Medical Board' project fund. I would also like to thank the CMB for its continued support.

Gonghuan Yang

Beijing, China
August 4, 2017

Summary of the Book

This book describes tobacco control in China from three aspects, China's attitude and position in the negotiations of WHO FCTC, and the scientific study on the harm of tobacco use for Chinese health impact in the first and the second chapter, trying to explain how the subject of "tobacco control" entered the agenda. The authors discuss how tobacco control to be accepted by the political system and society in China, how to be promoted by the social elite, and how to be assisted by the international community in Chaps. 3–7. Also, how have infrastructure of tobacco control been run in China in these chapters, including social mobilization, capacity building, public education, legal action, and surveillance and evaluation. Authors described the progress, challenges, and tobacco industry interference of a series of policy actions in China, including protection from secondhand smoke, support for smokers to quit, health warnings of cigarette package, tobacco product regulation, and comprehensive ban on all forms of tobacco advertising, promotion and sponsorship, as well as tobacco tax and tobacco economy separately in Chapters 8–13 of the book. In general, the policy progress of tobacco control has been weak during 2006–2010; after 5 years, especially after 2015, there were obvious breakthroughs of policies related to tobacco control in China.

The book provides an important perspective of understanding tobacco control for sustainable development when the Chinese economy comes to a new normal on the basis of analyzing and reviewing the history of tobacco control for 30 years, the book revealed that four main factors restricted the tobacco control in China. These factors are that (1) Tobacco industry grabbed the partial leading power on tobacco control in China; (2) The development ideology of GDP first restricted the Chinese governor's understanding on the significant of tobacco control; (3) Evaluating the performance of Government officials based on GDP made weakness of tobacco control in most provinces of China. (4) Political and financial resources have restricted the momentum of tobacco control campaign in China. The tobacco control will be in priority in China only to change the development ideology. China should focus on eight key issues: (1) To understand tobacco control from China's long term target and Sustainable development goals; (2) To adjust the Steering Committee, removing the obstruction of tobacco control; (3) To adopt a strong, comprehensive national smoke-free law urgently to ensure 100% smoke-free in indoor public and working places; (4) To regularly issue the national plan of tobacco control, and regularly increase tax and price of tobacco product, as well as include helping quit program into the primary health care and medical insurance; (5) To strength public education and place the pictorial warning on the cigarette package; (6) To regularly monitor, evaluate and report progress of tobacco control policy implement; (7) To strengthen capacity building and ensure financial support of tobacco control. (8) To expand the coalition of tobacco control and promote nation-wide tobacco. Fortunately, in 2018, National People's Congress approved the State Council's report on Institutional Reform, and the function of tobacco control has finally shifted from the Ministry of Industry Information to the National Health Commission. The National Health Commission should take the golden opportunity to reset up an effective the Steering Committee and to remove the interference of tobacco industry control.

Keywords: Tobacco control; WHO FCTC; Tobacco industry; China

Contents

About the Authors

Quan Gan is the director of Tobacco Control at the International Union Against Tuberculosis and Lung Disease. He holds a PhD in public health from the University of California at Berkeley with a concentration in tobacco control. Dr. Gan Quan has more than 10 years of experience in tobacco control policy advocacy and research. He joined the Union in 2009 as a technical advisor for tobacco control and was the director of the Union's China Office from 2014 to 2016.

Hanbing Guo is currently research associate at the International Union Against Tuberculosis and Lung Disease China Office. Her work on tobacco control focuses on both research and policy advocacy. She has conducted in-depth investigation into China's e-cigarette industry and collected evidence to lend support to China's proposed national smoke-free legislation. In addition, she helped design and carry out research that provided the scientific basis for the successful passage of the Shanghai smoke-free amendment. She received her Master of Public Health degree from Tufts University School of Medicine in the USA.

Jason Hsia is a senior statistician, from the Division of Population Health, the US Centers for Disease Control and Prevention. His primary interests are chronic diseases related surveillance methodology and applying biostatistics to medical research. He has designed a number of population-based complex surveys in the past 25 years and provided the technical lead in 2010 Global Adult Tobacco Survey, China.

Jie Yang is a Professor of public health. He held a PhD in environment health from Chinese Academy of Military Medical Sciences in 2006. His study focused the tobacco control and Health Law. He worked at the Tobacco Control Office of Chinese Center for Disease Control and Prevention and has been in charge of the tobacco control policy advocacy and promote the legislation of banning smoke in public places at national and local level since 2007.

Jinrong Huang was born in 1974. He is an associate researcher of Institute of Law of Chinese Academy of Social Sciences. His research mainly focuses on legal theory, human rights, and public interest law. His works include *The Limit of Judiciary in Human Rights Protection: A Study on the Justiciability of Economic and Social Rights* (2009), *Textbook on the Domestic Implementation of ICESCR* (Chief editor, 2011), and *Pro Bono Publico: A Study on the Practice of Public Interest Law in China* (coauthored, 2012). He also has been involved in a lot of public interest litigation cases on human rights and tobacco control in China since 2005 as a *pro bono* lawyer.

Pinpin Zheng is the professor and director of Tobacco Control Research Center in Fudan Health Communication Institute. She has been involved, as PI or investigator, in several tobacco control projects funded by the WHO, China National Natural Science, Bloomberg Global Initiative on Tobacco Control, and other international funding agencies. Her research filed in tobacco control includes smoking cessation, smoking prevention among adolescents, tobacco advertisement, tobacco industry monitoring, and health communication among the public.

Xia Wan is an associate professor of the Institute of Basic Medical Science at the Chinese Academy of Medical Sciences/School of Basic Medicine at Peking Union Medical College. She has taken part in four NIH projects, one Bloomberg and three China Medical Board (CMB) projects on tobacco control research. Among them, she is a PI for one NIH and Co-PI for two CMB projects. She has got five awards from Chinese Medical Association, Chinese Preventive Medicine Association, and the Ministry of Education. In addition, she got Global Tobacco Control Alumni Awards for Excellence by the Institute of Global Tobacco Control at JHSPH in 2012, CMB Faculty Development Award in 2013, and the State Scholarship Fund Award in 2014. She has published more than 60 papers in Chinese or English.

Chunhui Wang has more than 10 years of experience in journalism in China. From 2010 to 2014, she started to work at China office of Campaign for Tobacco-Free Kids as a media consultant, providing advice on domestic media advocacy strategies, coordinating and managing campaigns to make sure the policy objectives are achieved in China. During the year of 2014 and 2015, she studied public policy in the UK at King's College of London and obtained master's degree in 2015 and then worked for another year at Campaign for Tobacco-Free Kids as a senior media consultant in 2016. Also, Chunhui Wang has two bachelor's degrees of arts and law from Xi'an University of Arts and Science in 1995 and from China University of Political Science and Law in 1999.

Fan Wang is now the lecturer of School of Public Health, Fudan University. He also serves as the Assistant Director and the Secretary-General of the Health Communication Institute in Fudan University as well as the Communication

Advisory Member of Shanghai Health and Family Planning Commission. Dr. Wang' research interests are doctor–patient communication, health communication, and health mobilization in new media society and especially in tobacco control. He has obtained several research fundings including national social science program and international collaborating projects. Relevant papers were published on SCI journals and news magazines. Recently, he has tried to use psycho-scene drama for adolescent mental health promotion in China.

Lin Xiao works in tobacco control office of China CDC. In past 10 years, she has been involved in many tobacco control projects, such as Global Adult Tobacco Survey, Global Youth Tobacco Survey, China-U.S. Smoke-Free Workplaces Project, Study on tobacco advertisement and its effect on adolescents, International Tobacco Control Policy Evaluation Project, and Promoting Smoke-Free Environment Project. As a technical expert, she took part in the drafting of the National Smoke-Free Law and the Amendment of the National Advertisement Law, and participated in the development of many authoritative reports for tobacco control in China. In addition, she attended many WHO FCTC meetings as a member of the Chinese delegation.

Gonghuan Yang is a professor of public health and a senior epidemiologist. She studies the relationship between the chronic non-communicable diseases and related risk factors, especially tobacco use and environmental pollution. She did a lot of work on tobacco control, including assessing the hazards at an early phase of the growing epidemic of deaths from tobacco in China; organizing the national epidemiological surveys of tobacco use in 1996, 2002, and 2010; and having published the book *Tobacco Control and the Future of China* about performance evaluation on tobacco control policy implementation. She gained six Science and Technology Achievement Awards from the Ministry of Health, Ministry of Education, Chinese Medical Association, and Chinese Preventive Medicine Association. Also, she obtained the World Health Organization Award in recognition of outstanding contribution to tobacco control in 2006.

Yiqun Wu has been the executive director of Think-Tank Research Center for Health Development in Beijing and a professor and vice president at the Chinese Academy of Preventive Medicine. For nearly two decades, she has been a leading force in promoting strong tobacco control policies in China. 2010.5.31 World No Tobacco Day 2010 Award for tobacco control contribution was given by WHO.

Rong Zheng is a tax professor; she leads the WHO Collaborating Center for Tobacco and Economics based in the University of International Business and Economics in Beijing. She has served as a consultant for the World Bank Group and the World Health Organization, and she has been working with several other major global organizations on applying fiscal policies for health promotion in developing countries, particularly on applying taxes on tobacco, alcohol, and sweetened beverage. She has a strong commitment to health improvement and contributed directly to the Chinese tobacco tax reforms in 2009 and 2015 through a number of research projects in collaboration with the Chinese Ministry of Finance and the World Health Organization. In addition to her research and teaching activities, she devotes herself to policy advocacy through training of various administrations, organization of seminars/conferences, and regular interviews with the media.

Abbreviations

BCPHC	Beijing Committee of the Patriotic Health campaign
CAC	Cyberspace Administration of China
CATC	Chinese Association of Tobacco Control
CCHE	Chinese Center for Health Education
CCPPD	Central Publicity Department of the CPC
CFDA	China Food and Drug Administration
China CDC	Chinese Center for Disease Control and Prevention
CNTC	China National Tobacco Corporation
CPCI	China Public Communication Institute of Renmin University
CPHA	Canadian Public Health Association
CPSC	Central Politburo Standing Committee of the Communist Party of China
DSPs	Disease Surveillance Point system
FASC	China Automobile Association
GASC	General Administration of Sport of China
GATS	Global Adult Tobacco Survey
GTSS	Global Tobacco Surveillance System
GYTS	Global Youth Tobacco Survey
HCDC	Handheld Computers Data Collection
ITC	International Tobacco Control Policy Evaluation Project
LAOSC	Legal Affairs Office of the State Council
MIIT	Ministry of Industry and Information Technology
MOA	Ministry of Agriculture
MOCA	Ministry of Civil Affairs
MOE	Ministry of Education
NBQIQ	National Bureau of Quality Inspection and Quarantine
NEDL	National Essential Drug List
NHFPC	National Health and Family Planning Commission
NMLE	National Medical Licensing Examination
NPC	National People's Congress

NPHCC	National Patriotic Health Campaign Committee
PIL	Public interest litigation
PPD	Press and Publicity Department of NHFPC
Research on Counterproposals and Countermeasures	Research on Counterproposals to the WHO FCTC and countermeasures to address its impacts on the Chinese tobacco industry
SAPPRFT	State Administration of Press, Publication, Radio, Film and Television of the People's Republic of China
SHS	Secondhand smoke
SIIO	State Internet Information Office
STA	State Taxation Administration
STMA	State Tobacco Monopoly Administration
TAPS	Tobacco advertising, promotion, and sponsorship
TFI	Tobacco Free Initiative
The Steering Committee	Inter-Ministerial Coordination and Steering Committee for Implementation of WHO Framework Convention on Tobacco Control
Think-Tank	Think-Tank Research Center for Health Development
TQS	Tobacco Questions for Surveys
US CDC	S Centers for Disease Control and Prevention
WHO FCTC	World Health Organization Framework Convention on Tobacco Control
WNTD	World No Tobacco Day

Chapter 1
Introduction: China and the Negotiation of WHO FCTC

Gonghuan Yang

Abstract This chapter, as the introduction of the book *"Tobacco Control in China"*, described the response to the tobacco use pandemic from international public health community so as to understand the tobacco control in China by the international perspective. Tobacco use pandemic is a global problem and must be solved at the global level. It cannot be solved by traditional public health strategy, but should be solved based on the international law at the legal level! WHO Framework Convention on Tobacco Control (WHO FCTC) is the important weapon responding the tobacco pandemic under the Globalization. However, the attitudes and actions of the Chinese government during the negotiations on the WHO FCTC have shown that China's more pursuit of international recognition beyond pursuit of public health and safety, has presaged the setback of the implementation of WHO FCTC in China. Thirdly, the brief review of the tremendous progress made by the most Parties of WHO FCTC over the last 10 years reflects the status of China's tobacco control described in the following chapters as a mirror.

Keywords WHO Framework Convention on tobacco control · Globalization · Negotiation · Implementation · China

1.1 Tobacco Use: A Serious Public Health Problem at a Global Level

In 1951, a cohort study of British physicians on tobacco and health was initiated by Richard Doll and Bradford Hill. The study proved that physicians who were mild smokers were seven times more likely to die of lung cancer than non-smokers, while for 'moderate' smokers, the risk was 24 times higher.[1] By the late 1950s

---

[1] Doll R, Hill AB. The mortality of doctors in relation to their smoking habits: a preliminary report. *British Medical Journal* 1954; **1:**1451–1455.

G. Yang
Institute of Basic Medical Science Chinese Academy of Medical Sciences,
School of Basic Medicine Peking Union Medical College, Beijing, China

© Springer Nature Singapore Pte Ltd. 2018
G. Yang (ed.), *Tobacco Control in China*,
https://doi.org/10.1007/978-981-10-8315-0_1

and early 1960s, the mounting evidences on the health effects of smoking were formally reviewed and evaluated by government committees. In the United Kingdom, the 1962 report of the Royal College of Physicians concluded that smoking was a cause of lung cancer and bronchitis and a contributing factor to coronary heart disease.[2] In 1981, Professor Takeshi Hirayama published a prospective cohort study of 91,540 non-smoking Japanese women with smoking spouse.[3] The non-smoking wives were followed up for mortality, including mortality due to lung cancer, for 14 years. The risk of lung cancer was examined in relation to the level of smoking by the spouse, resulting in the finding of a statistically significant exposure-response relationship. This was the first study to assess the possible importance of passive smoking as one of the causal factors for lung cancer.[4]

Since 1964 a series of the Surgeon General's reports as a government scientific reports pointed out that cigarette smoking has been causally linked to diseases of nearly all organs of the body, to a poorer health status, and to harm to the fetus. Even 50 years after the first Surgeon General's report, research continues to find links between diseases and smoking, including such common diseases as diabetes mellitus, rheumatoid arthritis, and colorectal cancer.[5] Exposure to SHS has also been causally linked to cancer, respiratory, and cardiovascular diseases, and the adverse impact on the health of infants and children.[4]

By the 1990s, the tobacco epidemic was a severely public health problem and a leading cause of premature deaths. WHO reported "The escalation of smoking and other forms of tobacco use worldwide had resulted in the loss of at least 3.5 million human lives in 1998 and was expected at that time to cause at least 10 million deaths a year by 2030 if the pandemic was not controlled, with 70% of these deaths occurring in developing countries".[6] Tobacco use not only leads to a significant increases in morbidity and mortality, but also reduce productive powers and increase avoidable health expenditure.

---

[2] Royal College of Physicians of London. Smoking and Health. 1962. London: Pitman Medical.

[3] Hirayama T. Cancer mortality in nonsmoking women with smoking husbands based on a large scale cohort study in Japan. *Preventive Medicine* 1984;13(6):680–90.

[4] Hirayama T. Non-smoking wives of heavy smokers have a higher risk of lung cancer: a study from Japan. *British Medical Journal (Clinical Research Edition)* 1981 January 17; **282**:183–185.

[5] U.S. Department of Health and Human Services. *How Tobacco Smoke Causes Disease: The Biology and Behavioral Basis for Smoking-Attributable Disease: A Report of the Surgeon General.* Atlanta, GA: U.S. Department of Health and Human Services, Centers for Disease Control and Prevention, National Center for Chronic Disease Prevention and Health Promotion, Office on Smoking and Health, 2010.

[6] Resolution WHA52.18. Towards a WHO framework convention on tobacco control. In: *Fifty-second World Health Assembly: 22–27 May 1999. Volume 1. Resolution and decisions.* Geneva, World Health Organization, 1999 (WHA52/1999/REC/1). Available at http://www/who.int/tobacco/framework/wha52_18/en/index.html. Last accessed on 09 December 2009.

1.2 Response to the Challenge of the Global Tobacco Pandemic: WHO FCTC

The international community recognizes that past efforts to stem the global tobacco pandemic have proven in effective. The epidemic of tobacco use spread rapidly from the developed to the developing world, owing to driving force from the multinational industry and the addictiveness of nicotine. Globalization undermined the efforts of individual countries to control tobacco use. The traditional public health approach to reducing tobacco use were not match for the tobacco industry's power, transnational reach and economic strength. International experts have suggested that the WHO should use its unused constitutional authority to change the rules of tobacco control, by developing an international framework convention covering key aspects of tobacco control with cross-border. Dr. Brundtland, as Director General of the WHO from 1998 to 2003, allocated sufficient resources to support the protracted, complex work of preparing Member States for the WHO's first foray into treaty making.

Dr. Gro Harlem Brundtland (former WHO Director-General) point out "The tobacco habit is extensively communicated! It is communicated through the media, the entertainment industry, and most directly through the marketing and promotion of specific products. Global trade in tobacco has increased markedly over the last few years. Direct foreign investment by multinationals in developing countries has also increased. New joint ventures are announced every few months between multinationals based in a few developed countries and the governments from emerging markets." Also she continued "Tobacco control cannot succeed solely through the efforts of individual governments, national nongovernmental organizations and media advocates. We need an international framework convention that will cover key aspects of tobacco control that cross national boundaries. The framework convention will seek to address key areas of tobacco control such as: harmonization of taxes on tobacco products, smuggling, tax-free tobacco products, advertising and sponsorship, international trade, package design and labeling and agricultural diversification".[7] That is to say, tobacco epidemic is a global problem and must be solved at the global level. It cannot be solved by traditional public health strategy, but should be solved based on the international law at the legal level!

After six rounds of negotiations, WHO FCTC was developed, in 2003. On 21st May 2003, the 56th World Health Assembly unanimously adopted the WHO FCTC.[8] It took only 7 years to start negotiations to the Convention into force. The WHO FCTC is one of the fastest treaties to be negotiated, adopted and concluded, with unanimous adoption by the convention by the World Health Assembly, acceptance

---

[7] Brundtland GH. Seminar on tobacco industry disclosures; implications for public policy, World Health Organization, 1998.

[8] Resolution WHA 56.1. WHO Framework Convention on Tobacco Control. In: *Fifty-sixth World Health Assembly. 19–28 May 2003*. Volume 1. Resolutions and decisions. Geneva, World Health Organization, 2003 (WHA56/2003/REC/1). Available at http://www.who.int/tobacco/framework/final_text/en/. Last accessed 09 December 2009.

by the signatories, and rapid entry into force in February 2005, which means the Governments committed to creating a healthy, tobacco-free New World for future generations. As the preamble to the Convention, "The Parties to this Convention, *Determined* to give priority to their right to protect public health, *Recognizing* that the spread of the tobacco epidemic is a global problem with serious consequences for public health that calls for the widest possible international cooperation and the participation of all countries in an effective, appropriate and comprehensive international response; *Reflecting* the concern of the international community about the devastating worldwide health, social, economic and environmental consequences of tobacco consumption and exposure to tobacco smoke". When the treaty was closed to new signatories, on 29 June 2004, it had 168 signatories, making it one of the most widely embraced treaties in United Nations history. This suggests that governments agree to curb tobacco consumption is one of the priorities to protect people's health and health concern of the people is the basic part of the development goal of people-oriented. The governments have recognized the "people-oriented" social development goals. The WHO FCTC covers the key strategies of tobacco control. The core provisions for reducing demand are contained in Articles 6–14, which address both price and tax measures, and non-price measures to reduce the demand for tobacco, including protection from exposure to tobacco smoke; regulation of the contents of tobacco products, regulation of tobacco product disclosures, education, communication, training and public awareness, comprehensive banning of tobacco advertising, promotion and sponsorship, and measures to reduce tobacco dependence and help people to give up smoking. The core provisions for reducing supply are contained in Articles 15–17 and cover illicit trade in tobacco products, sales to and by minors, and support for economically viable alternative activities. The Framework Convention also covers other important areas, such as liability, and protection of public health policies from the interests of the tobacco industry with respect to tobacco control, protection of the environment, national coordinating mechanisms, international cooperation, reporting and exchange of information, and institutional arrangements (Article 5 and 18–26).[9]

1.3   China and the Negotiation of WHO FCTC

China's attitude and performance in the WHO FCTC negotiations were the result of the game between the health departments and the tobacco industry, but ultimately reflect the basic position of the Chinese government in international affairs.

Since reform and opening to the outside world in 1979, China began really to integrate into the international community, posing as a co-operator. China claimed to be an international responsible nation and to assume international responsibility.

---

[9]WHO FCTC, WHO Framework Convention on Tobacco Control.

Meanwhile, the health community of China very actively supported the idea that the WHO should take the lead in the development of an international convention to curb the prevalence of tobacco at the tenth conference of smoking or health held in Beijing in 1997.[10] The Ministry of Health (MOH) of China also actively responded to the negotiation of the first global public health treaty. However, as a country with a large state-owned tobacco production and consumption, the Chinese government has been concerned that a decline in tobacco consumption would affect China's economy. In summer 2000, the MOH organized a workshop, inviting officers from various ministries of the State Council.[11] At this workshop, several key points on tobacco control were clarified:

Firstly, the epidemic of tobacco use in China was so severe that it would be bound to cause serious health hazards. The serious health risk caused by the epidemic of tobacco use in China will inevitably lead to rising medical costs, exacerbating poverty and social instability. In addition, one of the important measures of tobacco control is increasing taxes and prices of tobacco products, which will be beneficial to the health of the people and increase the country's fiscal revenue. The 1999 report of the World Bank concluded that tobacco control is not only beneficial to people's health, but also valuable for the development of the national economy.[12] Secondly, based on international experience, even if effective tobacco control measures are implemented, the prevalence of smoking in the population can only drop by around 1% per year. Meanwhile, 1% of Chinese population is projected to increase annually from 2000 to 2020.[13] That means the number of smokers will not be reduced in the short term. Chinese tobacco companies therefore have 20–30 years to complete the transformation of their enterprises. China is also adjusting its industrial structure, and tobacco companies, as an industry that represents a health hazard, should fall into disuse or be transformed, in line with the State policy of industrial structure adjustment. The National Development and Reform Committee (NDRC) calls the tobacco industry a "Sunset industry"[14] to visually express its understanding for tobacco industry.

As has been claimed by China's Ministry of Foreign Affairs, "the Chinese delegation (to the WHO FCTC negotiation) not only safeguards China's rights and interests as a major power for tobacco production and consumption, but also establishes its image as a responsible major power".[15]

---

[10] Weng XZ The tenth session of the smoking or health conference was successfully held in Beijing, Journal Cardiovascular and Pulmonary diseases, 1998 17(1), P65.

[11] The author's memory as a witness.

[12] The World Bank, *Curbing the Epidemic: Governments and the Economics of Tobacco Control*, Washington DC, 1999, p. 2.

[13] State Statistical Bureau, Fifth census data (2000), http://www.stats.gov.cn/tjsj/ndsj/renkoupucha/2000pucha/pucha.htm.

[14] Xiong BL The status and trend of tobacco industry in national economy *Tobacco economy and tobacco control*, edited by Liu TN and Xiong BL, Economy and Science Press, 2004.

[15] Ministry of Foreign Affairs of China, "China and the Framework Convention on Tobacco Control", 9 July 2001.

Before going to Geneva, the Chinese delegation received clear instructions from the State Council to make efforts to actively contribute to the WHO FCTC, and not to quibble on the WHO FCTC text. The instruction, in essence, determined the direction of the efforts of Chinese delegation and criticized the officials of the STMA for their stubborn opposition towards the Convention. The head of China's delegation at the first session of the negotiating conference said that the Chinese Government supported the formulation of the proposed framework for the convention on tobacco control, and had elaborated its views at the two working group meetings. Anti-tobacco initiatives had already been introduced into the Chinese legislation. … China gave its full commitment to being involved in that process for the forthcoming 3 years.[16]

China's delegate repeatedly expressed the notion that "China devotedly supports the WHO's efforts to control tobacco, appreciating the great significance of the WHO FCTC, and presenting itself as a responsible power with a completely cooperative attitude towards the negotiation".[17]

However, the China National Tobacco Corporation (CNTC) did not want an international Convention on tobacco control. The CNTC is a state-owned monopoly over the tobacco industry, and also a government department: the State Tobacco Monopoly Administration (STMA). The CNTC and STMA are a unified organization, in charge of the management and production of tobacco. In October 2000, at the WHO hearing on the Framework Convention, the CNTC explicitly expressed its opposition: "*Firstly, as a legal product should have its existence in the market place and should not be 'eliminated'; … Secondly, individual countries are different in many aspects and can have their own choices and therefore tobacco control should respect these differences and should not violent their country sovereignty.*" The CNTC also described its other strategies and opinions, which are discussed later. Thus, the CNTC's intention was that the form, scope and scale of any tobacco controls should respect the different circumstances of each country, and that the choices made should not interfere with national sovereignty.

China' Delegation to WHO FCTC Negotiation was only the Delegation including representatives of the tobacco industry,[18] which roused suspicious over the real position of China's delegation to the WHO FCTC. The delegate from the STMA, in particular, professed[19] that the words "including a picture or pictogram illustrating the harmful consequences of tobacco consumption" should be deleted from text of WHO FCTC. They also said that as the health warning covering 10% of the area of

---

[16] World Health Organization, *Intergovernmental Negotiation Body on the WHO Framework Convention on Tobacco Control, First Session, A/FCTC/INB1/SR.* 16-21 Oct. 2000, p.34. http://apps.who.int/gb/fctc/.

[17] "An Interview with Xiong Bilin, Head of China's Delegation to FCTC Negotiation", http://www.tobaccochina.com/people/interview/wu/20037/2003721104721_164827.shtml.   Accessed   12 November 2011.

[18] List of participants from A/FCTC/INB1-INB6.

[19] World Health Organization, *Intergovernmental Negotiation Body on the WHO Framework Convention on Tobacco Control, Second Session, A/FCTC/INB2/SR.* 30 April–4 May. 2001, p.44. http://apps.who.int/gb/fctc/PDF/inb2/FINAL_FCTC_INB2_SR_COMPILATION.pdf.

packaging in China, we must respect domestic laws and practices and cannot agree to the requirements of the Framework Convention. Due to the speech on the pictorial health warning, China's delegate was offered the "Dirty Ashtray Award".

The head of the Chinese delegation, however, interpreted the opposition to the pictorial health warning as an attempt to get more member states to accept the Framework Convention. So Convention should be general and flexible enough to allow tobacco control measures to be implemented in accordance with the individual situation and economic conditions prevailing in different countries.[20] The explanation is logically absurd and the expresses was similar to the views of the CNPC at the WHO hearing.

On one hand, the Chinese government actively participated in the negotiations on the WHO FCTC as a result of the strong advocacy from the professional health community, and effort from the Ministry of Health, with the Chinese government hoping to be praised as a responsible great power in dealing with international affairs. On the other hand, the Chinese government was reluctant to embrace a treaty with the strict tobacco control measures, as it regards its tobacco industry as a good source of government revenue. In other words, China views tobacco control as an internal economic issue rather than a public health issue.

Regardless of the debate or compromise in the negotiation process, the Chinese government signed the treaty in November 2003. While signing the WHO FCTC on behalf of China, Wang Gunagya, China's UN ambassador, stated that China has played an active and constructive role in the negotiation of the WHO FCTC. By endorsing the international convention, China is once again demonstrating to the world its commitment to supporting the WHO and the government's strong determination to control tobacco.[21] The convention was ratified by the standing Committee of the National People's Congress of China, China's top legislative body, in 2005,[22] indicating that China should fulfill its legal obligation in accordance with the WHO FCTC.

Nevertheless, it remains to be seen how far the tobacco control strategies covered in WHO FCTC to be internalized into China' policies. As Sebastian Heilmann and Nicole Schulte-Kulkmann note, "in effect, Chinese policymakers try to utilize policy diffusion as an instrument for negotiating and promoting the nation's global rise. Yet, when it comes to implementation, global regulatory standards are weakened or even neutralized through discretionary enforcement. The depth and robustness of normative assimilation therefore remain uncertain".[23] It has been proved that the fear is well founded based on the implementation of the Convention after its entry into force in China.

---

[20] World Health Organization, *Intergovernmental Negotiation Body on the WHO Framework Convention on Tobacco Control, First Session, A/FCTC/INB1/SR.* 16-21 Oct. 2000, p.34. http://apps.who.int/gb/fctc/PDF/inb1/FINAL_FCTC_INB1_SR_COMPILATION.pdf.

[21] Xinhua News, "Wang Guangya signs the FCTC on behalf of Chinese Government", Dec 11, 2003, http://news.xinhuanet.com/world/2003-11/11/content_1170775.htm. Accessed Oct 18, 2011.

[22] The Standing Committee of the NPC approved the WHO FCTC, Sept. 200, 2005, 2005-09-20, http://news.163.com/05/0920/08/1U32OU4L0001124L.html.

[23] Sebastian Heilmann, Nicole Schulte-Kulkmann, "The limits of Policy Diffusion: Introducing International Norms of Anti-money Laundering into China's Legal System", *Governance*, Vol.24, No.4, 2011, p.639.

1.4   Implementation of the WHO FCTC

Significant progress has been made since WHO FCTC came into force in February 2005. With 180 party member states in March 2015, covering 90% of the World's population, the WHO FCTC has been among the most popularly and rapidly embraced global health norms in the history of the United Nations.[24] Meanwhile, the principal treaty bodies, the Conference of the Parties and the Permanent Secretariat, were established and are fully functional. The six sessions of the Conference of Parties (COP) have adopted the first protocol and several guidelines covering more than ten substantial Articles of the Convention, including the guideline of Article 6 adopted in the sixth Session of the COP. Eighty percent of the Parties have submitted their implement report of WHO FCTC to the reporting system of the treaty, the analyzed results were in the progress reports by the secretariat of WHO FCTC. The implementation of the Convention is on the track.

To expand the fight against the tobacco epidemic, the WHO has introduced the MPOWER package of six proven policies, which comprise the key Article of the WHO FCTC: **M**onitor tobacco use and prevention policies, **P**rotect people from tobacco smoke, **O**ffer help to quit tobacco use, **W**arn about the dangers of tobacco, **E**nforce bans on tobacco advertising, promotion and sponsorship, and **R**aise taxes on tobacco.[25]

In the decade since the WHO FCTC came into force, and 7 years after the introduction of MPOWER, there has been great progress in global tobacco control. Today, the number of countries that have implemented at least one MPOWER measure (not including Monitoring and Mass media measures) at the highest level has reached 103 countries, covering 2.8 billion people, or 40% of the world's population.[26] This proven that most countries worldwide, large and small, rich and poor, could combat the global tobacco epidemic and protect the health of their people.

The 2010, 2012, 2014 and 2016 global progress reports on the implementation of the WHO FCTC indicated that the Parties themselves have been taking extraordinary steps to implement the WHO FCTC. Most Parties have now reached the requirement of the Convention within the prescribed time limit of execution, particularly, Articles relating to the protection of people from SHS, the pictorial health warnings and comprehensive banning tobacco advertising, promotion and sponsorship. However, a third of Parties have not yet achieved full implementation of the related Articles since ratifying the WHO FCTC.[27]

---

[24] Parties to the WHO Framework Convention on Tobacco Control, http://www.who.int/fctc/signatories_parties/en/.

[25] WHO Report on the Global Tobacco Epidemic, 2008: the MPOWER package, Geneva, World Health Organization, 2008.ISBN 978 92 4 159628 2.

[26] WHO, WHO Report on the global Tobacco epidemic, 2015: Raising taxes on tobacco, http://apps.who.int/iris/bitstream/10665/178577/1/WHO_NMH_PND_15.5_eng.pdf?ua=1.

[27] 2014 global progress report on the implementation of the WHO Framework Convention on Tobacco Control.

Overall, the average rate of implementation of the treaty, when calculated by indicators comparable across all reporting cycles, increased steadily, from 52% in 2010 to 56% in 2012, 59% in 2014 and 65% in 2016. However, progress of the different Articles has been uneven, ranging from 15% to 88% varying, implement rate of two-thirds of Articles were over 50%, the highest is Article 8 (Protection from exposure to tobacco smoke), next is the Article 11 (Packaging and labeling of tobacco products) (76%).[28] Implementation rates are also very different among Parties.

1.4.1   General Obligations (Article 5)

Strengthening national capacity and legislation for tobacco control is one of the general obligations under the Convention; it is the first step of the WHO FCTC that the Party is legally obliged to internalize. The success or failure of tobacco control depends on how the WHO FCTC is explained and implemented at national and community levels.

Article 5 of the treaty requires Parties to develop, implement, periodically update and review comprehensive multi-sector national tobacco control strategies, plans and programmes in accordance with the Convention and the protocols; Towards this end, each Party shall, in accordance with its capabilities: (a) establish or reinforce and finance a national coordinating mechanism or focal points for tobacco control; and (b) adopt and implement effective legislative, executive, administrative and/or other measures and cooperate, as appropriate, with other Parties in developing appropriate policies for preventing and reducing tobacco consumption, nicotine addiction and exposure to tobacco smoke.

Based on a series of the Global progress report of the WHO FCTC, the proportion of Parties reporting the development and implementation of comprehensive multi-sector national strategies, plans and programmes (Article 5.1) has increased consistently from 49% in 2010 to 59% in 2012, 65% in 2014 and in 73% in 2016.[29] Sixty one percent of the Parties have strengthened their existing tobacco control legislation, or approved new legislation, since ratifying the Convention, but 39% Parties have still not put in place legislative measures in accordance with the requirements of the Convention in 2014.[30]

Appointing a national tobacco control focal point, strengthening the national coordination mechanism and international cooperation, are the basic national obligations with overarching impact. Most Parties have completed these aspects of their infrastructure.

---

[28] 2016 global progress report on the implementation of the WHO Framework Convention on Tobacco Control. P3.

[29] WHO FCTC. 2016 global progress report on implementation of the WHO Framework Convention on Tobacco Control.

[30] WHO FCTC. 2014 Global progress report on implementation of the WHO Framework Convention on Tobacco Control.

1.4.2 Protect Tobacco Control Policies from the Tobacco Industry

Parties to the WHO FCTC have understood the tobacco industry as the main pusher of the tobacco epidemic. The preamble of the WHO FCTC emphasizes the need for Parties to be vigilant of any efforts by the tobacco industry to impede or undermine tobacco control efforts, and to grasp any activities of the tobacco industry that have a negative impact on tobacco control efforts. Article 5.3 of the WHO FCTC states that "in setting and implementing their public health policies with respect to tobacco control, Parties shall act to protect these policies from commercial and other vested interests of the tobacco industry in accordance with national law."

In November 2008, the third session of COP adopted guidelines of Article 5.3, emphasizing the fundamental and irreconcilable conflict between the tobacco industry's interests and public health policy. The guidelines recommend that Parties "establish measures to limit interactions with the tobacco industry" and "reject partnerships and non-binding or non-enforceable agreements with the tobacco industry" and so on, especially "treat State-owned tobacco industry in the same way as any other tobacco industry".

In addition, Article 12.C stresses the importance of public education and awareness of the activities of the tobacco industry, and the Parties agree to promote "public access, in accordance with national law, to a wide range of information on the tobacco industry as relevant to the objective of this Convention." Article 12.E reiterates the importance of the "participation of public and private agencies and nongovernmental organizations not affiliated with the tobacco industry in developing and implementing inter-section programmes and strategies for tobacco control." Furthermore, Article 20.4C also mentioned to "cooperate with competent international organizations to progressively establish and maintain a global system to regularly collect and disseminate information on tobacco production, manufacture and the activities of the tobacco industry which have an impact on the Convention or national tobacco controlactivities."

In brief, the Parties should have a sense of closely monitoring the activities of the tobacco industry to interfere with public health policy-making, preventing the tobacco industry from interference with tobacco control policies, and regulating activities described as "socially responsible" by the tobacco industry, and so on.

The WHO has been trying to monitor and counterattack the activities of the tobacco industry to interfere with public health policymaking though setting up the database and publishing reports.

In 2000, the WHO committee of experts on tobacco industry documents published *Tobacco industry strategies to undermine tobacco control activities at the World Health Organization*.[31] The committee found that "the evidence shows that

---

[31] Committee of Experts on Tobacco Industry Documents, Tobacco industry strategies to undermine tobacco control activities at the World Health Organization, July, 2000, http://www.who.int/tobacco/en/who_inquiry.pdf?ua=1.

tobacco companies have operated for many years with the deliberate purpose of subverting the efforts of WHO to address tobacco issues."

The WHO report "Tobacco industry interference in tobacco control"[32] describes the spectrum of tobacco industry practices that interfere with tobacco control. Other reports, based on internal industry documents and companies' public pronouncements, give many examples of how the multinational tobacco companies interfere in tobacco control.[33,34,35]

The WHO provided the technical resource to support the implementation of the Article 5.3 Guidelines by sharing practical actions and best practices, and giving examples applicable to the implementation of Article 5.3 of the WHO FCTC.[36]

Almost two thirds of the Parties have provided additional information on their progress in implementing Article 5.3, including promoting and raising awareness of the need to implement Article 5.3 within governments, the development of codes of conduct, ethical guidelines and administrative policies for civil servants, and so on.[37]

There have been a few examples of litigation to promote tobacco control. A recent case was the successful legislation to prohibit tobacco industry logos, brand imagery, colors and promotional texts in Australia following the dismissal, by the highest court of Australia, of a challenge from transnational tobacco companies on Aug. 15, 2012.[38] Since December 1, 2012, cigarettes and tobacco products in Australia have been sold in plain olive green packets bearing graphic health warnings, such as pictures of mouth cancer and other smoking-related illnesses.

The global public health community has recently recognized the scope and intensity of interference from the tobacco industry and began to take protective action. The guideline of Article 5.3 of the WHO FCTC points out that "Treats State-owned tobacco industry in the same way as any other tobacco industry", which hit the mark in the countries with the state-owned tobacco industry, such as China. The STMA is a member of the Inter-Ministry Coordination and Steering Committee for the Implementation of the WHO Framework Convention on Tobacco Control in China in charge of tobacco control policies, including Articles

---

[32] WHO Tobacco industry interference with tobacco control. ISBN 978 924 159734 0.

[33] WHO Tobacco industry and corporate responsibility ... an inherent contradiction.

[34] WHO Evolution of the tobacco industry positions on addiction to nicotine.

[35] WHO The tobacco industry documents. What they are, what they tell us and how to search them. A practical manual (2nd edition).

[36] WHO Technical resource for country implementation of WHO framework convention on tobacco control article 5.3 on the protection of public health policies with respect to tobacco control from commercial and other vested interests of the tobacco industry. ISBN 978 92 4 150373 0.

[37] 2016 Global progress report on implementation of the WHO Framework Convention on Tobacco Control. P16.

[38] Australian court approves tobacco pack logo ban, http://www.reuters.com/article/us-australia-tobacco-idUSBRE87D0PI20120815.

9, 10, 11 and 15 of the WHO FCTC,[39] which is the main reason why China falls behind the majority of countries around the world in relation to tobacco control. Nonetheless, Parties with state-owned tobacco companies should find a way to separate the interests of the tobacco industry from tobacco control and health interests, and governments with state-owned tobacco companies must still give priority to protecting public health, through the effective implementation of the WHO FCTC, protecting the tobacco control policies from interference by tobacco industry interests.

1.4.3   The Reduction in Demand for Tobacco

Articles 6–14 are measures of reducing tobacco use, corresponding to five policies of WHO MPOWER package.

1.4.3.1   Price and Tax Measures to Reduce the Demand for Tobacco

Article 6 encourages price and tax measures as effective means to reduce the demand for tobacco. These include tax increases that result in an increase in the sale price of tobacco products; and prohibiting or restricting sales of tax- and duty-free tobacco products. Guidelines for the implementation of Article 6 were adopted at the COP 6 in October 2014.

First, the proportion of countries levying excise taxes has further increased (to 92% in 2014 and 2016, up from 67% in 2010 and 85% in 2012). Second, a combination of specific and ad valorem type taxes has become more widely used. Finally, the average proportion of all taxes in the retail price of tobacco products has further increased (to 67% in 2014, compared with 57% in 2012).[40] The worldwide simple average of total tax share on cigarette prices is 58% in 2016. This average is lower than in 2014. However, there are still significant differences between the Parties and regions in terms of levels of taxation and prices of tobacco products (minimum tax burden 5%; maximum tax burden 90%). Since 2012, seven countries (Bangladesh, Bosnia and Herzegovina, Croatia, Kiribati, New Zealand, Romania and the Seychelles) have raised taxes on cigarettes to more than 75% of the retail price; as up 2015, it is in a total of 33 countries covering 1/10 of world's population that levy taxes of tobacco products were over more than 75% of the cigarette retail price.[41]

---

[39] Reply from State Council on agreement to set up the Inter-ministerial leading group to be in charge of FCTC implementation State letter No. 41 2007. http://www.360doc.com/.

[40] 2014 global progress report on implementation of the WHO Framework Convention on Tobacco Control.

[41] WHO report on the global tobacco epidemic, 2015: raising taxes on tobacco, ISBN 978 92 4 069460 6 (PDF).

1.4.3.2   Protection from Exposure to Tobacco Smoke

Article 8 addresses the adoption and implementation of effective measures to provide protection from exposure to tobacco smoke in indoor workplaces, public transport, indoor public places and, as appropriate, other public places. In 2008, the COP 3 adopted guidelines for the implementation of Article 8, requiring that each Party should strive to provide universal protection within 5 years of the WHO FCTC's entry into force for that Party.[42]

Based on the 2016 progress report of the WHO FCTC, Article 8 has the highest average implementation rate by all substantive articles of WHO FCTC, and increasing from 78% by 126 Parties in 2012, 84% by 130 Parties in 2014 and 88% in 133 Parties in 2016. A noteworthy trend is the extension of ban on smoking in public places, such as beaches, transport stops, public parks, outdoor cafes, sheltered walkways and hospital compounds, outdoor markets and even some streets, prisons, and private vehicles when carrying children, as in Australia, Canada Singapore, New Zealand, South Africa, Fiji and other countries. The hospitality sector is still one of the least regulated sectors in relation to smoke-free policies. Although the hotel industry is the least smoke-free sector, nearly 50% countries still make bars and restaurants completely smoke-free since 2014.

By 2014, 55 countries had implemented a comprehensive smoke-free legislation, covering 1.5 billion people, or 20% of the world's population.[43]

1.4.3.3   Tobacco Product Regulation

Article 9 deals with the testing and measuring of the contents and emissions of tobacco products, Article 10 deals with the disclosure of information on such contents and emissions to governmental authorities and the public. Based on the 2016 progress report of WHO FCTC, only about half of the reporting Parties regulate the contents and the emissions of tobacco products, fewer than half of the Parties require the testing of contents and measurement of emissions of tobacco products. Over 60% of the reporting Parties required manufacturers or importers of tobacco products to disclose information on the contents and emissions of tobacco products to governmental authorities, and around half of the Parties required such disclosures to be made publicly available.[44]

---

[42] 3 session of COP GUIDELINES ON PROTECTION FROM EXPOSURE TO TOBACCO SMOKE, http://www.who.int/fctc/cop/art%208%20guidelines_english.pdf?ua=1.

[43] WHO report on the global tobacco epidemic, 2017: Monitoring tobacco use and prevention policies. Geneva: World Health Organization; 2017.

[44] WHO FCTC. 2016 global progress report on implementation of the WHO Framework Convention on Tobacco Control. P 30–2.

1.4.3.4 Packaging and Labeling of Tobacco Products

In general, most Parties are very active to implement Article 11 on package health warnings, with increasing warning size, more requiring pictorial warnings. And more and more countries consider for implementation of plain packaging. Also from the 2016 WHO FCTC progress report, the average of implementation of Article 11 of the Convention in 2016 reached 76%. In the 3-years deadline, close to 90% the Parties have health warning required with clear, visible and legible approved by authority, over three-quarter Parties' health warning in package are over 30% of areas, the percentage of Parties requiring health warnings covering 50% or more of the principal display area has increased since 2014. Fifty eight percent Parties (74 countries) require pictorial health warnings on tobacco product packaging in 2016.

1.4.3.5 Comprehensive Banning Tobacco Advertising, Promotion and Sponsorship

Tobacco Advertising Promotion and Sponsor briefly call TAPS. Article 13 of the WHO FCTC requires Parties to the treaty to implement and enforce a comprehensive ban on tobacco advertising, promotion and sponsorship, within 5 years of FCTC ratification.

According to the WHO Secretariat of the WHO FCTC 2016 global progress report, the average of the implementation rates for Article 13 was increasing year by year, from 59% in 2012, 63% in 2014, and 71% in 2016. In the 2016 reporting period, 96 Parties reported to have a comprehensive TAPS ban in place, but in fact, only 34 countries banned TAPS in global internet,[45] which is matched with finding of ***WHO REPORT ON THE GLOBAL TOBACCO EPIDEMIC, 2017***: only 25% (34 countries or regions) do a comprehensive ban of TAPS.[46] Except for this, there have been obvious progress on banning TAPS in 2016. One hundred and eight Parties (accounting for 83% of reports) has banned tobacco sponsorship of tobacco products. It is a more difficult to prohibit display at point of tobacco product sale, but 75 Parties (56% of reports) have banned tobacco product display at sale point.

1.4.3.6 Treatment of Tobacco Dependence

Average implementation of articles 14 of the Convention in 2016 was 50% based on 18 indicators,[47] which of these indicators are highly implemented. Besides the majority (over three quarters) of the Parties (133) utilized the

---

[45] WHO FCTC. 2016 global progress report on implementation of the WHO Framework Convention on Tobacco Control. P 39–40.

[46] WHO report on the global tobacco epidemic, 2017: monitoring tobacco use and prevention policies. Geneva: World Health Organization; 2017. P 12- License: CC BY-NC-SA 3.0 IGO.

[47] WHO FCTC. 2016 global progress report on implementation of the WHO Framework Convention on Tobacco Control. Annex 1 P77.

opportunities provided by events, such as the World No Tobacco Day or had run media campaigns, to promote tobacco cessation, 69% of the reporting Parties included tobacco dependence diagnosis and treatment and counseling services in their national tobacco-control strategies, plans and programmes, as well as had integrated diagnosis and treatment into their health-care systems. Seventy eight percent Parties covered the costs of services and treatment in primary health care fully or partially through public funding or reimbursement schemes. Seventy nine (59%) Parties offered assistance to improve the accessibility and affordability of pharmaceutical tobacco dependence products, including nicotine replacement therapy (NRT), bupropion and varenicline available in their jurisdiction.

1.5 Closing Remark

WHO FCTC has been developed in order to cope with the global epidemic of tobacco use, saving the huge loss of health around the world from the tobacco epidemic. The formulating process of WHO FCTC fully embodied the concern of the international community and governments for the health of the people, also showed determination and wisdom with using international law to cope with the negative effect of globalization. The Convention being into effect on February 27, 2005, quickly became international regulations with the most widely accepted in the history of the United Nations. Now, WHO FCTC as a powerful weapon to deal with the global tobacco epidemic, is playing a great role.

Today, following the WHO FCTC, the difficulties are not longer insurmountable. Numerous countries have passed, or are renewing and strengthening, their national legislations and policies to conform to the evidence-based interventions set forth in the Framework Convention. Tobacco control is now almost universally acknowledged as a significant public health priority, tobacco control policies and strategies are popularizing in the world and donor support is growing. The global tobacco control community has expanded, and tobacco control capacity continues to improve at various levels.

Now, WHO FCTC have set up the new rules, and the commitment of all the players will make a difference to change the world with tobacco epidemic.

However, the global public health community cannot relax its vigilance. The tobacco industry continues to thrive, and fuel the conflict between profit and health. The addictiveness of nicotine continues to enslave over a third of the world's adult population, and globalization continues to facilitate the spread of the tobacco epidemic, through trade, travel and communication.

Tobacco control is a marathon effort in public health, and the entry into force of the WHO FCTC is just one milestone in a long, ongoing struggle to address the tobacco epidemic effectively. It is the challenge to ensure that obligations and commitments under the treaty are successfully translated into effective national and Community actions.

China is the world's largest producer and consumer of tobacco. There are 360 million smokers among more than 1.3 billion population in China; about one-third of all smokers in the world are in China. A staggering 44% of the world's cigarettes are smoked in China. China is the epicenter of this epidemic, and thus lies at the heart of global efforts to stop it. However, The attitudes and actions of the Chinese government in the negotiations on the WHO FCTC described in the second section of this chapter, have shown that China focused on the pursuit of international recognition rather than public health and safety, which has presaged the setback of the implementation of WHO FCTC in China. The 10-year implementation process of the WHO FCTC in China will be described in this book confirms the above prediction. The focus of this book is how to promote tobacco control in China, let China make progress together with the whole World using the new rules of universal health coverage. It is useful for tobacco control, also inspiring for the other public affairs globally.

Chapter 2
Tobacco Epidemic and Health Risk in the Chinese Population

Gonghuan Yang

Abstract The prevalence of tobacco in Chinese men has peaked since the 1980s. The past 30 years, the smokers start to smoking more and more early, and a half of smokers did before 20 years old in 2010 survey; the prevalence of male smoking only fallen about 10% from 1984 to 2015, did not drop and still over 50% from 2002 to 2015. For female, its prevalence of smoking has been kept very low level. By 2015, after 10 years the entry into force of the Convention, the prevalence of SHS exposure at homes and in the public places were dropped to 46.7 and 54.3%, separately. However, there are still about half of the non smokers at home or in public places suffer from SHS exposure. Reviewing eight case-control or prospective cohort studies in different urban and rural of China from 1980s to 2005. The overall mortality of smokers was significantly greater than that of nonsmokers, relative risk (RRs) are from 1.1 in 1990s rural to 1.65 in 2010 urban. The urban male smokers who had started before age 20 years had twice the never-smoker mortality rate (RR 1.98, 1.79–2.19) and who daily smoked more than 25 cigarettes was closed twice (RR 1.93, 1.75–2.12). Based on these estimation, smoking caused about one million (840,000 male, 130,000 female) deaths in China in 2010. The female tobacco attributable mortality fraction may be over-estimated from GBD2010 study and WHO 2008 study, which is different with the results of all epidemiological studies. GBD study estimated that exposure SHS causes around 159,000 deaths in China in 2010. Although it is need to further approach and deepen for the scientific evidence on secondhand smoke, the current global and Chinese evidences were sufficient for public health intervention.

Keywords Epidemiology · Prevalence · Smoking · SHS · Health risk · China

G. Yang
Institute of Basic Medical Science Chinese Academy of Medical Sciences, School of Basic Medicine Peking Union Medical College, Beijing, China

© Springer Nature Singapore Pte Ltd. 2018
G. Yang (ed.), *Tobacco Control in China*,
https://doi.org/10.1007/978-981-10-8315-0_2

2.1   Introduction

The adverse effects of smoking and passive smoking on health have become a social consensus, and has promoted the WHO Framework Convention of Tobacco Control (WHO FCTC).

When individuals inhale cigarette smoke, whether active or passive, they inhale more than 7000 chemicals, including hundreds of poisonous substance and at least 69 known carcinogen. In 1964, the U.S. Surgeon General's Report concluded only that "cigarette smoking is causally related to lung cancer in men".[1] A solid evidence chain has been established, setting up the causal relationship between the health consequences and both active smoking and exposure to SHS. Cigarette smoking has been causally linked to diseases of nearly all organs of the body, diminishing health status, and harming the fetus.[2]

2010 US Surgeon General report "*How Tobacco Smoke Causes Disease: The Biology and Behavioral Basis for Smoking-Attributable Disease*" reviewed a lot of scientific evidence, and pointed out that the specific mechanisms of smoking-related diseases have been established.[3] In the biological processes of cigarette smoke inhalation and disease, chemicals are rapidly absorbed by the cells in the body and produce disease-causing cellular and gene changes. The way in which tobacco users become addicted to nicotine has also been documented. New evidence continues to be added for the long list of diseases caused by tobacco use and exposure to tobacco smoke.

The 2014 US Surgeon General's Report[4] concluded that "active smoking is now causally associated with age-related macular degeneration, diabetes, colorectal cancer, liver cancer, adverse health outcomes in cancer patients and survivors, tuberculosis, erectile dysfunction, or facial clefts in infants, ectopic pregnancy, rheumatoid arthritis, inflammation, and impaired immune function". In addition, "exposure to secondhand smoke has now been causally associated with an increased risk for stroke". According to the report, there are sufficient evidences to conclude that the risk of developing lung adenocarcinoma from cigarette smoking has increased since the 1960s related to changes in the design and composition of cigarettes since the 1950s.

---

[1] Smoking and health: report of the Advisory Committee to the Surgeon General of the Public Health Service. Washington, DC: Department of Health, Education, and Welfare, 1964:387. (PHS publication no. 1103).

[2] US Department of Health and Human Services. *The health consequences of smoking: a report of the Surgeon General*. Atlanta: US Department of Health and Human Services, Centers for Disease Control and Prevention, Office on Smoking and Health, 2004.

[3] U.S. Department of Health and Human Services. *How Tobacco Smoke Causes Disease: The Biology and Behavioral Basis for Smoking-Attributable Disease: A Report of the Surgeon General.* Atlanta, GA: U.S. Department of Health and Human Services, Centers for Disease Control and Prevention, National Center for Chronic Disease Prevention and Health Promotion, Office on Smoking and Health, 2010.

[4] U.S. Department of Health and Human Services. *The Health Consequences of Smoking: 50 Years of Progress. A Report of the Surgeon General.* Atlanta, GA: U.S. Department of Health and Human Services, Centers for Disease Control and Prevention, National Center for Chronic Disease Prevention and Health Promotion, Office on Smoking and Health, 2014.

According to the 2010 US Surgeon General's Report, "the constituents of tobacco smoke believed to be responsible for cardiovascular disease include oxidizing chemicals, nicotine, carbon monoxide, and particulate matter".[5] The report also shows that "even low levels of exposure to tobacco, such as a few cigarettes a day, occasional smoking, or exposure to secondhand tobacco smoke, are sufficient to substantially increase the risk of cardiac events". Based on these evidence, a causal relationship can be inferred between SHS exposure and increased risk of stroke. The increasing in risk for stroke from exposure SHS is estimated about 20–30%. The evidence is suggests that there is a causal relationship between the implementation of a smoke-free law or policy and a reduction in coronary events among people aged under 65 years.

Tobacco epidemic and health risk in Chinese population are discussed, including the prevalence of smoking and exposure of second-hand smoke (SHS), the health risk caused by smoking and SHS exposure.

2.2   The Pattern of Tobacco Epidemic in the Chinese Population

2.2.1   Model on Stages of the Cigarette Epidemic in the Developed and Developing Countries

The rise and fall in smoking and smoking-attributed mortality lagged about 20–30 years behind the change of smoking rates in men and women, which has been observed in Western countries such as the USA, the UK and Australia. Alan D Lopez and Richard Peto suggested a four-stage model[6] for describing the epidemic of cigarette smoking and its mortality risk in developed countries (Fig. 2.1). The four-stage model shows that female smoking rate began to rise after 30–40 years when the male smoking rate was increasing; tobacco-attributed mortality began to arise after 30 years the smoking rate in population has been increased. Especially, tobacco attributable mortality will continue to rise for 20–30 years even during the substantial drop of cigarette consumption. The difference in peak between tobacco attributed mortality and tobacco use is as that the main increase in smoking-attributed mortality in middle age occurred several decades after the main increase in smoking among adolescents and young adults.

---

[5] Chapter 3 Chemistry and Toxicology of Cigarette Smoke and Biomarkers of Exposure and Harm. In: U.S. Department of Health and Human Services. *How Tobacco Smoke Causes Disease: The Biology and Behavioral Basis for Smoking-Attributable Disease: A Report of the Surgeon General.* Atlanta, GA: U.S. Department of Health and Human Services, Centers for Disease Control and Prevention, National Center for Chronic Disease Prevention and Health Promotion, Office on Smoking and Health, 2010.

[6] Lopez AD, Collishaw N, Piha T. A descriptive model of the cigarette epidemic in developed countries. Tob Control 1994;3:242e7.

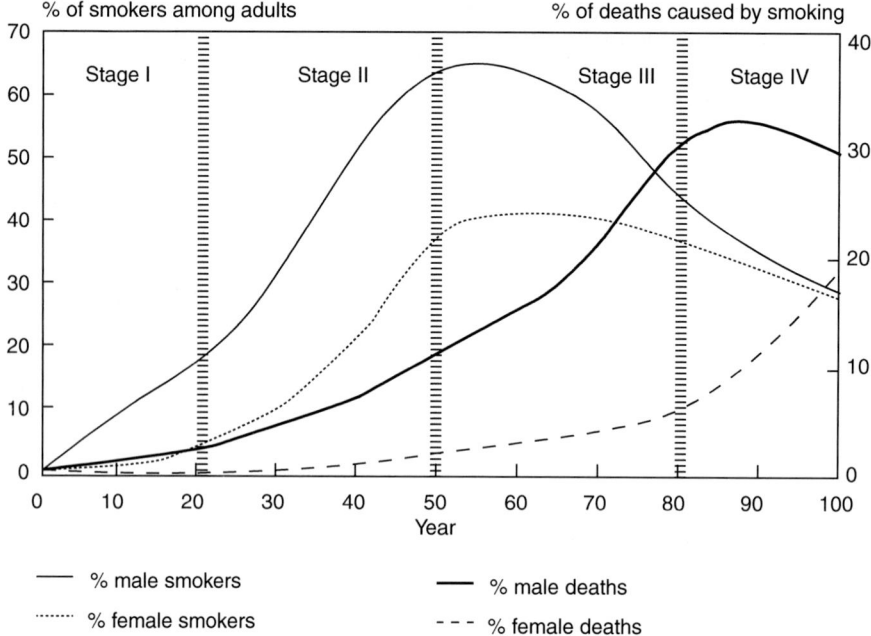

Fig. 2.1 Schematic diagram of a model of cigarette epidemic proposed in 1994 for economic developed countries. Reprint with permission from Lopez AD, Collishaw N, Piha T. A descriptive model of the cigarette epidemic in developed countries. Tob Control 1994;3:242e7

The epidemiological characteristics of tobacco use in the developing countries are different from those in the developed countries. The four-stage model cannot be directly applied to the developing countries, where prevalence of smoking in female did not follow the increasing rate in male, and female smoking-attributed mortality is little as the social customs do not encourage women's smoking in China and India. The original model was modified to allow the different stages to be described separately for male and the female epidemics in a particular country.[7] The second difference is that the diseases attributed tobacco use, are affected by other risk factors, mainly indoor burning, as co-factors. Ezzati et al. adapted and adjusted the model according to the regional characteristics of the epidemic for different sub-regions, divided the tobacco epidemic into five stages (early, rising, peak or maturity, declining and late).[8] The revised model chiefly emphasizes smoking-attributed proportions of all deaths in middle age (defined as 35–69 years old), although it also provides links to estimates of smoking-attributed proportions at older ages, and at

---

[7] Thun M, Peto R, Lopez AD et al. Stages of the cigarette epidemic on entering its second century, Tobacco Control 2012;21:96e101.

[8] Majid Ezzati and Alan D. Lopez, Smoking and oral tobacco use, in *Comparative Quantification of Health Risks Global and Regional Burden of Disease Attributable to Selected Major Risk Factors* (Volume 1) Edited by Majid Ezzati, Alan D. Lopez, Anthony Rodgers and Christopher J.L. Murray.

all ages. Thus, the indicators to used determine the stages of a tobacco use epidemic are: (1) prevalence of smoking among young adults (defined as current smoking), (2) age of starting smoking, (3) smoking-associated relative risks (RRs), (4) smoking-attributed proportions of all deaths in middle age (defined as 35–69 years old).

The model summarized the characteristics of the tobacco epidemic, i.e. that main increase in smoking-attributed mortality in middle age came several decades after the sharp increase in smoking among adolescents and young adults. The model is helpful to determine the prevalence of tobacco use and relative risk (RR) in order to estimate the Population Attributable Fraction (PAF) for a particular time period.

2.2.2 Characteristics of Smoking Prevalence in China

The national cross-sectional surveys on behavioral of tobacco use conducted in 1984, 1996, 2002, 2010 and 2015.[9,10,11,12,13] The 2010 survey was a part Global Adult Tobacco Survey (GATS). The criteria used in these surveys to define ever smoker, current smoker, former smoker, and never smoker were similar, except that there was no definition of ever smoker in the 1984 survey. Ever smoker was defined as a person who, in the 1996, 2002, 2010 and 2015 surveys, reported smoking more than 100 cigarettes during their lifetime, including current smoker and former smoker. The difference between current smoker and former smoker is smoking or not smoking within 30 day of the interview. The questionnaire used in these surveys included frequency, type, amount (current and past), age first began smoking, age of cessation, and main reason for cessation. Figure 2.2 shows the annual prevalence of current among adults aged 15 and over at 1984, 1996, 2002, 2010 and 2015.

These findings indicate that smoking patterns were relatively similar among men in several surveys conducted in the past 30 years. The prevalence of current smoking increased among men aged 15–30 years, which was matched the falling average age of starting smoking. The prevalence of tobacco use remained fairly high, over 50%, and did not change with age until the age of 60 years due to illness. Except

[9] Weng XZ, Hong ZG, Chen DY (1987) Smoking prevalence in Chinese aged 15 and above. Chin J (Engl) 100:886–892.

[10] Yang GH, Fan LX, Tan J et al (1999) Smoking in China: findings of the 1996 national prevalence survey. JAMA 282:1247–1253.

[11] Yang GH, Ma JM, Liu N, et al (2005) Smoking and passive smoking in Chinese, 2002, Zhong Hua Liu Xing Bing Xue Za Zhi 26:77–83.

[12] 2010 Li Q, Xia JS, Yang GH, Prevalence of Smoking in China in 2010 Nengl j med 364;25 nejm. org June 23, 2011.

[13] Liang XF, ed. 2015 China Adult Tobacco Survey Report. China (Beijing): People's Medical Publishing House. 2016 [in Chinese].

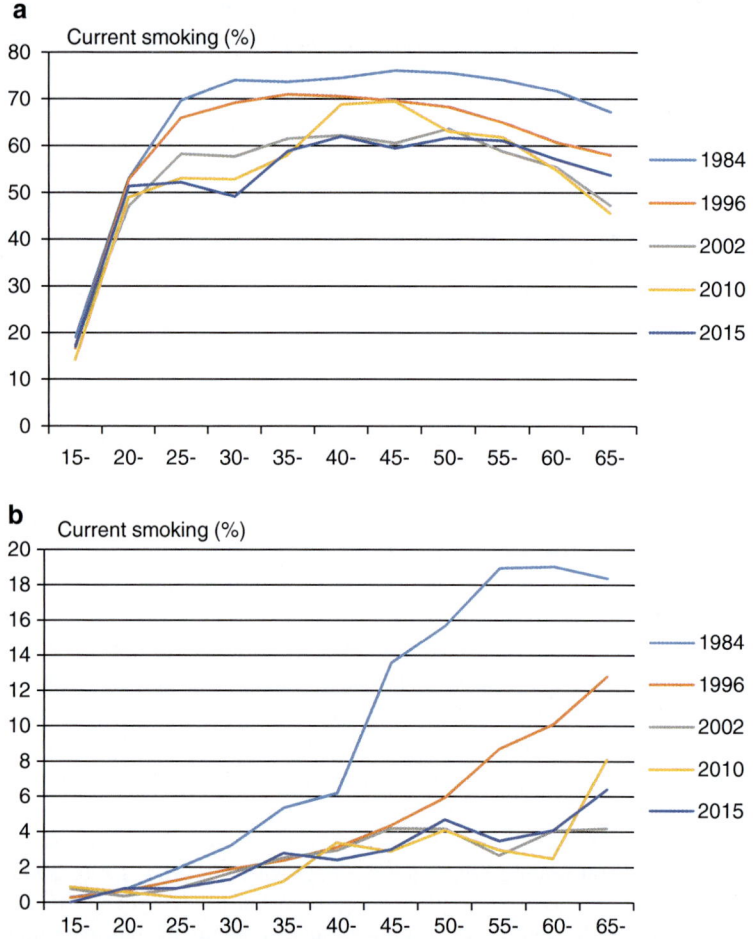

Fig. 2.2 (**a**) Prevalence of tobacco use in Chinese Men by age group in different years. (**b**) Prevalence of tobacco use in Chinese Women by age group in different years. Source: The figures are made by authors according to five national surveys

people aged 15–19, the prevalence of current smoker among men by age group was decreasing since 1984, but prevalence continued to decline in men aged 20–39, and not obvious change in med aged 40 and over after 2002. Also, prevalence was still over 50% in adults aged 20–60.

The prevalence of current smoking was relatively low among Chinese women, the levels among male is about more than 20–30 times that in the female. The results of 1984 and 1996 surveys showed the higher the rate of smoking while the older the age. Especially 1984 survey showed that the prevalence of smoking in women aged 45 and over (before born in 1940s) achieved 14–18%; the prevalence of smoking in women was still increasing while the older age, but the prevalence level at 1996 survey was the one quarter in women at the same age group and a half if women born in same years in 1984 survey. The results predicted that prevalence level in Chinese women born in the 1920–1930s may be higher than that in women born in 1940s and later, increasing speed of prevalence while older age in Chinese women born in the 1920–1930s may be quicker than that in women born in 1940s and later. The prevalence of smoking in women were the lower. The prevalence of women by age group were about 4% after 2002 (Fig. 2.2b).

The tobacco epidemic stage is more affected by socio-economic factors and public health interventions. The prevalence of tobacco in Chinese men has peaked since the 1980s, fallen about 10% since that time, which reached the maturity stage. However, the prevalence of smoking in Chinese males was only fallen about 10% last 30 years, it is estimated that the period of maturity would be last the longer than 40 years. After 2000 the smoking rate of young adult decreased from 70 to 50%. If the tobacco control measures is effectively implemented, the smoking rate of young male rate dropped to below 40% in the next 10–20 years, the pattern of male smoking may fall into the declining stage. For female, its prevalence of smoking is very low as influenced by various social and economic factors after 1950s. The change in future remain to be observed.

2.2.3 Exposure to Secondhand Smoke in China

The prevalence of exposure to secondhand smoke (SHS) has been a serious problem in China. In national surveys on smoking behavior conducted in 1984, 1996, 2002, 2010 and 2015, a similar questionnaire was used to measure exposure to SHS. However, the judgment standard on exposure to SHS has become increasingly stringent as understanding of the health risks of SHS exposure has increased among the medical community. As a result, the prevalence of SHS exposure reported has also increased accordingly. As shown in Table 2.1, the judgment standard of SHS exposure changed from "*exposure to SHS for more than 15 minutes per day*" to "*exposure to SHS for more than 15 minutes at least one day per typical week*", the prevalence of SHS exposure increased from 39.8% in the 1984 survey to 53.5% in the 1996 survey (the standards and results in the 2002 survey were the same as in 1996). The standard then changed from "*exposure to SHS for more than 15 minutes at least one day per typical week*" to "*exposure to SHS for at least one day per typical week*" without the limitation of more than 15 min. The prevalence of SHS exposure increased from 53.5% in the 1996 survey to 72.4% in the 2010 survey, the prevalence of SHS exposure was not reported in 2015 survey.

We choose the same standard of exposure to SHS "*Exposure to SHS for more than 15 minutes per day*", as that used in the 1984 survey, i.e. we measured the prevalence of the most serious exposure to SHS in the population. Therefore, the data in the various surveys can be used. As shown in Table 2.1, only the 2010 Survey

Table 2.1 Questions, standard and results of exposure to SHS in four national smoking behavior surveys

Survey year	Question	Scale	Standard exposure to SHS	Rate of exposure to SHS (%)
1984	*Exposure to SHS for more than 15 min per day*	1 = Yes at home, 2 = Yes at working and public places, 3 = Yes Both, 4 = No, including for *less than 15 min per day*	1 + 2 + 3	39.8
1996	*Exposure to SHS for more than 15 min at least one day per typical week*	1 = every day 2 = 4–6 days 3 = 1–3 days 4 = No	1 + 2 + 3	53.5 (53.2–53.8)
2002	The same as 1996	The same as 1996	1 + 2 + 3	53.9 (50.9–55.8)
2010	*Exposure SHS at least one day per typical week*	The same as 1996	1 + 2 + 3 without limitation of exposure time	72.4 (69.2–75.5)

did not have the limitation of more than 15 min, but were not obvious difference between the results with or without this limitation, for people exposed to SHS every day. The results of several surveys showed that daily exposure to SHS remained the same, without change. However, more and more people, whether male or female, urban or rural, reported themselves to exposure SHS at least 1–3 days per week over the past 25 years (1984–2010), especially with the implementation of the WHO FCTC after January 2006 (Fig. 2.3a, b). By the end of 2015, the WHO FCTC had been effective for 10 years, about half of non-smokers were being exposed to SHS, either at home or in public places, although the proportion of every day exposure to SHS had a little declined.[14] By 2015, after 10 years the entry into force of the Convention, the prevalence of SHS exposure at homes and in the public places were dropped to 46.7 and 54.3%, separately. However, there are still about half of the non smokers at home or in public places suffer from SHS exposure.

2.3 Epidemiological Study on Mortality Attributed Tobacco Use in China

Over the past 30 years, several prospective, retrospective and cohort epidemiological studies on mortality attributed tobacco use have been carried out in China.

---

[14]China CDC, 2015 report of tobacco survey for adults in China http://www.tcrc.org.cn/UploadFiles/2016-03/318/201603231215175500.pdf.

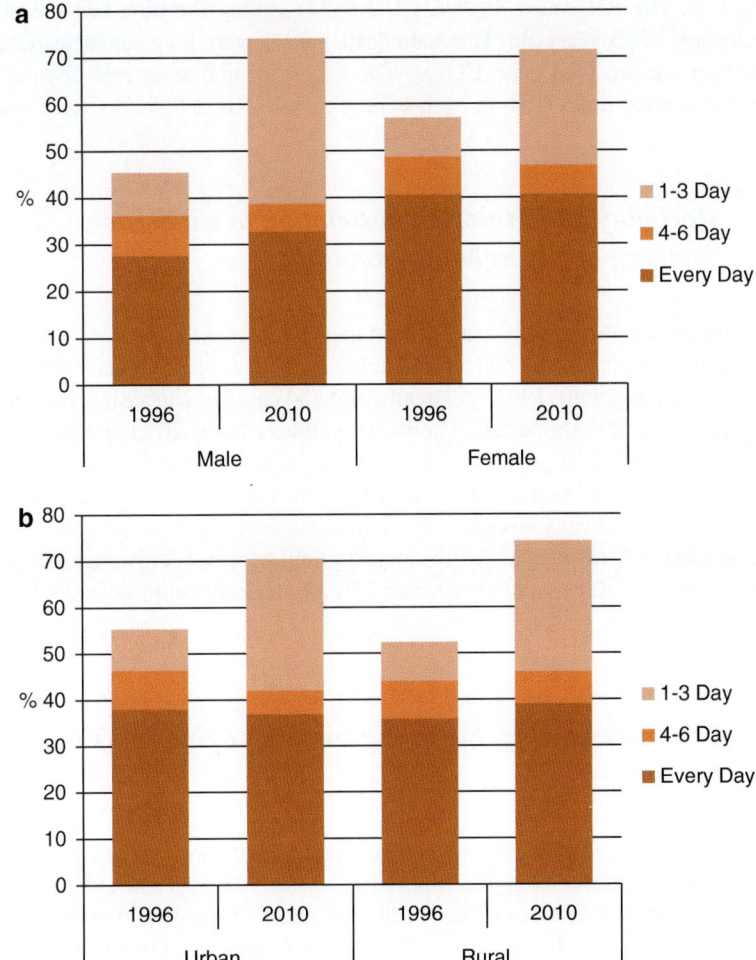

Fig. 2.3 (**a**) Percentage of adults aged 15 and over to exposure SHS in a typical week by gender, 1996 and 2010. (**b**) Percentage of adults aged 15 and over to exposure SHS in a typical week by area, 1996 and 2010. Source: the figure is made by author according to the 1996 and 2010 surveys

2.3.1 Early Health Effects of the Emerging Tobacco Epidemic in China: A 16-Year Prospective Study

The earliest prospective research was carried out in 11 factories in Shanghai, China at beginning of economic reform and opening up to the outside world. That study covered a total of 9351 adults (6494 men and 2857 women) aged 35–64 years. Sixty one percent of men were smoking at the baseline survey in the 1970s. During an average follow-up of 16 years (1978–1994), 881 men and 207 women died, Their overall mortality of smokers was significantly greater than that of nonsmokers (RR: 1.4; 95%

CI: 1.2–1.7). The RR was 1.8 (95% CI, 1.5–22) among the men begun smoking before the age of 25 years old. The main death causes were lung cancer, esophageal cancer, liver cancer, CHD and COPD. The excess of above several disease were almost one to three times (RR-1), such as lung cancer (RR, 3.8; 95% CI, 2.1–6.8).[15]

2.3.2 Morbidity and Mortality in Relation to Cigarette Smoking in Shanghai Community

The prospective cohort study was follow death and incidence of cancer among 18,244 male residents in the resident community of Shanghai, China from 1986 to 1993.[16] By September 30, 1993, 852 deaths and 554 cases of cancer had been identified during the follow-up period. The heavy smokers (over 20 cigarettes per day) had a 60% greater risk of death relative to lifelong nonsmokers; the RR of mortality of lung cancer and CHD associated with heavy smoking were 1.9 and 2, separately. The relative risks in heavy smokers after adjustment for alcohol consumption were 2.2 for incidence of any cancer, 9.4 for incident lung cancer. Totally, cigarette smoking caused 36% of all cases of cancer and 21% of all deaths in middle aged men of the study population.

2.3.3 Mortality Attributable to Cigarette Smoking in Xi'an Factory

The study assessed mortality among smokers and non-smokers were carried out by following a cohort at the Xi'an machinery factory for 20 years. The cohort involved 1696 people aged 35 years or older (1124 men and 572 women) recruited in May 1976. A total of 56% of the men and 12% of the women were ever-smokers at baseline. Up to August 31, 1996, 218 persons (173 men and 45 women) had died. The relative risks of male and female ever smokers for total deaths, adjusted by demographic factors and diastolic blood pressure, and blood lipid levels, were 2.42 and 2.32, respectively.[17] The relative risk of all cancer, and coronary heart disease associated with smoking in male and female were described in Table 2.2.

---

[15]Chen Z M, Xu Z, Collins R, Li W X, Peto R (2007) Early health effects of the emerging tobacco epidemic in China. A 16-year prospective study. JAMA 1997 Nov 12; 278: 1500–1504.

[16]Yuan JM, Ross RK, Wang XL, Gao YT, Henderson BE, Yu MC. Morbidity and mortality in relation to cigarette smoking in Shanghai, China. A prospective male cohort study. JAMA 1996; 275: 1646–50.

[17]Lam TH, He Y, Li LS, Li LS, He SF, Liang BQ. Mortality attributable to smoking in China. *JAMA* 1997;278:1505–8.

Table 2.2 Summary of Relative risks and PAF for adult mortality of the selected diseases with tobacco use in China

Study code	All causes RR	PAF (%)	Lung cancer RR	PAF (%)	Ischemic stroke or IHD RR	PAF (%)	COPD RR	PAF (%)
2.3.1 SH F	1.4 (1.2–1.7)	20 (12–29)	3.8 (2.1–6.8)	63 (52–78)	1.8 (1.0–3.2)		2.5 (1.4–4.4)	
2.3.2 SH C mortality	1.6	21	6.5		2.0			
2.3.2 SH C incidence		34	9.4					
2.3.3 X'A factory Male	2.42 1.72–3.42		2.50 (cancer) 1.41–4.43		3.61 1.35–9.67			
2.3.3 X'A factory Female	2.32 1.18–4.56		1.98 (cancer) 0.50–7.92		4.67 0.78–27.8			
2.3.4 1 million Case-control Male	1.23 (0.01)	13%	2.72 (0.05)	52.3	1.28 (0.03)	14.7	1.43 (0.03)	22.6
2.3.4 1 million Case-control Male urban	1.29 (0.03)		2.98 (0.05)		1.28 (0.03)		1.57 (0.03)	
2.3.4 1 million Case-control Male rural	1.22 (0.02)		2.57 (0.08)		1.28 (0.05)		1.41 (0.03)	
2.3.4 1 million Case-control Female	1.23 (0.03)	2.7	2.64 (0.08)	19.4	1.3 (0.05)	1.5	1.72 (0.05)	9.3
2.3.4 1 million Case-control Female urban	1.40 (0.03)		3.24 (0.06)		1.37 (0.04)		2.51 (0.06)	
2.3.4 1 million Case-control Female rural	1.14 (0.04)		1.98 (0.12)		1.22 (0.09)		1.50 (0.06)	
2.3.5 Hypertension male	1.28 (1.23–1.33)	12.9	2.44 (2.01–2.96)	50.6	1.21 (1.03–1.42)	12.9	1.19 (1.05–1.35)	12.1
2.3.5 Hypertension female	1.33	5	2.76 (2.18–3.49)	14.8	1.41 (1.15–1.71)	3.8	1.61 (1.37–1.89)	17.1
2.3.6 0.25 million Urban (1999)	1.32 (1.28–1.37)	17	2.32 (2.08–2.59)		1.35 (1.23–1.47)		1.42 (1.30–1.55)	
2.3.6 0.25 million Rural (1999)	1.13 (1.11–1.15)	9	1.76 (1.62–1.91)		1.13 (1.07–1.20)		1.25 (1.21–1.30)	

(continued)

Table 2.2 (continued)

Study code	All causes		Lung cancer		Ischemic stroke or IHD		COPD	
	RR	PAF (%)	RR	PAF (%)	RR	PAF (%)	RR	PAF (%)
2.3.7 0.5 million Urban	1.65 (1.59–1.73)	26	2.98 (2.66–3.33)		1.63 (1.49–1.77)		4.61 (3.71–5.71)	
2.3.7 0.5 million Rural	1.22 (1.20–1.25)	14	2.30 (2.13–2.48)		1.24 (1.17–1.32)		1.41 (1.31–1.51)	
2.3.8 Hong Kong Male	1.92 (1.7–2.16)	33	4.99 (4.0–6.22)		1.58 (1.27–1.97)		3.68 (2.58–5.26)	
2.3.8 Hong Kong Female	1.62 (1.4–1.88)	10	3.06 (2.3–4.07)		1.96 (1.3–2.96)		13.27 (7.19–24.49)	

Source: Author tabulated according to relevant literature

2.3.4 Retrospective Proportional Mortality Study of One Million Deaths in the 1980s

Family member or informants of 429,852 death cases were visited by interviewers in 98 areas of China during 1989–91, reviewing death causes, as well as smoking and the other health status of the decedent and control. The study firstly systematically reported the relative risk and death for the main diseases associated with tobacco use, including a various of cancer, respiratory disease, especially COPD, vascular disease, especially stroke and coronary heart disease in such crowds.[18] It is a very important study on the relationship between smoking and its health consequences among Chinese people.

Nearly 70% of the male dead, 22.5% of the urban female and 12% rural female dead were smoker before death. The both relative risk for total mortality associated with smoking in the male and female aged 35–69 were 1.23, the proportion of attributable tobacco use was 13% of deaths in men but only 3% of deaths in women. The relative risk for lung cancer related to tobacco use 2.64 and 2.72 in male and female aged 35–69, separately; 52.3% lung cancer in male and 19.4% lung cancer in female were attributed to tobacco use.

The study estimated that 0.6 million deaths was attributed to tobacco use in 1990 and would increase at least 0.8 million in 2000 and about 3 million a year by 2050 on the basis of current smoking patterns.

---

[18] Liu B Q, Peto R, Chen Z M, Boreham J, Wu Y P, et al. (1998) Emerging tobacco hazards in China: 1. retrospective proportional mortality study of one million deaths. BMJ 317: 1411–1422.

2.3.5 Mortality Attributable to Tobacco Use from National Hypertension Survey in 1991

National Hypertension Survey of China was carried out in 1991, including 169,871 Chinese adults aged 40 years of age or older. The basic data were collected on smoking and other risk factors and 71.1% of men and 9.9% of women were smokers. The follow-up survey was carried out in 1999 and 2000, with a response rate of 93.4%. The 17,863 deaths reported during follow-up, 98.6% were verified by death certificates or medical records. The overall risk ratios (RR) associated with smoking were estimated at 1.21 (1.16–1.26) in men and 1.33 (1.25–1.41) in women, after adjusting for multiple risk factors. The PAFs were 12.9% in men and 3.1% in women in 2005. The relative ration of lung cancer in male and female aged 40 and over were 2.44 and 2.76, separately, more than 50% of smoking-attributable lung cancer in men and 14.8% in women. The risk ration (RR) values of cancers other than lung cancer, cardiovascular disease and respiratory disease were about 1.5.[19] It was estimated that a total of 673,000 deaths were attributable to smoking in Chinese adults aged 40 years or older in 2005.

2.3.6 The Chinese Prospective Smoking Study in a Population of 250,000

The Chinese prospective smoking and its health impact study has been carried out in 45 nationally representative Disease Surveillance Points (DSPs) from April 9 to Dec 31, 1991 as baseline survey, with follow-up to Dec 31, 1999. In the baseline survey of the study the data of smoking and other risk behavior and environment factors of 225,721 men aged 40 and over were collected. There were 74% were smokers (73% current, only 1% former), but few of this cohort born before 1950 would have smoked substantial numbers of cigarettes since early adult life. Medical death certificates are routinely collected by staff trained in DSP.

Up to end of 1995, 9233 male aged 40–79 dead in the cohort. Overall relative risk associated with smoking were 1.19 (95% CI 1.13–1.25). Twelve percent mortality was attributed to tobacco use in 1995. Compared with lifelong non-smoker, relative risk of death for neoplasm, respiratory, or vascular diseases were 1.26, 1.38 and 1.13. Their PAF were 16%, 22% and 9% in 1995.[20] Up to 1999, 25,111 male aged 40–79 (Urban: 5033, Rural 20,078) dead in the cohort. The relative risk of total death in urban and rural population associated with smoking was 1.32 and 1.13 respectively, which increased than that in 1995. The RR of the main chronic disease

[19] Gu D, Kelly T N, Wu X, Chen J, Samet J M, et al. (2009) Mortality attributable to smoking in China. N Engl J Med 360: 150–159.
[20] Niu SR, Yang GH, Chen ZM, et al. Emerging tobacco hazards in China: 2. Early mortality results from a prospective study. *BMJ* 1998; **317:** 1423–24.

in urban and rural male of the cohort were 2.32 and 1.76 for lung cancer, 1.35 and 1.13 for coronary heart disease and 1.42 and 1.25 for COPD.[21]

2.3.7   A Prospective Study of 0.5 Million Adults in China

A large blood-based prospective study (the China Kadoorie Bio-bank) was start-up in 2004, in order to assess the complex interplay of lifestyle, environmental and genetic factors as determinants of chronic disease, by following 0.5 million people (210,222 men and 302,669 women) in four urban and six rural or semi-rural areas. The baseline survey of the study took place during 2004–08, with follow-up to Jan 1, 2014. The study administered laptop-based questionnaires on tobacco and other risk behavior factors, measured physiological indicators, height, weight, etc., and took blood samples for long-term storage.[22,23] The 63% male and 3.5% women were smokers in the cohort.[24] Up to Jan. 2014, The 13,281 deaths reported during follow-up (Urban: 3318, Rural 9963). The overall risk ratios (RR) in male of the cohort associated with smoking were estimated at 1.65 in urban and 1.26 in rural. The relatively risk of the major diseases, such as lung cancer, CHD and COPD, were list in Table 2.2. It is particularly meaningful that the relative risk of people started smoking before the age of 20 has reached 1.98. In general, the PAF of tobacco use was increasing, achieved 18.3% in men, but was dropped to 4% owing to decreasing prevalence of tobacco use in female. These findings of the study inspire to understand in further the relationship between smoking and health in the Chinese population.

2.3.8   Case-Control Study of Mortality and Smoking in All Adult in Hong Kong

The study collected data of 27,507 cases of death and 13,054 spouse or relative aged >35 years as live controls in 1998.[25] The death cause for each victims has been confirmed from the registry about the medical cause of death; the smoking habits 10

---

[21] Chen, ZM, Richard Peto, Maigeng Zhou, et al. Contrasting male and female trends in tobacco-attributed mortality in China: evidence from successive nationwide prospective cohort studies, *Lancet* 2015; 386: 1447–56.

[22] Chen ZM, Chen J, Collins R, et al. China Kadoorie Biobank of 0.5 million people: survey methods, baseline characteristics and long-term follow-up. *Int J Epidemiol* 2011; 40: 1652–66.

[23] Chen, ZM, Richard Peto, Maigeng Zhou, et al Contrasting male and female trends in tobacco-attributed mortality in China: evidence from successive nationwide prospective cohort studies, *Lancet* 2015; 386: 1447–56.

[24] Chen ZM, Peto R, Lona A., et al. Emerging Tobacco-Related Cancer Risks in China: A Nationwide, Prospective Study of 0.5 Million Adults, Cancer 2015;121:3097–106.

[25] Lam TH, Ho SY, Peto R. at el. Mortality and smoking in Hong Kong: case-control study of all adult deaths in 1998. BMJ 2001; 323: 361.

years earlier of death cases and live control were attained. The proportion of ever smokers in male was over 60% (case: 69%, control: 60%), that in female over 10% (case: 21%, control 13%). The risk ration of main disease associated with smoking were reported, which was higher than that reported in mainland of China. Smoking caused about 33% of all male deaths and 5% of all female deaths in the study population aged 35–69 in 1998.

2.3.9 The Characters of Epidemiologic Studies on Tobacco Use and the Impact of Health in Chinese Population

Table 2.2 summarizes the results for all study on tobacco use and impact of health in China. Of these, sample size of 4 studies were smaller, between 10,000 and 20,000 observing subjects, only 2000 people in Xi'an study. The sample size of the other four studies were bigger, from 0.17 million, 0.25 million, 0.5 million and 1 million. The small scale study were located in the metropolis, such as Shanghai, Hong Kong and Xi'an. The other four studies covered more cities and rural areas. Except the results of Xi'an study, the finding of these studies were consistent based on tobacco use history, observing time and district.

The relative risk (RRs) and PAF for total death and main disease associated with tobacco use were similar to those for other Asian countries[26]; However, these results were substantially lower than those from studies conducted in Europe and North America,[27,28,29] but were close to results reported in early years of follow-up (1951–1971), in the British Doctors Study.[30] The finding from Hong Kong study was similar that in the United States in 1990.[31]

However, in the China Kadoorie Biobank cohort study, urban male smokers who had started before age 20 years had double the never-smoker mortality rate (RR 1.98, 1.79–2.19) and those who smoked more than 25 cigarettes daily was nearly

---

[26] Zheng W, McLerran DF, Rolland BA, et al. Burden of Total and Cause-Specific Mortality Related to Tobacco Smoking among Adults Aged >=45 Years in Asia: A Pooled Analysis of 21 Cohorts, PLOS Medicine, e1001631 April 2014, Volume 11.

[27] US Department of Health and Human Services, (1989) Reducing the health consequences of smoking: 25 years of progress. A report of the Surgeon General. DHHS Publication No. CDC 89–8411. Rockville (Maryland): US Department of Health and Human Services.

[28] IARC Working Group on the Evaluation of Carcinogenic Risks to Humans, (2004) Tobacco smoke and involuntary smoking. IARC Monogr Eval Carcinog Risks Hum 8: 1–1438.

[29] Pirie K, Peto R, Reeves G K, Green J, Beral V, et al. (2013) The 21st century hazards of smoking and benefits of stopping: a prospective study of one million women in the UK. Lancet 381: 133–141.

[30] Doll R, Peto R , Wheatley K, Gray R, Sutherland I (1994) Mortality in relation to smoking: 40 years' observations on male British doctors. BMJ 309: 901–911.

[31] Thun M J, Carter B D, Feskanich D , Freedman N D, Prentice R, et al. (2013) 50-year trends in smoking-related mortality in the United States. N Engl J Med 368: 351–364.

double (RR 1.93, 1.75–2.12), which is close to the RRs for western countries.[32] China's 2010 survey[33] showed that more than half of men aged 15–34 years in China are the regular current smokers; more than a half of these younger smokers started smoking before the age of 20. Based on these estimation, smoking caused about one million (840,000 male, 130,000 female) deaths in China in 2010.

2.4 Estimating Health Risk of Tobacco Use in Chinese Population

In previous section, the relative risk and PAF from several large-scale epidemiological studies between tobacco use and health consequences have been introduced in China past several decades. However, the results of these study cannot be extrapolated directly to other population as there are more than one billion adults, vast in terrene, different smoking pattern and different co-factors in different areas of China, such as indoor coal burning pollution. In recent years, the GDB study used the indirect method to estimate health hazards attributable tobacco use in China.

2.4.1 Method Used to Estimate the Health Hazards of Tobacco Use

2.4.1.1 To Estimate the Population Attributable Risk of Tobacco Use Population

Attributable Fraction (PAF) method is defined as the proportion of deaths than can be attributed to exposure some risk factor, here refers to tobacco use. The PAF method can also be thought of as the proportional reduction in population disease or mortality that would occur if nobody were exposed to tobacco over a specified time interval while distributions of other risk factors in the population remained unchanged. There are three steps to calculating PAF: (1) Developing relative risk (RR) estimates for diseases that affect current and former smokers compared to lifetime nonsmokers; (2) Developing estimates of smoking prevalence and smoking patterns for the populations and years of interest; (3) Estimating disease- and gender-specific PAFs by age group; and applying the PAFs to disease-specific mortality data to estimate smoking-attributable mortality in different age-sex

---

[32] Chen ZM Peto R Zhou MG et al Contrasting male and female trends in tobacco-attributed mortality in China: evidence from successive nationwide prospective cohort studies Lancet 2015; 386: 1447–56.

[33] China CDC Global Adult Tobacco Survey (GATS) China 2010 Country Report, edited by Yang GH, China San Xia Press, 2011 Nov.

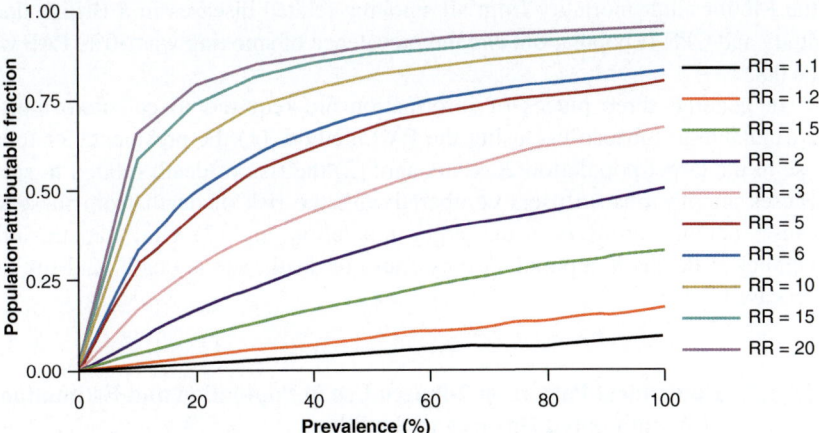

Source: Michael Thun, unpublished data.

Fig. 2.4 The relationship of relative risk (RR) to the population-attributable fraction at different prevalence levels.
Source: Figure is from Chapter 12, 2014 Report of the Surgeon General, P 650.
Note: *RR* relative risk

populations.[34] Several formulas are commonly used to estimate PAF. Some of these formulas are valid only under the assumption of no-confounding for the association between exposure and disease.[35]

The typical formula used to calculate PAF is as:

$$PAF = \frac{P(RR-1)}{P(RR-1)+1} \tag{2.1}$$

where P is the prevalence of exposure in the population and RR is the relative risk for disease associated with exposure assumed for the population. Smoking-related diseases have been identified, with plenty of scientific evidence.

By the above formula, PAF is determined as two components: the relationship of relative risk (RR) and the prevalence of tobacco use. The figure below (Fig. 2.4) shows the relationship between relative risk (*RR*) and the population-attributable fraction at different prevalence levels. As shown in the figure, when the relative risk is low, such as RR = 1.5–3.0, the rate of smoking prevalence is 60% in male, PAF may be between 0.20 and 0.50 (It may be tobacco attributable mortality for Chinese male in the current and next 20 years). When the relative risk (RR) is 10, which was

---

[34] U.S. Department of Health and Human Services. *The Health Consequences of Smoking: 50 Years of Progress. A Report of the Surgeon General.* Atlanta, GA: U.S. Department of Health and Human Services, Centers for Disease Control and Prevention, National Center for Chronic Disease Prevention and Health Promotion, Office on Smoking and Health, 2014.

[35] Rockhill B, Newman B and Weinberg C, Use and Misuse of Population Attributable Fractions, American Journal of Public Health, January 1998, Vol. 88, No. 1 15–19.

the RR for adult mortality from all smoking-related diseases in a British doctors study and CPS-II population, and the prevalence of smoking was 50%, PAF would be 0.8.[36]

In general, three pieces of information are required to calculate mortality attributable to tobacco use using the PAS method: (1) the prevalence of tobacco use in the target population 20 years ago; (2) the risk of death related to specific causes among tobacco users compared with the risk of death from these same causes among non-users in the target population; and (3) Vital statistics on the number of deaths in a population by cause of death, age at death, and sex of the deceased.

2.4.1.2 Epidemical Pattern of Tobacco Use in Population and Estimation of Accumulated Hazards of Smoking

The current prevalence and characteristics of smoking, even where data are available, is not sufficient to determine cumulative hazards of smoking. The smoking pattern directly affects the degree of relative risk attributable smoking. In addition, the absence of data on the prevalence and history of tobacco use at the same time point, in many countries, makes it difficult to estimate tobacco-attributable deaths for any one particular year.

It is not realistic to obtain such complex data in all parts of the world. It is therefore necessary to arrive at an indirect estimation. To resolve this problem, many methods on the indirect estimation have been produced in past decades.

Many famous classic studies revealed that the more cigarettes smoked, the longer smoking period, the greater risk of the lung cancer.[37,38,39] The increasing gradient of cancer risk associated with increased exposure level, often called the dose-response relationship, provides a sound basis for assessing the causality. Based on the observation, Peto et al. pointed that lung cancer deaths reflect the cumulative risk of tobacco use over time and defined the proxy indicator–the smoking impact ratio (*SIR*), referred to as the "Peto-Lopez approach".[40] *SIR* is equal the ration of the difference between population lung cancer mortality and that of never-smokers in

[36] U.S. Department of Health and Human Services. *The Health Consequences of Smoking: 50 Years of Progress. A Report of the Surgeon General*. Atlanta, GA: U.S. Department of Health and Human Services, Centers for Disease Control and Prevention, National Center for Chronic Disease Prevention and Health Promotion, Office on Smoking and Health, 2014. P650.

[37] Doll R, Peto R. Cigarette smoking and bronchial carcinoma: dose and time relationships among regular smokers and lifelong non-smokers. *J Epidemiol Community Health* 1978; 32: 303–13.

[38] Freund KM, Belanger AJ, D'Agostino RB, Kannel WB. The health risks of smoking. The Framingham Study: 34 years of follow-up. *Ann Epidemiol* 1993; 3: 417–24.

[39] Naohito Yamaguchi Yumiko Mochizuki-Kobayashi Osamu Utsunomiya, Quantitative relationship between cumulative cigarette consumption and lung cancer mortality in Japan, *International Journal of Epidemiology*, 2000 29(6), 963–968.

[40] Peto R, Lopez AD, Boreham J, et al Mortality from in developed countries: indirect estimation from national vital statistics, Lancet 1986, 339:1268–78.

target population, to the difference between smoker lung cancer mortality and that of never-smokers in reference population.

$$SIR = \frac{C_{LC} - N_{LC}}{S^*_{LC} - N^*_{LC}}$$
(2.2)

C_{LC}: (age-sex-specific) lung cancer mortality rate in the study population (for example, country of analysis)

N_{LC}: lung cancer mortality rate for never-smokers in the same population

S^*_{LC} and N^*_{LC}: lung cancer mortality rates for smokers and never-smokers, respectively, in a reference population.

Thus, *SIR* as a proxy for prevalence in the PAF formula. The resulting *SIR* estimate is then used instead of P in the PAF formula:

$$PAF = \frac{P(RR-1)}{P(RR-1)+1} = \frac{SIR(RR*-1)}{\left[SIR(RR*-1)+1\right]}$$
(2.3)

To calculate the *SIR*, 4 parameters are needed in (Eq. 2.1). The national vital statistics system provides the number and rate of lung cancer deaths by age and sex for each target country. The lung cancer mortality rates for smokers (S^*_{LC}) and never-smokers (N^*_{LC}) can be obtained from the Cancer Prevention Study II (CPS-II) as a reference population (Table 2.3). The only parameter to be estimated indirectly is N_{LC}, since direct estimates of never-smoker lung cancer mortality are not known for most countries (this parameter is only known from the USA and China studies).

The non-smoker lung cancer mortality was higher in China, India and other developing countries. The higher mortality of lung cancer mortality in the non-smokers was related to the Chinese patterns of household cooking and heating using coal as fuel over the past few decades.[41,42] For example, the highest morbidity and mortality of lung cancer has closely been associated with using coal as household fuel and without adequate ventilation in Yunnan Xuanwei of China.[43,44]

---

[41] Smith KR, Shuhua G, Kun H, et al. One hundred million improved cookstoves in China: how was it done? World Development 1993;21:941–61.

[42] Du YX, Cha Q, Chen XW, et al. An epidemiological study of risk factors for lung cancer in Guangzhou, China. Lung Cancer 1996;14:S9–37.

[43] He XZ, Chen W, Liu ZY, Chapman RS (1991) An epidemiological study of lung cancer in Xuan Wei county, China: current progress. Case-control study on lung cancer and cooking fuel. *Environmental Health Perspectives,* **94**:9–13.

[44] Wang TJ, Zhou BS, Shi JP (1996) Lung cancer in nonsmoking Chinese women: a case control study. *Lung Cancer,* **14**:S93–98.

Table 2.3 Mortality rate to lung cancer by smoking status in the CPSII reference population ($1/10^5$)

Age group (years)	Smokers		Never-smokers	
	Men	Women	Men	Women
30–44	8.9	9.4	1.7	1.6
45–59	124.0	81.6	7.1	6.8
60–69	496.6	246.6	17.3	6.8
70–79	985.5	375.3	31.0	29.8
80+	1183.5	409.7	42.3	40.3

Source: From Table 1 of the *WHO Global Report: Tobacco Attributable Mortality*

Meanwhile, the relative risk of mortality from lung cancer as a result of smoking is relatively constant in different cities in which non-smoker lung cancer mortality rates varied in China.[45]

A constant relative risk over a large range of background mortality rates means that the death rate of lung cancer in non-smokers is high, that in smokers is higher proportionally (synergistic effect with other factors), which provided a raison for adjusting *Smoking Impact Ratio* (*SIR*) in areas where the mortality of lung cancer in non-smokers. Therefore, Ezzati and Lopez adjusted *SIR* though multiplying the numerator of the (Eq. 2.2) by $\dfrac{N^*_{LC}}{N_{LC}}$ so as to take off proportionally death of lung cancer due to indoor air pollution by coal burning in China and India.[46]

$$SIR = \frac{C_{LC} - N_{LC}}{S^*_{LC} - N^*_{LC}} * \frac{N^*_{LC}}{N_{LC}} \qquad (2.4)$$

C_{LC}: (age-sex-specific) lung cancer mortality rate in the study population (for example, country of analysis)
N_{LC}: lung cancer mortality rate for never-smokers in the same population
S^*_{LC} and N^*_{LC}: lung cancer mortality rates for smokers and never-smokers, respectively, in a reference population.

2.4.1.3 Relative Risk (RR) Estimates

Next, it is need to estimate the relative risk (RR) for those diseases for current and former smokers in comparison to lifetime nonsmokers. The relative risk (RR) measures the risk of dying from a specific cause among those exposed to a factor relative

---

[45] Liu BQ. 1990 *Retrospective proportional mortality study of one million deaths* to estimate tobacco attributable mortality in China, *BMJ* 1998;317:1411–22.
[46] Majid Ezzati and Alan D. Lopez, *Chapter 11* Smoking and oral tobacco use, in *Comparative quantification of health risks: global and regional burden of disease attributable to selected major risk factors* edited by EzzatiM, Lopez AD, Rodgers A and Christopher J.L. Murray.

to those not exposed to the same factor. If the risk of dying from a specific disease, when exposed to tobacco use, is equal to the risk among those not exposed to tobacco use, then the ratio of the two risks (RR) will be equal to one. If the risk is higher among those exposed then relative risk will be greater than one. It is important to note that the *Relative Risk* in (Eq. 2.3) is not the ordinary RR, but is the *RR** for each unit of *SIR*. It need to be converted from *RR* for each smoker by back calculation.[47]

The use of a relative risk approach for common risk factors for common diseases is standard in epidemiological literature based on its ability to capture the "risk magnification" role of most risk factors. In the particular case of smoking, Liu et al. (1998) found that in China, the relative risks for mortality from lung cancer and other major diseases are approximately constant in different cities and villages where background (non-smoker) mortality rates for the same disease varied significantly.[48] This finding also has been confirmed in studies which stratified on serum cholesterol for cardiovascular diseases.[49]

Taking the CPS-II as their reference base, without adjusting these relative risks for potential confounding factors, they realized that the level of calculated risk may be biased and could, in theory, result in upwardly biased estimates of mortality attributable to tobacco. To minimize this potential source of bias, Peto et al. conservatively halved the excess mortality in smokers from all diseases other than lung cancer and chronic obstructive pulmonary disease. The Global Disease Burden (GBD) study and WHO report made some changes to the Peto/Lopez approach.

2.4.2   To Estimate the Health Consequence Attributable Tobacco Use for Chinese Population

2.4.2.1   The Roadmap to Estimate Health Hazards Associated with Tobacco Use

The health hazards attributable tobacco use during 1990–2000 were related to tobacco use during 1960–1970. Based on the epidemiological study introduced earlier, the average age of starting smoking was after the age of 20, the cigarettes amount of smoking was fewer although the prevalence of smoking was higher than that after 2000 in both male and female. It was support the judgment that the tobacco

[47] Majid Ezzati and Alan D. Lopez, Table 11.2 and 11.3 from Smoking and oral tobacco use, in *Comparative Quantification of Health Risks Global and Regional Burden of Disease Attributable to Selected Major Risk Factors* (Volume 1) Edited by Majid Ezzati, Alan D. Lopez, Anthony Rodgers and Christopher J.L. Murray.

[48] Liu BQ. 1990 *Retrospective proportional mortality study of one million deaths* to estimate tobacco attributable mortality in China, *BMJ* 1998;317:1411–22.

[49] Jee SH, Suh I, Kim IS, Appel LJ (1999) Smoking and atherosclerotic cardiovascular disease in men with low levels of serum cholesterol: the Korea Medical Insurance Corporation study. *Journal of the American Medical Association,* **282**:2149–2155.

product in 1960–1970 was one fifth to two fifth of tobacco product in 1984 when the first epidemiological survey on smoking behavior carried out. We can calculate *SIR* based on the (Eq. 2.3) in order to estimate the accumulated smoking risk in those years. By the way *SIR* was used to the accumulated smoking risk to estimate the cancer and chronic respiratory diseases, 10-years lagged tobacco smoking prevalence for the other health outcome in GBD 2010.[50] The data sources for calculating the four parameters of *SIR* are as follows. The mortality rate of lung cancer in lifelong non-smokers in Chinese population is directly from Liu' study.[51] GBD study also referred to the other results of non- smokers' lung cancer in the Asia Pacific Region.[52]

1. The data on lung cancer mortality in Chinese population were from the death causes registration systematic, DSP system or cancer registry system. The completeness of death registration in China were estimated about 20%.[53] The completeness of non-national death registry system was poor, under reporting about 30%.[54] GBD 2010 reappraise a series of strategies on mortality and death causes, focused to adjust the mortality level and to estimate cause fractions of total causes in China. The difference of lung cancer between in total objective population and in non-smokers are vary after adjustment, so It is certain to affect the *SIR* value.
2. The numerator and denominator of equation for calculating *SIR* is adjusted with the respective never-smoker lung cancer mortality rates in target population and reference population due to indoor smoke in China and India.[55]
3. Lung cancer mortality rates for smokers and never-smokers in a reference population were from CPS-II.

Some relative risks of disease related to tobacco use have been obtained from several epidemiologic studies in previous section since 1980'. At present the international studies on disease burden attributed to tobacco use mainly refer to the results of Retrospective proportional mortality study of one million deaths in the

---

[50] *Stephen S Lim‡, Theo Vos, Christopher J L Murray†, et al,* A comparative risk assessment of burden of disease and injury attributable to 67 risk factors and risk factor clusters in 21 regions, 1990–2010: a systematic analysis for the Global Burden of Disease Study 2010, *Lancet* 2012; 380: 2224–60.

[51] Liu BQ. 1990 *Retrospective proportional mortality study of one million deaths* to estimate tobacco attributable mortality in China.

[52] Thun MJ, Hannan LM, Adams-Campbell LL, et al. (2008) Lung Cancer Occurrence in Never-Smokers: An Analysis of 13 Cohorts and 22 Cancer Registry Studies. PLOS Medicine 5(9): e185. https://doi.org/10.1371/journal.pmed.0050185.

[53] Wang L, Wang LJ, Zhou MG et al Analysis of under-reporting of mortality surveillance from 2006 to 2008. Chin. J Prov. Med. 45(12) Dec. 2011, 1061–4.

[54] Chen GB, Huang HC, Yang GH, et al Investigation on under-reported deaths in Xuan Wei, Yunnan Province during 2011-2013. Chin. J Prov. Med. 49(6) 541–5.

[55] Majid Ezzati and Alan D. Lopez, *Chapter 11* Smoking and oral tobacco use, in *Comparative quantification of health risks: global and regional burden of disease attributable to selected major risk factors* edited by Ezzati M, Lopez AD, Rodgers A and Christopher J.L. Murray.

1980s.[56] The upper aero-digestive cancer category was constructed from esophageal cancer and cancers of five minor sites (mouth, pharynx, larynx, pancreas and bladder), using weights based on the number of deaths in each disease category.

1. Some smoking-related causes of death were not included in Liu' study; in these cases, the relative risks from CPS-II were used.
2. With the change of smoking epidemic pattern in Chinese, the RR of the main disease associated with tobacco use is need to infer the results of the prospective Study of 0.5 Million Adults in China. Or estimate the trend of relative risk by Meta-analysis so as to select the appropriate RR value. in the future.

So PAF and death number of mortality associated with tobacco use by age group, gender and diseases can be calculated.

2.4.2.2 Estimation of Attributable Mortality in Smoking in Chinese Population

M Ezzati and Lopez AD reported the accumulated risk of tobacco use in 2000 by country and districts. The *SIR* for male and female in China was 63% and 4%,[57] the *PAF*s of tobacco use were 13% in men and 4% in women in 2000, It was estimated that 490,000 male and 100,000 female deaths were attributable to smoking in Chinese adults aged 40 years or older in 2000.[58]

The WHO reported that in 2004, about one million deaths (12% of total deaths) attributable to tobacco use occurred in adults aged 30 years and older in China, with 12% of deaths in men and 11% of deaths in women in 2000.[59]

GBD 2010 estimated that 1.2 million smokers died to diseases attributed to tobacco use (accounted for 14.54% of the total deaths), 911,000 men and 2,950,000 women among these victims, accounted for 18.33% and 8.87%, separately.

The estimated results of tobacco attributable mortality in the Chinese population by the *PAF/SIR* indirect method are shown in Table 2.4.

The methods used in these assessments are similar, but the PAF of tobacco use were a big difference for women.

According to the results of the three studies, the PAF of tobacco use for men were about 13% in 2000 and 18% in 2010, which was relatively reasonable; However, the PAF values of tobacco use for women were 11% in 2005 by the WHO

[56] Ezzati M, Lopez AD. Measuring the accumulated hazards of smoking: global and regional estimates for 2000, Tobacco Control 2003;12:79–85.

[57] M Ezzati, A D Lopez, Measuring the accumulated hazards of smoking: global and regional estimates for 2000, Tobacco Control 2003;12:79–85.

[58] Majid Ezzati and Alan D. Lopez, Smoking and oral tobacco use, in *Comparative Quantification of Health Risks Global and Regional Burden of Disease Attributable to Selected Major Risk Factors* (Volume 1) Edited by Majid Ezzati, Alan D. Lopez, Anthony Rodgers and Christopher J.L. Murray.

[59] World Health Organization, WHO Global report: Mortality Attributable to Tobacco, 100–101.

Table 2.4 Summary of the number and PAF for adult mortality from smoking-related diseases, for male adults 35 years of age and older in China by PAF/*SIR* indirect estimating methods

Cause of death	2000 by Ezzati et al.[a] (over 35 years)	2004 by WHO[b] (over 30 years)	2010 by GBD 2010[c] (over 35 years)
Total population			
All causes	7,500,000	8,375,603.7	8,303,700
Attributable to tobacco	590,000	968,318.74	1,206,977
Proportion of death attributable to tobacco (%)	7.87	11.56	14.54
Trachea, bronchus, lung cancer		381,673.08	513,300
Attributable to tobacco		183,768.52	172,273
Proportion of death attributable to tobacco (%)		48.15	33.56
Ischemic heart disease		720,938.04	948,700
Attributable to tobacco		28,272.08	238,235
Proportion of death attributable to tobacco (%)		3.92	25.11
Chronic obstructive pulmonary disease		1,406,535.98	934,400
Attributable to tobacco		508,897.44	207,527
Proportion of death attributable to tobacco (%)		36.18	22.21
Male			
All causes	3,770,000	4,532,967.14	4,972,800
Attributable to tobacco	490,000	549,995.22	911,547
Proportion of death attributable to tobacco (%)	13.00	12.13	18.33
Trachea, bronchus, lung cancer	490,000	258,821.28	360,100
Attributable to tobacco	98,000	143,789.6	128,565
Proportion of death attributable to tobacco (%)	20.00	55.56	35.70
Ischemic heart disease		363,068.74	533,900
Attributable to tobacco		14,378.96	197,265
Proportion of death attributable to tobacco (%)		3.96	36.95
Chronic obstructive pulmonary disease	493,939	683,001	534,400
Attributable to tobacco	163,000	230,063	97,447
Proportion of death attributable to tobacco (%)	33.00	33.68	18.23
Female			
All causes	3,330,000	3,837,742.35	3,330,900
Attributable to tobacco	100,000	420,241.47	295,430
Proportion of death attributable to tobacco (%)	3.00	10.95	8.87

Table 2.4 (continued)

Cause of death	2000 by Ezzati et al.[a] (over 35 years)	2004 by WHO[b] (over 30 years)	2010 by GBD 2010[c] (over 35 years)
Trachea, bronchus, lung cancer	94,444	121,557	153,200
Attributable to tobacco	17,000	38,204	43,708
Proportion of death attributable to tobacco (%)	18.00	31.43	28.53
Ischemic heart disease		354,253	414,800
Attributable to tobacco		13,892	40,970
Proportion of death attributable to tobacco (%)		3.92	9.88
Chronic obstructive pulmonary disease	98,361	725,872	400,000
Attributable to tobacco	60,000	281,319	110,080
Proportion of death attributable to tobacco (%)	61.00	38.76	27.52

[a]Majid Ezzati and Alan D. Lopez, Smoking and oral tobacco use, in *Comparative Quantification of Health Risks Global and Regional Burden of Disease Attributable to Selected Major Risk Factors* (Volume 1) Edited by Majid Ezzati, Alan D. Lopez, Anthony Rodgers and Christopher J.L. Murray
[b]World Health Organization, WHO Global Report: Mortality Attributable to Tobacco, 2012
[c]Yang GH Yang GH, Wang Yu, Christopher J L Murray, et al Rapid health transition in China, 1990–2010: findings from the Global Burden of Disease Study 2010, Lancet 2013; 381: 1987–2015
Note: Compiled by the author, based on related reports and literature

2008 and 8.7% in 2010 by GBD 2010, which was not match the smoking pattern in Chinese women. Past decades, the prevalence of smoking in women aged 35–69 was very low, about 3–4%, and has been on a downward trend. The explanation of the results perhaps is not in line with the adjustment for background mortality of lung cancer. As Ezzati points out, "if we had not accounted for the Chinese specific never-smoker rates, the *SIR* would be similar to that of the men in SEAR-B, and higher than that of women in any other developing country for women."[60] Whether this is true or not, further studies are needed.

2.5 Estimation of SHS Exposure-Attributed Mortality

Since 1970s, scientific community has been concerning the health consequences of health exposed SHS. Besides a series of US Surgeon General reports, the National Research Council of USA, International Agency for Research on Cancer (IARC), U.S. Environmental Protection Agency (EPA), National Health and Medical Research Council of Australia, California EPA (Cal/EPA), Office of Environmental

---

[60]Ezzati M, Lopez AD Measuring the accumulated hazards of smoking: global and regional estimates for 2000, Tobacco Control 2003;12:79–85.

Health Hazard Assessment, Scientific Committee on Tobacco and Health of UK, and World Health Organization have published that exposure SHS causes lung cancer, coronary heart disease, COPD in adults, and respiratory infection, otitis media in the children.

2.5.1 Assessment of Exposure of SHS

First of all, it is important to understand the exposure of the SHS assessment to choose a reasonable level of relative risk and prevalence of SHS exposure. SHS as an risk factor caused disease, its exposure assessment includes the time and place of the exposure, cumulative exposures, and so on.[61,62] One of methodological difficulties inherent to the exposure assessment is the lengthy interval of SHS exposure. For example, exposures to SHS across the full life span may be related to lung cancer, while only more recent exposures may be relevant to the asthma attack. Second, assessments of exposure are further complicated by the multiplicity of environments risk factors, such as indoor coal burning pollution. Additionally, levels of exposures may be changed owing to the difference in location and time between smokers and passive smokers. Over time and across locations because of temporal changes and geographic differences in smoking patterns.

To select surrogate indicators, such as marriage to a smoker or the number of cigarettes smoked in the home, the usual practice to describe and assess a source of exposure may also be used to assess the exposure in epidemiological studies.[63] This approach has been used this study to assess the relationship between SHS exposure and health effects in China, which is detailed below. Another commonly method is epidemiological investigation by using questionnaire to measure epidemic level of secondhand smoke exposure in general population and exposure levels in the main places, workplaces and public places, and public transports. Questionnaires are used in series of national surveys on tobacco use, as described above. The measurement still is subject to errors, because these instruments and respondent' false memories. Two studies evaluated the reliability of questionnaires on lifetime exposure of SHS.[64,65] Both studies showed that the repeatability for questions concerning whether a spouse had smoked was very higher, but the reliability for responses

[61] Jaakkola MS, Jaakkola JJ. Assessment of exposure to environmental tobacco smoke. *European Respiratory Journal* 1997;10(10):2384–97.

[62] Jaakkola MS, Samet JM. Environmental tobacco smoke: risk assessment. *Environmental Health Perspectives* 1999;107(Suppl 6):823–904.

[63] Hirayama T. Cancer mortality in nonsmoking women with smoking husbands based on a large scale cohort study in Japan. *Preventive Medicine* 1984;13(6):680–90.

[64] Pron GE, Burch JD, Howe GR, Miller AB. The reliability of passive smoking histories reported in a case-control study of lung cancer. *American Journal of Epidemiology* 1988;127(2):267–73.

[65] Coultas DB, Peake GT, Samet JM. Questionnaire assessment of lifetime and recent exposure to environmental tobacco smoke. *American Journal of Epidemiology* 1989;130(2):338–47.

concerning the quantitative aspects of an exposure was lower. Emerson et al. assessed the repeatability of information from parents of children with asthma. They found high reliability of their smoking status and the number of cigarettes at home reported by children's parent during the past week.[66]

Biomarkers can also provide an indication of exposure or possibly exposure level. Exposure to secondhand smoke can occur in a number of different places, such as the home, the workplace, public places, and transportation environments, often referred to as "microenvironments" (NRC 1991).[67] Using the micro-environmental model, total exposure can be estimated as the weighted average of the concentrations of secondhand smoke or indicator compounds, such as nicotine, or the time spent in the microenvironments.[68] China used similar model to estimate SHS exposure in restaurants and bars.[69]

2.5.2 Quantitative Estimates of Potential Health Consequences of SHS: Relative Risk of SHS Exposure in Different Situations

Generally speaking, all assessment studies on the relative risk of the association between SHS exposure and health outcomes or disease were mainly derived from meta-analysis studies for the different categories of disease.

2.5.2.1 Lung Cancer

As early as 1980s epidemiologic evidences of an association between SHS exposure and lung cancer appeared in a prospective cohort study in Japan[70] and a case-control study in Greece.[71] There are sufficient evidences to infer a causal relationship between SHS and lung cancer among lifelong nonsmokers, which extends to the

---

[66] Emerson JA, Hovell MF, Meltzer SB, Zakarian JM, Hofstetter CR, Wahlgren DR, Leaderer BP, Meltzer EO. The accuracy of environmental tobacco smoke exposure measures among asthmatic children. Journal of Clinical Epidemiology. 1995;48(10):1251–9.

[67] National Research Council. *Human Exposure Assessment for Airborne Pollutants: Advances and Opportunities.* Washington: National Academy Press, 1991.

[68] Klepeis NE. An introduction to the indirect exposure assessment approach: modeling human exposure using micro-environmental measurements and the recent National Human Activity Pattern Survey. *Environmental Health Perspectives* 1999;107(Suppl 2):365–74.

[69] Liu R., Jiang Y., Li Q. et al An Assessment of Health Risks and Mortality from Exposure to Secondhand Smoke in Chinese Restaurants and Bars. PLOS ONE, Volume 9 Issue 1, e84811, 2014, January.

[70] Hirayama T. Cancer mortality in nonsmoking women with smoking husbands based on a large scale cohort study in Japan. *Preventive Medicine* 1984;13(6):680–90.

[71] Trichopoulos D, Kalandidi A, Sparros L. Lung cancer and passive smoking: conclusion of Greek study [letter]. *Lancet* 1983;2(8351):677–8.

link between all cancers and SHS exposure. The 2006 US Surgeon General's Report pointed out that nonsmokers increased a 20–30% risk of lung cancer from SHS exposure associated with living with a smoker by the pooled evidences.[72] The results from China were similar with the pooled relative risk.

2.5.2.2 Cardiovascular and Other Chronic Diseases

2006 report of US Surgeon General pointed that a 25–30% increase in the risk of coronary heart disease from exposure to SHS.[73] Fischer and his colleagues published study "Meta-analysis of the association between second-hand smoke exposure and ischemic heart diseases, COPD and stroke" including 24 credible papers. The paper reported the extra risk of IHD with exposure of SHS was still within 25–30%, and the relative risk of stroke with exposure SHS was 1.35 (male: 1.40 and female: 1.43).

Meanwhile Oono et al. published a Meta-analysis study covering 20 eligible studies showed that[74] the pooled estimate of stroke risk was 1.25 (95% CI: 1.12–1.38). The RR of stroke in Hong Kong was higher than the pooled RR. Also the relative risk (RR) of stroke risk with SHS exposure was non-liner dose-response, there is no safe lower limit of exposure, 1.16 (95% CI 1.06–1.27) for exposure SHS from 5 cigarettes per day.

PD risk related to SHS exposure was 1.66 (male 1.50, female 2.17), which is a little higher that reported by China.[75]

2.5.2.3 Risk of SHS Exposure in Child

The evidences is sufficient to increase the risk of lower respiratory infection (LRI) in infants with SHS exposure.[76] Jones et al. provided an updated systematic review and meta-analysis of 60 studies of the association between passive smoking and

---

[72] U.S. Department of Health and Human Services. *The Health Consequences of Involuntary Exposure to Tobacco Smoke: A Report of the Surgeon General.* Atlanta, GA: U.S. Department of Health and Human Services, Centers for Disease Control and Prevention, Coordinating Center for Health Promotion, National Center for Chronic Disease Prevention and Health Promotion, Office on Smoking and Health, 2006.

[73] U.S. Department of Health and Human Services. *The Health Consequences of Involuntary Exposure to Tobacco Smoke: A Report of the Surgeon General.* Atlanta, GA: U.S. Department of Health and Human Services, Centers for Disease Control and Prevention, Coordinating Center for Health Promotion, National Center for Chronic Disease Prevention and Health Promotion, Office on Smoking and Health, 2006. Chapter 7.

[74] Oono IP, Mackay DF, Pell JP. Meta-analysis of the association between secondhand smoke exposure and stroke. *J Public Health (Oxf)* 2011; **33**: 496–502. 21 March 2011.

[75] Yin P, Jiang CQ, Cheng KK, Lam TH, Lam KH, Miller MR, et al. Passive smoking exposure and risk of COPD among adults in China: the Guangzhou Biobank Cohort Study. Lancet. 2007;370(9589):751–7.

[76] U.S. Department of Health and Human Services. *The Health Consequences of Involuntary Exposure to Tobacco Smoke: A Report of the Surgeon General.* Atlanta, GA: U.S. Department of

LRI.[77] The meta-analysis found that paternal smoking, both parents smoking, as well as other household members significantly increased the risk of LRI: the odds ratios (OR) were 1.22 (95% CI 1.10–1.35), 1.62 (95% CI 1.38–1.89), and 1.54 (95% CI 1.40–1.69), separately.

2.5.3 Estimating the Accumulated Hazards of Passive Smoking for the Chinese Population

The mortality caused by passive smoking has been examined in many countries,[78] but only a few studies systematically estimate the mortality of passive smoke in China.

In view of the differences in type of exposure to SHS, and the fact that these differences cause different diseases in adults and children, it is necessary to assess the exposure levels in adults and children separately. The prevalence of involuntary smoking and exposure information in adults is based on the results of a series of national surveys. The exposure information for Children is based on a literature review.

The relative risk of lung cancer and other diseases due to passive smoking among non-smokers was obtained from a meta-analysis.

Gan Q et al.[79] reported that in China, passive smoking causes around 22,200 deaths from lung cancer: 5700 men and 16,500 women, and 33,800 deaths from IHD: 6300 men and 27,500 women. The added risk that passive smoking puts on exposed non-smokers was 20/100,000 in 2002.

Wang JB et al.[80] estimate that passive smoking by the spouse was responsible for 5.2% of lung cancer deaths among non-smoking women, while passive smoking in the workplace was responsible for 6.2% of lung cancer deaths in 2005. A total of 11,507 lung cancer death among non-smoking women (11.1%) were attributable to passive smoking from the spouse or in workplace, in that year.

Health and Human Services, Centers for Disease Control and Prevention, Coordinating Center for Health Promotion, National Center for Chronic Disease Prevention and Health Promotion, Office on Smoking and Health, 2006.

[77] Jones LL, Hashim A, McKeever T, Cook DG, Britton J, Leonardi-Bee J. Parental and household smoking and the increased risk of bronchitis, bronchiolitis and other lower respiratory infections in infancy: systematic review and meta-analysis. *Respir Res* 2011; **12**: 5.

[78] Woodward A, Laugesen M. How many deaths are caused by secondhand cigarette smoke? Tob Control 2001;10:383–8.

[79] Quan Gan, Kirk R Smith, S Katharine Hammond et al Disease burden of adult lung cancer and ischaemic heart disease from passive tobacco smoking in China, Tobacco Control 2007;16:417–422.

[80] Wang JB, Jiang Y, Wei WQ, et al Estimation of cancer incidence and mortality attributable to smoking in China Cancer Cause Control (2010) 21:959–965.

GBD 2010[81] estimated that exposure to SHS causes around 159,000 deaths, which accounted for 1.9% of the total deaths (total deaths 8,303,700) in 2010. There were 15,662 deaths (3.6%) from lung cancer: 5540 men and 10,122 women. The more than 53,000 coronary heart disease deaths: 18,744 among men and 34,258 women, were attributable to passive smoking in 2010. Meanwhile 27,000 deaths in children aged 0–5 in 2010 were due to infections of the lower respiratory tract and otitis media, and among these, about a quarter were attributed to exposure to secondhand smoke.

As mentioned earlier, there is a lack of detailed information on environmental tobacco smoke exposure (with scant data, for example, on the number of hours of exposure) and the information on morbidity and mortality of disease. Although further studies are needed, to improve the scientific evidence on the effects of secondhand smoke, the current data, both global and for China are sufficient to enable some public health interventions.

---

[81] Yang GH, Wang Yu, Christopher J L Murray, et al Rapid health transition in China, 1990–2010: findings from the Global Burden of Disease Study 2010, Lancet 2013; 381: 1987–2015.

Chapter 3
Action Subject and Surroundings of Tobacco Control and Anti Tobacco Control in China

Gonghuan Yang

Abstract The tobacco control has been carried out in China with 1.3 billion population under the leadership of a single party, the Communist Party of China with multi-party cooperation and political Consultation. The delegates of NPC and CPPCC are an approach to contact the process in decision-making, the issues related to tobacco control are important topic in their bills or proposals. In the Inter-Ministry Coordination and Steering Committee for Implementation of WHO FCTC (the Steering Committee) in China, the most ministries advocates positive tobacco control, but it was a fatal mistake that STMA has become a member of the Steering Committee, in charge of implementing the WHO FCTC items regarding packaging, labeling, and regulation of the contents disclosures of tobacco products, which provides convenient conditions for tobacco industry to blockade tobacco control in China. Many medical, public health experts, and legal experts participated in tobacco control campaigns, which are important tobacco control force. The experts in the name of a professional organization, a non-governmental organization or an individual, expressed their views and suggestions by publishing research or investigation report, letter of appeal, and so on. Mass media communicated their comments to influence public opinion, then influence policy making. The tobacco companies is a strong anti tobacco control interest group. STMA/CNTC used their considerable economic and political influence to interfere the legislation of tobacco control at the national and local levels with a series of strategies and tricks. In addition, some government leaders don't really want to implement policies related to tobacco control and worry about tobacco control reducing the government's income from cigarettes. The anti tobacco control force is very strong at present.

Keywords NPC · CPPCC · Tobacco control · Non-government organization · STMA · CNTC · China

G. Yang
Institute of Basic Medical Science Chinese Academy of Medical Sciences, School of Basic Medicine Peking Union Medical College, Beijing, China

© Springer Nature Singapore Pte Ltd. 2018
G. Yang (ed.), *Tobacco Control in China*,
https://doi.org/10.1007/978-981-10-8315-0_3

47

The success of the WHO FCTC depends on the energy and political commitment devoted to implementing it by governments of countries. The most Parties of WHO FCTC follow their political commitment as which matched the principle that it is the right of "everyone to the enjoyment of the highest attainable standard of physical and mental health" in the International Covenant on Economic, Social and Cultural Rights, adopted by the United Nations General Assembly on 16 December 1966.[1] So *Article 4 Guiding principles* **of WHO FCTC** mentioned: "Strong political commitment is necessary to develop and support, at the national, regional and international levels, comprehensive multi-sectional measures and coordinated responses, taking into consideration". "Each Party shall develop, implement, periodically update and review comprehensive multi-sectional national tobacco control strategies, plans and programmes" in accordance with *Article 5 General obligations* of this Convention.[2]

How is WHO FCTC implemented, how is Laws related to tobacco control updated and performed in China, as a country with 320 million smokers and 740 million passive smokers among 1.3 billion population? In order to answer these questions, it is very necessary to understand the characters of the polity regime, social power and tobacco industry in China in order to promote development and implement of the Law or regulations related to tobacco control under the decision-making system in China.

3.1   The Polity Regime and Tobacco Control in China

The politics of the People's Republic of China takes places in a framework of a socialist republic run by a single party, the Communist Party of China with multi-party cooperation and political Consultation. The leadership of the Communist Party is stated in the Constitution of the People's Republic of China. State power within the People's Republic of China (PRC) is exercised through the Communist Party, the Central People's Government and their provincial and local representation.[3] The Structure of the State includes the National People's Congress (NPC), The State Council, The State Central Military Commission, The Supreme People's Court, and The Supreme People's Procuratorate.[4] The Party commands the overall situation and integrates the works in all aspects, and the Party shall play the leadership role as the core of among all kinds of organizations at corresponding levels. **Central Politburo Standing Committee of the Communist Party of China (CPSC)** serves as top

[1] United Nation, International Covenant on Economic, Social and Cultural Rights, http://www.ohchr.org/EN/ProfessionalInterest/Pages/CESCR.aspx.

[2] World Health Organization, Framework Convention of Tobacco Control http://apps.who.int/iris/bitstream/10665/42811/1/9241591013.pdf.

[3] Multiparty cooperation and political consultation under the leadership of the Communist Party of China, Chinese government network, http://www.gov.cn/test/2005-05/25/content_18182.htm.

[4] Current constitution of People's Republic of China, (2004 Amendment) http://www.npc.gov.cn/npc/xinwen/node_505.htm.

policy-making body in China. In practice, members of the CPSC are in charge of NPC, State council, The State Central Military Commission and the Chinese People's Political Consultative Conference (CPPCC) as the head, and set up party committees in each institution. Article 15 of Constitution of Communist Party of China: "Only the Central Committee of the Party has the power to make decisions on major policies of a nationwide character. Party organizations of various departments and localities may make suggestions with regard to such policies to the Central Committee, but shall not make any decisions or publicize their views outside the Party without authorization".[5]

The National People's Congress (NPC) is China's unicameral legislature. Based on the Article 62 and 63 of the State Constitution, the NPC has the power to amend the state constitution, supervise its enforcement, enact and amend laws, ratify and abrogate treaties, approve the state budget and plans for national economic and social development, and elect and impeach top officials of the state and judiciary and so on.[6] The NPC is the highest organ of state power in China; but in reality, the NPC is led by the Communist Party and many powers and responsibilities given by Constitution exist in name and procedure only. Each Congress lasts 5 years. Every March, about 3000 "elected" delegates from all over the country to Beijing attend the National People's Congress, what has become a familiar annual ritual. The 12th **Standing Committee** usually has 161 members and convenes every 2 months. Many of the NPC's top officials are retired senior officials from governmental system.

There are nine **special committees** in the 12th NPC (全国人大).[7] Among them, Education, Science, Culture and Public Health Committee, Law Committee, and Financial and Economic Affairs Committee are related to tobacco control. The 17th session of the Standing Committee of the 10th National People's Congress has ratified the WHO Framework Convention on Tobacco Control (WHO FCTC) on August 28, 2005.[8]

The Chinese People's Political Consultative Conference (CPPCC), also known as the **People's PCC** (人民政协) or just **the PCC** (政协), is the United Front organization as representing the multi-party cooperation and political advisory body under the leadership of the Communist Party just as stated in the preamble of the PRC Constitution.[9]

The delegates of NPC and CPPCC are regards as an approach to contact the process in decision-making, and an important force for tobacco control. Since WHO

---

[5] Article 15 of Party Constitution of Communist Party of China, Beijing: People's Press, 2012, http://www.12371.cn/special/zggcdzc/zggcdzcqw/.

[6] Constitution of the People's Republic of China(2004 Revision) http://www.people.com.cn/GB/shehui/1060/2391834.html.

[7] NPC of China, *Organization, functions and powers and rules of procedure of the Standing Committee of the National People's Congress,* http://www.npc.gov.cn/npc/xinwen/rdlt/rdjs/2008-05/26/content_1430161_3.htm.

[8] Decision of the Standing Committee of the National People's Congress about Ratifying the Framework Convention on Tobacco Control http://www.tobaccocontrollaws.org/files/live/China/China%20-%20FCTC%20Ratification%20Decision.pdf.

[9] Li ZH, The history of The Chinese People's Political Consultative Conference. Research division of United Front Work Department of CPC Central Committee, Sept. 20, 2014 http://news.china.com/zh_cn/history/all/11025807/20140920/18802915_all.html.

FCTC came into force in China in 2006, Tobacco control always is an important issue in delegates' proposals or bills at national and provincial People's Congress and Political Consultative Conference. The bills and proposals covered wider topics: banning smoking in the indoor public or working places, increasing tax and price of tobacco products, package warning, comprehensive banning advertisement of tobacco, and mechanism of tobacco control, and so on. Although most issues have not been accepted, the representatives still persistently their responsibility. Such as the joint proposal for tobacco control provided by 281 members of the CPPCC had caused the great echo in 2011,[10] the National delegate of NPC, Madam Huang XH, provide bill to speed up national legislation of banning smoking in indoor public or working places for 5 years.[11] The proposals of pictorial warnings on the cigarette package had been submitted for 10 years, but not making any progress.[12]

The State Council of the People's Republic of China, namely the Central People's Government, is the highest executive organ of State power, as well as the highest organ of State administration. The State Council is composed of a premier, vice-premiers, State councilors, ministers in charge of ministries and commissions, the auditor-general and the secretary-general. The second-ranked CPSC member serves as Premier of the State Council. On the procedure, the premier of the State Council is nominated by the president, reviewed by the NPC, and appointed and removed by the president. Other members of the State Council are nominated by the premier, reviewed by the NPC or its Standing Committee, and appointed and removed by the president. Under the State Council, there are 25 Ministries and Commissions and 38 centrally administered government organizations that report directly to the state council. It should be mentioned that all the major and important policy and major matters in government work must be reported to Party Central Committee and approved by Party Central Committee based on the stipulates of Party Central Committee in 1953.[13] In 2007, the State Council approved the establishment of an Inter-Ministry Coordination and Steering Committee for Implementation of WHO FCTC (the Steering Committee).[14] It is a the major mistakes to appoint the STMA as a member of the leading group of the tobacco control owing to violating Article 5.3 of WHO FCTC although we have not judge

---

[10] Li QM,281 CPPCC members jointed proposal for the State Council to set up implement WHO FCTC group,BeijingTimes,March,12,2011.http://news.sina.com.cn/c/2011-03-12/025722098783.shtml.

[11] Liu HY, Hail to persistence of delegation of NPC and CPPCC. Xinhua network, March, 4, 2013. http://news.xinhuanet.com/2013lh/2013-03/04/c_114883570.htm.

[12] Tobacco tracking letter, Suggestion provided for 10 years—Health China: call for the pictorial warning on the cigarette package, 2017, No. 1 Sohu Health http://www.sohu.com/a/128467351_608541.

[13] Decision on strengthening the central government departments' reporting system to the central government and the leadership of the central government on the work of the government (Draft), The selected important literature (4) since 1953 http://cpc.people.com.cn/GB/64184/64186/66658/4492923.html.

[14] Reply from State Council on agreement to set up the Inter-ministerial leading group to be in charge of FCTC implementation State letter No. 41 2007. http://www.360doc.com/content/09/0524/09/128196_3628618.shtml (accessed December 27, 2016).

that the appointment is belong to negligence of duty or intentional decide of protecting the tobacco industry.

After more than 20 years of rapid economic development, the Chinese government has gradually been aware that the "health endangering" economy development pattern at present stage should be transformed into a "health friendly" one in face of a large number of environmental and health problems. Protecting and improving people's health has become a new and the most important standard for industrial restructuring and economic transformation. However, the leadership of government obviously have not link the health development pattern to curb tobacco economic.

3.2 Push Forward a National Action on Tobacco Control

The national coordinated and strategic efforts will result in substantial decline of tobacco consumption. The development of a national tobacco control action, establishment of a coordination mechanism and strengthening the infrastructure and capacity to implement the plan of action are key steps in the successful curb the tobacco epidemic.

3.2.1 The National Coordinating Mechanism on Tobacco Control in China

Institutional capacity building is the key step to the long-term sustainability of tobacco control efforts. It is crucial to the formulation and successful implement of a comprehensive national action plan for tobacco control. Article 5 of WHO FCTC pointed out "Each Party shall develop, implement, periodically update and review comprehensive multi-sectoral national tobacco control strategies, plans and programmes" and "establish or reinforce and finance a national coordinating mechanism or focal points for tobacco control". The national coordinating mechanism includes the creation of a multisectoral national committee, task force, working group or steering committee for tobacco control. WHO suggested that the agencies or institutions, possible as a composition of the multi- sectional national committee should be carefully evaluated for their potential to advance the development of the national plan of action for tobacco control, based on the function of these agencies or institution in the country. The aim is to keep the broadest possible representation, effective implement capacity but take care not to include those who would impede or counter the committee's efforts at controlling the tobacco epidemic. Select only the essential members to keep the size of the committee manageable. In addition, it is may be necessary to establish multi-sectoral committees for tobacco control at the state, district and provincial levels in order to set up an appropriate plan of action at those administrative levels in large countries.[15]

---

[15] WHO Tobacco Free Initiative, Building block for tobacco control: a handbook. http://www.who.int/tobacco/publications/building_capacity/building_blocks/en/.

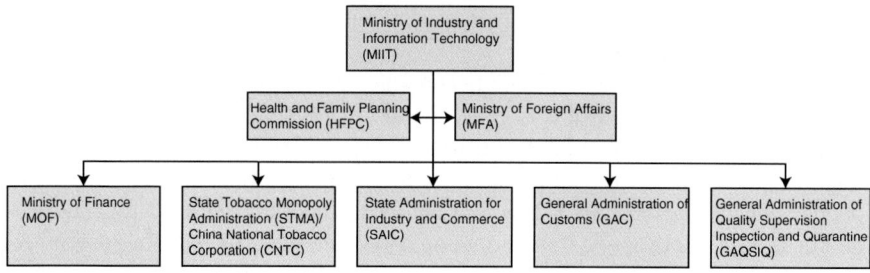

Fig. 3.1 Inter-Ministry Coordination and Steering Committee for Implementation of WHO Framework Convention Tobacco Control.
Source: Figure is made by author on the basis of information provided by the State Council

The Inter-Ministry Coordination and Steering Committee for Implementation of WHO FCTC (the Steering Committee) in China includes major government departments related to the fulfillment of the Convention (Fig. 3.1), but the composition of the Committee has several fatal weaknesses.

First, there were not the representative sectors from civil society in the committee. The WHO FCTC recognizes the important of participation of civil society to achieve the goal of reducing tobacco-related mortality and morbidity, such as Media, NGOs involved tobacco control, health professional, lawyers, economists, and so on. However, representative of civil society is hard to join such as decision-making body.

Second, the leader unit of the Steering Committee is not the Ministry of health, but the Ministry of industry and information technology (MIIT). The MIIT's responsibilities include to develop of new industrialization strategy and policy, formulate and organize the implementation of professional layout, plan and industrial policies of manufacturing and communications industries, supervise and analyze running situation of industry, communications industry, comprehensively promote the national informatization, and so on, total 15 responsibilities.[16] Obviously, the MIIT is not a suitable, right head unit of the Steering Committee. The only reason is MIIT is the competent department of STMA. The head unit of the Committee is changed along with the adscription institute of STMA. Then the Director General of STMA is also the leadership member of MIIT. It means that, the hegemony of tobacco control is essentially handed over to STMA in China. In 2018, the matter took a turn for the better. The 13th NPC has reviewed the report on institutional reform of State Council. The Tobacco control has shifted to the upcoming National Health Commission. It is obvious that the head of the Steering Committee will be replaced by National Health Commission.

The third, the worst of it is, STMA, in the name of a government sector, has also been a member of the Steering Committee (Fig. 3.1), and was placed in charge of implementing the FCTC items regarding packaging, labeling, and regulation of the

---

[16]The general office of the State Council on the issuance of the Ministry of information industry and the main functions of internal structure and staffing requirements of the notice issued [2008] 72, http://www.miit.gov.cn/n1146285/c3722514/content.html.

contents disclosures of tobacco products, which directly violate Article 5.3 of the WHO FCTC. WHO strongly urgent its Member States not to engage the tobacco industry when designing, implementing and evaluating plans of action for tobacco control. However, Chinese Government believes that STMA, as a government department, should involve everything related to tobacco, so to form the current situation. The practice of implement of WHO FCTC over 10 years in China has shown that STMA has been hindering the implementation of the Convention, especially those Articles is in charge of STMA. The obstacle behaviors will be introduced in detail in tobacco advertising (Chapter 11) and cigarette packaging and labeling (Chapter 10) and so on.

3.2.2   Developing and Implementing National Action Plan for Tobacco Control

Article 5.1 of WHO FCTC points out: "Each Party shall develop, implement, periodically update and review national tobacco control strategies, plans and programmes in accordance with this Convention and the protocols to which it is a Party".

The 2012–2015 China Tobacco Control Action Plan was published by the Steering Committee in December, 2012.[17] Although the planning goals were ambitious on reducing tobacco smoking prevalence, the Plan lack relevant policy measures to support these goals. In fact, by the end of 2015, these goals have not been achieved. In general, there are many problems in the tobacco control plan.

- On tobacco control measures, it's important to highlight the fundamental problem of the Plan does not preclude tobacco industry's role in tobacco control policy development and implementation. This is a violation of Article 5.3 of the WHO FCTC and has led to the weakened FCTC measures stated in the Plan.
- Second, the Plan does not require the graphic health warnings on cigarette packs, and lacks specific commitment and plan to increasing tobacco taxes and prices as a tobacco control measure.
- The Plan does, however, contain relatively strong language on banning tobacco advertising, promotion and sponsorship and implementing smoking ban in public places, but it does not have a specific timeline for the national government to enact such policies.

So tobacco control circle criticized the Plan, and push to make a truly effective national plan for tobacco control.[18]

---

[17] Ministry of Industry and Information Technology of the People's Republic of China. China Tobacco Control Plan, 2012–2015. Issued by Dec 22, 2012. http://www.miit.gov.cn/n11293472/n11293832/n12843926/n13917012/15071046.html (accessed Oct 7, 2014).

[18] Beijing Evening News, "Tobacco control experts criticized six problems in Chinese tobacco control plan" 2013,2,22 http://news.xinhuanet.com/health/2013-02/22/c_124377561.htm.

Reviewing tobacco control action in China during 2012–2015, Ministry of Finance has performed tobacco control policy to increase tax and price of tobacco products although without the issue in the tobacco control plan; NPC approved the Advertising Law with comprehensive banning advertisement of tobacco products; Local Laws of banning smoking in indoor public places and workplaces have been issued in many cities, especially in Beijing.

Compared with the objective of Plan, the adult smoking rate did not decrease from 28.1% in 2010 to below 25%, still kept 27.7% in 2015; the objective of improving the awareness of health hazards of smoking has not been reached. It is directly related to no having used the pictorial health warning on the cigarette package, which is hinder from the STMA as STMA as a member of WHO FCTC implementation committee, has a seat at the tobacco control policy table. This arrangement is the biggest mistake in the implementation of China's tobacco control. As of 2018, the 2016–2020 action plan for tobacco control has not yet been launched.

3.3 Tobacco Control Action Among Governments

The routine tobacco control work is responsible by the NHFPC (former MOH). As early as February 1979, the MOH and the MOF, Ministry of agriculture and Ministry light industry jointly issued the notice *"Health education on smoking is harmful and control smoking"*. During 1988–1998 years, the MOH united a number of Ministries to carry out the campaigns of smoke-free hospital, smoke-free schools, smokeless public transport, and successfully banned smoking in both international and domestic airplanes. Health promotion action on banning smoking in indoor public places, helping smokers to quit carried out in the main cities under international assistance, such as WHO and World Bank. In August 1997, China held the 10th World Conference on tobacco or health in Beijing, with "tobacco: the continuous spread of plague" as the theme of the conference, to promote the WHO developed under the auspices of the international convention, to promote global tobacco control, to curb the tobacco epidemic spread in developing countries.

The MOH actively instigated Chinese governmental to join the negotiations on the FCTC. After 2006 WHO FCTC took effect in China, MOH, in compliance with the duties of performance, created smoke-free medical and health system nationwide, as a demonstration of tobacco control, and assisted Beijing and Shanghai to achieve the target of "Smoking Free Olympics" and "Smoking Free Expo", respective, as well as supported local legislation on smoke-free in indoor public places, push forward national legislation on smoke-free in indoor public places. Second, MOH order the medical and public professional organization to develop health education of health hazards of smoking and second-hand smoking, and published the first official report on the harms of smoking in 2012.[19] Third, MOH communicated

---

[19] Ministry of Health. China report on the health hazards of smoking edited by Chen Zhu. Beijing, China: People' Health Press, 2010.

the key points of WHO FCTC through the World Tobacco Free Day theme activities; and in forth, formulated "Chinese clinical smoking cessation guidelines", set up cessation clinic and hotline, and improve service capacity of medical staff. The implement of key issues of WHO FCTC, such as improving the clinical service of quite have list in *the Plan for the Prevention and Control of chronic diseases in 2012–2015*, as the key measures for the prevention and treatment of chronic diseases. The MOH advocates positive tobacco control. Before negotiations of Convention, MOH successfully held the workshop on significance of WHO FCTC, which get the support of NDRC and several ministries. The Chinese government delegation basically took positive line to promote WHO FCTC. In the negotiations, the views and suggestion of the MOH often were in priority, while the opinions of STMA cannot control the negotiating delegates in general. However, when MIIT became the head, the MOH was in a weak position, and its propositions were not understood and supported at the Steering committee.

In eight ministries of the Steering Committee, the MFA and the GAC generally do not participate in tobacco control affair discussion, the MOF, the SATC relatively took positive performance, their performance in tobacco taxes and a ban on tobacco advertising, promotion and sponsorship are described in detail. GAQSIQ is close to STMA, position on tobacco control of GAQSIQ was obvious from notice on domestic packaging and labelling of cigarettes packages[20] issued in 2008, which will be described in the chapter of cigarette package and health warning.

Other ministries, such as the Ministry of education (MOE) and the Ministry of civil affairs (MCA), have a positive attitude towards tobacco control, such MOE and MOH issued in alliance the regulation of tobacco control in schools in 2010[21]; MCA canceled Charitable Awards for six tobacco companies in 2008[22] after understand the WHO FCTC. More ministries and agencies directly under State Council, Such as the NDRC, the Ministry of science and technology (MST), the Ministry of culture (MOC), the Ministry of environmental protection (MEP), the Ministry of agriculture (MOA), the Chinese Academy of Social Sciences (CASS), the Academy of engineering, and the State Council Development Research Center, as well as agencies and departments directly under CPSC, such as the Central Civilization Guidance Office under the Central Propaganda Department, and all kinds of the Executive Leadership Academy, Party School, do not join the Tobacco Control Campaign. We believe that they contact the topic of tobacco control, they will support these strategies of tobacco control, such as Central Party School and National School of Administration have done past years.

---

[20] STMA. QAQSIQ, the domestic regulations on cigarette packaging and labeling in the territories of the People's Republic of China, April 16, 2008. http://www.tobaccochina.com/law/nation/wu/20084/20084153948_297463.shtml.

[21] General Office of Ministry of Education, General Office of Ministry of Health, Opinions on Further Strengthening tobacco control work in schools, Dept. Teach, Sport and Art 5 (2010) http://www.moe.edu.cn/publicfiles/business/htmlfiles/moe/s4667/201007/92850.html.

[22] Ministry of Civil Affairs, Publicity List of "China Charity Award" in 2008 http://news.xinhuanet.com/politics/2008-11-26/content_10415537.htm.

3.4 Professional Department, Experts and Non-government and Tobacco Control

Reviewing the history or tobacco control in China, it is impossible to separate the roles of health professional institute, experts, scholars and non-governmental organizations (NGOs). The reason is that well-known NGOs relevant to tobacco control were most founded by experts and retired officials from health departments, and the tobacco control activities of the NGOs were promoted by experts and scholars. Although roles of NGOs slightly differ from that of the professional institutes, their functions on tobacco control are basically similar, therefore, the merger is described in this section.

Before 2000, tobacco control campaigns in China were mainly lead by experts and scholars. Around 1970, studies by scientists across the world showed that smoking is harmful to health, the famous professors Ye GS, Weng XZ, Wu YK and Wu JP et al. as the leading figures of the medical community wrote to Qian XZ, the Minister of Health, suggesting national tobacco control campaign and urging the government to take tobacco control actions.[23] In 1990, professor Chen MZ, the Minister of MOH at that time, proposed to found the Chinese Association on smoking or Health (CASH), renamed Chinese Association on Tobacco Control (CATC) in 2004, to start tobacco control in China.

During 1990s, CASH held many national seminars on smoking or health. The ministry of health and the other organizations jointly announced the finding of 1996 National prevalence survey of smoking pattern that the current smoking prevalence reached 63% in Chinese male, the prevalence of SHS exposure was 53.5% in Chinese non-smokers.[24] The several large-scale retrospective and prospective studies were published in BMJ estimated that 0.6 million deaths was attributed to tobacco use in 1990 and would increase at least 0.8 million in 2000 and about three million a year by 2050 on the basis of current smoking patterns in China.[25] At the same time, about 40%, 133 cities introduced the regulation of banning smoking in indoor public places.[26] The 10th World Conference on tobacco or health was held successfully in Beijing in 1997, Jiang ZM, the top leader, Former General Secretary of the Communist Party of China and Dr. Hiroshi Nakajima, Former Director-General of WHO made an important speech at the opening ceremony of the Conference.[27] Mass media widely reported the activities, pushing the campaign of tobacco control to the upsurge in China.

---

[23] Xu Guihua, The historical role of Non-government organization in tobacco control, The 15th National Academic Symposium on Tobacco Control, Xi'an, 2011, http://cpfd.cnki.com.cn/Article/CPFDTOTAL-XYJK201104001002.htm.

[24] MOH, CAPM, CASH, the National Patriotic Health Campaign, 1996 National Prevalence Survey of Smoking Pattern, The Chinese Science and Technology Press, Beijing, 1997.

[25] BBC news, China's cigarette threat, http://news.bbc.co.uk/2/hi/health/216998.stm.

[26] Wang JL The current status about Laws of protection from exposure to tobacco smoke in China, Master's degree thesis of Jilin University, R197.3, 2006722019.

[27] Headline Today, The World Conference on tobacco or health was held in Beijing, August, 24, 1997 http://www.todayonhistory.com/8/24/ShiJieYanCaoHuoJianKangDaHuiZaiBeiJingJuHang.html.

On 2000, the negotiation for the WHO FCTC was formally initiated. After six rounds over 3 years, the Convention was finally adopted by universal vote at the 56th World Health Assembly on May 2003. The WHO FCTC became effective on February 27, 2005. On November 10, 2003, Wang GY as the Permanent Representative of China to the United Nations signed the WHO FCTC on behalf of China, which is the 77th signatory country. In August 2005, the 17th National People's Congress approved the WHO FCTC, which came into force in China on January 8, 2006. From then on, China started tobacco control campaign under the guidance of the WHO FCTC. Thereafter, not only more and more medical and public health experts, but also many legal experts participated in tobacco control campaigns. Among all the NGOs and professional departments related to tobacco control, some institutes were especially active in tobacco control. A few organizations and departments are described in detail as following.

Chinese Association on Tobacco Control: with the advocating and support of Former Minister of MOH Chen MZ, Chinese Smoking or Health Society was founded in 1990. It is a national organization of academicians and social mass group, focuses on tobacco control, consisting of officials, experts, scholars, journalists and celebrities in the show business. Professor Wu JP, former vice-chairman of the NPC Standing Committee, was the first president of the association, and He LL and Han QD, both vice-chairmen of the NPC Standing Committee, as well as Qian ZY, vice chairman of the CPPCC, served as the honorary presidents successively. The second, third and fourth presidents of the association were all retried vice Ministers of MOH. Because the Chinese government forbids officials to serve as presidents of associations after 2015,[28] currently Professor Hu DY, an expert in cardiovascular diseases, holds the president's position. The association includes five panels, namely smoking and disease control, hospital tobacco control, adolescent tobacco control, tobacco control in media and show business and tobacco control product. "Chinese Tobacco Control Ambassadors" include famous singer Peng LY (the Wife of Xi Jinping, the supreme leader of China), sport stars Yao M, Zhang YN and Liu X, and celebrities in the show business such as Jiang K, Pu CX, Ju P, Yang L, Feng YZ, Niu L, etc.[29] the CATC entrusted academic institutions to perform epidemiological surveys on tobacco, organized national seminars on smoking and health, and especially achieved a great success in hosting the 10th World Conference on Tobacco or Health and the Cross-strait Conferences on Tobacco Control. It also took the initiative to promote campaigns such as Smoking Free schools and hospitals, as well as Tobacco Free advertising cities, etc. CATC also plays a crucial part in policy advocating with its extensive governmental resources and political network. In the beginning, CATC could even issue documents and work together with the government agencies. The most honorary presidents and presidents of the CATC are incumbent or retired officials at various levels, and many experts and

---

[28] General Office of the CPC Central Committee, General Office of the State Council, The overall plan on disconnecting Industry Association, chamber of Commerce from the Administration, General Government Network, 2015,7,8. http://www.gov.cn/zhengce/2015-07/08/content_2894118.htm.

[29] Chinese Association on Tobacco Control, www.catcprc.org.cn/.

scholars are also chairmen and representatives of NPC and CPPCC and provincial People Congress and Political Consultative Conference. CATC also brought together a large number of experts and scholars from the medical community, who bring authoritativeness to communicate health hazards of smoking. More importantly, CATC invited many international experts, so that the tobacco control in China has been concerned and supported by the international society from the beginning. Each province also has its own tobacco control association. Especially, the tobacco control associations of Shanghai, Beijing, Guangdong, etc. played crucial role in facilitating local tobacco control legislation. The following chapters of this book will describe campaigns of CATC in detail.

Chinese Center for Disease Control and Prevention (China CDC): From 1990s, experts and scholars from Chinese Academy of Preventive Medicine (rename China CDC in 2002) carried out epidemiological surveys on tobacco use, and a prospective cohort study on smoking and health including 250,000 subjects. In 1999, entrusted by the Ministry of Health (MOH), Chinese Academy of Preventive Medicine did a lot of work for the WHO FCTC negotiation, and Professor Yang GH joined the WHO FCTC negotiation as one of the experts of Chinese government delegation. In May 2009, China CDC integrated tobacco control forces to the Tobacco Control Office including four divisions, General/Project management, Policy advocacy, Surveillance and Intervention. The responsibility of Tobacco Control Office is assisting the MOH to implement of WHO FCTC, establishing surveillance system and tobacco control network, training professionals, and assessing the impact of tobacco control programs. China CDC has organized national surveys of tobacco for adults in 2010 and 2015, as well as survey for Youth in 2014. They also provide scientific evidence and consultation for relevant government departments to develop laws, regulations, norms, policies, standards and plans concerning tobacco control.[30] China CDC and China University of Political Science and Law banded into the "League of Legal Expert for tobacco control", promote legislation of smoke-free at province and city and carried out smoke-free campaign at hospital, school, as well as set up quit hotline to provide quit service, and so on. Some provincial and local CDC have list tobacco control as their core work of chronic disease control, however, most provincial and local CDC have not put tobacco control on the their agenda.

Think Tank Research Center for Health Development (Think Tank) is a social service institute (a non-governmental non-enterprise entity) founded in 2001 and registered under the Ministry of Civil Affairs. Its operation is under the supervision of the NHFPC. It was initiated and founded by Chen CM, the first president, and Wang KA, the third president of Chinese Academy of Preventive Medicine (the predecessor of China CDC), and the other retired officers of MOH. From 2005, Think Tank began to engage in tobacco control, and become a very influential force in the tobacco control of China. In the last 10 years, Think Tank has made prominent contribution to policy advocating and defending tobacco control from tobacco industry. Especially, Think Tank made tremendous achievement in advocating pic-

---

[30] China CDC Tobacco Control Office, http://www.notc.org.cn/.

torial warning on cigarette boxes, and promoting comprehensive prohibition of tobacco advertising, promotion and sponsorship. With financial aids from international organizations, Think Tank pushed forward local legislation of tobacco free city, helped improving capacity of enforcement, and gathered media league and volunteer team, to spread tobacco control campaigns from experts to the public.[31,32] Leadership of Think Tank has the great influence in the medical science community to attract a great number of experts into tobacco control campaign.

The Other Medical Organization and Experts That smoking causes lung cancer has been recognized health hazards of tobacco more than 50 years ago. Medical experts in the Chinese oncology community also early participated in tobacco control campaign. In 1980s, Professor Liu BQ of the Cancer Hospital, Chinese Academy of Medical Sciences conducted a case control study on smoking and health among 1,000,000 subjects, and provided research evidence on health hazards of tobacco use among Chinese population.[33] On October 26, 1984, Cancer Research Foundation of China (renamed as Cancer Foundation of China in 2005) was founded. This foundation comprises mainly retired officials of high rank from the healthcare system and famous oncologists. It is a NGO affiliated to the government. Several retired Ministers and vice ministers of MOH are members of the foundation. The foundation announced 2007 Beijing Declaration "Stop Lung Cancer—Prevention, Research and Treatment", and appealed for "Strict enforcement of WHO FCTC and initiative in legislation for further tobacco control", as well as "Tobacco Control Promotion" to prevent lung cancer.[34] During each cancer summit and forum, tobacco control is an important topic.

Smoking is a risk factor for cardiovascular diseases, however, Chinese knows little about the relationship between smoking and cardiovascular diseases. Diseases such as coronary heart disease, stroke, peripheral vascular diseases and abdominal aortic aneurysm are all directly related to smoking. Proposed by Professor Hu DY, an expert of cardiovascular diseases, on the 18th Great Wall International Congress of Cardiology, smoking cessation was included in the agenda of the conference. During the opening ceremony, all cardiovascular specialists made "Declaration of Smoking Cessation of Chinese Cardiovascular Specialists".[35] From then on, tobacco control is always an important theme of the annual Great Wall Congress. Participants increased from a dozen to several hundred and the number of themes also grew year

---

[31] Think Tank Research Center for Health Development, tobacco control, http://www.healthtt.org.cn/Item/list.asp?id=1544.

[32] China CDC, NGO promotes China tobacco control campaigns, http://www.chinacdc.cn/ztxm/jksn_9678/mlhc/201611/t20161122_135961.html.

[33] Liu BQ, Peto R, Chen ZM, et al. Emerging tobacco hazards in China: 1. Retrospective proportional mortality study of one million deaths. BMJ, 1998, 317(7170): 1411–1422.

[34] "Beijing Declaration" of the Second South-North Forum of Lung Cancer in China, September 24, 2005, Beijing, http://www.cfchina.org.cn/show.php?contentid=108.

[35] Tobacco Control Pioneers Build the Great Wall together–Summary of Smoking Abstinence Forum on The Great wall Conference, http://www.100md.com, December 9 2017,*China Medical Tribune*.

by year. Following this, associations such as Chinese Medical Doctor Association also made declaration of tobacco control.[36]

Legal Experts support Tobacco Control On May 29, 2009, the Chinese Legal Expert Panel of Tobacco Control with 59 legal experts was formed in Beijing. The experts are from China University of Political Science and Law, Peking University, Tsinghua University, as well as state and local cities legislatures, and will strive to promote national and local tobacco control legislation and to urge implement of WHO FCTC.[37] Legal experts took the initiative in local legislation. Especially, officials and leaders of governmental Legislative Affairs Offices of Harbin, Tianjin and Shenzhen played key roles in promoting local legislation and accelerating issue of smoking free laws of these cities. Since 2013, Professors Ying SN and Ma HD of China University of Political Science and Law, together with a dozen of legal experts from universities and research institutes such as Peking University Law School, Nankai University School of Law and Shanghai University of Political Science and Law, proposed that "the central government issues national tobacco control legislation as soon as possible."[38] When the draft regulations on comprehensive banning smoking in indoor public places and working places was blocked in the State Council, the Chinese University of Political Science and Law hosted a seminar to support the draft submitted by NHFPC in 2004 at reasonableness of legislative procedures and provisions to counter accusations from the tobacco industry. Legal experts believe that comprehensive banning smoking in all indoor public places is one of the criteria of well-off China.

Academicians of Chinese Academy of Sciences and Chinese Academy of Engineering (CAE) are also concerned about the tobacco control in China. Xie JP, the vice director of Zhengzhou Tobacco Research Institute adopted wrong parameters and claimed that "cigarettes with low tar and Chinese herbal medicine cigarettes could reduce the harm of tobacco to human health", and was granted academician of CAE for major achievement "having developed a China specific research area of reducing tar and harm of cigarettes". This became a scandal of academician selection of CAE and blemished the reputation of CAE and even the scientific community. In December 2012, when the scandal happened, 26 academicians jointly questioned this result and requested reevaluation. Up to May 2013, nearly 100 academicians had written jointly to the presidium of CAE and requested reconsidering and reassessing the qualification of tobacco expert Xie JP as an academician.[39]

---

[36] Chinese Doctors' Tobacco Control Declaration–A Proposal by Chinese Medical Doctor Association, http://www.360doc.com/content/11/0712/05/128196_133015361.shtml.

[37] Xinhua News Agency, Beijing, May 29, Legal Expert Panel is Formed to Promote Tobacco Control Legislation, http://www.iolaw.org.cn/showNews.asp?id=22297.

[38] Tens of Chinese Legal Experts Jointly Advocate National Tobacco Control Legislation, The Beijing News, January 28, 2013, http://health.sina.com.cn/news/2013-01-28/091670787.shtml.

[39] Mingyan Wei, Yanxin Jiang, Ru Wen, Nearly 100 Academicians Jointly Request Reevaluating the Qualification of "Tobacco Academician", The Beijing Newspaper, 2012-05-30 http://news.163.com/12/0530/02/82NHNTV000014AED.html.

At present some social groups, including public health professionals, officials, lawyers, journalists, social and academic celebrities, ordinary citizens and non-governmental organizations have participated in tobacco control. However, for a country with a population over 1.3 billion, there are only very few professional agencies and NGOs paying attention to tobacco control.

Currently, there have already been 310,000 Chinese NGOs, in which health organizations alone are over 10,000.[40] Over 20 nationals associations such as Chinese Medical Association and Chinese Preventive Medicine Association, 50 NGOs under the supervision of NHFPC, and All-China Women's Federation, All-China Federation of Trade Unions, the Central Committee of Communist Youth League of China, All-China Journalists Association, and Chinese Society of Ideological and Political Work could be potential tobacco control NGOs. In summary, only more and more people participate in the social movement changing unhealthy norms so as to create a new situation of tobacco control.

3.5 Tobacco Industry and Strategy Against Tobacco Control in China

3.5.1 Tobacco Industry in China

China National Tobacco Corporation (CNTC) was founded in January 1982, as the state-owned business enterprise of the tobacco monopoly. CNTC is mainly responsible for centralized and unified management of staff, finance, properties, products, supply, sale, import and export business and foreign economic and technological cooperation of the country's tobacco industry.[41] In 1984, The State Council agreed to rename Tobacco Monopoly Bureau of Ministry of light industry to the State Tobacco Monopoly Bureau (STMA), and merged into the CNTC, but kept two name: CNTC and STMA, which has formed a unified leadership, vertical, monopoly franchise management system,[42] and determines the overall government tobacco policy, including tobacco leaf quotas, pricing, cigarette production quotas, and more.

STMA/CNTC is the umbrella organization for 58 affiliated institutions, 446 Municipal Bureau (company), 2283 County Bureau (Sales section), 105 cigarette manufacturing enterprises, and many branches, with totally around 550,000

---

[40] The Ministry of Civil Affairs of the People's Republic of China, Statistical Report of the People's Republic of China on the Social Services Development in 2014, 2015-06-10 16:43, http://www.mca.gov.cn/article/zwgk/mzyw/201506/20150600832371.shtml.

[41] Baidu Encyclopedia, China Tobacco Corporation, http://baike.baidu.com/view/1036717.htm.

[42] STMA/CNTC, Memorabilia on Chinese Tobacco, China Tobacco online http://www.tobacco.gov.cn/html/10/1003/56860_n.html.

employees.[43] Between 1998 and 2009, this consolidation reduced the number of companies to one sixth (from 185 to 31).[44] In 2013, consolidation had reduced cigarette brands from around 2000 in the late 1990s to 90.[45] CNTC and STMA are, in effect, one organization with the same leadership and structure,[46] even sharing one government website (www.tobacco.gov.cn), so-called a set of institutions, two brands. So, the Chinese government plays conflicting roles in China's tobacco sector, as both owner and regulator of the industry.

With nearly one-third of the world's smokers (more than 300 million), and 42% of global tobacco production (average annual 2.53 trillion cigarettes) during 2011–2015,[47] CNTC is the world's single largest producer of cigarettes, and serves the largest domestic tobacco market in the world. Annual cigarette production in China from 1952 to 2015 is shown in Fig. 3.2. Cigarette production was about 500 billion cigarettes in 1976, and substantially rose to 2·6 trillion in 2015, an increase of 5.2 times in 1976.[48] China is also the world's largest cultivator of tobacco, producing about three million tons of tobacco leaf (43% of the global total) since 2009,[49] and 3.4 million tons in 2012.[50]

The retail sales volume of cigarettes grew by almost 6% (from 2.34 trillion sticks to 2.49 trillion sticks) between 2010 and 2015, decreased about 2.5% between 2014 and 2015.[51] In addition, the retail value of China's cigarette market in 2015 was RMB 1422.3 billion ($206.1 billion), up 54% from RMB 922.1 billion (USD 136.2 billion) in 2010. The tobacco industry has become one of the most profitable state-owned enterprise, with annual net profits of 165.0 billion RBM ($26.2 billion) back in 2012, only next to Industrial & Commercial Bank of China and Construction bank, far

[43] STMA/CNTC, General situation of tobacco in China, China Tobacco online. http://www.tobacco.gov.cn/html/10/1004.html.

[44] STMA, A series of China Tobacco Almanac 2000–2010. Beijing: China Economic Publishing House.

[45] Anon. (2014, August 6). Analysis of market competitiveness of Chinese cigarette brands. Tobacco Market. http://www.etmoc.com/market/looklist.asp?id=31733.

[46] Central People's Government of the People's Republic of China. Chinese Government's Official Web Portal: Management Structure of State Tobacco Monopoly Administration and China National Tobacco Corporation. Beijing2006; Available from: http://www.gov.cn/english//2005-09/15/content_63766.htm.

[47] National Bureau of Statistics of China, National Data http://data.stats.gov.cn/search.htm?s=卷烟产量.

[48] Industry information network. Statistics on cigarettes output by province in China, 2015. http://www.chyxx.com/data/201402/229234.html (accessed Jan 3, 2017).

[49] Eriksen M, Mackay J, Ross H. The Tobacco Atlas (Fourth Edition). American Cancer Society and World Lung Foundation. http://www.tobaccoatlas.org/ (accessed Oct 7, 2014).

[50] Data of industry of China, Tobacco product. http://d.qianzhan.com/xdata/detail?d=x2Hy6yG&di=xex8xByaynHy6yG (accessed Oct 7, 2014).

[51] STMA/CNTC, Summary of the national cigarette market in 2015, China Tobacco online. http://www.tobacco.gov.cn/html/56/4889035_n.html.

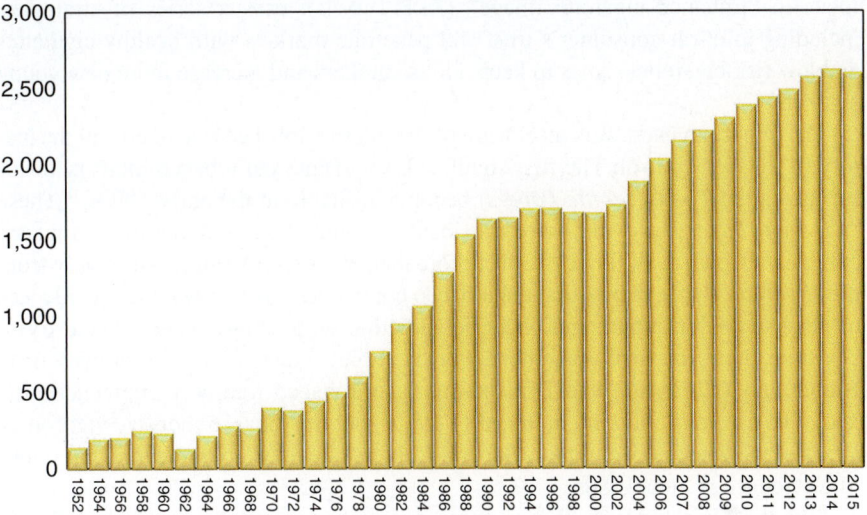

Fig. 3.2 Annual cigarette production by the China National Tobacco Corporation between 1952 and 2015*.
Resource: The figure is made by author based on the National Bureau of Statistics of China National Data http://data.stats.gov.cn/search.htm?s=卷烟产量

bigger than the Bank of China or the Petro China Company.[52] The major excuse of the tobacco industry to argue against tobacco control is that they turned over the great taxes revenue to the State. In 2015, the tobacco industry paid revenues taxes of 1095 billion RBM ($158.6 billion), up to 20.2% than that in 2014. Many government leaders don't really want to practice polities related to tobacco control to impact the government's income owing to higher revenues and taxes from tobacco company; STMA/CNTC use their considerable economic and political influence to create an environment that encourages the continued consumption of cigarettes and to influence the political process at the local and national levels with a series of strategies and tricks in order to obstruct the implementation of WHO FCTC in China.

3.5.2   Strategies Against Tobacco Control by Chinese Tobacco Industry

The powerful tobacco industry has counteracted the effort of tobacco control community with open or covert way so as to promote tobacco use, despite the health hazards of tobacco use has been evident to anyone in China. The STMA/CNTC

---

[52] National Audit Office. Tobacco China gained profit 165.0 billion RBM in 2012, far beyond Petro China. http://money.163.com/14/0620/10/9V66GKTL00252G50.html (accessed Oct 7, 2014).

focus to "Enhance cigarette image" (卷烟上水平), uses a series of strategies, including to cheat consumer's trust and penetrate markets with healthy cigarettes and low risk cigarettes, so as to keep adults smokers and increase more new young smokers.[53]

The important event was disclosure of the internal tobacco documents in the history of tobacco control. The first significant set of internal tobacco industry documents (called *The Cigarette Papers*) become available in the early 1990s.[54] These *"Cigarette Papers"* provide a shocking inside account of the activities of one tobacco company, Brown & Williamson, over more than 30 years. Quoting extensively from the *Cigarette Paper,* shows that the tobacco companies have known these evidences of adverse health impact and Nicotine addiction with using cigarettes, and try to cover up them, cheated customers. For example, scientists and executives from Brown and Williamson and British American Tobacco routinely appreciated the addictive nature of nicotine in the early 1960s, but the tobacco industry vigorously attacked the a series of Surgeon General Reports since for going beyond the scientific evidence in later 1980s.

Like the Multinational tobacco companies, tobacco industry in China (STMA/CNTC), make all effort and devoted to the promotion of cigarettes' use and keep high epidemic levels and cultivate the new generation smokers. Since 2000, the STMA has paid more attention how to block the implementation of the WHO FCTC and draft the countermeasures of WHO FCTC: *The study on Counter-proposals to the WHO FCTC and countermeasures to address its impacts on the Chinese tobacco industry in China (Research on Counterproposals and Countermeasures)*,[55] which was praised by STMA.[56] More than 400 pages of report showed off how the representatives of STMA do defend the tobacco industry's benefits at negotiation of WHO FCTC mainly by translation of Chinese Version of WHO FCTC, and have provide the coping strategies against each substantial Article of WHO FCTC when implement of Convention in China. The Chinese tobacco industry, as a state-owned tobacco company, has many unique strategies against tobacco control under the specific political regime in China. The *Research on Counterproposals and Countermeasures* is important for understanding the STMA/CNNC' coping strategies against WHO FCTC. Its importance for tobacco control in China is similar to *the Cigarette Paper* for global tobacco control. International community, Governments, public health workers as well as tobacco control advocates concerned

---

[53] STMA/CNTC Overview tobacco in China中国烟草概况, http://www.tobacco.gov.cn/html/10/1004.html.

[54] Glantz S et al. The cigarette paper. Burkeley, University of California Press, 1996. http://publishing.cdlib.org/ucpressebooks/view?docId=ft8489p25j&brand=ucpress.

[55] Zhou RZ, Cheng YZ, eds. The Study on Countering Tactics for Implement of WHO Framework Convention on Tobacco Control and Convention' Impact to Tobacco Industry in China. Beijing, China: Economic Science Press, 2006:13.

[56] Department of Science and Education. STMA. No. 06. Summary table of project winning award for science and technology of CNTC, 2008. http://www.tobaccoinfo.com.cn/images/zhxx/szgdgg/Uploadpdf/2009/20090330.doc (accessed 31 Jan 2013).

China, are necessary to understand STMA/CNTC' strategies against tobacco control in China.

The coping tactics and strategies against WHO FCTC by tobacco industry of China are summarized below. The detail description of these tactics will be shown in various Chapter. Although strategies are presented here separately, it is important to note that the tobacco industry often use one or more of these strategies at the same time so as to achieve their target.

The STMA/CNTC undermine the political and legislative processes on tobacco control by exaggerating the economic importance of the industry,[57] by organizing support through so-called front groups (such as China Tobacco Society), and by funding research, including in universities, to promote pseudoscience (e.g., research on so-called safe cigarettes with low tar and Chinese herbs) to create doubt about the health effects of tobacco use.

3.5.2.1 Exaggerating the Economic Importance of the Tobacco Industry

SMTA/CNTC always strengthen that tobacco industry has made a significant contribution to economics and social development by directly increasing revenue, finance and foreign exchange, indirectly developing related industries and lowering employment pressure.[58,59] The authors of the book of *Research on Counterproposals and Countermeasures,* strengthened that tobacco industry is an important pillar industry in china, "... Any influence factors on the development of tobacco industry, must be paid high attention to, and carefully and cautiously dealt with. When to concern smoking and health, we have to consider the development of the tobacco industry, State's financial revenues, local economic growth, benefits and interests of smokers and employees. Therefore, the whole society should more gently, impersonally but conservative carry out for tobacco control ....".[60]

Although the revenue of tobacco industry ranked in front, it only showed that China was still kept an inefficient economic module in China. The inefficient module is need to reform in future. Back in 2000, the officer from Development and Reform Commission, who joined negotiation of WHO FCTC, clearly pointed out that tobacco industry is the sunset-industry.[61] Many scholars have elaborated the issue in different dimensions over past few years.

---

[57] Tobacco China online Tobacco had taken up important position in national economy of China. http://www.tobaccochina.com/news/data/20045/z_3437815_521162230.htm (accessed Oct 7, 2014).

[58] Meng Z, Effect of Yunnan Tobacco Industry on Economic Growth, Journal of Heffi University of Technology, Vol 25, No. 2, April 2011.

[59] Che K, Contribution of Tobacco Farming to economy and agriculture in China http://www.tobacco.org.cn/news/yczzy.htm.

[60] Zhou RZ, Cheng YZ, eds. The Study on Countering Tactics for Implement of WHO Framework Convention on Tobacco Control and Convention' Impact to Tobacco Industry in China. Beijing, China: Economic Science Press, 2006:13.

[61] Liu TN, Xiong BL Tobacco Economy and Tobacco Industry, P 168,Science and Economy Press, 2004.

- The tobacco industry's business turnover tax, 80% of total revenues and tax of tobacco industry, is contributed by Chinese 350 million smokers, not by the tobacco industry. The STMA/CNTC only report the total revenue and tax in order to confuse and exaggerate its contribution to government finance.[62]
- Tobacco platting is not most economic crop; If the capital of Tobacco industry switches to the other industries, the greater output value will be obtained.[63]
- The social contribution of tobacco industry is obviously over-estimated. If the capital of tobacco industry switches to agricultural products process, food manufacture and textile industries, quantity of employee will increase by ten times.[64]
- The direct and indirect health-related economic costs attributable to tobacco use in China is to offset the considerable extent of contribution of revenues from tobacco industry.[65]

In conclusion, even if only from the economic considerations, the tobacco industry's "profit contribution" is far from sufficient to compensate for the cost of the whole society to pay with the tobacco bring harm to society. The more great and stronger tobacco industry is, the more distant the health and happiness of Chinese is.

3.5.2.2 Manipulating and Affecting the Political and Legislative Process of Tobacco Control

STMA/CNTC is an agency with function of a tobacco enterprise and a government department. Different from other tobacco industries, STMA/CNTC directly snatched leadership and interfered the tobacco control in China. In the negotiation stage of WHO FCTC, STMA blocked the negotiation process as described in Chapter 1, then weakened the Article of WHO FCTC though official translation of Chinese version of Convention, just as described in the book of *Research on Counterproposals and Countermeasure*. For example, Article 13.2 of WHO FCTC: Each Party shall, in accordance with its constitution or constitutional principles, undertake a **comprehensive** ban of all tobacco advertising, promotion and sponsorship. "**Comprehensive** 全面" was translated "**extensive** 广泛" in order to leave room for tobacco advertisements.[66]

[62]Zheng R The puzzle and the truth of revenues and tax contributed by tobacco industry, Cai Xin Website, April, 4, 2016. http://mini.eastday.com/a/160429145356902-2.html.

[63]Yu H, Reevaluate on tobacco economy and financial benefit in China, 2012, http://finance.cnr.cn/gundong/201205/t20120530_509746889.shtml.

[64]Yu H, Reevaluate on tobacco economy and financial benefit in China 2012, http://finance.cnr.cn/gundong/201205/t20120530_509746889.shtml.

[65]The bill China cannot afford: health, economic and social costs of China's tobacco epidemic. Manila, Philippines: World Health Organization Regional Office for the Western Pacific; 2017.

[66]Zhou RZ, Cheng YZ, eds. The Study on Countering Tactics for Implement of WHO Framework Convention on Tobacco Control and Convention' Impact to Tobacco Industry in China. Beijing, China: Economic Science Press, 2006:13. P 220.

After implementation of WHO FCTC, as mentioned earlier, STMA/CNTC successfully become a member of into the Steering Committee of tobacco control. On April, 2008, at 1 months after the Steering Committee was established, the STMA and the General Administration of Quality Supervision, Inspection, and Quarantine (AQSIQ) issued the departmental notice on domestic packaging and labeling of cigarettes packages in the name of implementing the WHO FCTC,[67] which is expected by the tobacco industry and described in *Research on Counterproposals and Countermeasure*. Article 11 of WHO FCTC mentioned *"shall be approved by the competent national authority"*, National Authority is defined "STMA" in the department notice. It is clearly that the Government' public power has been heavily influenced by the tobacco industry.

3.5.2.3   Sponsorship for Researches and Marketing Pseudo-Science

The tobacco industry has been offering financial support to scientists and some academics and research institutes. The history of researches funded by tobacco industry has shown that researchers often use the wrong method or misinterpret the results to support the wrong conclusions, or do not publish the results so as to suit the needs of the tobacco industry. In China, STMA/CNTC financed Institute of toxicology, Chinese Academy of Military Sciences to provide scientific fig leaf to make up their "Low tar, low risk" myths.[68]

The scientific evidences indicates that changing cigarette designs over the last five decades, including filtered, low-tar, and "light" variations, have not reduced overall disease risk among smokers and may have hindered prevention and cessation efforts.[69] While the 'low-tar' scheme has been widely recognized as a misleading tactic used to deceive the public about the true risks of low tar and light cigarette smoking by the tobacco industry. The a similar, even more crazy campaign using the slogan of 'less harmful, low tar' was launched by the STMA/CNTC. Despite no any evidence supports the claims that these cigarettes are safer, the STMA/CNTC has continued to market low tar, low risk cigarettes supported by "pseudo-science",

---

[67] STMA. QAQSIQ, the domestic regulations on cigarette packaging and labeling in the territories of the People's Republic of China, April 16, 2008. http://www.tobaccochina.com/law/nation/wu/20084/20084153948_297463.shtml (accessed Oct 7, 2014).

[68] Institute of Basic Medical Study PUMC and Think Tank, Assemble of symposium on "Is Science or Hoax the reducing harm of cigarette by low tar", Jan. 15,2015.

[69] U.S. Department of Health and Human Services. *How Tobacco Smoke Causes Disease: The Biology and Behavioral Basis for Smoking-Attributable Disease: A Report of the Surgeon General.* Atlanta, GA: U.S. Department of Health and Human Services, Centers for Disease Control and Prevention, National Center for Chronic Disease Prevention and Health Promotion, Office on Smoking and Health, 2010.

which was propped up with national award[70,71] and researcher of tobacco industry has the title of Academia. Such absurd farce has been widely reported by a lot of mass media, including that *Science* said that Tobacco scientist's election tars academy's image.[72] The ludicrous consequence remain uncorrected, whether it was public protests or experts appeal, including appeal of 100 academicians of the Chinese Academy of Engineering, which saddens me deeply.[73] This is a typical case supported by the pseudo science, corruption in the scientific community and abuse of public power, to help China's tobacco industry to most successfully promote the "low tar strategy" in China.[74]

3.5.2.4 Discrediting and Distort the Proven Scientific Information

Questioning the scientific evidences of health hazards caused by smoking and SHS exposure is a popular tactic used by the tobacco industry. In China, STMA/CNTC communicates that "Low tar, low risk" cigarettes make smoker from harmful smoking to healthy smoking, to mistake the people. Tobacco industry even communicated that the some cigarettes with some Chinese medical herb have functions and efficiencies of relieving cough and reducing sputum, delaying senescence and prolong life.

3.5.2.5 Disseminating Tobacco Culture, Oppose Tobacco Control

STMA/CNTC tries in vain to make up smoking into a positive, elegant, fashionable image by dint of a series of efforts in order to "let consumers form such a concept that smoking is a normal behavior of adults". Building the Tobacco Museum of China, the largest tobacco museum in the world, features smoking stories and images of the great personage, leaders and famous people, to promote and celebrate Chinese culture and civilization related to tobacco use.[75] The packages of Chinese cigarettes are designed very magnificent, gorgeous and resplendent with "cultural connotation", which become an excuse to refuse placing picture warning in cigarette

[70] Ministry of Science and Technology, P. R. China. List of National Scientific and Technological Progress Awards. 2003: No. J-211-2-03. Research on improving burley tobacco quality and its application in low-tar cigarettes. http://www.most.gov.cn/cxfw/kjjlcx/kjjl2003/200802/t20080214_59048.htm (accessed 20 Mar 2012).

[71] Ministry of Science and Technology, P. R. China. List of National Scientific and Technological Progress Awards. P. R. China: Ministry of Science and Technology, 2004. No. 54. Technology research and application on reducing the harmful ingredients. http://www.most.gov.cn/cxfw/kjjlcx/kjjl2004/200802/t20080214_59054.htm (accessed 20 Mar 2012).

[72] Hvistendahl M. Tobacco scientist's election tars academy's image. Science 2012;335:153–4.

[73] About 100 Academicians ask reviewing Xie' reconsider his validation as a qualified Academician. Xinhua News. http://news.163.com/12/0530/02/82NHNTV000014AED.html (accessed 31 Jan 2013).

[74] Yang GH, Marketing 'less harmful, low-tar' cigarettes is a key strategy of the industry to counter tobacco control in China, Tobacco Control, Published Online, First 24 January 2013.

[75] China Tobacco Museum. http://www.tobaccomuseum.com.cn/maincontrol?url=&linkType=AbstractCategory&id=8 (accessed Oct 7, 2014).

package. At the third session of COP of the WHO FCTC, the Chinese Government delegation prevented Guideline of Article 11 of WHO FCTC, was against placing graphic warnings on cigarette packs. The speaker of the delegation said: "There are the famous mountains and great waters, beautiful scenery in Chinese cigarette package. If playing the warning picture on package, these picture will hurt the feeling of Chinese people." Of course, China was awarded the Dirty Ashtray Award by Framework Convention Alliance for attempting to make a mockery of Article 11 guidelines, including preferring beautiful cigarette packages over the health of its citizens.[76]

3.5.2.6 Manipulating Public Opinion to Improve the Tobacco Industry's Social Image

In the name of sponsorship, charity, and social responsibility, direct or indirect marketing of tobacco products or promotion of tobacco use by supporting cultural and sports activities, donations to schools, donations to the disaster area, etc. and to gain a veneer of social respectability. Many cases in these areas will be introduced in the relevant chapters.

3.5.2.7 Political Intimidating Tobacco Control Advocators

Political threats and putting political labels on people are a popular tactic to intimidate some organization or individuals that promote social progress, but move cheese of the certain departments or groups in China. STMA/CNTC also accused of advocating tobacco control as a traitorous act, communicating western liberal thoughts, break down tobacco industry, and so on.

As early as in negotiation of WHO FCTC, a member of the Chinese delegation from STMA, pointed to officer of Ministry of Health and cursed that "Do you want to tobacco control? I tell you, it is the betray China, you are public servants, one tenth of your salary is from our tobacco industry."[77]

STMA entrusted the Chinese Academy of Social Sciences to complete the internal report information communication to Central Government. In the report, the some tobacco control NGOs were described as that "... These NGO try to break down Chinese tobacco industry and spread the Western liberal ideological thought in name of tobacco control under manipulation by foreign investors and transnational tobacco companies...".[78] The purpose is try to threaten them so as to curb the active action of Tobacco Control Advocators.

---

[76] Baid du Bai ke Dirty Ashtray Award. http://baike.baidu.com/view/4165080.htm?fr=Aladdin (accessed Oct 7, 2014).

[77] Finance.ifeng.com The tobacco industry is over 8%on the financial contributions, STMA said tobacco control is quislism behavior. http://finance.ifeng.com/news/bgt/20120607/6573906.shtml.

[78] Shi D, A number of the contentious subjects and suggestions on tobacco control (Extract), The Important Report (Inter reference) of Chinese Academy of Social Science, Feb. 23, 2012 (Secret 3 Months).

3.6 Summary

The description on action subjects and surroundings of tobacco control clarified several issues. The tobacco control is carried out in China with 1.3 billion population under leadership of the Communist Party of China with multi-party cooperation and political Consultation. The national policy formulation generally experiences three steps, at the ministry level, inter ministerial coordination and top layer protocol, State Council or CPSC. Legislation or amendment may be listen to the advice of public and approved by NPC. Many medical and public health experts are also the delegates of NPC and the members of CPPCC, even Vice chairman of NPC and CPPCC who all concerned tobacco control. In the past more than 10 years of tobacco control process, experts can directly communicate with leaders at various levels, and even send letters to the top leaders to promote legislation and policy of tobacco control. The professional organization, such as China CDC commonly provided the robust evidences and suggestions by publishing research or investigation report. In addition, the views and suggestions of expert groups express though the NGO platform, such as Chinese Association of tobacco control and Think-Tank Health Development Center, communicated by mass media, influenced public opinion, then influenced policy making. The China tobacco control movement is dramatic and vivid, but the substantive policy changes were few until 2015.

The powerful tobacco companies is a strong anti tobacco control interest group. STMA/CNTC use their considerable economic and political influence to influence the political process and legislation of tobacco control at the national and local levels with a series of strategies and tricks in order to obstruct the implementation of WHO FCTC in China. In addition, some government leaders don't really want to practice polities related to tobacco control as to worry reducing the government's income from cigarettes. So, the anti tobacco control force is very strong at present.

STMA/CNTC enjoys special advantages by combining government function and business management. The STMA/CNTC, as a department of government, is easy to connect with other national governmental agencies very well and to find influential supporters within governments to counter the development of tobacco control legislation. In especial, after the STMA had a seat at the tobacco control policy table and sat on the central Government's WHO FCTC implementation committee, the cases of curbing legislation related to tobacco control are very common in China. As criticized by international community, to control tobacco use by STMA is just as the fox sat in a hen coop to discuss how to protect the chicks.

While coordination among ministries, as they are same rank, the other ministries, just discuss, not command the STMA do something, such as the increase the tax of cigarettes. If the superior leadership, such as the National Development and Reform Commission (NDRC), supports tobacco control, the STMA somewhat restrained, just as in the negotiation of the WHO FCTC. Now MIIT supports the SMTA, STMA is recklessly violated WHO FCTC.

Analysis on the political framework, and strength and advantage of tobacco control and anti tobacco control in China shows that the decision-making process was always bargaining and very lower efficiency owing to the STMA/CNTC interest or benefit and without supervision of public opinion. The stalemate between tobacco control and anti tobacco control was broke a little until 2013 to issue the notice on prohibiting Party and government officials from smoking in public to set an example for all to follow.[79] Recently, Xi Jinping, chairman of the CPC Central Committee pointed out that health should be in all policies. These steps are notable in the history of China's tobacco control, which suggest that the political will of the top leadership in China is to take tobacco control more seriously than they have done previously. The tobacco control community also needs to use its own expert strengths to convey the knowledge and push more government organization to understand the strategy of tobacco control, so as to make a significant breakthrough of tobacco control in China.

---

[79] Xinhua network. The circular from General Office of the Communist Party of China Central Committee and the General Office of the State Council, to prohibit Party and government officials from smoking in public in order to set an example for all to follow 29 Dec 2013, Beijing. http://news.xinhuanet.com/politics/2013-12/29/c_118753701.htm.

Chapter 4
International Assistance and Tobacco Control in China

Gonghuan Yang

Abstract Since 1980s, the tobacco control campaign has been supported by financial assistance of international community. Tobacco control donation from major American foundations has increased considerably after China ratified the WHO FCTC in 2006. The research grants are to support the study of health risk of tobacco use, prevalence pattern of smoking and secondhand smoke exposure (SHS), as well as policy assessment of tobacco control. Next, tobacco control as a significant public health measure was introduced project activities in an early health loan of the World Bank. For the past century, such distinguished philanthropies as the Rockefeller foundation (China Medical Board), Ford Foundations have pioneered many fields in China, especially in medicine. The Bloomberg Initiative (BI) Grants and the Bill & Melinda Gates Foundations provided the biggest support for tobacco control in China. During 2007–2016, BI grant has provided 21.4 million US$ fund to China for tobacco control with 96 projects for national professional organization, local agency of tobacco control, university and non-government organization (NGO). The Grant supported to promote national and local tobacco control legislation, including 100% smoke free environments in project cities, and so on. The Bill and Melinda Gates Foundation continues to provide more than $34 million (US) to support policy interventions, social marketing and building the evidence base in tobacco control in China. Meanwhile, it is important for tobacco control community should consider how to promote domestic charitable donations to tobacco control.

Keywords Foreign philanthropy · The Bloomberg initiative grant · Bill & Melinda gates foundations · Tobacco control · China

G. Yang
Institute of Basic Medical Science Chinese Academy of Medical Sciences, School of Basic Medicine Peking Union Medical College, Beijing, China

© Springer Nature Singapore Pte Ltd. 2018
G. Yang (ed.), *Tobacco Control in China*,
https://doi.org/10.1007/978-981-10-8315-0_4

4.1   Introduction

International engagement, including technical assistance and financial support, has been an important dimension of tobacco control in China. International engagement includes a variety of sources of assistance, such as the world bank's loan projects, the WHO's funding projects, and the research fund from USA and the other countries, as well as the private Philanthropic donations.

WHO Collaborating Centre for Tobacco or Health was set up in China in 1986, which located in Beijing Chao Yang Hospital.[1] It was the first cooperation on tobacco control with World Health Organization. The Center organized the first survey of tobacco use in 1984,[2] conducted educational campaigns on various topics related to tobacco control, especially among medical professionals, set up the smoking cessation clinics and quit lines.[3] Since then, the tobacco control movement in China has been supported by technical support and financial assistance of international community. More significant international donation from major American foundations has been into China to tobacco control, after China ratified the WHO Framework Convention on Tobacco Control (WHO FCTC) in 2006. Here the effort on research, behavior interfere and policy advocacy related to tobacco control are introduced in the chapter.

4.2   Epidemiological Study of Tobacco Control Supported by International Community

The most significant epidemiological studies related to tobacco use have been completed by international experts and domestic experts together. These studies focused the threat of health caused by tobacco use and prevalence pattern of smoking and secondhand smoke exposure (SHS), and the surveillance on knowledge, attitude and behavior related to tobacco use, as well as interfere studies so as to provide evidences for promoting the smoke-free policy. Most of the funding of these research projects have been applied by international experts or/and Chinese scholars. The Chinese government' investments in study related to tobacco use and tobacco control were a few, almost zero at that time.

Table 4.1 list the sources of funding for the major epidemiological studies with significant impact for tobacco control in China. From Table 4.1, there are several characters of the international engagement related to scientific study of tobacco control. First, the sources of funds are very wider, but the funds from the National

---

[1] WHO Collaborating Centre for Tobacco or Health http://www.who.int/tobacco/global_interaction/collab_centers/tob_cc_china/en/.

[2] Weng XZ, Hong ZG, Chen DY (1987) Smoking prevalence in Chinese aged 15 and above. Chin J (Engl) 100:886–892.

[3] www.smokefreehealthcare.org.

Table 4.1 The major epidemiological study of tobacco use with international cooperation in China

Time	Project	Funding
1985–1990	A prospective male cohort study for Smoking Health Risk in Shanghai	US NIH Grants R01 CA43092 and R35 CA53890 from the NIH[a]
1986–1989	Retrospective proportional mortality study of one million deaths	1. Medical Research Council and Imperial Cancer Research Fund in Britain 2. US NIH grant 5R01 CA33638 3. Chinese Academy of Medical Science and Ministry of Health[b]
1994–2005	Prospective study on health risk of smoking in Chinese	1. The Ministry of Health in China 2. The British Medical Research Council and Imperial Cancer Research Fund 3. The World Bank loan to China 4. The Canadian International Development Research Centre(IDRC)[c]
2005-	Prospective Study of 0.5 Million Adults in China	Welcome Trust, MRC, BHF, CR-UK, Kadoorie Charitable Foundation, Chinese MoST and NSFC[d]
1984	Smoking prevalence in Chinese aged 15 and above	WHO funding[e]
1996	1996 National Prevalence Survey of Smoking Pattern	1. Smithkline Beecham (Philadelphia, PA) 2. The Rockefeller Foundation (New York, NY)[f]
2010	Prevalence of Smoking of adult in China in 2010	1. The Bloomberg Global Initiative to Reduce Tobacco Use, a program of Bloomberg Philanthropies 2. The Bill and Melinda Gates Foundation for the implementation of GATS China[g]
2003–2012	Reducing Secondhand Smoke Exposure in China: A Tobacco Control Capacity Building Project	US NIH Grants R01–HL–73699[h–j] and R01TW007949
2006–2008	The International Tobacco Control Policy Evaluation Project(ITC)—China	The Bloomberg Global Initiative to Reduce Tobacco Use
2003–2012	The taxation in tobacco control and its potential economic impact in China	US NIH Fogarty International Center (R01-TW05938) and 1R01TW009295-01[k]

[a]Yuan JM, Ross RK, Wang XL, Gao YT, Henderson BE, Yu MC. Morbidity and mortality in relation to cigarette smoking in Shanghai, China. A prospective male cohort study. JAMA 1996; 275: 1646–50

[b]Liu B Q, Peto R, Chen Z M, Boreham J, Wu Y P, et al. (1998) Emerging tobacco hazards in China: 1. retrospective proportional mortality study of one million deaths. BMJ 317:1411–1422

[c]Niu SR, Yang GH, Chen ZM, et al. Emerging tobacco hazards in China: 2. Early mortality results from a prospective study. *BMJ* 1998; 317:1423–24

[d]Chen ZM Peto R Zhou MG et al. Contrasting male and female trends in tobacco-attributed mortality in China: evidence from successive nationwide prospective cohort studies Lancet 2015; 386:1447–56

[e]Weng XZ, Hong ZG, Chen DY (1987) Smoking prevalence in Chinese aged 15 and above. Chin J (Engl) 100:886–892

[f]Yang GH, Fan LX, Tan J et al (1999) Smoking in China: findings of the 1996 national prevalence survey. JAMA 282:1247–1253

(continued)

Table 4.1 (continued)

^{g}2010 Li Q, Xia JS, Yang GH, Prevalence of Smoking in China in 2010 Nengl J Med 364;25 nejm. org June 23, 2011

^{h}Stillman F, Navas-Acien A, Ma J, et al. Second-hand tobacco smoke in public places in urban and rural China. Tob Control 2007;16:229–34

^{i}Wang CP, Ma SJ, Xu XF, et al. The prevalence of household second-hand smoke exposure and its correlated factors in six counties of China. Tob Control

^{j}Ma SJ, Wang JF, Mei CZ, et al. Passive smoking in China: contributing factors and areas for future interventions. Biomed Environ Sci 2007;20:420–5

^{k}Project Information in NIH https://projectreporter.nih.gov/project_info_description.cfm?aid=833 3920&icde=13481850

Institutes of Health (NIH) in the United States are relatively covered more research projects, which may be explained that US NIH set up the International Tobacco and Health Research and Capacity Building Program.[4] The aims of the Program is "to encourage trans-disciplinary research on the international tobacco epidemic, and focuses on reducing the global burden of morbidity and mortality caused by tobacco use". The programs were designed to "promote international research collaborations between investigators in the U.S. and scientists/institutions in low- and middle-income countries (LMICs) to pursue research on tobacco control and prevention in LMICs".

Second, The amount of funds for study was not sufficient, so a project often have multiple sources of support from Table 4.1.

Third, the most important is that the protocols of these projects have been reviewed by qualified experts on the strict project application procedures; and the findings of that these studies have very high academic value, and many papers published in the famous internationally journals, so the conclusions of these research are convincing, to affect the policy oriented. For example, an important conclusion from a series of epidemiological studies on health impact of smoking in China was that "**smoking caused about 1 million deaths per year in China**". Another important finding from 1984, 1996, 2002 and 2010 epidemiological surveys on prevalence of tobacco use (2002 survey was supported by Ministry of science and technology of China) that the "**prevalence of tobacco use in men is one of the highest in the world, with more than 300 million smokers and 740 million non-smokers exposed to second-hand smoke**". The two findings directly lead to an important conclusion that tobacco use is a leading risk factor for health hazards of Chinese. The tobacco control should be the important strategy for government of China. A series of studies of policy implement and assessment impact on cigarettes tax, smoke-free environments, the packages of cigarettes and other tobacco control policy implementation in China, strongly promote WHO FCTC policy implementation in China. In a word, the research results has a decisive impact of tobacco control in China.

---

[4] International Tobacco and Health Research and Capacity Building Program, https://www.fic.nih. gov/Programs/Pages/tobacco.aspx.

Of course, a lot of scientific problems related to tobacco control need to be further studied in China, which need more research funding support. At the same time, we also know that, tobacco control in China is very complex, related to many factors. The findings of scientific research cannot be directly change situation of tobacco control in China, but it provides evidences for validity and necessity of tobacco control in China, nobody can argue against tobacco control in a flagrant and open way.

4.3 World Bank Early Loan Project Related to Tobacco Control

Tobacco control as a significant public health measure was introduced project activities in an early health loan to China of the World Bank. The **World Bank** is an international financial institution that provides **loans** to developing countries for capital programs. The current World Bank comprises five institutions, the International **Bank** for Reconstruction and Development (IBRD), the International Development Association (IDA) and so on. IDA provides financing, risk management products, and other financial services to middle-income countries with conditional preference.[5] Since 1980s, China has been experiencing an epidemiological transition shifting from the infectious to the chronic non-communicable diseases (NCD) in much shorter time than many other countries. The most important health risk factors were identified as tobacco use, hypertension, unhealthy diet, overweight and obesity, and pollution based on the assessment on health status of Chinese population by World Bank in 1989.[6] Chinese government hopes to improve the capacity of the health sector to design and implement health promotion programs to prevent and control the rising prevalence of NCDs, Sexually Transmitted Diseases (STDs), Human Immunodeficiency Virus (HIV) and injury, which fitted in well with Bank strategies.

The health promotion component of disease preventive project (Health 7) was highly successful in introducing, for the first time, modern theory and practice of health promotion into the Chinese context. Total funding for **The Health Promotion component** was US$22.43 million (IDA US$10.88 million), including: (1) institutional development and policy reform, (2) human resource development (HRD), (3) surveillance, especially for behavioral risk factor surveillance (BRFS) and (4) interventions. **The National component** with a total cost of US$2.49 million (IDA US$2.25 million) would provide support to coordination management and technical support for local components, in recognition of the complexity of the Project.[7] As pointed out in the implementation completion report, "The participation of

[5] World Bank, Who we are, http://www.worldbank.org/en/who-we-are.

[6] World Bank, The China: *Long-Term Issues and Options in the Health Transition* (No. 7965-CHA), http://www-wds.worldbank.org/external/default/WDSContentServer/WDSP/IB/1990/06/2 5/000009265_3960929024734/Rendered/PDF/multi0page.pdf.

[7] The World Bank, China: Disease Prevention Project, IMPLEMENTATION COMPLETION REPORT (TF-25197 IDA-27940 TF-52892), Report No: 30613.

Australian Agency for International Development (AusAID) in the project was very helpful in the success of the health promotion component. Their funding supported technical assistance, which contributed significantly towards increasing high level understanding of health promotion concepts and towards improving the capacity to design and implement health promotion programs. This increase in management commitment and technical capacity not only helped in bringing about a good outcome for the project, but also helped to ensure the sustainability of the health promotion efforts".[8]

Seven project cities selected tobacco use as one of behavior risk factor of NCD to carry out activities. The capacity on the principles and practice of health promotion has been improved among a large number of core workers in the process.

The internal and external evaluation report of Health promotion component of Health 7 project pointed: "The greatest concentration of effort and the most impressive outcomes were achieved in the tobacco control area". From today's perspective, there are still a lot of highlights of health 7 projects. A scale of health education on health hazards and tobacco use, advocacy of banning smoking in public places, banning on sale cigarettes to minors, and bans on tobacco advertising were as City-wide strategies; implement of banning smoking in public places and help smokers to quit as strategies for neighborhoods, schools, hospitals and workplaces. However, policy changes at city-level were not obvious owing to not concern legislation in the project cities. Health 7 project still was a large-scale tobacco control project with standard design, implemented and strictly evaluated in China, which laid the foundation for the standardized tobacco control activities in China.

The BRFS System recorded some change in awareness of tobacco hazards and smoking behavior in project population from 1996 to 2002, but prevalence of current male smoking felled from 59.3% to 44.3%, prevalence of current smoking in male aged 15–19 come down from over 11.5% to 7.5%. In Kunming with HIV prevention, without tobacco control, as control population, there was not significant change for prevalence of male current smoking, and the prevalence of male aged 15–19 was increasing 10.5% to over 20% in same year. Meanwhile, the level of SHS exposure in the 7 project cities dropped by over 15% over 7 years, but the decreasing scope was larger than that in Kunming although there were some decrease in Kunming.[9]

Look back to the project' achievement is that the policy makers at all levels have pay more attention to bring health promotion and prevention of NCDs and a steady increase in the funds available for NCD work at national and local levels. Tobacco control strategies, as one of the important strategies have been included in "*Working Plan on NCD Control and Prevention of China, 2012–2015*".[10]

---

[8] The World Bank, China: Disease Prevention Project, IMPLEMENTATION COMPLETION REPORT (TF-25197 IDA-27940 TF-52892), Report No: 30613 P7.

[9] The World Bank IMPLEMENTATION COMPLETION REPORT, Report No: 30613.

[10] Ministry of Health and 14 other ministries and state administrations, *Working Plan on NCD Control and Prevention of China, 2012–2015,* May 8, 2012, http://www.chinacdc.cn/en/ne/201207/t20120725_64430.html.

The following points explained why Health promotion component of Health 7 project was quite successful:

1. The objectives of Health 7 project was in line with the Government's requirement, which was supported by Government.
2. A well-prepared Plan Implement Plan (PIP) with Institutional Development, Surveillance, Human Resource Development (HRD) and Intervention provided the good roadmap.
3. Guided by the theories and methods in health promotion, general public has been mobilized to join in practice against tobacco use and other risk factor so that these control measures were implemented very well.
4. BRFS provided assessment timely for impact of intervention.
5. The training of a large number of officers of administrative, management and professional staff in the theory and practice of health promotion and disease prevention has been to bring them to understand and support for priority of NCD prevention and control, as well as innovative intervention activities.

4.4 Assistance of Foreign Philanthropy Related to Tobacco Control in China

Recent high-profile international aid for Tobacco Control in China is from the major American foundations.

4.4.1 Review of Philanthropies of American Foundation in China

For the past century, such distinguished philanthropies as the Rockefeller, Ford Foundations have pioneered many fields in China. Then the Bill and Melinda Gates Foundations is the most prominent one.

Rockefeller Foundation (RF) focused on health philanthropy. In order to modernize medical education and to improve the practice of medicine in China, during 1915–1951, RF endowed China Medical Board (CMB) spent well over $50 million on medical initiatives in China, nearly $45 million of it to establish Peking Union Medical College (PUMC) and Peking Union Hospital. RF set up the fellowships helped doctors and nurses to travel abroad for advanced training. Also Foundation supported to translate the medical texts and build the medical libraries.[11] It is important that RF created the modern medical, nursing and public health education, cultivated a group of outstanding talents of modern medicine who obtained some outstanding achievements, so that PUMC become a center spread the modern medi-

---

[11] 100 years the Rockefeller Foundation, Medicine in China, http://rockefeller100.org/exhibits/show/education/china-medical-board.

cal science in Asia. On public health, it is who John Grant and CC Cheng, as pioneers of rural barefoot, created the Ding Xian model and the embryo of three level of medical and health network, which is one of great RF legacy.[12] Today, PUMC has been making its own unique contributions in terms of fighting tobacco epidemics and other health problems under financial support of CMB and other international funding.

CMB accepted the Chinese government's invitation to return to China, embarking on a new era of collaboration with 8–13 Chinese medical schools in 1981. Tibet Medical College was established from a provincial training school under CMB support in 1995. Under stewardship of President Lincoln Chen, CMB has focused on strengthening capacity in health policy and systems sciences since 2006. CMB Rural Health Network, consisting of 12 schools mostly in Western China, has been established.[13] Some colleges and universities began to explore the curriculum of tobacco control, promote the male doctor to quit in medical education by the CMB support, and join to the social campaign of tobacco control. These are some good start, but also need long-term continuous efforts.

At present, WHO, UN agencies, multilateral banks, and new foundations also pay close attention China' health attention. For example, Ford worked with Chinese partners to promote a paradigm shift in family planning, paid more attention to reproductive health than an exclusive focus on population. The fund on the Sexuality and Reproductive Health *Education* achieved 1.62 million US$ in 2010.[14] The Bill & Melinda Gates Foundation's efforts in China include fighting HIV/AIDS and tuberculosis (TB), improving tobacco control, and investing in agricultural research since 2007. Totally the Bill & Melinda Gates Foundation supported more than $175 million for above efforts, including $100 million to HIV prevention, $33 million to help improve TB control, $18 million (U.S.) grant to develop "green super rice" hybrids, $24 million to tobacco control as well as $1.3 million to assist the Ministry of Health of the People's Republic of China with emergency relief activities following the Sichuan earthquake on May 12, 2008.[15]

4.4.2   Investing in Tobacco Control in China by American Foundation

In February, 2015, WHO FCTC came into force, a new era started by international law as a weapon to tobacco control. But compared with the powerful resources of the international tobacco industry, global tobacco control funding was very shortage. In 2008, Michael Bloomberg and Bill Gates announced joint

---

[12] Chen CC. Medicine in rural China: a personal account. Berkeley: University of California Press, 1989.

[13] Norris L. The China Medical Board: 50 years of programs, partnerships, and progress, 1950–2000. New York, NY: China Medical Board of New York, Inc., 2003.

[14] Ford Foundation. China. http://www.fordfoundation.org/pdfs/library/China-brochure-2011.pdf (accessed 27 Nov 2012).

[15] Bill& Melinda Gates Foundation—China Office Fact Sheet. http://www.gatesfoundation.org/global-health/Documents/china-office-fact-sheet.pdf (accessed 27 Nov 2012).

efforts to combat the global tobacco epidemic. The both jointly invested US$500 million to help low- middle income countries to effectively implement WHO FCTC.[16]

Since 2007, Michael R. Bloomberg, philanthropist and former Mayor of New York City, started "Bloomberg initiative to reduce tobacco use Grant Program". Up to now Bloomberg has promised US$1 billion to support tobacco control, which is the greatest financial support. The objective, the working contents and the aid objects of the charitable grant program are very clear. The objective is to reduce tobacco use; the supporting areas of program focused to promote the policy improvement in protecting people from SHS smoking, warning about the danger of tobacco use, comprehensive banning tobacco advertising, promotion and sponsorship, and raise taxes on tobacco products and strong mass media communication. Also the funding support to implement Article 5.3 of WHO FCTC so as to improve MPOWER police package. The aid objective is any low or middle-income countries in Open Grant Round (OGR), and priority ten countries in Strategic Grant Round (SGR). The ten countries included China, India, Indonesia, Bangladesh, Pakistan, Vietnam, Philippines, Brazil, Ukraine, Mexico.[17] In order to effectively promote "the reduce tobacco use Grant Program", the Foundation invited some partners to work together, now has increased from the original five organizations to seven ones: Campaign for Tobacco-Free Kids and Tobacco-Free Kids Action Fund, International Union Against Tuberculosis and Lung Disease, Johns Hopkins University Bloomberg School of Public Health, University of Illinois at Chicago, Vital Strategies, CDC Foundation, World Health Organization Tobacco-Free Initiative.[18] The project has made a big difference: among 69 countries obtained the grant and technical support from Bloomberg Grant program, 54 countries have passed national tobacco control legislation.[19] In the third round, Bloomberg and Gates launch legal fund to help countries fight big tobacco: Philanthropists donate initial $4 million towards legal advice for nations whose health measures are challenged by tobacco industry, as in Uruguay and Australia.[20]

The Bill and Melinda Gates Foundation has provided about US$210 million for supporting tobacco control. The supporting areas focused in policy Interventions, social Marketing and building the Evidence Base in China, Africa and South-east Asia areas.[21]

---

[16] Michael Bloomberg and Bill Gates Join to Combat Global Tobacco Epidemic http://www.prnewswire.co.uk/news-releases/michael-bloomberg-and-bill-gates-join-to-combat-global-tobacco-epidemic-156069425.html.

[17] Bloomberg Initiative to reduce tobacco use, https://tobaccocontrolgrants.org/About-the-BI-Grants-Program.

[18] Bloomberg Initiative partners, https://tobaccocontrolgrants.org/BI-Partners.

[19] Bloomberg Initiative to reduce tobacco use Grant Program https://tobaccocontrolgrants.org/.

[20] The Gardian, Bloomberg and Gates launch legal fund to help countries fight big tobacco, Wednesday 18 March 2015 13.06 EDT, https://www.theguardian.com/society/2015/mar/18/bloomberg-gates-foundation-fund-nations-legal-fight-big-tobacco-courts.

[21] The Bill and Melinda Gates Foundation, Tobacco Control Strategy overview, http://www.gatesfoundation.org/What-We-Do/Global-Policy/Tobacco-Control.

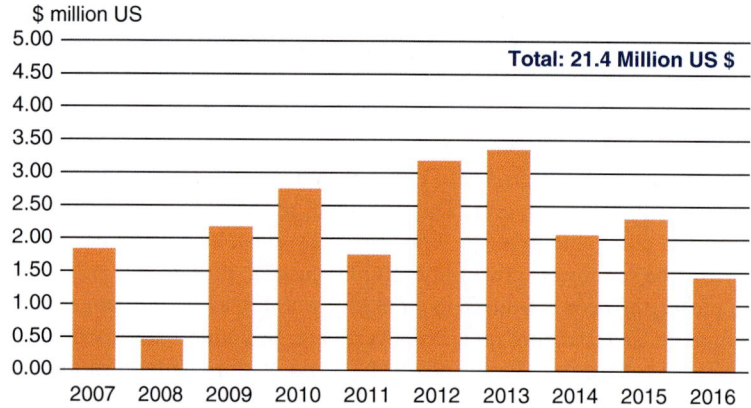

Fig. 4.1 BI Grant to China by year

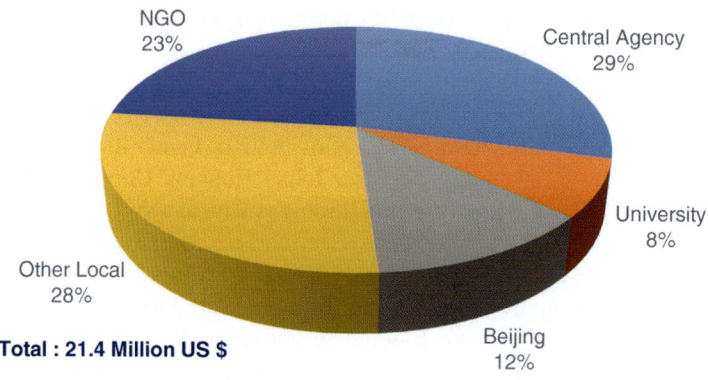

Fig. 4.2 BI Grant to China by organization

4.4.2.1 Bloomberg Initiative and Tobacco Control in China

BI grant have provided 21.4 million US$ fund to China for tobacco control with
96 projects between 2007 and 2016.[22] Despite some fluctuations, the average
annual funding for tobacco control is between $200–300 million. BI grant of
tobacco control were provided to different organization, central agency, local
agency, university and non-government organization (NGO) (Figs. 4.1 and 4.2).
Grant awarded supported to Chinese Center for Disease Control and Prevention
(China CDC) 4.27 million US$ with 14 projects to strengthen the China CDC
National Tobacco Control Office and support its efforts in creating a smoke-free
China, to improve and implement smoke-free policies in Olympic cities. The
Grant supported to promote national and local tobacco control legislation, includ-
ing 100% smoke free environments in project cities, and so on. The fund is many
times larger than the regular budget of tobacco control from the government.

---

[22] Author compiled by data from Bloomberg Initiative To Reduce Tobacco Use Grants Program for
China,   http://tobaccocontrolgrants.org/Pages/40/What-we-fund?who_region=WPRO&country_
id=3&amount=&date_type=&date_from=&date_to=&submit=Search.

Table 4.2 Bloomberg Initiative Grant to local areas to reduce tobacco use in China, 2007–2016

Area	BI grant		Project number
	Amount (US$)	Percentage (%)	
Beijing	2,630,024	30.6	11
Guangzhou	1,051,458	12.2	5
Harbin	754,950	8.8	3
Tianjin	713,902	8.3	3
Shenzhen	701,757	8.2	4
Lanzhou	552,171	6.4	3
Shenyang	398,437	4.6	2
Nanchang	390,772	4.5	2
Chongqing	231,510	2.7	1
Jinan	200,000	2.3	1
Shanghai	180,006	2.1	2
Zhuhai	178,181	2.1	1
Luoyang	51,279	0.6	1
Hangzhou	37,170	0.4	1
Guangdong	535,247	6.2	2
Total	8,606,864	100.0	42

Among BI Grant for China, 40% ($8.61 million) have been supported to local areas, including Beijing, Tianjin, Shanghai, Chongqing, six provincial capitals, and Shenzhen, Zhuhai and Luoyang, as well as Guangdong province. 2.63 million US$ fund has been supported to smoke-free campaign in Beijing last 10 years (Table 4.2). Many cities have not any regular budget for tobacco control, these funds is very useful to promote tobacco control legislation at local levels. The legislation actions of smoke-free public places and working places in China will be describe in the related chapter.

BI Grant spent about $5 million to non-government organizations, $1.53 million and $2.22 million of it supported to Chinese Association of Tobacco Control and Think-Tank, respectively. The support' objective is to advocacy of policy and media to promote FCTC Implementation in China.

4.4.2.2   The Bill and Melinda Gates Foundation and Tobacco Control in China

The Foundation continues to provide more than $34 million (US) to tobacco control in China. The foundation has selected CMB, Emory university, The China Red Cross and Beijing Normal University as partners in different time. The successful implementation on smoke-free Olympic projects and smoke-free environmental projects in 25 China City laid the foundation for promoting smoke-free legislation. Also CMB support to strengthen anti-tobacco teaching in China's medical universities, and so on.[23] The Emory Global Health Institute was in charge of two main programs:

---

[23] Bill& Melinda Gates Foundation—China Office, working plan, 2011, http://www.chinanpo.gov.cn/1803/59847/xxgkindex.html.

Tobacco-Free Cities Program and Programs of Excellence.[24] **Tobacco-Free Cities Program** provided grant funding to 17 selected cities to focus on smoke free in hospital, school, business, and a lot of public places, such as airport, restaurant and hotel and so on. In addition, grant supported to strengthen mass media communication on hazards of tobacco use. These efforts were vital important and necessary in China where smokers were so huge and prevalence of smoking was so high, to promote legislation and the compliance of smoke-free laws of whole society. **Programs of Excellence** supported five Chinese universities/research institutions to carry out academic research on tobacco control and foster the academic leaders, experts of tobacco control and promote academic attention of tobacco control.

Under supported by Bill and Melinda Gates Foundation Established, CMB and Emory university jointly launched a smoke-free campus, developed curricula on hazards of smoking and SHS, and increased cessation among physicians. The textbook *"The Certified Physician and Tobacco Control* supported by CMB, has been designated the refer list for national professional physician examination by National Medical Examination Center.[25] It is a good case to change knowledge and awareness on tobacco control of new young generation of physicians. Although it is hard to emerge significant results, these efforts could be slowly and gradually affect the awareness and change knowledge on tobacco control of professionals, as well as students—future professionals, push them to become an social example of tobacco control.

In addition, there are same international foundations, such as American Cancer Society are all involved in tobacco control campaign in China.

In general, these philanthropic funds play a huge role by building up a tobacco control workforce and increasing their capacity to develop and deliver effective tobacco control interventions, supporting national and local governments to adopt and enforce Smoke Free policies, comprehensive forbidden tobacco advertisement, and increasing cigarettes tax, deliver effective media campaigns although implement of some projects is not very successful.

4.5 Significance and Challenge of International Aid to China's Tobacco Control

Guided by the belief that every life has equal value, the American Foundation works to help all people lead healthy, productive lives, which is American history, American culture, moreover one of important element of development and progress of American. Why does international donors focus on tobacco control in China? The reason is very simple as China is a great country of cigarette consumption, one third of cigarettes in the World are smoked by Chinese every year. China is the area with severe tobacco epidemic, China also is the main field to stop tobacco epidemic.

---

[24] Emory Global Health Institution. Emory Global Health Institution—China Tobacco Control Partnership. http://www.ghi-ctp.emory.edu/ (accessed 27 July 2016).

[25] National Medical Examination Center, *The Certified Physician and Tobacco Control*, *chief-edited* Yang GH, Beijing: People Health Press, Jan., 2013.

In this chapter, the epidemiological study supported by international communities, the World Bank' project on tobacco control in 1990s, the strategy and focus areas on tobacco control of Bill & Melinda Gates Foundation, as well as the 96 projects supported by Bloomberg Initiative Grant have been reviewed. Through the review, the above questions are answered. Whether international foundation is making a difference to tobacco control in China? how to measure? What are the challenges of international aid of tobacco control in China? Then, how to expand the donation for tobacco control in China?

4.5.1 The Role of International Aid to China's Tobacco Control

Whether international foundation is making a difference to tobacco control in China? The answer is YES. The progress of tobacco control in China were related to international aid.

The tobacco control is very hard and complex work in China. Although Chinese government ratified the WHO FCTC, it is hard to say that tobacco control is the priority of disease control in China. Many Chinese public leaders and famous professional experts have been advocating tobacco control as important strategy of disease control, especially of non-communicable disease control.

The advocacy has been strengthened by support of international community. Meanwhile, tobacco control cannot succeed solely through the efforts of individual governments, national nongovernmental organizations and media advocates play an important role. But China does not have a diverse and pluralistic civil society or many non-governmental advocacy organizations in tobacco or any other field. A few organizations are lack activity funds of tobacco control.

Over the past 30 years, due to various reasons, China tobacco control funding has always been shortage, international aid provided support for China' tobacco control campaign in different periods. These timely sources of help promoted greatly tobacco control in China with forming the professional team, increasing the capacity of policy advocacy, project design, plan and management, surveillance and assessment, public information, education and communication. Especially these aid strongly help non-government organization, civil society jointed into tobacco control social movement.

4.5.2 Tobacco Control Legislation and International Financial Aid

It is International community that could not replace government' responsibility to legislation and enforcement. All policy developments need to be internalized by the Chinese government. A series of researches completed by the Chinese scientists have proved the health risk attributable to tobacco use, the effective and impact of implement strategy of tobacco control. It forcefully refuted the erroneous view that international experience did not apply to China. Under support from BI grant to China CDC and local cities, Harbin, the capital city of Heilongjiang province, issued 100% smoke-free rules to protect people from SHS exposure in 2011.[26] The new law in Harbin has been honored as the first law to accord with Article 8 of the WHO FCTC in China. Since then, the other project cities Tianjin, Lanzhou, Shenzhen and Guangzhou have similarly legislated between 2011 and 2013. Qingdao, Changchun and Tangshan supported by Gates Foundation have legislated the similar law or mayoral command. Beijing passed the strictest smoking control law: banning smoking in all indoor public and working places, including the single office of building, bar, and eliminating smoking rooms at airports on Nov 28, 2014.[27] All of these achievements were results of endeavors from tobacco control community in China, which are not separated from international engagement. Many Chinese officer in central and local governments, famous experts, and common staff worked on tobacco control admire the foreign foundation work and appreciate for their contribution.

4.5.3   The Challenges of International Charity Foundation for Tobacco Control in China

In general, any charity foundation faced the challenge on of choosing goals, roadmap, and focus of aided programs, also and project management. Some foundations have obviously improvement rooms in these areas. In addition, the work of the international foundation will face some special challenge in China, when the control of civil social organization becomes more and more strict and tight.

For example, the American Foundation's investment in China has been blamed for bringing down Chinese tobacco companies for the sake of the American industry.[28] The charge of foreign interference is obvious slander from tobacco industry. These accusations cannot be put on the table, because it does not conform to the facts. The foreign foundation just support the many Chinese public leaders and experts to advocate for tobacco control in China. But in a sensitive social environment, there is still a market for such accusations among an unknown crowd.

---

[26] Public announcement (No. 11th) by the Standing Committee of 13th People's congress in Harbin: Rules to protect people from secondhand smoke exposure Sept 5, 2011. http://wenku. baidu.com/view/02c3b46eaf1ffc4fff47ac04.html (accessed Oct 7, 2014).

[27] No. 8 Proclamation by Beijing municipal People's Congress standing committee: Beijing control smoking ordinance. http://210.75.193.155/rdzw/information/exchange/Laws.do?method=showInf oForWeb&id=2014321 (accessed Jan 25, 2015).

[28] Redmon P, Chen LC, Wood L J, et al. Challenges for philanthropy and tobacco control in China (1986–2012), Tob Control 2013, 22: ii4–ii8 originally published online May 25, 2013.

4.5.4 Expand Donation to Support Tobacco Control in China

The financial resource plays important role in implementation of the WHO FCTC. Just Article 26.2 pointed that "Each Party shall provide financial support in respect of its national activities intended to achieve the objective of the Convention, in accordance with its national plans, priorities and programmes". However, many Parties of the WHO FCTC are low- and middle-income countries, where funds of tobacco control has often been very short. On the other hand, some Parties are not paying enough attention to tobacco control, so there is very little investment in tobacco control, such as China. In 2012, central government invested 368 million RBM (US$57 million) to screen the breast cancer and cervical carcinoma,[29] but investment for tobacco control was less 1% of the Breast cancer screening funds by central government. The investment of International Foundation can provide support for tobacco control when regular budget of government is insufficient, but promote government' further investment. In addition, the international fund support the civil society' tobacco control so as to broader social mobilization.

Rapid economic expansion over the past decades has resulted in a generation of highly concentrated wealth holders in China. Their action displayed that they start to give back to their community. China's top 100 donors accounted for $3.8 billion of both pledges and donations in 2015, which accounted for about 0.03% of China's 2014 GDP, and their actual giving equaled just under one-quarter of total national giving that year.[30] Either individual or China Charity Federation, donation programs cover disaster-relief, poverty-alleviation, aiding the old, orphans, people with disabilities, aid education, tuition assistance and medical assistance. The donation of social development, such as the environment protection was a markedly low level, nothing for public health. Not to mention the support of tobacco control.

China Charity Federation (CCF) is a national non-profit public organization (non-government organization) founded in 1994, which receives donation and transfer to the other though different programs. CCF received money and materials worth RMB17.482 billion Yuan in 2014,[31] less than three-quarter of donation from China's top 100 philanthropists. All mean that CCF has not enough influence on the donation of civil society.

All means that Chinese philanthropy need to adapt its objective, methods and procedure to the international practice. Global leaders in the sector such as Bill Gates and Warren Buffett have sought to recruit counterparts of the developing

---

[29] China Women Screening Breast Cancer and cervical carcinoma, protect rural women' health. Dec. 22, 2013, People's network http://acwf.people.com.cn/n/2013/1022/c99013-23289718.html.

[30] Edward Cunningham, *CHINA'S MOST GENEROUS UNDERSTANDING CHINA'S PHILANTHROPIC LANDSCAPE,* Ash Center for Democratic Governance and Innovation Harvard Kennedy School, https://chinaphilanthropy.ash.harvard.edu/.

[31] China Charity Federation, 2014 China Charity Federation annual report, P4-5, http://files2.mca.gov.cn/cszh/201603/20160330102809948.pdf.

world into "The Giving Pledge"[32] and other forms of phased planning that enables donors, so as to remedy social inequality and promote social development. The public welfare actions, such as environmental protection, tobacco control will attract the growing Chinese philanthropic community.

Meanwhile, the tobacco control community should consider how to promote the domestic charitable donations to tobacco control.

---

[32] The Giving Pledge is a commitment by the world's wealthiest individuals and families to dedicate the majority of their wealth to philanthropy, http://givingpledge.org/.

Chapter 5
Tobacco Control Mass Communication in China

Chunhui Wang and Jie Yang

Abstract This chapter describes the model, the network and the main features of mass communications of tobacco control in China since 2006, when the "Framework Convention on Tobacco Control" (FCTC) came into effect in China. It also introduces the implementation and influences of tobacco control activities in China through 9 case studies of representative tobacco control communication events. These case studies include campaigns such as "I want to tell you, because I love you" and "giving cigarettes is giving harm" that are promoting the knowledge of harms of tobacco use, attempting to change the social norms. It also includes important media events regarding tobacco control policy change and legislations that help the public to comprehend tobacco control policies of FCTC, as well as its implementation in China—for example, the WNTD events, the communication activities of Beijing tobacco control legislation, and the release of "Tobacco Control and China's Future", a critical report that evaluate the FCTC implementation in China during the past 5 years. Communication events such as "Tobacco Academicians" and "Dirty Ashtray Award" are also highlighted because its critical effect of disclose the tobacco industry's interferences with China's tobacco control movement.

The analysis of China's tobacco control communications shows that the joint efforts of government departments (primarily the National Health and Family Planning Commission, NHFPC), tobacco control experts teams, media and non-governmental organizations in the past 10 years have achieved good results in tobacco control. However, the task of tobacco control in China is arduous. The most important reason for the success of tobacco control is the interaction between experts and scholars, opinion leaders and the media. Therefore, how to maintain this positive and interactive model so that more and more people can join in, approve, and supervise the implementation of tobacco control policies—this is the key to the success of tobacco control communications and the major challenge facing the tobacco control experts in the future. At the same time, how the government department more actively participate in and provide financial support; and how to develop

C. Wang (✉)
Foodthink, Beijing, China
e-mail: chunhui@foodthink.cn

J. Yang
Chinese Center for Disease Control and Prevention, Beijing, China

© Springer Nature Singapore Pte Ltd. 2018
G. Yang (ed.), *Tobacco Control in China*,
https://doi.org/10.1007/978-981-10-8315-0_5

the most effective communication strategies that adapt into the new era of information technology, are also key challenges of tobacco control communication in China.

Keywords Mass communication · Tobacco control · China

5.1 Introduction

In this chapter, *"tobacco control mass communication"* is defined as the actions and
campaigns that are designed and conducted by governmental or non-governmental
organizations through making use of various mass media channels, in order to promote the knowledge of harms of tobacco use, to form the consensus among the
public, as well as to appeal to decision makers adopting tobacco control policies,
which are recommended by *World Health Organization Framework Convention of
Tobacco Control* (WHO FCTC). This chapter will discuss and outline the pattern,
network, case studies, and key features of tobacco control mass communication
work in China since 2006 when the FCTC came into force in the country. Through
the analysis of these communication activities, the achievements made by tobacco
control mass media in China are summarized, the existing problems and challenges
are discussed, and specific suggestions for improving China's tobacco control activities are put forward.

As a complex and interdisciplinary issue that involves the knowledge of epidemiology, medical science, economics, and health policies, "tobacco control" is
faced with the challenge on how to help public to fully understand the problem of
excessive tobacco use and its solutions (evidence-based tobacco control policies). It
also requires long-term public engagement that can help laws or regulations which
leads to substantial reduction of smoking rate being formulated effectively. In the
U.S., the 2012 Report of the Surgeon General, *Preventing Tobacco Use Among
Youth and Young Adults*,[1] concluded specifically and unequivocally: mass media
campaigns "prevent the initiation of tobacco use and reduce its prevalence among
youth." The recently released 2014 Surgeon General's Report, *The Health
Consequences of Smoking 50 Years of Progress*,[2] affirms this conclusion and recommends, among other actions, that "high impact national media campaigns…at a
high frequency level and exposure for 12 months a year for a decade or more." The
importance of tobacco control mass communication has also stressed in the WHO
FCTC, of which the Article 12 requires Parties of the treaty to promote public
awareness and provide access to information on the addictiveness of tobacco, the

---

[1] U.S. Department of Health and Human Services, 2012. Preventing Tobacco Use Among Youth
and Young Adults: A Report of the Surgeon General. Atlanta, GA: U.S. Department of Health and
Human Services, Centers for Disease Control and Prevention, National Center for Chronic Disease
Prevention and Health Promotion, Office on Smoking and Health.

[2] US Department of Health and Human Services, 2014. The Health Consequences of Smoking–50
Years of Progress: A Report of the Surgeon General. Atlanta, GA: US Department of Health and
Human Services, Centers for Disease Control and Prevention, National Center for Chronic Disease
Prevention and Health Promotion, Office on Smoking and Health.

health risks of tobacco use and exposure to smoke, the benefits of cessation, and the actions of the tobacco industry.[3]

Since WHO FCTC has globally come into effect in February 2005, a considerable number of Parties have introduced educational and public awareness programs, as recommended by the treaty. China signed the treaty in 2003, and the treaty has officially come into legal force for China in 2006. In order to fulfill the implementation work of FCTC, an "Inter-Ministerial Leading Group" (hereinafter referred to as the Leading Group) composed by eight Ministries and Commissions has been established by the approval of the State Council in 2007. The eight Ministries include the Ministry of Industry and Information Technology (MIIT), the National Health and Family Planning Commission (NHFPC), the Ministry of Finance (MOF), the Ministry of Foreign Affairs (MAF), State Administration for Industry and Commerce (SAIC), General Administration of Quality Supervision, Inspection and Quarantine (GAQSIQ), General Administration of Customs (GAS), and State Tobacco Monopoly Administration (STMA). The State Council stipulates the job responsibilities of the eight ministries' coordination mechanism. It is clear that public education to tobacco control is attributed to the National Health and Family Planning Commission.[4] In 2012, the Leading Group introduced its first *National Tobacco Control Strategy (2012–2015)*, including a set of tobacco control communication plans. It is suggested that tobacco control campaigns should be encouraged to prevent youth from smoking and to change the social norms regarding smoking as well (see Footnote 4).

Directly led by the government, nationwide tobacco control activities such as *"Tobacco Control Mass Media Award"* and the annual event on World No Tobacco Day can be seen as a part of China's obligations to fulfill the requirements of FCTC on mass communication. Meanwhile, a few years before the plan was carried out, organizations in non-governmental sectors have already taken considerable campaigns and communication activities, in both way of criticizing the Government's negligent in the performance of duties, and exposing tobacco industry's interference in health policy-makings. Since the Chinese cigarette market is dominated by a state-owned monopoly (China National Tobacco Corporation, CNTC), STMA actually controls all aspects of the tobacco industry.[5] There is an obvious conflict of interest that STMA is included into the Leading Group of tobacco control. It is particularly crucial that the critiques can be heard by both the public and decision-makers, taking it as the right "diagnosis" to help China moving forward in the way of creating smoke-free environments.

---

[3] World Health Organization, 2007. WHO Framework Convention on Tobacco Control. [pdf] Geneva: WHO Press. Available at: http://apps.who.int/iris/bitstream/10665/42811/1/9241591013.pdf?ua=1 [Accessed 31 May 2017].

[4] Ministry of Industry and Information Technology, 2012. China Tobacco Control Plan, 2012–2015. [pdf] Beijing: Ministry of Industry and Information Technology of the People's Republic of China. Available at: http://www.tobacco.gov.cn/history_filesystem/2013yckz/fj/449995.pdf [Accessed 31 May 2017].

[5] He, P., Takeuchi T., Yano, E., 2013.An overview of the China National Tobacco Corporation and State Tobacco Monopoly Administration. Environmental Health and Preventive Medicine, 18(1), pp. 85–90.

The chapter will provide a review and brief analysis over China's tobacco control mass communication efforts in four aspects. First topic is an overview on China's media industry and the communication environment of tobacco control. Then a tobacco control communication network will be illustrated as topic two, in order to demonstrate the relationship and the respective roles of government, NGOs, media and academic institutions. The third topic is the main body of this chapter, in which some of the important tobacco control communication events and campaigns are reviewed. The chosen cases are taken as representatives of tobacco control communication achievement in a broader sense. Finally, some of the key characteristics of tobacco control mass communication practices will be summarized, trying to explain why it works in China. The last session is about some of the reflections and challenges facing in the future.

5.2   Communication Environment and Media Capacity

Before proceeding, two conceptions—"traditional media" and the "new media" are needed to be clarified. In this chapter, "traditional media" is closely connected with journalism, encompassing television, radio, newspapers, magazines, newsletters, other print publications, and some of the portal websites that having been entitled by the government to do reporting. As for those large commercial portals in China, such as QQ.com, Sohu.com, Sina.com.cn, although they do not have the certification to work on news writing and reporting, much of their content-related business focuses on secondary spreading of news—to exchange the "traffic" with copyrights of news from TV and printed media. The nature of such business for these portals is more equivalent to those traditional ones. Therefore they are also included into the field of "traditional media". While "new media" in this chapter has similar meaning with "social media"; it refers to those emerging new technology platforms in digital era that the users can create and share their own content, such as Weibo, Wechat, and domestic streaming video sites such as Youku.com, Tudou.com, and Aiqiyi. com, etc. For tobacco control campaigners, methods of how to utilize social media are entirely different from those of traditional media engagement.

China is the largest media market in the world, and has the world's largest online population. According to State Administration of Press, Publication, Radio, Film and Television (SAPPRFT), by 2015, China has 1906 newspapers, 10,014 magazines and journals,[6] some of which are directly issued by the China's Communist Party, such as *People' daily*. There are more than 2520 local, regional and national public broadcast and television channels by 2013.[7] State-run Chinese Central TV (CCTV) is China's largest media company, although its dominance is challenged by provincial TVs,

---

[6] State Administration of Press, Publication, Radio, Film and Television, 2015. *Basic Information of the National News and Publication Industry, 2014* (00A17-00000-2015-00699). Beijing: SAPPRFT.

[7] State Administration of Press, Publication, Radio, Film and Television, 2014. General Situation of the Development of National Radio, Film and Television, 2013. [online] Beijing: SAPPRFT. Available at: http://gdtj.chinasarft.gov.cn/showtiaomu.aspx?id=43a1f7c3-1d45-4ab5-b381-edeebfac5c46 [Accessed 31 May 2017].

which are on the air nationally via satellite. All of China's 2207 radio stations are state-owned (see Footnote 7). Although the market is still large, the profits of many traditional media outlets and their influence have been on decline. On one hand, traditional media groups and outlets are forced to compete with social media platforms for readership; on the other hand, traditional media is challenged to transform in the digital era. In 2015, Shanghai United Media Group launched two online media platforms, The Paper and Jiemian, to meet the readers' demand for integrated function of news portal with APPs. They soon have become the most promising media platforms, setting a model for the transformation in the media industry.

Meanwhile, China represents the world's biggest digital market, with 688 million active netizens and 620 million active mobile social accounts.[8] In the first decade of twenty-first century portal websites competed with publications; more and more readers become "net surfers" who read news on portals and websites rather than newspapers. In the recent 10 years, the emerging power of social media has quickly dominated the market, where more people tend to create their own content and share with friends. The once-popular portal sites are soon declined and become "old-fashioned". Social media in China is more local than global (due to the firewall settings of central government). WeiBo and WeChat are the two top popular social media platforms, with more than 300 million[9] and 889 million monthly active users[10] respectively. More and more social media Apps such as various live broadcast platforms became popular in 2016, and about half of new online users are under 19 years old. The "Post-90s generation" has been the main crowd on social media.

Journalism in China is subject to the "press certification" system. There are two meanings: only the media that is registered and approved by the government have rights to do reporting and editing; only the media practitioners with the press card that is issued by the government has right to interview and report, especially in the field of political news. Since 2014, the news portals and website has also been formally incorporated into the management of the press certification system. There is not much news portal with independent reporting rights in China, however. Most of the certificated sites such as *people.com.cn* and *xinhuanet.com* are affiliated of state-owned media companies.

Both traditional and social media contents are under the scrutiny of Chinese government. Three competent departments are taking the responsibilities: the Central Publicity Department of the CPC (CCPPD) controls all traditional media/ publications; Cyberspace Administration of China (CAC) is responsible for news portals and online press; the State Internet Information Office (SIIO) which shares the same set of personnel with CAC is also responsible for online and traditional press censorship, and particularly on those online press affiliated with traditional

---

[8] China Internet Network Information Center, 2016. The 37th statistical report on the development of China's Internet network. [pdf] Beijing: CNNIC. Available at: http://www.cnnic.net.cn/hlwfzyj/hlwxzbg/hlwtjbg/201601/P020160122444930951954.pdf [Accessed 31 May 2017].

[9] Wu, J.M., 2017. The number of Weibo's active user has broken through 300 million. *Securities Times*, [online] 23th, Feb. Available at: http://finance.sina.com.cn/stock/t/2017-02-23/doc-ify-avwcv8648272.shtml.

[10] Statista, 2017. Number of monthly active WeChat users from 2nd quarter 2010 to 4th quarter 2016 (in millions). [online] Available at: https://www.statista.com/statistics/255778/number-of-active-wechat-messenger-accounts/ [Accessed 31 May 2017].

media. These departments have the power to prescribe the reporting "caliber" on certain issues; it can also decide whether or not to prohibit reporting over certain topics, too. But as some of the studies have pointed out, not all the news content in China are necessarily to be censored. Rigorous bans are often replaced by "soft approaches", such as constructing conditional public opinion guidance on certain agenda setting, rather than exerting absolute control.

Despite the challenges mentioned above, operative communication activities around this issue are able to be continued over the past 9 years with sound achievements. The credibility and legitimacy of tobacco control have been constantly improved through large amount of public mobilization and engagement. According to the monitoring data collected by the China Public Communication Institute of Renmin University (CPCI) from 2010 to 2015, the volume of tobacco control report on traditional media has been steadily increased from 28,784 to 68,492.[11]

5.3   Tobacco Control Mass Communication Networks

As mentioned earlier, mass education on tobacco control is one of the main duties of NHFPC, as stipulated in the Inter-ministerial Leading Group on Coordination of the FCTC.

China Tobacco Control Network includes agencies and organizations in different departments and at different levels (Figure 5.1). The NHFPC is the well-deserved "node" of the network. In addition to being responsible for formulating policies and rules and regulations in the field of public health (including tobacco control), the NHFPC also undertakes the duties of publicizing and promulgating health news, public health education and so on. Under the direct supervision and management of the NHFPC, the two directly affiliated institutions, the China Center for Disease Control and Prevention (CDC) and the China Center of Health Education (CCHE), have provided concrete technical support in its tasks of mass communications and tobacco control. CCHE is the national health education institution that is responsible for organize large scale health education campaign, as well as the news promotion of NHFPC. China CDC has established the Tobacco Control Office in 2002, and it is the first (and the only) professional tobacco control office in China. The Tobacco Control Office plays a crucial role in tobacco control communications, tobacco control policy advices and the monitoring of tobacco use. In the past decade or so, it can be said that the vast majority of mass tobacco control communication activities are directly or indirectly related to these three core agencies.

At the local level, tobacco control communications are under the jurisdiction of NHFPC respectively from provinces (including autonomous regions and municipalities), cities, and counties. Normally there will be a Disease Control or Health Education institution under the supervision of the corresponding health and family planning department. They are also commissioned to propose and carry out com-

---

[11] China Public Communication Institute of Renmin University, 2016.*Annual Media Monitoring Report on Tobacco Control*. [in press] Beijing: China Public Communication Institute of Renmin University.

munication plans. All the local tobacco control communication works are, of course, eventually supervised by NHFPC. But it is important to note that the local government and institutions in China usually have high degree of autonomy on personnel and financial power. The investment on tobacco control programs at local level are highly depended on the government's overall financial planning and the average level of the region's economic development. Sometimes the personal willingness could also become a decisive factor: the issue will be prioritized if any individual key officials are interested in (tobacco control).

Besides the governmental departments and its affiliated health education/disease control departments, there are also a number of related institutional organizations in this network, including hospitals and universities. Chinese universities such as Tsinghua University, Peking University, Fudan University, and Renmin University have been played important role in conducting researches and training journalists. Hospitals such as Peking Union Medical College, Chaoyang Hospital and China-Japan Friendship Hospital have been taking the lead in conducting smoking cessation programs in China.

Non-governmental organizations in China are active participants in tobacco control progress. Although the number of tobacco control NGOs in China is small, they have given the tobacco control communication work huge support, and have contributed enormous passions and expertise into this area for years. Most importantly, these social organizations are more independent from the government; they take great initiatives to alert the public about tobacco harms, as well as to urge the government adopting tobacco control policies. They are not afraid of speaking up towards unreasonable phenomenon or omissions of the government during the process of tobacco control. It can be said that these organizations from the dimension of civil society in China has hold up "half the sky" in the world of tobacco control. Representative NGOs include: China Association of Tobacco Control (CATC), Think-Tank Research Centre for Health Development (Think-Tank), Yunnan Pioneers for Health Consultancy Center (Pioneers), Nature University, etc. In this network international organizations e.g. WHO, World Bank, and some professional tobacco control NGOs from foreign countries are also critical components. Although most of them cannot directly conduct campaigns or activities in China, but during the past decade they have offered considerable and valuable technical support to tobacco control community in China, including funds and professional advising on communication strategies.

Chinese media should also have a place in this network. For years the tobacco control organizations have constructed broad and long-term partnerships with state-owned news agency and media, such as the *Xinhua News Agency, People's Daily, CCTV, Guangming Daily, China Youth Daily, Workers Daily, Health News*, etc. Also it has broadly involved those media companies who are relatively independent and liberal like the *Southern Week, the Southern Metropolis Daily, Beijing News, Caxin Media, Life Weekly*, and *China News Weekly*, etc. In recent years, the media industry has been dramatically transformed and reformed, from the traditional pattern focusing on newspapers, magazines, TV, and radio stations, to a more integrated one combining the old with the new in digital era. In practice, tobacco control campaigners are taking online campaigns on most of the social media platforms in China, such as Weibo, Wechat, and some major streaming video site, etc. (Fig. 5.1).

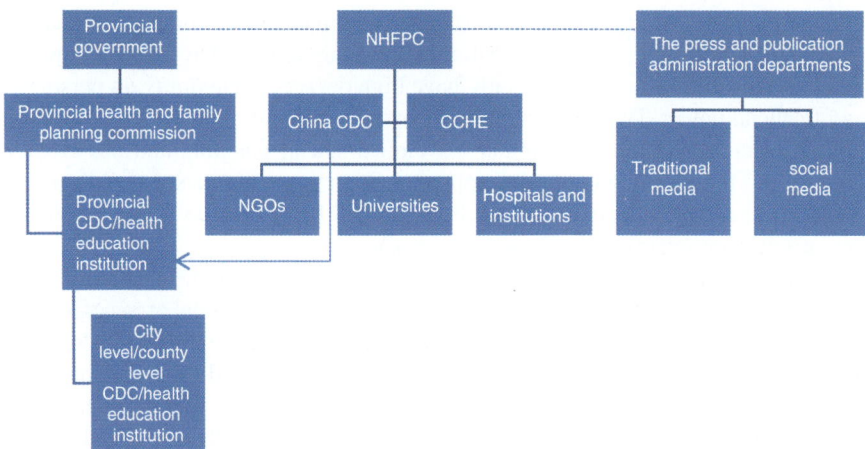

Fig. 5.1 Tobacco control mass communication networks
Source: drawn by authors according to the administrative attribute of the organization and the practice of tobacco control

5.4 Tobacco Control Mass Communication Practices

This section reviews and analyzes the tobacco control mass media activities conducted in China in the past 10 years. Since it is impossible to make an overall review of all the conducted activities or events, the selected cases are considered as most representative ones that can help to explain why tobacco control in China so far is able to achieve good result and fulfill the Article 12 of FCTC.

The tobacco control activities included in this section include four aspects: disseminating tobacco health hazards, helping the public to understand tobacco control policies, exposing the tobacco industry's interference and disruption to tobacco control, and the trainings that aim to enhance media's capacity in reporting tobacco control issues. All these activities are assessed to some extent by media monitoring data.

5.4.1 World No Tobacco Day in China

World No Tobacco Day (WNTD) is a worldwide campaign taking place on 31st May of every year. Created by WHO in 1987, the aim of WNTD is to draw a global attention to the excessive tobacco use, as well as the preventable death and disease it causes. Each year there will be a specific theme for tobacco control campaigners all over the world to conduct their own WNTD activities. Most of the themes are associated with policy measures in FCTC and its guidelines; including: protecting people from tobacco smoke (for example, by banning smoking in indoor public places), offering tobacco users help to quit, increasing warnings about the dangers of tobacco (through graphic pictorial warnings on packaging), enforcing bans on

Fig. 5.2 The "no smoking" logo over the "Bird's Nest"
Source: Beijing office of WHO, http://www.wpro.who.int/china/mediacentre/multimedia/bj_sf_20150604/zh/ (accessed on April. 18, 2018)

tobacco advertising, promotion and sponsorship, and raising taxes.[12] For example, in 2016 the theme is "get ready for plain packaging"—a measure that is designed to reduce the attractiveness of tobacco products to the minimal level, and clearly notify the health warnings to consumers. The theme of World No Tobacco Day also targets specific groups of people, such as "Gender and tobacco with an emphasis on marketing to women", "Tobacco-Free Youth", or tobacco industry interventions such as the 2012 WNTD Theme: Tobacco industry interference (see Footnote 12).

Every year around WNTD, NHFPC will launch a communication event. This is so far the official tobacco control communication activity in China with the highest level of administration. Government officials, usually director or deputy director from NHFPC will attend the event and give speeches. In recent years the launch event is more to be combined with celebration campaign of WHO office in China, and to largely involve WNTD events conducted by other tobacco control organizations. For example, in both 2014 and 2015 NHFPC co-hosted the WNTD event with WHO, CCHE, and Beijing government to celebrate the pass of *Regulation of Beijing Municipality on the Control of Smoking*. Meanwhile, as the response of the coordinative mechanism between central and local government, health educational campaigns stressing tobacco control topic will be held by local health departments across the country[13] (Fig. 5.2).

---

[12]World Health Organization, 2017. *World No Tobacco Day*. [online] Available at: http://www.who.int/tobacco/wntd/previous/en/ [Accessed 31 May 2017].

[13]World Health Organization, 2014. Fact Sheet: Tobacco taxation in China. [online] Geneva: WHO. Available at: http://www.wpro.who.int/china/mediacentre/factsheets/tobacco_taxation/en/ [Accessed 28 April 2017].

The key messages of these WNTD activities do not always keep the same with WHO's theme and slogan. For example, in 2015 the theme is "Protocol to Eliminate the Illicit Trade in Tobacco Products"; but in China most of the activities were about promoting smoke-free environment—to echo the policy progress that Beijing government has passed the law to ban smoking in all indoor public places. In 2016 the WNTD theme is "Get Ready for Plain Packaging"; still most of the tobacco control activities in China are irrelevant to the subject. Sometimes, the WHO's official slogan will be translated into another Chinese expression to conform to the reality of Chinese society. In 2013 the topic was "Tobacco Industry Interference", which focuses on the industry's specific actions to prevent or undermine tobacco control programs. In China it has replaced with "the confrontation between lives and tobacco"—with a much more softened tone that avoided direct opposition with the tobacco industry.

No matter what the slogan is, the media outcome of each year's WNTD is considerable productive. The volume of tobacco control related media stories always peaks around May 31st every year. It shows the significant capacity of NHFPC in mobilizing Chinese media resources. But on the other hand it is also decided by the wide collaborations and coordinated actions from the whole tobacco control community on that day, that are able to converge resources in all aspect and effectively expand the communication impacts.

5.4.2 Joint Assessment Report "Tobacco Control and China's Future"

Released on 6th January, 2011, the joint assessments report "*Tobacco Control and China's future*" set a perfect example on how the entire tobacco control network collaborate with people from various areas to speak up and push for the policy change. The scale of engagement for this event has been ranged from the public sector to civil society, from inland tobacco control organizations to international tobacco control communities, involving experts with multiple professional backgrounds. Most importantly, it has laid a solid communication foundation by clarifying a number of key controversial issues of tobacco control, warning about the disastrous health consequence of excessive tobacco use in China, as well as recommending the solutions of the problem.

The report was released before a deadline for China to implement international commitments to curb smoking yet failed to meet. Two Joint Editor-in-Chiefs: Yang GH and Hu AG from Tsinghua University, cooperated with more than 60 Chinese public-health experts, officials and economists to systematically review and assesse the implementation work that have been done over the past 5 years. Four key facts have been clearly delivered in the report: (1) the total number of smokers in China has surpassed the one in 2002 and reached to more than 300 million. The exposure rate of secondhand smoke is particularly high, with a total of 738 million non-smokers suffering from secondhand smoke hazards. (2) More than 3/4 of the people did not fully aware the hazards of smoking; 86% of them believe that "low tar is equal to low harm"; (3) Tobacco industry has become China's largest health hazard industry with huge negative externalities which has exceeded the revenue and other positive externalities that the industry has provided. (4) after a series of evaluation, China only scored 37.3 out of 100, low ranked among over 100 Signatories of FCTC. It is concluded in the report that China has failed to keep its commitment to reduce tobacco use in its first five-year's implementation. It is argued that state ownership of the tobacco industry continues to stymie real progress in fighting tobacco—despite the mounting health and financial costs. The report finally made a clear policy recommendation: besides keep working on FCTC implementation works, the Government should also put the goal of comprehensive control on tobacco use into the "12th five-year plan", and make it as one of the key indicators for all levels of government to evaluate the performance on achieving health targets.

The launch event has generated a large amount of media report, focusing on the poor implementation performance and the inner conflict of tobacco control mechanism. Over 129 media stories have been printed in newspapers, 39 TV stations have made feature programs, and over a thousand of reprints in news portals have been generated within 1 week.[14] The Institute of Public Communication (IPC) of Renmin University has collected and analyzed the media report, the forum posts and microblogs that discuss the event within two weeks after the conference. It shows that "China has only attained 37.3 points in five years of tobacco control" , "China has failed in compliance of FCTC" have generated high volume of discussion, indicating that FCTC and China' implementation has caused widespread concern among the public. The number of media coverage exceeded 4,000 in half a month, of which 391 articles were original stories.[15]

In addition, with the exception of China's tobacco control organizations, experts and scholars in the field of public health as the main information output groups, law and economics experts have also participated in discussions as the leaders of public opinions, successfully aroused the wider concern of the whole society.

The spread of the report has been continued nationwide until the following year, as a number of tobacco control reports were published consecutively. On December 27th of 2011, Think-Tank released its annual shadow report "A Civil Society Perspective on Tobacco Control in China 2011", it is highly recommended policies to ban smoking on indoor public places, as well as pictorial warning labels to be printed on the package of cigarettes. The China CDC releases the "2011 China Tobacco Control Report" in the May 26th 2012; called for 100% smoke-free public places (where there are no smoking areas or district).

The combination of internal system (e.g. China CDC and Tsinghua University) and external system (such as Think-Tank and other NGOs) has enhanced the communication effectiveness of the event. Key information and essential data in the report has been widely quoted by media for long time after it has been released. The

---

[14]Yang, G.H., and Hu, A.G., 2011. *Theme Analysis Report of Media Monitoring on Tobacco Control and China's Future.* [in press] Beijing: China CDC.

[15]China Public Communication Institute of Renmin University. Summary report on communication results of the five year implementation of FCTC in China [in press]. Beijing: China Public Communication Institute of Renmin University; 2012.

clear solution pattern that integrated FCTC guidelines and the reality of China also facilitates the policy-making progress at certain point. The bold criticism to the state ownership of tobacco industry has revealed the core contradiction. It was not the first attempt but was a rather convictive and accurate diagnosis with the support of sufficient evidence and case studies from various disciplines. The report has gained wide recognition including NHFPC officials: the launch event was selected as one of the top ten tobacco control news events in 2011. Later, the narrative of "carry out full-implementation of smoking ban in public places" was indeed put into China's 12th Five-Year Plan,[16] as it has recommended in the report. It can be said that the release of *Tobacco Control and China's Future* should be regarded as an early milestone of tobacco control progress in China.

5.4.3 *"Tobacco Academician": Uncover the Anti Tobacco Control Strategy of the Tobacco Industry*

In China's early tobacco control process, there have been continuous criticisms coming from civil society level towards the controversial implementation mechanism of tobacco control, especially the tobacco industry's improper interferences. In this case of "tobacco academician" it can be observed how organizations and influential individuals from different fields achieved consensus to act against questionable scientific research endorsed by tobacco industry.

Here the "tobacco academician" was a nickname given to Xie JP—the Vice Director of Zhengzhou Tobacco Research Institute of CNTC. In the December 2011, he developed a "low tar and low harm" cigarette containing Chinese herbal medicine, and put forward the "Tobacco Hazard Index" to evaluate the harm of tobacco to human health, which has proved that the harms of cigarette made in China have declined year by year. As the result, he was elected as academician of Chinese Academy of Engineering (CAE) in that year. But since the first day of election, Xie Jianping's research and the him membership of CAE academician have become a contentious topic, as the international scientific evidence has shown that "changes in cigarette design, including filters, low tar, and 'bland' taste over the past 50 years, do not reduce the overall health risk of smokers. No sufficient evidence has demonstrated whether new tobacco products reduce individual and population's health risks (U.S. Department of Health and Human Services, 2010). Therefore, the results of Xie's research were widely questioned, and it was found that the study used the primary and conventional lethal acute toxicity index, which was not possible to draw conclusions about the reduction of the health hazard of Chinese herbal cigarettes at present. Actually the result was denied by the following epidemiological study of higher evidence level. Xie, violating the basic knowledge of scientific research, extended the lethal hazard index to the "tobacco hazard index" to assess the health of the population. A large number of scientists and tobacco control experts

---

[16] National Health and Family Planning Commission, 2011. *Top Ten News Events of Tobacco Control in China, 2011*. [online] Available at: http://www.moh.gov.cn/wsb/pxwfb/201212/769e27 dc159444d999f0a7445d4ba8df.shtml [Accessed 31 May 2017].

believe that Xie's research and invention is a false proposition suspected of decep-
tion. The essence of the matter is to endorse the STMA's "Low tar low harm" business strategy. In addition, how such study (which is obviously contrary to the
scientific research method) has won the National Science and Technology award for
so many times? It also aroused widespread skepticism in the community.

The news about Xie's election was initially posted on Weibo by a Weibo ID "Liu
Zhifeng", who believes Xie's invention is more of a concern for commercial return
by attracting more people to smoke. The Weibo post was soon echoed by tobacco
control organizations immediately. In 10th December, 2011, former director of
TCO Yang GH said publicly that the election is one of the manifestations of dishon-
esty and misconduct in academic world of China. If Xie's study and the extract have
not been fully examined and demonstrated, it could lead to disastrous health consequences once it was used and developed by tobacco industry.[17] Following Yang
GH's comment, the China Association of Tobacco Control (CATC) formally sent a
letter to the CAE in December, requires a re-evaluation to both Xie's study and his
academician qualifications. CATC also asks CAE to consider not to approval any
project related with tobacco industry background in the future.[18]

The issue has greatly gained media's attention across the country from the very
beginning; and it has been upgrading till the next year. In May, seven social organizations in the area of medical and health include the China Medical Association
(CMA), Chinese Preventive Medicine Association (CPMA), Chinese Medical
Doctor Association (CMDA), CCHE, and Think-Tank sent letter to the CAE again,
urging to re-examine Xie JP's academician qualifications. In response to CAE's
reply to media that the election result is in accord with the "election procedures",[19]
Wu YQ, executive deputy director of Think-Tank pointed out that the procedure is
not flawless, the problematic mechanism of CAE's academician system should be
accountable for introducing his invention to the public. In an interview of a CAE
member Qin BY, he further explained that the election procedures was haste and
closed, which make it difficult for people from science community to aware the real
problem (see Footnote 18).

By the end of May, just before the "World No Tobacco Day", nearly 100 academics of CAE have addressed a joint letter to CAE, requested a thoroughly re-
examination and reconsideration of Xie's membership, which formed a small
climax of the spread. The series of communication activities have mobilized almost
all the important tobacco control civil societies, scientific academics in science
communities, and even the governmental officials from NHFPC have publicly

---

[17] Shang, X., 2011. The vice President of tobacco institution was elected as a member of the academician whose research was accused of pseudoscience. *Beijing Times*, [online] 12th December
Available at: http://news.xinhuanet.com/society/2011-12/12/c_122408381.htm [Accessed 31 May
2017].

[18] Wang, L.K., 2013. The "tobacco academicians": behind the tobacco control war. *Life Week*,
[online] 20th March. Available at: http://www.lifeweek.com.cn/2013/0320/40298.shtml [Accessed
31 May 2017].

[19] Zhang, G., 2017. Chinese academy of engineering: no active revocation of "tobacco academicians". *ScienceNet*, [online] 8th March. Available at: http://news.sciencenet.cn/html-
news/2013/3/275414.shtm [Accessed 28 April 2017].

suggested Xie to resign from the CAE.[20] It has repeatedly become the reporting focus of Chinese media, and has triggered a large number of articles even in the respectful domestic scientific journal *Science*.[21] Being faced with the questioning and disputes, CAE promised in 2013 that they will not accept any academician applications from the tobacco industry.[22]

There is no substantive action regarding Xie JP's election, and his membership of CAE still remained till today, the demands of the tobacco control community, including the requests of over 100 academicians, eventually failed. However, the media's in-depth coverage and positive response, as well as the two public responses of the CAE, including government officials, have all been seen as great success in the confronting the "harm reduction" strategy of the China Tobacco. By reviewing this event it can be observed the worrying fact of how the tobacco industry's private interest has been deeply entwined in (public) area in China, with strong support and endorsement from the state. But on the optimistic side, the drastic spread of debate and discussion of this case also indicate that the topic of "tobacco control" has been accepted by the media industry and the public on a large scale. The state's ownership of tobacco industry has also been fully disclosed and deepened the public awareness on tobacco hazards. Another point to note is that the issue of "tobacco academician" actually goes beyond the simple tobacco control's domain; other area of science, medicine, health care, and even toxicology and food safety have been mobilized and collaborated to joining into actions. Finally, the continuous communication engagement has efficiently push it forward to an essential change by strategically keep the public and the media updated.

5.4.4   Communication Activities That Support Smoke-Free Legislations and Mobilize Social Norm Change

There are two major tobacco control programs that have been carried out by China CDC: one is *Toward a Smoke-free China* which was launched in 2007. The main goal of the project is to advocate smoke-free policies with FCTC standard in 20 provinces and 40 cities/counties of China, as well as to ensure effective enforcement. Meanwhile, rather than a single communication event, a series of integrated communication activities focusing on health education and public engagement have

---

[20]Li, M.Y., 2013. The "tobacco academicians" should leave the academicians voluntarily. *The news website of the Chinese people's political consultative conference (CPPCC)*, [online] 5th March. Available at: http://cppcc.people.com.cn/n/2013/0305/c34948-20674754.html [Accessed 28 April 2017].

[21]Ren, C.X., 2013. "Science" focuses on the Chinese academy of engineering for "tobacco academicians". *ScienceNet*, [online] 15th March. Available at: http://news.sciencenet.cn/htmlnews/2013/3/275691.shtm [Accessed 28 April 2017].

[22]Yu, X.J., 2013. Chinese academy of engineering: no longer accept the nomination of academician candidate in the field of tobacco research. *XinhuaNet*, [online] 1st February. Available at: http://news.xinhuanet.com/politics/2013-02/01/c_114586785.htm [Accessed 28 April 2017].

been developed, including routine press conferences and paid media campaigns to promote key messages such as *"Three Do-Nots"* – the campaign slogan which advocate "do not smoke in public place", "do not smoke in front of non-smokers", and "do not offer cigarettes to your guests". Also, to keep strengthening the idea of "do not offer cigarettes to your guests", a paralleled annual campaign called *Giving cigarettes is giving harm* which also conducted by China CDC was released at the same time.

Another program is called *Promoting Smoke-free Environment* (also named as *Strengthening capacity building of the National Office of Tobacco Control in China CDC*). This project is designed particularly for the purpose of policy change in seven cities of China in order to facilitate the government adopting new rules/laws. The most significant achievement among the communication activities is the journalism workshop that dedicates to improve media capacity and professional news writing on tobacco control.

The communication efforts around these two projects will be reviewed respectively in this case.

- *Mass communication efforts for "Toward a Smoke-free China" Project: "Three Do-Nots" and "Giving cigarettes is giving harm"*

The communication team of this project has developed a set of standard spreading materials that can be used by various tobacco control organizations. It includes: (1) a standard logos for the *"Three Do-Nots"* campaign (Fig. 5.3); (2) an official statement of the project; (3) the educational content regarding smoking and health. The materials are disseminated through media trainings, media seminars, and paid

Fig. 5.3 The poster "Three Do-Nots" is displayed outdoor in program cities Source: provided by project of "Towards a Smoke Free in China, of China CDC"

media advertisement. Local government and health agencies can also use the materials to conduct street activities. In addition to promote the idea of "Three Do-Nots", local health departments in program cities have arranged activities related to smoke-free environment and social-norm change, such as smoke-free weddings, smoke-free "two sessions"—The National Committee of the Chinese People's Political Consultative Conference (CPPCC), and the National People's Congress (NPC), and smoke-free tea parties for the spring festivals.

As a result, a total of 988 media coverage including reprints has been generated by December 7th, 2008; 177 of them are the original news works. Regarding the key notion of "Three Do-Nots" as a critical indicator of the communication work, the awareness rate in 40 program cities has reached a high level of 40%.[23]

To further strengthen the concept of *"Three Do-Nots"*, China CDC also proposed a paralleled campaign called *Giving cigarettes is giving harm*. From the name of the campaign it can tell that cigarettes are often presented as a gift in China, especial in festivals. It is also taken as a friendly gesture in some social occasions when you pass a cigarette to friend or stranger. The original intention of this campaign is to carry out a subtle intervention by associate cigarettes with ominous sickness and negative images so that people will be less willing to buy it as a gift[24,25] (Figs. 5.4 and 5.5).

The campaign is funded by an American NGO "Vital Strategies" (VS, used to be called "World Lung Foundation" at the time); and it is conducted annually by the China CDC before the Spring Festival—a good timing to promote healthy life style and persuade people to quit. After years of running, the impact of the campaign has been increased among the people. The exposure rate of the campaign poster is getting higher. Especially in Beijing, posters can be seen not only in neighbourhood or gated communities, but also began to be shown in the light box advertising at more attractive public places. Also, communication channels for the campaign go beyond the printed traditional media, and the key messages have got promoted in carious social media platforms such as Weibo and Wechat. In this year's campaign China CDC even launched a creative mobile games to promote the key message. Players need to identify and avoid touching cigarettes while keep receiving other items as gifts to gain the score. Although this is a rather small project, it is undoubtedly an attempt to meet the current trend of the times, as well as to embody an old notion in China that "to combine education with recreations."

- *Mass communication efforts for "Promoting Smoke-free Environment" Project*

During the implementation of this project, the local municipal people's congress, or the city level legislative affairs office have been greatly involved. According to the proposed project, the first batch of 7 "smoke-free cities"—including Tianjin,

[23] China CDC, Peking Union Medical College, and Johns Hopkins Bloomberg School of Public Health, 2009.*Towards A Smoke-free China: Program Summary Report (January 2007–December 2008)*. [in press] Beijing: China CDC.

[24] Poster of "Giving cigarettes is giving harm" campaign, 2017a. [image online] Available at: http://www.sohu.com/a/125117429_480174 [Accessed 20 June 2017].

[25] Poster of "Giving cigarettes is giving harm" campaign, 2017b. [image online] Available at: http://www.zscdpc.org.cn/Item/4385.aspx [Accessed 20 June 2017].

Fig. 5.4 A special version of the campaign poster for the Spring Festival, 2017
Source: China CDC. http://www.lwscdc.cn/fangzhi/ShowArticle.asp?ArticleID=6769. 2016/02/03
(accessed on April, 18, 2018)

Fig. 5.5 The campaign poster of "Giving cigarettes is giving harm" was displayed at the main
street of Beijing Xi Zhi Men in 2016
Source: provided by Tobacco Free Kids' stuff

Chongqing, Shenyang, Harbin, Nanchang, Lanzhou, and Shenzhen should issue new or revised law to prohibit smoking in indoor public places within 2 years. The accompanied communication efforts around the project have been developed in two dimensions: one is led by TCO and local health institutions to directly conduct press conference and mass media campaign on TV and radio stations; another one is the journalism workshops that were hosted by professional communication institutions, telling journalists about knowledge and facts of tobacco control policies. The two dimensions will be reviewed respectively.

In order to inform the public about government's legislative plan on smoke-free environment, each of the cities will not only have regular media conference to announce the launch of the program, but also the local health bureaus put much energy into developing and spreading smoke-free PSA (broadcast-ready public service ads for TV and radio), including videos, as well as posters and printed advertisement that usually will be largely disseminated before the law is enacted. The dissemination of such videos and posters, however, are expensive. Although local government usually has access to release campaign in media at much lower price, it was still not enough if only depend on the department's own budget. Under the extra financial and technical support of VS, a series of smoke-free PSA were finally able to be aired on local satellite televisions and mobile television in all the seven cities of this project.

The content and messages carried by these PSAs are usually being tested through standard testing methodologies to guarantee the communication effectiveness. According to VA's monitoring data and evaluation report, about ten PSAs have been aired in smoke free cities. To take Ha'erbin as an example, the "arrival rate" (percentage of the interviewees who have seen the video) of the PSA was 31% after 3 months it has been disseminated. More than 80% of the respondents realized that smoking was harmful to health. The majority of respondents said they would support the government's tobacco control actions.

Another dimension of the communication effort is to conduct tobacco control journalism workshops—a more indirect but increasingly effective way of improving media's capacity on tobacco control. Funded by "Campaign for Tobacco-Free Kids" (CTFK), a professional tobacco control organization based in Washington DC, these workshops are organized by Tsinghua University International Center for Communication (TICC). TICC was established in 1999, it has been very experienced in health communication, crisis management, and news education. TICC is such a highly prestigious and politically powerful department that it is one of the main institutions that cultivate China government news spokesman. It also is quite influential in the field of journalism.

Normally the training takes 1–2 days, and covers 20–40 reporters who are mostly from traditional media across the country. Tobacco control experts and academics (domestic and international) give courses on the topics of tobacco control from various perspectives, such as health consequences of smoking, smoking-related social/disease burdens, tobacco economics, legal theoretical basis of the smoke-free laws, and case studies on FCTC policy implementations, etc. Besides trainers and trainees, Tsinghua will also invite key decision makers and head of the local health department of the target city to give the opening speech. In 2 years, the workshop has been conducted in all the seven cities and has trained more than 200 journalists. Many of the trainees later have been highly engaged and dedicated in reporting tobacco control.

TICC is not the only institution that organizes such workshops. Professional communication institutions such as TICC and CPCI are both experienced tobacco control partners that have dedicated in training journalists for years; media agencies and companies such as Xinhua News Agency, Caixin media, Nanfang Daily Group have also been engaged in hosting media trainings. It is a common method for CCHE as well to develop health educational programs. However, the media workshops in *Smoke-free Environment Construction Project* has played a particularly important role as it links the three parties together—media, tobacco control community, and the local government.

In 2008 when China CDC started its two programs, the scales of the media activities were relatively small, and were still in its early stage of explorations. However, the collaborative frameworks among different sectors and the evidence-based key messages have already been well developed. A tobacco control network that contains a large number of organizations and its practitioners from public sectors, NGOs, academic institutions, and media has been woven together during this period. It has laid a good mass communication foundation for the future tobacco control campaigners to carry out more efficient activities that gradually make tobacco control a professional and popular issue in China.

5.4.5   China Mass Media Tobacco Control Communications Initiative

Conducted by CCHE since 2008, "China Mass Media Tobacco Control Communication Initiative" is another program with support of the Chinese government (NHFPC). It is composed of a series of communication activities, includes the annual *China tobacco control mass communication awards*, tobacco control journalism workshop which trains Chinese reporter about the facts and scientific research regarding tobacco control, the launch of tobacco control advertisement (including posters and TV ads), and social media tobacco control campaigns designed to engage celebrities and key opinion leaders becoming "tobacco control ambassadors".

Among the set of the activities, *China tobacco control mass communication award* is the main program. The award gives prizes to the writers of the most outstanding media works on tobacco control of the year, which have been evaluated and selected by a professional committee made up of tobacco control and communication experts. The evaluated works are massively collected by two ways: the tobacco control media monitoring that has been conducted every year, and the admission system that directly accept works from applicants (individual journalists or media agencies). The content of the awarded media works ranges from the harms of tobacco products, smoke-free legislations, tobacco advertisement and sponsorship, pictorial warnings, tobacco economy, to cessation services. Like WNTD event, every year in the award ceremony officials from NHPFC will be attending and giving speeches.

The award has established the branding effect after years' of practices. Nine years ago, tobacco control in China is still a relatively unpopular health topic (especially compared to other health issues such as food safety, air pollution); in 2008 when the award was initially organized, the total amount of the original traditional media stories (not include reprints) was only 2345, which has jumped to 11,084 after 7 years in 2015. Especially the number of works that are recommended for admission has been significantly increased.[26] Not only does the number indicate that the media capacity of tobacco control issue has been improved (by the increased gross number of press articles); the fact that the award are recognizing by more journalists also proved its branding effect, that it has helped to promote the professional news writing in tobacco control area.

The award has also played a positive role particularly in strengthening the collaborations between the tobacco control community and the field of communication studies. Every year CCHE will organize several meetings to select and evaluate the selected works, and vote for the final winners. These works are done by professionals from both of the two areas: tobacco control experts with abundant knowledge on public health, epidemiology, public policy; renowned scholar from communication departments of universities in China. It provides good opportunity for people to exchange ideas on how to improve tobacco control mass communications work in the future.

5.4.6 Beijing Smoke-Free Legislation: Successful Communication Campaigns That Combines Multiple-Communication Channels

In 2014 when Beijing has passed *the Regulation of Beijing Municipality on the Control of Smoking*, mass communication campaigns to introduce and to promote the policy appear to be even more creative and integrated, compared with the former smoke-free activities. At that time, the department Beijing Patriotic Health Campaign Committee (BPHCC) takes in charge of the policy implementation; it cooperated with The Beijing Smoking & Health Association (BASH)—a non-profit organization under the supervision of BPHCC, released an integrated communication plan about 1 month before the law come into effect. In this process, various tobacco control organisations and institutions have been greatly involved in and well collaborated with Beijing government. The communication plan covers almost all the media channels such as Wechat, newspapers, TV, radio stations to conduct online and offline activities.

BATC plays crucial rule in implementing activities contained in the communication plan. These activities include: (1) to launch an official Wechat account named "smoke-free Beijing" in order to keep the public informative, as well as to engage the public to participant in by sending complaint online; (2) to create three recommended symbolic gestures to discourage smoking, inviting citizens to vote for their

---

[26] National Health and Family Planning Commission, 2016. *China Mass Media Tobacco Control Communications Initiative*. [online] Available at: http://www.nhfpc.gov.cn/xcs/s3582/201611/998 799f05d7349c9a8c1d3186aa4bf0c.shtml [Accessed 31 May 2017].

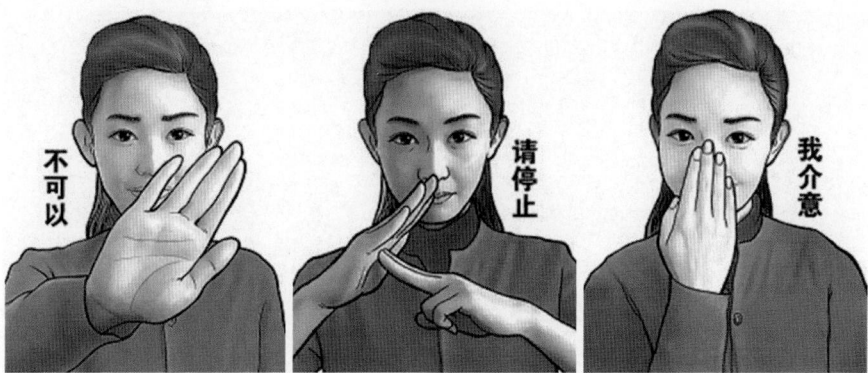

Fig. 5.6 The three recommended symbolic gestures to discourage people from smoking. BATC creates three recommended symbolic gestures to discourage people from smoking: "no, you can't", "please stop", and "I do mind (you smoking)". Beijing citizens are invited to vote for their most recognized one
Source: Xinhuanet.com.   http://www.xinhuanet.com/politics/2015-05/12/c_127790384.htm (accessed on April, 18, 2018)

most recognized one. It has attracted a lot of attention from the public. According to the government's statistics, the number of the people voting through the "smoke-free Beijing" WeChat is about three million[27]; (3) to adapt the important provisions of the regulation into a more popular narrative that can be easily memorised by the public. For example BATC created a Beijing dialect jingle to explain the penalties.[28] Also, BATC rewrote a popular Chinese dance song "little apple" into another version telling people about harms of smoking and the new law. The song has been widely accepted by local retirees who take "square dancing" as a main way of leisure and exercise. Except for these creative attempts, the routine ways to promote the law have also been strengthened. Media channels such as TV, radio stations, traditional media, new media, and mobile media have been fully utilized (Figs. 5.6 and 5.7).

In addition to the BPHCC and BASH, other tobacco control institutions and organizations have also been fully mobilized. In the World No Tobacco Day in 2015, the World Health Organization (WHO) has placed huge posters with "no-smoking" sign over the Bird's Nest, supporting Beijing's new law. Local and foreign NGOs such as Think-Tank, Nature University, CTFK, International Union against Tuberculosis and Lung Disease (Union), as well as a large number of tobacco control volunteers have participated into the city's tobacco control work in different ways, formed the foundation of Beijing tobacco control alliance. Along with the coordinated communication activities, the amount of media article regarding Beijing's smoke-free law has been

---

[27] National Health and Family Planning Commission, 2016. *The introduction and implementation of the Regulation of Beijing Municipality on the Control of Smoking—a case study.* [online] Available at: http://www.nhfpc.gov.cn/xcs/s3582/201611/c5c0212a7a054876a130dcb9d198483e. shtml [Accessed 31 May 2017].

[28] Du, Y. and Yin, L., 2015. Beijing "the strictest" tobacco control regulations: there is no place for smoking in places with rooftops. *ChinaNews*, [online] 13th April. Available at: http://politics.people.com.cn/n/2015/0413/c70731-26833999.html [Accessed 28 April 2017].

Fig. 5.7 In a primary school of Beijing, children are practising the dissuasion gestures
Source: from online at: http://health.huanqiu.com/pictorial/2015-05/2775822_4.html author is remained asanonymous

increasing since April, and peaked at June with approximately 339 original stories. The average number of reprints has reached 16.9 times/per article (compared to the annual reprints rate at 6.4 times/per article of 2014). It can be concluded that the smoke-free law of Beijing has become one of the focal points not only in the area of public health, but also in the whole society during that period of time (see Footnote 11).

Well-designed communication activities and widely collaborated network have sufficiently improved the awareness of the policy in the public. According to the China Association of Tobacco Control's survey data in August 2015, The Beijing people's awareness rate on the "Regulations" achieved 82.64%, compared to 43.43% before the regulation 3 month ago. 81.30% of the respondents are satisfied with the implantation.[29]

5.4.7 Communication Efforts on Tobacco Taxes

Ideally, when the tobacco taxes increase, it can effectively lead to an increase of the retail price, and thereby reducing tobacco consumptions gradually. But in China, one of the biggest challenges facing policy change to raise tobacco taxes is that the current tobacco tax system is too complicated to effectively reduce the retail price.

---

[29] China Association of Tobacco Control, 2015. *CATC published the results of a survey of smoke-free environments in Beijing.* [online] Beijing: CATC. Available at: http://www.catcprc.org.cn/index.aspx?menuid=4&type=articleinfo&lanmuid=122&infoid=6593&language=cn [Accessed 28 April 2017].

It involves more than five categories of taxes: tobacco leaf tax, value added tax (VAT), excise tax and urban construction/educational supplemental tax.[30] The tax rate of different categories varies, too. As one of the consequences, a single and minor adjustment of tobacco taxes just cannot sufficiently increase the retail price. Not to mention that in China, although the sales weighted tax share as percentage of retail price had been increased from 52% in 2014 to 56% in 2015 after a tax reform, it is still lower than the recommended standard provided by the World Health Organization, which should be at least 70% of the retail price (see Footnote 30). The price of cigarettes in China continues to be low and affordable, with the retail price of only 5 yuan (about 0.80 US dollars) per pack for the best-selling cigarette brand in 2014 (see Footnote 13). According to the analysis of International Tobacco Control Policy Evaluation Project (ITC project), China's current tobacco price has a very small effect on smokers' smoking cessation, with only 22% of smokers saying that the they may consider retail prices as a motivation to quit (see Footnote 13).

In general, the communication activities and the public engagement around the topic of tobacco taxes are not as highly "visible" as those of smoke-free environment or the warning labels, since to develop effective communication and public engagement strategies on tax issue is not an easy task. Any idea of increasing tax on certain item can be normally subjected to criticism and opposition. The risk of misinterpretation or misunderstanding of critical messages during the spread of messages is relatively high. Also, since tobacco taxes are concerned with fiscal policies, there is still a long way to go to reach consensus and trust among the public health experts, the public, and "technocrats" in the financial departments.

But the efforts have never stopped. Quite a few media seminars or press conferences based on professional research and findings have been conducted during the past 10 years, with the result of engaging more and more Chinese experts and academics in the area of tax, finance, and fiscal policies, such as Mao ZZ, Hu AG, Shi J, and even people from within the governmental department. International organizations like WHO and World Bank have provided substantial technical support, including drafting professional reports, country case-studies, and comparative research. Since technical terms of tax system does not help making it more understandable, it is crucial to replace it with popular language that is more acceptable by the audiences. A good example was an American Professor HU TW, who has been dedicated over years on tobacco taxation studies, putting forward the concept of "one more Chinese Yuan for a pack of cigarettes can save 3.4 million people." in 2010.[31] It has been repeatedly strengthened in the following years, and also widely cited by the media until 2015, when the government decided to moderately increase the tobacco taxes in China. However, due to the lack of a targeted communication strategy,

---

[30] World Bank, 2016. Taxing to Promote Public Goods: Tobacco Taxes. [pdf] Available at: http:// pubdocs.worldbank.org/en/799981480947591462/Taxing-to-Promote-Public-Goods-tobacco-taxation-chapter-conference-25-nov-2016-final-version-pmarquez-002.pdf [Accessed 28 April 2017].

[31] Gu, Q. J., 2010. Experts calculate that an increase of 1 yuan per pack of cigarettes will save 3.4 million lives in China. *International Herald Leader*, [online] 25th October. Available at: http:// finance.ifeng.com/news/special/yancaozhuanmai/20101025/2762246.shtml [Accessed 28 April 2017].

people still do not understand the tax increase on tobacco products, and there is still a large proportion of people who do not support or even oppose the policy.

Another communication effort on tobacco taxes is that it also helps to construct the environment of tobacco industry "denormalization"—a public health strategy to alert the public about industry's role in the tobacco epidemic.[32] For example, economist Hu AG has stated publicly in 2009 that tobacco industry is the largest health-risky industry in China that should not be taken as a major "economic pillar"; to continuously adopt tax raise on tobacco products is an important measure to smoothly transform this tobacco-dependent economy in China.[33]

5.4.8 "I Want to Tell You Because I Love You" Campaign: Highlighting the Role of Civil Society in China

Starting from September 2011, an integrated pack warning campaign called "I want to tell you because I love you" is launched by "Think-Tank Research Centre for Health Development" (Think-Tank)—one of the most prominent public health NGO in China, and had been originally promoted in residential communities of Beijing, as well as some public places and schools. The objective of the campaign is people living in mainland China who are not to be protected by strong warning labels that are supposed to be printed on the packs of cigarette, to understand the messages of smoking dangers, as well as know how the outside world notifies the health hazards of tobacco use so as to promote the pictorial warning on cigarette package in China.

It immediately becomes a multicity campaign that tours over 40 cities across China within 1 month.[34] The core element of this campaign is a set of large-scale exhibition panels with printed pictorial warnings from different countries, revealing the health hazards caused by smoking. As a comparison, one of the panels put together the pictures of the same tobacco brand that are sold respectively in China and in other countries/regions (where require a strict packaging policies). In order to attract more people's attention, additional educational elements such as short drama performance and square dancing about the hazards of smoking are added into the campaign, as well as on-site investigations regarding the public opinion towards tobacco control knowledge and policies (Fig. 5.8).

The campaign was such a huge success that its core messages and designs are refined into a set of standard health educational toolkit, along with some small funds that have been provided to city-level and provincial-level health educational bureaus,

---

[32] Malone1, E. R., Grundy, Q., and Bero, A. L., 2012. Tobacco industry denormalisation as a tobacco control intervention: a review. *Tobacco Control*, [online] Available at: http://tobaccocontrol.bmj.com/content/21/2/162 [Accessed 28 April 2017].

[33] Sun, Z.F., 2010. Tobacco becomes the biggest killer to Chinese' health, professor of Tsinghua called for a comprehensive tobacco control. *China News*, [online] 23th August. Available at: http://www.china.com.cn/news/txt/2010-08/22/content_20765406.htm [Accessed 28 April 2017].

[34] Redmon P, et al., 2013. Challenges for philanthropy and tobacco control in China (1986–2012). *Tobacco Control*, 22(s2) [online] Available at: http://tobaccocontrol.bmj.com/content/22/suppl_2/ii4 [Accessed 28 April 2017].

Fig. 5.8 One of the exhibition panels of Think-Tank's campaign
Source: provided by Think Tank

in order to repeatedly conducting the campaign in more local places of China. According to Think-Tank's monitoring data, the campaign has been toured in over 200 cities/counties of 30 provinces (including municipalities and autonomous regions) across the country.[35]

Think-Tank's campaign has "re-activated" the local health offices' capacity to carrying out community-based and face-to-face health educational campaign. To conduct the community based campaign is used to be one of the most skillful practices of Chinese health educational offices. But for a time it could not be fully applied to tobacco control issue due to the shortage of resources. Now Think-Tank's campaign has become good replenishment for local health bureaus. The standard toolkit has guaranteed the consistency and accuracy of key messages; but it also provides great flexibilities: some local health sectors has developed more forms of mass communication activities based on the toolkit, for example, they made T-shits, badges, and stickers as incentives to engage more people to participant in.

Crucial information that the campaign has delivered is that it puts emphasis on government's role in introducing new packaging policies. By comparing different packages of the same Chinese brand of cigarettes, it is strongly suggested that the government should introduce more measures to reduce the attraction of tobacco products.

5.4.9   "Dirty Ashtray Award": How the Chinese Media Become Both a Reporter and a Participant in the Tobacco Control Process

Policies regarding cigarette packs are indeed an attractive issue to the public. Media are often willing to take the initiative to report the communication activities on this topic; sometimes they even become important advocates and witness some of the

---

[35] National Health and Family Planning Commission, 2016. *NGO help to accelerate tobacco control movement in China*. [in press] Beijing: National Health and Family Planning Commission.

important progress of China's tobacco control. In 2008, a story about how the "Dirty Ashtray Award" has been given to Chinese delegation on the Conference of the Parties (COP) to the WHO FCTC in Durban, South Africa has become a remarkable event in the process of tobacco control communication in China.

"Dirty Ashtray Award" is assigned by Framework Convention Alliance (an international alliance of tobacco control NGO) in every FCTC COP conference, along with the Orchid Award. The Orchid Award recognized leadership in the negotiations for a strong FCTC, while the Dirty Ashtray Award "highlighted behavior undermining it".[36] At the Durban COP in 19 November 2008 in which the implementation standard of Article 11 of the WHO FCTC on "Packaging and labelling of Tobacco Products" were discussed. When most countries strongly agree the terms of using pictorial labels on cigarette packs, China showed objection, by giving the reason that to combine the pictures containing health hazards of smoking (e.g. rotten teeth or lung) with the China's tobacco packaging design, which in most cases are illustrating well-known landscapes of China, will "hurt the feelings of Chinese people". This speech was laughed at by delegates at the time.[37] In that evening, China was granted the "Dirty Ashtray" award by 200 delegates from the global NGO. The introductory speech was: "(the government) would prefer beautiful cigarettes packs rather than people's health". At the same time, the fact that the tobacco industry joined the Chinese delegation group to join the negotiations on tobacco control policies was again criticized by the international tobacco control expert, describing the practice as "a fox is sitting in the chicken cottage discussing how to protect them" (see Footnote 37).

In the media story which is written by a journalist from Xinhua News Agency, the circumstance of that night has been vividly reproduced, by highlighting the awards speech issued to China for the "dirty ashtray" and the critique of the tobacco control mechanism of China by international tobacco control experts. The two sentences (the introductory speech and the "fox – chicken" metaphor), which were so infectious that it have been widely spread once the story was published. Even in 2016 when other newspapers wrote stories about packaging policy in China, the article was still cited in the articles. As China's major state news agency, the Xinhua News Agency's voice often represents an attitude and tone in a more authoritative way, regarding certain topic. It will be read, valued and stressed by both the normal readers and the policy makers in China. Therefore, this story also marks the legitimacy and justice of tobacco control has been acknowledged by the media and the majority of Chinese people.

In fact, with more and more journalists and editors have been engaged and participant in the progress of China's tobacco control, Chinese media has become a much crucial factor to influence policy makers. Some of the reporters of Xinhua

---

[36] Mamudu, H. M. and Glantz, S. A., 2010. Civil society and the negotiation of the Framework Convention on Tobacco Control. Glob Public Health. 2009; 4(2): 150–168. [online] Available at: https://www.ncbi.nlm.nih.gov/pmc/articles/PMC2664518/ [Accessed 28 April 2017].

[37] Gu, Q. J., 2008. China's tobacco control becomes a negative example in the world. *International Herald Leaders*, [online] 27th November. Available at: http://news.xinhuanet.com/herald/2008-11/27/content_10419853.htm [Accessed 28 April 2017].

later become tobacco control volunteers and have helped organizing media trainings within the Xinhua News Agency. They also gave speeches in other tobacco control journalism workshops on how to accurately deliver tobacco control knowledge when writing articles.

Much of this result should be credited to the media trainings and workshops organized in China. In addition to the previously mentioned media training courses in smoke-free project cities, there are also at least 3–4 workshops focusing on other policies being hosted every year in China. According to CTFK—one of the main funders of these trainings, tobacco control media workshop have been held over 40 times in the past 9 years, covering nearly a thousand of Chinese journalists and editors.[38] It has strengthened the media's capacity regarding tobacco control, also enhanced the trust between the tobacco control network and media. As a result, journalists do not just passively report on communication events conducted by TC organizations; they can also track problems on a long-term basis, and take the initiative to discover and explore new tobacco control topics by using the knowledge and analysis frameworks they have learnt from the trainings.

5.5 Effects and Challenges of Tobacco Control Mass Communication in China

5.5.1 Effects of Tobacco Control Mass Communication in China

The tobacco control communication activities described in the previous section showed great success in disseminating the hazards of secondhand smoke from smoking, improving the social climate, informing and facilitating the public to understand various tobacco control policies, especially the smoke-free environmental policy.

In general, people's awareness of the dangers of smoking and second-hand smoke has greatly improved in China. For example, in 1996 the epidemiological survey of smoking showed that only 4% of Chinese people realized that smoking was the overall risk factor for death from heart disease. After 20 years, the 2015 survey shows more than 40% recognized smoking and secondhand smoke can cause heart disease and even death. Some changes have taken place in the social climate, but the change is still limited. Under the years of engagement by tobacco control communication strategies, the rate of public support for a total ban on smoking in public venues (bars and nightclubs) has reached more than 85%.

As mentioned previously, the coverage of "Tobacco Academician" and "Dirty Ashtray Award" have widely attracted the public's concern. Compared with 2010, the public's understanding of the hazards of low tar cigarettes has been significantly improved. "The proportion of misconceptions about the harm of low-tar cigarettes

---

[38] The number is estimated based on CTFK's work memos.

has dropped from 37.3% in 2010 to 28.1% in 2015; the percentage of correct under-standing has risen from 16.2% in 2010 to 24.5% in 2015" (see Footnote 39).

A societal problem can be openly discussed, debated, and disclosed through a series of campaigns, and made substantial policy progresses—it may seem quite incredible considering the unique communication environment in China. However, if we take an in-depth look into the reviewed ten representative cases, some of the key features are observed that can be also taken as main reasons why tobacco con-trol mass media communication in China can make such achievements.

First of all, the communications of tobacco control in China has become more than just a one-way spread of knowledge. Public's perceptions are formed jointly by the government department, the media, and individuals in assessing the effective-ness of tobacco control and the outspoken criticism of the tobacco industry.

Also, it is crucial to note that tobacco control communication work in China are conducted within a quite developed cooperative network, which involves public sectors, civil society organizations, academic institutions, media, as well as indi-vidual experts and opinion leaders. Each part of the network has been fully mobi-lized and play different role. Governmental departments (decision makers) are the protagonist (NHFPC and its Subordinate institutions) in this network, legally lead-ing the policy progress. However in the practice, a large volume of appeals, espe-cially the voice of criticism and public engagement are mostly coming from the non-governmental sectors. The role of academic institutions is to conduct research and capacity buildings for both the media and tobacco control campaigners. The long-term and sustained cooperation with the media is essential to ensure the exposure rate of the issue, and the accuracy of the tobacco control knowledge. Key opinion leaders and prestigious experts are highly valued in the area of public engagement. The collaborative and fully mobilized framework have guaranteed a wide consensus on this issue, so that the spread of key messages can be much more effective and smooth, and the risks of being disturbed (mostly for the reason of incomprehension) is largely reduced.

Third, long-term and continuous tobacco control media training in China has been proved to be a critical factor of successful mass communication strategies. The advances of this media engagement can be summarized as follows: (1) to help jour-nalists taking a deeper dive into the topic, where the debates and controversial ques-tions regarding tobacco control are fully exposed and discussed. (2) To strengthen transparency of policy-making by keeping journalists updated of the recent progress on legislation, law making, or policy formulation. (3) Increase social interaction of experts and scientists with media, which in turn reinforces the credibility of the topic. Despite the media industry has been dramatically changed, it is important to note that, at least so far, traditional media (newspapers, magazines, news agencies, TV, radio stations, and new portal with rights of journalistic interview) still play a vital role in the field of public policy communications, especially those state-owned media organizations such as *People's Daily, Xinhua News Agency, Healthy Times (* 健康时报*), Guangming Daily (*光明日报*), China Central Television (CCTV)*, and the affiliated websites. Stories published by these media can simultaneously raise public interest and decision-makers' attention. Also, professional policy interpretations and credible interviewing methodologies are still a big advantage of traditional media, that it cannot be replaced at present by new media where the "User Generated Content" (UGC) is dominating.

Of course the new media platforms cannot be ignored. This chapter has not included detailed case review on tobacco control new media campaigns. But tobacco control organization shave in fact began a large-scale exploration in using new media platforms since 2013, including Weibo, WeChat, video websites, etc. Until now, a number of campaigns have been carried out, which mainly focused on spreading the knowledge of tobacco harms, introducing measures to solve the problem, inviting netizens to express their opinions and to participate in policy discussions. The user oriented nature of new media platform has decided a more relaxing and flexible role in mobilizing public's participation. Sometimes new media platform also serves a function of "sources provider", where some of the unpredictable events or first-hand information can be found for traditional media and tobacco control campaigners to follow up and respond—such as the case of "tobacco academician".

As it has been mentioned in the previous session, during the past 8–9 years, the volume of tobacco control media reports has been impressively increased. The policy areas have also been improved, whether it is the smoke-free environmental legislation in Beijing and other cities, the increase in tobacco taxes, or the stricter provision regarding tobacco advertising and promotions—these progresses are closely related to the efforts of tobacco control mass media communication. It can be said that the above characteristics have determined the present achievement.

5.6 Challenges Facing Tobacco Control Mass Communication in China

The primary reason for the success of tobacco control mass communication is the interaction between media, tobacco control experts. How to maintain such a positive and interactive situation so that more people can communicate, supervise and help proving the implementation of tobacco control measures is the key challenge of tobacco control experts. The dissemination of knowledge about the harms of tobacco is of course critical, and is one of the main tasks of tobacco control. Communication activities such as "I want to tell you that I love you" shall continue. However, it is equally important to put more effort on the promotion and monitoring of tobacco control policies, as well as to expose the interference of the tobacco industry.

Second, direct participation from the other ministries is still inadequate. In the past 10 years tobacco control programs are basically remained within NHFPC and the related health sectors. Other ministries or departments seldom speak publicly to support the issue. But as an interdisciplinary issue, tobacco control actually needs more than a dozen of relevant public sectors to be involved in, such as MOF and MAF. Without other departments' participant, it would be difficult to achieve consensus among the ministries, and increase the difficulties of policy change in turn. How to effectively coordinate all the ministries and establish a truly effective mechanism with private interests groups being excluded—this becomes the fatal challenges for tobacco control people control issues can continue to achieve substantial progress in the future.

The third challenge is the insufficient financial investment from China government. The current funding for city-level tobacco control programs has two main sources, one is the government's special subsidy; another is the financial support from non-governmental sectors. As it can be seen from the previous case analysis, most of the tobacco control communication programs—whether it is mass media campaigns in smoke-free cities, journalism workshops, or specific communication event, are mostly funded by non-governmental organizations, especially foreign NGOs and foundations. In addition, in those cities that passed the smoke-free law, administrative agencies has not allocated extra budget on tobacco control enforcement. This does not only affects the law enforcement, but further reduces the effectiveness of tobacco control communications. If the state's administration cannot ensure stable and sufficient investment on tobacco control, it would be difficult for tobacco control people in China to carry on and build up truly sustainable networks in a long run.

Also, the radically changing media industry has created uncertainties and challenges. In reviewing the practices and case studies of tobacco control communications, we have learned that traditional media engagement has always been the focus of the work. However, as the print media industry has changed drastically with the growth of the Internet, new digital platforms provide distinctly different opportunities for people to engage with news and information than traditional print and broadcast media formats. For example, "net surfers" are increasingly abandoning the news platform, and spend more time hiding in online social spaces which are usually more private and closed, such as online amination communities. It would be a big challenge for tobacco control campaigners to reach such audiences, and to continue engaging them into public policy discussions.

Along with the drastic changing of information technologies, the dynamic of message spreading and receiving has changed, too. Tobacco control experts have devoted much of the energy into producing scientific evidence, facts, and data-based content, in order to maintain high level of accuracy and reliability—which is an incredible accomplishment. But it should be also realized that the content with strong "emotional appeals" is becoming unprecedented "eye-catching" than dry facts under the domination of social media. Without giving up accuracy and precision, tobacco control communication experts perhaps need to work harder on understanding the emotional needs of their internet audiences, so that the idea of a smokeless world will keep spread widely in the future as something distinct and valuable.

Chapter 6
Public Interest Litigation and Tobacco Control in China

Jinrong Huang

Abstract Public Interest Litigation (PIL) on tobacco control is relatively a new phenomenon in China. The rapid development of PIL in this area is the result of the close cooperation between Chinese *pro bono* lawyers and tobacco control NGOs. PIL on tobacco control in China is very different from that in the U.S. in terms of types of cases due to different legal systems and legal environments. Few lawsuit cases on tobacco control can be regarded as 'successful' in China. Nevertheless, the defeat in most PIL cases on tobacco control does not mean a total failure for law advocacy on tobacco control. PIL has the great potential to continue to play a significant role in tobacco control advocacy in future, although there are some restraints and uncertainties that may bring negative impact on PIL on tobacco control.

Keywords Public interest litigation · Tobacco control · Rule of law · China

6.1 Introduction: Public Interest Litigation and Tobacco Control in China

Public interest litigation (hereinafter referred to as PIL) usually means litigation used or designed to promote social and legal change through court. It has become part of larger law advocacy movement since it emerged in late 1990s in China. Unlike private interest litigation PIL is intended to obtain wider social or legal impact beyond the individual case. The activists for PIL usually have clear goal for public interest when taking part in or initiating PIL cases. The goal for public interest could be advocacy for legal reform, policy change, enforcement of law, or exposing unlawful or unreasonable practices or policies. Unlike that in the U.S., PIL is often understood in a broader sense in the context of China. PIL is not just referring to 'litigation' in courts. It also refers to other forms of public interest law practice, including administrative application to the state agencies (for administrative review

J. Huang
Institute of Law of Chinese Academy of Social Sciences,
Beijing, China

© Springer Nature Singapore Pte Ltd. 2018
G. Yang (ed.), *Tobacco Control in China*,
https://doi.org/10.1007/978-981-10-8315-0_6

or governmental information, for instance), arbitration, and law petitioning to the legislatures for compatibility review of conflicting laws and regulations. For legal activists, any legal means that can be used to advocate social justice, human rights and rule of law are PIL.

The emergence and prosperity of PIL in China, to a large extent, is the result of the development of rule of law and civil society in last three decades. The increasing emphasis on rule of law in Chinese society has enhanced tremendously the awareness of law in the public, and more and more legal professionals and NGOs have begun to take up legal tools to address all kinds of social problems which otherwise may not be highlighted. To some extent, PIL is also the strategic choice of legal professionals and NGOs in current political environment in China. The over-emphasis of the Chinese authorities on social stability has made them very sensitive to any action which has political implications, while the persistence of the civil society in using legal tools is widely regarded as a relatively safe way to advocate social justice, legal reform and human rights protection. Most law practitioners usually carefully choose cases that are not too politically sensitive but with the potential to have widespread social impact. It is understandable that most PIL cases so far are on consumer protection, anti-discrimination, educational rights, environmental protection and public health, which are usually not so sensitive as to provoke government intervention. It is also possible for the media, which on the whole are controlled by the government, to cover these legal actions and make these cases influential. There are some legal professionals and NGOs who choose to adopt a relatively radical approach in PIL. They some times may choose cases that directly challenge fundamental state or Party interests by focusing on sensitive political issues, or become involved in collective lawsuits or local unrest. These radical actions along with the following suppressions by the government, often receive significant media attention in Western countries. But they are often invisible to the general public in China due to the restraint of mass media. So generally speaking, the mild approach towards PIL is the mainstream of this undertaking, it is more sustainable and effective in the Chinese context.

Compared with PIL in other areas, PIL on tobacco control is relatively a new phenomenon in China. Although there had been sporadic PIL cases on tobacco control in early 2000s, most cases took place in last decade. To a large extent, the rapid development in this area is the result of the close cooperation between Chinese *pro bono* lawyers who are good at PIL and tobacco control NGOs who are in the hope that law may bring about a real change for tobacco control advocacy.

As we know, China is a country with biggest tobacco production and largest number of tobacco consumers in the world and it is also the country that suffers most from tobacco epidemic. However, tobacco control had not been put in the state agenda until in 1991 when the Law on Tobacco Monopoly was adopted and claimed that 'the state and society shall intensify the publicity of and education in the fact that smoking is hazardous to health', and it did not gain full momentum until WHO Convention on Tobacco Control (WHO FCTC) entered into effect in China on 9 January 2006. Since WHO FCTC was adopted by WHO in May 2003, there have surged a wave of legislation on tobacco control worldwide and more and more funds and resources have been devoted to tobacco control in China. For instance, international NGOs like Campaign for Smoke-free Kids, the International Union against Tuberculosis and Lung Disease and Bill & Melinda Gates Foundation have been very active in funding tobacco control programs of local governments and NGOs in China ever since the WHO FCTC took into effect. Under such a circumstance, Chinese NGOs on tobacco control became increasingly active in advocating law making as well as law enforcement on tobacco control. But their work on law didn't go well until they found their natural alliance in law professionals.

For legal professionals who are keen on *pro bono* work, tobacco control is a perfect topic for PIL. Firstly, the spread of the tobacco epidemic is a global problem with serious consequences for public health and China is one of the biggest victims of tobacco hazards in the world, so advocacy of tobacco control in law is wholly justified and well received by the general public. Secondly, there is relatively solid legal foundation in some areas of tobacco control despite the fact that many more laws and regulations need to be made or strengthened. Even more encouragingly, it is easy for the advocates on tobacco control to take moral as well as legal high ground with WHO FCTC in place. Thirdly, for *pro bono* legal professionals, tobacco control is relatively a safe area in which there is much room to operate in PIL. It's especially true in a time when the Chinese authorities have kept a harsher eye on PIL and *pro bono* lawyers.

The cooperation between tobacco control NGOs and *pro bono* lawyers in PIL is beneficial for both advocacy groups. For the former, *pro bono* lawyer can help them use the legal tools to advocate tobacco control. In an era that rule of law is frequently hailed by the Chinese authorities and society as the national goal, advocacy on tobacco control will not be strong enough without the involvement of law and legal professionals. For the latter, NGO can provide them with almost endless information on tobacco control that makes it possible to initiate various public interest legal actions. The skills and experiences in making use of mass media on the part of the NGOs is also very valuable for *pro bono* lawyers, since media is an essential part of any PIL in the context of China.

6.2   General Picture of PIL on Tobacco Control in China

The concept of PIL originated in the United States, so did PIL on tobacco. There have been three waves of PIL on tobacco since 1950s in the U.S. The first wave of cases took place during 1954–1970s in which individual plaintiffs had tried to establish that the tobacco industry's products caused their illnesses in court. But most cases failed in this stage. The second wave happened in 1982 to early 1990s. Cases in the second wave still involved individual plaintiffs seeking damages but had better results than that in the first wave. *Cipollone v. Liggett* was the most influential case in this stage, and a few similar cases won after the victory of this case. The third wave characterized by class actions began in1994.At this stage, the cases focused more on accusing the tobacco industry of hiding the known health consequences of smoking and the harms caused by exposure to secondhand smoke. These tobacco lawsuits in the U.S. have played an important role in establishing that tobacco use cause serious health problems in the U.S. as well as in the whole world. They also made public the dirty tricks the tobacco industry uses to promote tobacco products and cover up the harm of tobacco smoke. The success of part of these lawsuits also inspired activists worldwide to take similar actions. China is no exception, although at a much later time.

The first PIL case known to the public in China on tobacco control was Mr. *Yan v. State Tobacco Monopoly Bureau, Longyan Cigarette Factory et al.*[1] which was brought by an activist on PIL and two *pro bono* lawyers in a legal aid NGO for minors in Beijing in June 2001. The plaintiff, the son of an activist, was 17 years old and was a middle school student in Wuhan City. He claimed that he started smoking at 13 years old under the misleading publicity on tobacco in the websites of the defendants, and his right to know as a consumer had been violated. He demanded that the court order the State Tobacco Monopoly Bureau and 24 cigarette factories to explicitly carry in their websites such warnings as 'smoking is harmful to health', 'sale of cigarette to minors is prohibited' and 'students in primary and secondary schools are not allowed to smoke'. The case was declared in admissible on the ground that the dispute was not in the jurisdiction of court by both levels of courts, although it was widely covered by mass media. Legally speaking, the legal basis in this case was not very solid and the lawsuit against 25 state agencies and factories a time was too extraordinary in the context of China, but it was the first of its kind by *pro bono* lawyers. However, the real wave of PIL did not come until the entry into effect of WHO FCTC in China in 2006.

PIL in China is similar to that in the U.S. in seeking damages from tobacco industry, exposing tobacco industry wrongdoing and highlight law enforcement. But PIL in two countries is very different in term of reliance on court. Most PIL cases are lawsuits in the U.S. But in China, going to court is just part of PIL. There are much more administrative applications to the state agencies for law enforcement than lawsuit cases. Most PIL cases in China start with applications to the state agencies for its response to the complaint of the applicants. If the applications are successful, there is no need to file lawsuits at all. Even if the applications fail, there is only a small percentage of such applications will be followed by lawsuits out of the consideration of cost.

PIL in China is also very different from that in the U.S. in terms of types of cases due to different legal systems and legal environments. In the U.S., most PIL cases involve victims of tobacco smoke seeking damages directly from the tobacco industry, while the scenario in China is much more complicated. While there are a few suits for damages as well in China, much more tobacco cases involve law enforcement on advertisement, trademark, labeling and packaging, and governmental information on tobacco. Furthermore, majority of PIL cases on tobacco in China do not directly challenge tobacco companies, they instead mainly pointed the finger at state

---

[1] China News Service, "The first case of minors taking legal action to STMA in violation of the right to know was finalized. Sept. 8, 2001 Beijing. http://news.sina.com.cn/s/2001-09-08/351261.html.

agencies who fail to enforce tobacco control laws and regulations. Generally speaking, there are five types PIL cases on tobacco control. Typical lawsuits and administrative application cases are as follows.

6.2.1 Cases on Seeking Damages for Smoking Harm and Ensuring Smoke Free Environment

Although there are not as many cases as that in the U.S. regarding victims of tobacco smoke seeking damages from tobacco industry in China, several attempts did have been made to do so. Apart from challenging tobacco industry, a few cases also try to hold the workplaces to be accountable for their failure to ensure smoke free environment.

6.2.1.1 Mr. Liu v. Nanjing Cigarette Factory and Beijing Guohua Plaza[2]

It was a case brought by a law teacher in the Law School of Capital University of Economics and Business in 2007. Mr. Liu claimed that he had been a royal consumer of the cigarette brand 'Nanjing' produced by Nanjing Cigarette Factory since 1992. His teeth discolored and became yellow due to long time smoking. He claimed that two defendants should compensate him for his expense on tooth scaling and cleaning, since neither the manufacturer nor the seller had specifically warned him of such adverse effect in the cigarette packets or by other means in advance. Beijing First Intermediate People's Court ruled that as a well-educated person, Mr. Liu himself should take full responsibility for the damage caused by smoking, since Nanjing Cigarette Factory had warned him that Smoking Is Harmful To Your Health on the cigarette packets according to law.

6.2.1.2 Ms. Wang v. Mr. Chen and Xuchang Radio and TV University[3]

Ms. Wang is a teacher in Xuchang Radio and TV University and an active activist in initiating public interest cases. In late 1990s and early 2000, she was famous for bringing a few cases against liquor manufacturers for failing to give consumers health warnings of the harm of drinking liquor on the packages. In 2008, she brought a case against her colleague who shared an office room with her and the university she was working for. She claimed she had suffered allergy, cough, and chest

---

[2] China Court, A law teacher sued the cigarette factory for a fee of washing teeth and lost the lawsuit, July, 7, 2007. http://news.sina.com.cn/s/l/2007-07-12/140713432200.shtml.

[3] Henan, Business Daily, A female teacher was unbearable SHS exposure, and sued the colleagues and the cigarette factory. Dec. 3, 2009. http://news.sina.com.cn/s/2009-12-03/110019181769.shtml.

tightness for a long time because of the secondhand smoke produced by her colleague Mr. Chen and no change had ever made after she made repeated protests to him and to the university. She was to seek 100 RMB apiece for damages. But the local court did not admit the case on the ground that smoking was a moral rather than a legal issue. It was the first case seeking compensation for the health damage of secondhand tobacco smoke in workplace in China. In 2009, Ms. Wang filed another case against a tobacco company demanding the defendant to pay her 9800RMB for damages and add more specific health warnings like Secondhand Smoke Is Harmful to Your Health on the packets. This case also did not get admitted by the local court.

6.2.1.3 Mr. Huang v. Dongguan City Coal Mining Machinery Manufacture Limited[4]

This case may not be called PIL in strict sense, but it did demonstrate the importance for the workplace to ensure a smoke free environment. Mr. Huang was arranged by the company to live with a heavy smoker in a dorm. In less than a year, secondhand smoke made him suffered a lot and he eventually was diagnosed hypertension. However, the company not only chose to ignore his complaints and requests for a change of dorm mate on the ground that the company could not interfere in the freedom of smoking of an employee, but also fired him for his repeated complaints. He filed a lawsuit to the court against the company and demand damages for the health problem caused by the secondhand smoke. But the court eventually rejected his claim on the ground that his claim on health damage by the secondhand smoke did not belong to labor dispute and was thus not in the jurisdiction of that court.

6.2.1.4 Administrative Applications on Law Enforcement of Smoking Ban

While there are numerous complaints everyday made to the state agencies for law enforcement in smoke free cities in China, complaints for the purpose of public interest by NGOs and *pro bono* lawyers in this regard are still a rare phenomenon. However, such an investigatory legal action did had been taken in late 2010 by Beijing Dong fang Public Interest and Legal Aid Law Firm with a view to learning the situation of compliance of the smoke free regulations in Beijing and testing the responses of the different state agencies to complaints. A series of administrative applications were made to state agencies by volunteers from the law firm when violations of smoking bans were found. Eventually, a report on the compliance and

---

[4] Dong Z, An engineer cannot bear roommate' SHS exposure, frequently complained, but was fired. Oct. 21, 2010, http://news.ifeng.com/society/2/detail_2010_10/21/2848021_0.shtml.

enforcement of the smoke free ban in Beijing based on the results of the administrative applications was published on Jan. 5, 2011.[5]

6.2.2 Cases on Tobacco Advertisement

Tobacco advertisement is an area most frequently targeted by public interest actions. There are a few public interest lawsuits, but much more are cases of administrative application for law enforcement. There are two reasons behind the prosperity of PIL in this regard. Firstly, there has been a relatively rigorous law regulating tobacco advertisement since 1994 and an even more rigorous regulation made by the State Administration Bureau for Industry and Commerce since 1995. Secondly, the Administration Bureaus for Industry and Commerce at various levels are often lukewarm in enforcing the law and regulation on tobacco advertisement since there are usually no obvious victims are involved. So it is very important for the civil societies to push the Bureaus to take actions against unlawful tobacco advertisement. The civil societies also can play a role in pushing for further clarification of rules regulating tobacco advertisement by initiating public interest actions.

6.2.2.1 Ms. Zhu v. Beijing Administration Bureau for Industry and Commerce[6]

This case was initiated by the volunteers and lawyers of Beijing Dong fang Public Interest and Legal Aid Law Firm in 2010. It targeted a tobacco ad in Chinese Central Television channel 10 which was released in an elusive way. According to law, Tobacco advertisement in TV shall be prohibited. However, this ad only promoted the name and image of Hongta Group, the largest tobacco company in China. Furthermore, it was funded by one of subsidiary company of Hongta Group which mainly focused on investment. So it seemingly only publicized the image of the non-tobacco subsidiary company, although what it conveyed to the public was the whole Hongta Group. An application made to Beijing Administration Bureau on Industry and Commerce for law enforcement was rejected on the ground that the ad was not tobacco ads. The further application to State Administration Bureau for Industry and Commerce for administrative review of the decision was also denied based on the same reason. A lawsuit then was filed to Haidian District People's Court against Beijing Administration Bureau for

---

[5] Xu LG, clouds of cigarette smoke swirled in Beijing Internet Bar, weak enforcement of Government agency is the biggest obstacle of smoke-free. Jan. 5, 2011. http://news.ifeng.com/gundong/detail_2011_01/05/3994723_0.shtml.

[6] Administrative Award of People's Court in Haidian district, Beijing (2010) Hai-Hang-Chu-Zi No. 00308.

Industry and Commerce. The court admitted the case but eventually dismissed the case on the ground that the plaintiff lacked standing. It ruled that the plaintiff had no direct interest with the advertisement, so she was not qualified to file a lawsuit against the defendant. The Beijing Intermediate People's Court also upheld the ruling of the first instance.

6.2.2.2 Think-Tank Research Center for Health Development v. Beijing Administration Bureau for Industry and Commerce

This case was initiated by Think-Tank Research Center for Health Development (hereinafter referred to as Think-Tank), a prominent NGO on tobacco control based in Beijing, and a *pro bono* lawyer in Hebei Province in 2014. The case targeted the same tobacco ad as that in *Ms. Zhu v. Beijing Administration Bureau for Industry and Commerce*. The only difference was that the tobacco ad in this case was placed on the entrance to Beijing West Railway Station rather than on Chinese Central Television. The lawsuit also followed almost the same approach of that in *Ms. Zhu v. Beijing Administration Bureau for Industry and Commerce* and suffered the same defeat. Both Courts of two levels declared the case inadmissible on the ground of lack of standing.

6.2.2.3 Mr. Li v. Ms. Wang and China Tobacco Jiangxi Industrial Limited Company[7]

It was initiated by lawyers from Beijing Yipai Law Firm in 2013. It Challenged the deceptive conception of 'low tar, low harm' which had been long publicized by tobacco industry. It was the first lawsuit concentrating on this issue in China. The defendant, China Tobacco Jiangxi Industrial Limited Company, claimed in its website that the tar in its tobacco brand 'Jinsheng' had been reduced to a great extent through high-techs and 'low tar means low harm'. It also claimed that this statement had been approved by the scientific research of the Chinese Society of Toxicology and Military Medical Academy of PLA. The plaintiff bought a packet of 'Jinsheng' and filed a lawsuit against both the seller and the tobacco company on the ground that he had been cheated by the illegal tobacco ad and demand for damages. The court declared the case admissible, but dismissed the claim of the plaintiff that the tobacco ad was deceptive on the ground that reducing tar in tobacco had been encouraged by the Tobacco Monopoly Law, and 'low tar means low harm' was not groundless under such a circumstance that the defendant had shown scientific evidences provided by relevant research institutes. The second and third instance of trial also upheld the verdict in the first instance.

---

[7]The civil judgment of First middle People's Curt (2014), Yi-Zhong-Min-Zhong-Zi No. 125.

6.2.2.4 Mr. Xie v. China Tobacco Shanxi Industrial Limited Company and Shanxi Gaochuang Leshi Trade Company[8]

This case was devised by a *pro bono* lawyer in Shanxi Province in 2014. It also targeted deceptive tobacco ads by tobacco companies and adopted the similar strategy in *Mr. Li v. Ms. Wang and China Tobacco Jiangxi Industrial Limited Company*. The plaintiff in this case claimed that he saw several tobacco ads of the tobacco brand 'Haomao' (or 'good cat') placed by the tobacco company which exaggerated the benefits of smoking to health. He bought two packets of 'Haomao' under the deceptive ads and brought the lawsuit to the court against the tobacco company as well as the seller, demanding compensation for the price he paid for the packets of cigarette. However, the local court rejected the plaintiff's claim on technical reasons. The court ruled that the tobacco ads on 'Haomao' the plaintiff provided to court were not identical to the authorized tobacco ads of the defendant in other places and the plaintiff failed to prove that these ads were placed by the defendant. The court also ruled that the plaintiff failed to prove there was deceptive publicity under such a circumstance that the defendant had printed 'smoking is bad to your health' on each packet of its products.

6.2.2.5 Ms. Tian v. Guangdong Wuyeshen Industrial Development Limited Company[9]

It was also a PIL case planned by Beijing Yipai Law Firm and followed almost the same approach as that in *Mr. Li v. Ms. Wang and China Tobacco Jiangxi Industrial Limited Company*. In 2014, an activist called *Ms.* Tian brought a case against Guangdong Wuyeshen Industrial Development Limited Company for damages in Shenzhen City Yantian District Court, claiming that she bought a carton of 'Wuyeshen' cigarettes under the influence of false tobacco ads in the website of the defendant which claimed that its tobacco products had been tested by authoritative research institutes and proved that smoking 'Wuyeshen' could substantially reduce such side effects of smoking as cough and helped to improve the flow of blood. The court of the first instance ruled against the plaintiff on the ground that the defendant's ads were justified since some contents of the ads did had been authorized by the Chinese Society of Toxicology. However, the court mediated an agreement between the two parties during the trial of second instance in April 2015. According to the agreement, the defendant paid 9935 RMB to the plaintiff and bore the burden of legal fare. This is the first case with partly positive legal

---

[8] The civil judgment of People' Court in Yan Ta district, Xi'an (2014), Yan-Min-Chu-Zi No. 06213.

[9] Wang GP, The first case on consumer sued the tobacco enterprises' cheat and get compensation of 10,000 RBM. July, 15, 2015. http://www.chinacourt.org/article/detail/2015/07/id/1668380.shtml.

result in PIL on tobacco control in China so far, although the court did not rule the tobacco company should be blamed for its false or exaggerated publicity of its tobacco products.

6.2.2.6 Administrative Application Cases

There are much more administrative application cases than lawsuits on tobacco ads and the results of the former are also much more satisfactory. There are a few NGOs and activists with successful practices in this regard. Take Think-Tank as example. In 2010, upon the application of Think-Tank, Beijing Industrial and Commercial Bureau investigated the illegal tobacco ads in a Parkour competition event co-sponsored by Beijing Cigarette Factory and some other institutes in a Beijing park and imposed a fine on the advertisement company. In Sept. 2012, upon the application of Think-Tank, the Sichuan Province Industrial and Commercial Bureau removed all of the tobacco ads in two notorious tobacco schools to which tobacco companies had donated a lot of money. In December 2012, more tobacco ads in some primary and secondary schools in Sichuan Province were removed upon a similar action by the Think-Tank. In May, 2013, thanks to Think-Tank's application, Jiangxi Province Industrial and Commercial Bureau also removed the illegal tobacco ads in the website of Tobacco Jiangxi Industrial Limited Company.

6.2.3   Cases on Tobacco Trademark

For tobacco companies, trademark is an important way to promote their products. Article 11 of WHO FCTC obligates the state parties to ensure that tobacco product packaging and labeling do not promote tobacco products by any means, including trade mark, that are false, misleading, deceptive or likely to create an erroneous impression about its characteristics, health effects, hazards or emissions. The Trademark Law of China revised in 2001 prohibits that trademarks that 'identical with or similar to the State name, national flag, national emblem, military flag, or decorations, of the People's Republic of China, with names of the places where the Central and State organs are located, or with the names and designs of landmark buildings' or 'detrimental to socialist morals or customs, or having other unhealthy influences'. Article 41 further provides that 'where a registered trademark stands in violation of the provisions of Articles 10', 'the Trademark Office shall cancel the registered trademark in question; and any other organization or individual may request the Trademark Review and Adjudication Board to make an adjudication to cancel such a registered trademark.' These provisions make it possible for activists and NGOs on tobacco control to challenge some tobacco trademarks that are suspected of being in violation of both the Trademark Law and WHO FCTC. There are two typical cases on this issue.

6.2.3.1   Mr. Wang v. Trademark Review and Adjudication Board[10]

This case targeted the tobacco brand 'Zhonghua' (meaning 'China') which is one of the most famous tobacco trademarks in China. Mr. Wang is a *pro bono* lawyer based in Shanghai. He made an application in 2008 to the Trademark Review and Adjudication Board, demanding the trademark be cancelled according to the Trademark Law in 2001 on the ground that the name 'Zhonghua' as well as the picture of Tiananmen in the trademark should not be used to promote tobacco which was harmful to health. The Trademark Review and Adjudication Board rejected his application in 2011 on the ground that the trademark was approved at a time far before the entry into effect of the Trademark Law in 2001. The ruling was also upheld by the Beijing First Intermediate Court.

6.2.3.2   Think-Tank Research Center for Health Development v. Trademark Review and Adjudication Board[11]

This case challenged another famous tobacco trademark 'Zhongnanhai' in China. It was initiated by Think-Tank and Beijing Dongfang Public Interest and Legal Aid Law Firm without the knowledge of the *Mr. Wang v. Trademark Review and Adjudication Board case*. Think-Tank made an application in 2009 to the Trademark Review and Adjudication Board claiming that the trademark should have been cancelled when it was reviewed by the Board for renewal in 2007 on the ground that 'Zhongnanhai' was the place 'where the Central and State organs are located' and was prohibited both by the Trademark Law of China and WHO FCTC. The Trademark Review and Adjudication Board rejected the claim in 2011 on the ground that the trademark should be protected since it was approved far before the entry into effect of Trademark Law in 2001. Both the Beijing First Intermediate Court and Beijing High Court dismissed the claims of the plaintiff on the same ground and ruled that the trademark licensed before the Trademark Law in 2001should be renewed even if it contradicted the new law according to the no retrospective principle of law.

6.2.4   Disclosure of Government Information on Tobacco Control

Since the Regulation on the Disclosure of Government Information was promulgated in 2007. Activists in China have frequently used this regulation to initiate public interest actions, since it provided citizens with cost-effective way to access to

---

[10]Zhang Y, A lawyer sue the Zhonghuacigarettes, claimed ornamental columns (Hua Biao) on the cigarette package is harm socialist morality, Feb. 18, 2017. http://news.timedg.com/2011-11/26/7427160.shtml, 2017年2月18日.

[11]The administrative Arbitral Award of Beijing Superior People's Court (2012), Gao-Hang-Zhong-Zi No. 310.

the government information. The access to court has also been greatly facilitated thanks to the low standard of standing the regulation requires. In this context, activists on tobacco control also take up this legal tool to promote the agenda of tobacco control.

6.2.4.1   Mr. Li v. State Tobacco Monopoly Bureau[12]

The case was brought by the *pro bono* lawyer Mr. Li from Beijing Yipai Law Firm in 2013. It was devised to acquire government information supposedly owned by the State Tobacco Monopoly Bureau and push it to clarify its stance on certain issues on tobacco control like whether it approved of putting picture health warning on the packets of tobacco in China. Before the case was brought, Mr. Li had successfully acquired affirmative answers about the picture health warning issue from some other state agencies among the so called Leading Group of Eight Ministries and Committees on Tobacco Control. The State Tobacco Monopoly Bureau, which is also the China Tobacco, is well-known for its elusive or even negative attitude towards tobacco control. One of aims of this case was to expose the agency's true attitude and its disqualified position as one of the leading ministries on tobacco control. Mr. Li filed a lawsuit against the State Tobacco Monopoly Bureau on the ground that it failed to properly disclose some information he applied for. The court eventually dismissed all of Mr. Li's claims. The court ruled that the information Mr. Li applied for about the 'sum of money donated by domestic tobacco companies since 2006' and the question that 'are you for or against the advocacy on putting picture health warning on tobacco packets in China' was not the information that the defendant was obliged to provide according to the Regulation on the Disclosure of Government Information.

6.2.4.2   Ms. Wang v. State Administration Bureau for Industry and Commerce[13]

It was a case planed by a *pro bono* lawyer in Hebei Province in 2015. Similar to *Mr. Li v. State Tobacco Monopoly Bureau*, the case was designed to get information on what the members of Leading Group of Eight Ministries and Committees on Tobacco Control had done to implement the Plan of Tobacco Control in China (2012–2015) which was made and published by the Leading Group in 2012. But the Plan had not been implemented rigorously. The division of work among the Leading Group on tobacco control was also vague and the coordination within was poor. The plaintiff made an application to the State Administration Bureau for Industry and Commerce,

---

[12]The administrative written judgment of Beijing First Middle People's Court (2014), Yi-Z Hong-Hang-Chu-Zi No. 6099.

[13]The administrative written judgment of Beijing First Middle People's Court (2015), Yi-Z Hong-Hang-Chu-Zi No. 1565.

demanding the disclosure of the information on measures that had been taken to achieve the goals of substantively reducing smoking rate and increasing the awareness of tobacco harm in China set in the Plan. However, the State Administration Bureau for Industry and Commerce replied that the information related matters were not within its jurisdiction. The Court eventually supported the stance of the defendant.

6.2.4.3 Administrative Applications on Disclosure of Government Information

There are also a lot of administrative applications on disclosure of government information for the purpose of advocacy of tobacco control. For instance, Beijing Yipai Law Firm published a report on the implementation of smoking bans in 15 cities based on the government information acquired from administrative applications in 2015. In 2016, it further published a report on the implementation of smoking bans in 18 cities based on the government information obtained through the same approach in 2016.

6.2.5 Tobacco Labeling and Packaging

Well-designed health warnings and messages are one of the most effective measures to communicate health risks and to reduce tobacco use. The WHO FCTC imposes strict regulation on the labeling and packaging of tobacco products. However, the tobacco labeling and packaging has been poorly regulated in China. In 2008, the STMA and the General Administration of Quality Supervision, Inspection and Quarantine (GAQSIQ) jointly promulgated a regulation on labeling and packaging of tobacco products in order to implement the WHO FCTC. But the regulation fall short of the requirements of the WHO FCTC, and the implementation of it also has been lax. While GAQSIQ was involved in the making of the regulation and the Law on Products Quality provides that the GAQSIQ should be in charge of law enforcement of the rules regulating labeling and packaging of industrial products, the role of it in making and enforcing rules on tobacco labeling and packaging is far from clear. A public interest action thus was designed by Think-Tank and the *pro bono* lawyer from Beijing Dong fang Public Interest and Legal Aid Law Firm to push the two state agencies to clarify the division of work in enforcing the Regulation on the labeling and Packaging of tobacco products and expose the inappropriate role of the State Tobacco Monopoly Bureau in enforcing the Regulation under such a circumstance that there is conflict of interest between selling tobacco products and enforcing rules on tobacco control.

Mr. Wang and Ms. Wu from Think-Tank made two applications respectively to the State Tobacco Monopoly Bureau and the GAQSIQ in March 2012, demanding investigations on some tobacco packages which seem to be promoting 'low tar, low harm' or other good natures of tobacco. The Tobacco Monopoly Bureau made a reply to Ms. Wu, denying there were any violations on the tobacco packages concerned as expected. However, the GAQSIQ also replied to Mr. Wang claiming that investigation of tobacco packages was the responsibility of the Tobacco Monopoly Bureau. On June 25, 2012, an application was made to the Legal Office of the State Council for an administrative review on the decision of GAQSIQ. But it was declared by the Office inadmissible on the ground that the subject was not within the scope for administrative review. No further legal action was taken on this issue.

6.3   Impact Evaluation: The Scenario Changed and Unchanged

From the PIL cases shown above, we can see that PIL on tobacco has been prosperous since 2006. It's been an important part of wider advocacy movement on tobacco control. However, prosperity does not necessarily mean successful. From the perspective of law, apart from the case of *Ms. Tian v. Guangdong Wuyeshen Industrial Development Limited Company* in which part positive result has been achieved, no lawsuit cases on tobacco control can be regarded as 'successful' in China. Most lawsuit cases were either declared by the courts inadmissible, or failed to gain the support of the courts in law.

This fact is in stark contrast to that in the U.S. or India in terms of PIL on tobacco control. It's true that in the first wave of PIL in the U.S. before 1970s, most PIL cases for damages ended in failure too due to the restraint of tort law and lack of experiences. These cases also did not change much in corporate behaviors although they generated much publicity. However, since the breakthrough of landmark case *Cipollone v. Liggett* in the second wave of tobacco litigation in early 1980's, the victims of tobacco smoking in a series of cases had been awarded huge sum of money for compensation and these cases also succeeded in exposing industry's bad behaviors in covering up the risks of tobacco. In the third wave of tobacco litigation, a few class action cases against the tobacco industry on personal injury and consumer fraud also were very successful in forcing the tobacco companies to pay for damages or special foundation set up to support tobacco control research.

In India, PIL on tobacco control also has an excellent record. Indian courts, the Supreme Court of India in particular, are famous for its tremendous judicial activism. There have been quite a few successful PIL cases on tobacco control driven by such activism. For instance, in *Murli S. Deora v. Union of India and Others* in 2001, the plaintiff won a landmark case that facilitated the making of a national smoking ban in public places in India. The Supreme Court of India held in this case that allowing smoking in public places would amount to an indirect violation of the right to life of non-smokers since smoking in public was harmful to the health of passive smokers. The Court ordered Indian government to issue a smoking ban in public places like auditoriums, hospital buildings, educational institutions, libraries, public offices and public conveyances.[14] The case partly prompted India to pass the

---

[14] Murli S. Deora v. Union of India and Others, WP 316/1999 (2001.11.02) (Public smoking case).

Cigarettes and Other Tobacco Products Act in 2003 which prohibited smoking in some public places. In a series of PIL cases on the use of Gutka (a chewing tobacco product which can cause oral cancer), the Indian courts also banned the use of plastics in Gutka and prompted many Indian states to ban the sale of Gutka.

The startling contrast in legal results of PIL cases on tobacco control between China and U.S or India shows that PIL in China in no way can compare with that in the U.S. or India. Although the pitiful results of PIL on tobacco control in law can be partly attributed to its infant stage of development of PIL, it's fair to attribute the low rate of success to unfavorable legal environment which the Chinese activists have to face. There are quite a few elements that restrain the odds of success of PIL on tobacco control in court.

6.3.1   The Issue of Standing

Standing (or *locus standi*) is a common issue in PIL. Like PIL in other areas, a considerable number of PIL cases on tobacco control were not admitted or ruled against the plaintiffs by the courts on the ground that the plaintiffs lacked standing. Just as the cases of **Ms. Zhu v. Beijing Administration Bureau for Industry and Commerce** and *Think-Tank Research Center for Health Development v. Beijing Administration Bureau for Industry and Commerce* show, the restriction on the standing of activists to challenge the decisions of state agencies in court on law enforcement means the state agencies enjoy a final say on the enforcement of law when there are no obvious victims are involved in the violations of law. This legal restriction has greatly discouraged the activists or NGOs to challenge the state agencies further when they found the state agencies failed to enforce law. The only possible way for the activists to avoid the lack of standing is to play 'victim' sometimes, as did in the cases of *Mr. Li v. **Ms.** Wang and China Tobacco Jiangxi Industrial Limited Company* or *Ms. Tian v. Guangdong Wuyeshen Industrial Development Limited Company*. That's the common strategy adopted by activists, but it will depend on the court to decide whether this strategy can be supported.

6.3.2   Unfavorable Laws and Regulations

China has made tremendous progress in term of tobacco control since WHO FCTC took effect in China in 2006. However, it still falls short of the requirements of WHO FCTC in many respects. There is no comprehensive tobacco control law in China. The national smoking ban in public places is still not in place. No law regulates the contents of tobacco products. No law regulates packaging and labeling of tobacco products other than a loose regulation made by the State Tobacco Monopoly Bureau. These facts all hinder effective advocacy of tobacco control through PIL.

The Law on Tobacco Monopoly in 1991 was also a negative factor for PIL on tobacco control. Apart from those provisions that intend to protect the monopoly of tobacco production and sale, there are also a few provisions that reflect some old conceptions on tobacco control. For instance, article 5 of the Law stipulates that 'T(t)he State shall strengthen the scientific research and technical development of tobacco monopoly commodities, so as to improve the quality of tobacco products and reduce the content of tar and other hazardous ingredients in such products'. This provision means the efforts made by the tobacco industry to reduce the content of tar and other hazardous ingredients through scientific research are commendable and the slogan of 'low tar, low harm' that has been denied by WHO FCTC and proved baseless by modern scientific evidences, is not groundless in law. It is this provision that partly contributed to the failure in the case of *Mr. Li v. Ms. Wang and China Tobacco Jiangxi Industrial Limited Company* which was initiated to challenge the 'low tar' strategy of tobacco industry.

Even in the area of tobacco ads with most vigorous law, there is a great deal of restraints for advocacy on tobacco control. Regardless of the Advertisement Law in 1994 or the more vigorous new law in 2015, there is no provision on the definition of tobacco ads. This leaves the Administration Bureaus for Industry and Commerce huge power to define tobacco ads. Furthermore, the fact that the Advertisement Law does not forbid tobacco promotion and sponsorship leaves a huge loophole enabling tobacco industry to advertise tobacco through tobacco promotion and sponsorship. That's why quite a lot of tobacco ads placed in the name of sponsorship can't be removed through legal actions. A case in point is that a lot of 'tobacco schools' which are sponsored by tobacco companies and carry the names of tobacco companies or tobacco brands still remain firm in China.

The vague legal status of international law in Chinese legal system is a negative factor as well for law advocacy on tobacco control. WHO FCTC is a very useful but not so powerful legal tool to advocate tobacco control in China. There is no general provision in Constitution or other laws on the relationship between domestic law and international law in China, although quite a lot of laws stipulate that the international laws shall prevail when they are conflicting with domestic laws. There is also no unitary legal theory on the justiciability of international law in domestic courts. So the Chinese courts or the executive branches of government are usually reluctant to enforce international law directly unless there is a specific law instructing them to do so. This situation makes it hard for the activists to win a case by simply invoking WHO FCTC regardless of the provisions in domestic laws in terms of tobacco advertising, promotion and sponsorship or packaging and labeling of tobacco products.

6.3.3　Weak Courts

The role of courts is essential to PIL in any countries. But unlike U.S. or India models of PIL which to a large extent are based on the capacity of courts to make law through interpreting and invalidating existing laws and to order sweeping reforms of public institutions, the courts are playing a much less important role in PIL in China.

Chinese courts explicitly do not have the authority to invalidate laws and regulations. The remedies that Chinese courts can award are very limited and weak. The lack of judicial independence, the inability of the court to directly apply the Constitution and the limitation of the laws themselves all add up to the low rate of victory in PIL.[15]

The weakness of courts makes them vulnerable to outside pressures and reluctant to interpret laws and regulations in a way favorable to the activists rather than to the established interests. It is especially true when it comes to powerful tobacco industry which is so heavily protected by the laws and government. For instance, in *Mr. Li Enze v. Ms. Wang and China Tobacco Jiangxi Industrial Limited Company*, the court not only narrowly interpreted laws and regulations on the evidence issue, but also took measures to prevent the trial accessible to media and other activists. It deliberately held the trial in a tiny courtroom with only two extra seats available to visitors. Furthermore, it even went as far as to arrange two court clerks to occupy the only two visitor's seats, which essentially had made the trial be held in camera.

Nevertheless, the defeat in most lawsuit cases on tobacco control does not mean a total failure for law advocacy on tobacco control. Lawsuit cases are only part of PIL on tobacco control. There are far more administrative application cases which have higher rate of legal success. What's more, even those legally unsuccessful PIL cases often can make a difference on tobacco control in the long run.

First of all, there are quite a lot of administrative applications that yield a lot of positive results despite the fact that most lawsuits on tobacco control do not end well. As mentioned above, activists and NGOs in China have played a key role in ensuring compliance with laws and regulations on tobacco control. They have achieved quite a lot of positive results in ensuring the state agencies to enforce laws and regulations by legal means. The achievements are especially tremendous in the area of tobacco ads. We can see what difference the NGOs and activists have made in enforcing the law and regulation on tobacco ads in the two following cases.

6.3.4 'Tobacco Schools' Case

There had been two notorious 'tobacco schools' in Sichuan province. They were established under the auspices of Sichuan Tobacco Company. Both of the two primary schools were named after the tobacco company and carried the logos of the company and the slogan of 'tobacco helps you to become a useful person' on the walls. The blatant tobacco ads in the schools had been widely and constantly criticized by media including the China Central TV Station since they were revealed in 2009. But no change had been made until Think-Tank made a formal legal application in Sept. 2012 to the Sichuan Province Industrial and Commercial Bureau for an

---

[15] See Huang Jinrong, Hatla Thelle, and Wang Fang, China under Transition to Rule of Law: the Role of Legal Aid and Advocacy organizations, in *A Human Right to Legal Aid*, Handy-Print A/S, skive, Denmark 2011, p. 93.

investigation and made a threat to take further legal actions against it if it failed to do so. Upon the applications of Think-Tank, the state agency removed all of the tobacco elements in the two schools and some other schools in similar situations in Sichuan Province. So it was the legal actions that made a difference.

6.3.5 · Cases on Internet Tobacco Ads

The big change on the scenario of rampant internet tobacco ads also can attribute to the legal actions of activists and NGOs on tobacco control. According to the State Administration Bureau for Industry and Commerce in 1995, if tobacco ads were to be published or placed in the media and the places beyond the explicit ban of the Advertisement Law, a special authorization was needed to obtain from the Administration Bureaus for Industry and Commerce above provincial level or the Administration Bureaus for Industry and Commerce authorized by them. This provision meant that without prior approval, it was illegal to publicize tobacco ads in internet, the new media developed a few years after the making of the Regulation. Since 2000, internet had increasingly become the main venue for the tobacco industry to publicize tobacco ads. However, for a long time, the state agencies had almost done nothing to monitor, investigate and punish the violations of this rule for reasons unknown and most of tobacco ads in internet were illegal for lack of approval. It was the legal actions of NGOs and activists on tobacco control that had activated this rule. Quite a lot of internet tobacco ads had been removed and punished ever since the rule was pushed for enforcement. It's worthwhile to mention that although both lawsuits on the deceptive tobacco ads in *Mr. Li v. Ms. Wang and China Tobacco Jiangxi Industrial Limited Company* and *Ms. Tian v. Guangdong Wuyeshen Industrial Development Limited Company* failed in courts, the administrative applications to state agencies intended to remove the unlawful tobacco ads in internet were all quite successful. The tobacco companies were eventually punished heavily for both of the deceptive ads.

Secondly, while winning cases in PIL is desirable for activists or NGOs, legal failure by no means indicates that the efforts are completely futile. Actually, all PIL cases, no matter what legal results are, can bring about some changes on tobacco control in the long run. Like that in other areas, PIL on tobacco control usually involves multi-purpose. For one thing, many legal actions are designed to test the response of state agencies and ascertain their real altitudes on certain issues. No matter what the results are, they can be used as a basis for further legal advocacy in the future. For instance, the investigatory legal action planned by Beijing Dongfang Public Interest and Legal Aid Law Firm in late 2010 was intended to learn the situation of compliance of the smoke free regulations in Beijing and to test the responses of the different state agencies to complaints. This coordinated action found out that the enforcement of smoke free regulations in Beijing at that time was very weak. The most astonishing finding was that no state agencies were willing to impose fines on the violating internet cafés according to law even though the violations had been found twice. The complaint mechanism was also clumsy, since there was no convenient way to complain for the violations. These findings were eventually covered by the media, and could have been used as a factual basis for Beijing to update the smoking ban and strengthen law enforcement in 2015.

Furthermore, the role of PIL in increasing the awareness of the general public on tobacco control and building support for lawmaking or law enforcement on tobacco control also can't be underestimated. PIL is always aiming bigger and is never only a legal issue. It intertwines with media and publicity. It's especially true in the area of tobacco control where the awareness of the general public on the tobacco harm and tobacco control is of paramount importance. For NGOs on tobacco control, PIL can be used as an effective way to mobilize media since it provides the media with a vivid story and a reportable event. PIL itself also is heavily reliant on media, without which it's hard to generate social impact. It's true in particular in the context of China where the activists usually have to practice law in a harsher legal environment than their counterparts in the U.S. or in India. For instance, although it's regretful that the local courts did not admit the cases brought by Ms. Wang from Xuchang Radio and TV University against her colleague and working institute for the harm of secondhand tobacco smoke, these widely covered cases carried positive information to the general public that tobacco smoke is harmful to your health and you should stand up for your own interest. By the same token, although the case of *Mr. Li v. State Tobacco Monopoly Bureau* failed in court, it conveys the brutal information that State Tobacco Monopoly Bureau itself is also a tobacco company. You can never count on it to take proactive attitudes towards tobacco control. It is completely an irony to have it in the Leading Group of Ministries and Committees on Tobacco Control. In sum, without PIL together with other means of advocacy, it is hard to imagine that China would have made so much progress on tobacco control in the last decade.

6.4 Prospect of PIL on Tobacco Control Under New Legal Environment

Last decade has witnessed the rapid development of PIL and tremendous progress in law making and enforcement on tobacco control. Considering there is still a long way to go before China can fully reach the goals set by the WHO FCTC on tobacco control, PIL has the great potential to continue to play a significant role in advocating tobacco control.

Among the areas of PIL that had been explored by the activists and NGOs on tobacco control, most are worth strengthening further in future. There is limited room for activists and NGOs on tobacco control to continue to challenge tobacco industry on tobacco trademarks which supposedly contravene the Trade Mark Law and the WHO FCTC, since most similar trademarks have been challenged and the odds of winning lawsuits in future are also slim. However, there are plenty of potentials to pursue PIL in seeking damages for tobacco harm. There is also much room to initiate PIL to prompt the state agencies to enforce laws and regulations on tobacco ads, smoke free environment, tobacco labeling and packaging and disclosure of government information.

China has a population with one of highest smoking rate in the world. The smoking rate remains high despite of the progress made on tobacco control in recent years. The culture of smoking and taking tobacco products as valuable gifts still is well embedded in Chinese society. Most people remain in the dark about the real health risks (including dreadful lung cancer) carried with tobacco smoke. Under such a circumstance, China is really in need of anti-tobacco activists like Barb Tarbox in Canada to stand up to tell people what deadly decease smoking can cause and what dying of lung cancer looks like. We need more victims of smoking or secondhand tobacco smoke like Rose Cipollone in *Cipollone v. Liggett* or Norma Broin in *Norma Broin v. Philip Morris, et al.* to sue against tobacco industry for its deceptive promotion of tobacco. We also need more activists in China to sue the workplaces for failing to protect their employees from secondhand tobacco smoke. Whatever the legal results may be, constant lawsuits brought by victims of tobacco use, especially those with serious deseases caused by tobacco smoke, will bring about a big change to the awareness of the general public on the risks of tobacco smoke. It is the awareness of the public that will play a key role in forcing the authorities to take more stringent measures on tobacco control in the long run.

The possible PIL on tobacco ads and smoke free environment is also worth mentioning in particular. Although tobacco ads are well regulated under the Advertisement Law in 2015 in China, violations are still rampant in some grey areas, especially under such a circumstance that tobacco promotion and sponsorship is still lawful. Activists and NGOs on tobacco control need to keep a close eye on those possible tobacco ads in the name of sponsorship and make sure they do not trespass into the forbidden area of law. Furthermore, the enforcement of Administration Bureaus for Industry and Commerce at various levels is often lax without close monitoring of activists and NGOs on tobacco control. A case in point is that after the Advertisement Law in 2015 was passed, the State Administration Bureau for Industry and Commerce have tried to make an exception for the tobacco stores in enforcing the new Law despite the fact the Law itself does not explicitly exempt them. Activists and NGOs need to use PIL to challenge any of such signs on the part of Administration Bureaus for Industry and Commerce to loosen enforcement.

Smoke free environment is also an area worthy of more attention for PIL. Smoke free legislation has been prosperous in Chinese cities since 2006 and the national smoke free regulation of the State Council is also reportedly forthcoming. However, the implementation of smoking bans has been notoriously poor. The lack of effective law enforcement led to low compliance of smoking bans in most Chinese cities and weak confidence of the general public on smoking bans. Although considerable progress has been made in term of enforcement in some cities, the implementation in quite a lot of cities is still unsatisfactory. Even in those cities like Beijing, Shenzhen and Shanghai with relatively rigorous enforcement, the compliance rate of smoking ban can't be comparable to that in developed countries like Canada, Australia and Britain. This situation, to a certain extent, attributes to a lack of enough political will of the authorities to implement smoking bans, but no effective monitoring on the state agencies from civil society is also a big factor. In fact, unlike in the area of tobacco ads, very few PIL cases have been initiated to prompt the state agencies to strengthen law enforcement in past. So there is a great potential for PIL to play a role in this regard in future.

Nevertheless, there are some restraints and uncertainties ahead that may bring negative impact on PIL in future despite the great potentials. How far PIL can go, to a large extent, will depend on a few elements.

First of all, the cautious attitude of the authorities and courts on PIL and *pro bono* lawyers remains an unfavorable factor on the PIL on tobacco control. Legally speaking, the concept of PIL has gained substantial legitimacy since the Environment Protection Law in 2014 and the Law on Protection of Consumer Rights and Interests in 2013 grants some NGOs the standing to initiate PIL in court. However, this positive development does not necessarily mean the prosperity of PIL in broad sense in China. Since PIL is often closely related to general rights advocacy movement, the authorities have strengthened control on public interest lawyers and NGOs out of public safety concern in recent years. PIL on tobacco control is relatively "safe" compared with that in some other areas, but it is still discouraging for *pro bono* lawyers and NGOs under such a political atmosphere.

Apart from the authorities, Chinese courts are also not so friendly to PIL. Many courts, to a certain extent, still regard PIL cases as frivolous and think *pro bono* lawyers as 'trouble maker' both in terms of law and politics. For instance, in the ruling of **Mr. Li v. Ms. Wang and China Tobacco Jiangxi Industrial Limited Company**, the court implied that this PIL case was a frivolous lawsuit since the cost the plaintiff paid for the lawsuit was far more than the price he paid for the tobacco products. The court also played a negative tune towards PIL by saying that 'law encourages consumers to actively protect their own interests in just way, but it does not certainly support those demands that pursue the interests beyond interests of consumers'.[16] It court also deliberately restricted the presence of media in the trial. Under such a circumstance, high rate of no admission and defeat of PIL cases in court is almost inevitable. The activists and NGOs will continue to use court as a legal platform to advocate social justice against all odds, but they have to do so in a court system not so friendly to them.

The interference and counterattack of Chinese tobacco industry can also never be underestimated in the respect of law advocacy in China. China has the most powerful tobacco industry in the world. Article 5.3 of WHO FCTC provides that 'in setting and implementing their public health policies with respect to tobacco control, Parties shall act to protect these policies from commercial and other vested interests of the tobacco industry in accordance with national law'. But in China, such interference in setting and implementing the public health policies with respect to tobacco control is not only widespread, but also public, since tobacco industry itself is part of the government. What's more, it is also authorized to partly 'lead' the

---

[16]The administrative written judgment of Beijing First Middle People's Court (2014), Yi-Z Hong-Hang-Chu-Zi No. 6099.

cause of tobacco control in China. With the progress made in recent years, the counterattack from the tobacco industry is also intensified. The leaders of the tobacco industry has labeled the advocacy of activists on tobacco control for comprehensive ban of tobacco advertisement, promotion and sponsorship and 100% smoke free environment as unilateralism, extremism, and expansionism.[17] Under such a circumstance that the Chinese economy is on the downturn, 'ensuring the national revenue' has increasingly been used as an excuse of the industry to delay or undermine the efforts to strengthen tobacco control. The accusation that activists and NGOs on tobacco control 'take foreign money to undermine national interest of China' is also frequently used to demonize and politicize the advocacy on tobacco control. Chinese government or the public may not always buy such nonsense, but the chilling effect of such accusation on tobacco control can't be underrated. Under the strong influence of tobacco industry, the Charity Law passed in March 2016 failed to ban all tobacco sponsorship as required by WHO FCTC and NGOs on tobacco control.

Furthermore, the Law on the Management of Activities of Overseas Non-governmental Organizations is also an uncertain element for PIL on tobacco control in future. It's undeniable fact that PIL on tobacco control in China is heavily dependent on foreign funds. Quite a lot of PIL cases so far are directly or indirectly funded by Foreign NGOs on tobacco control or public health. So it is of paramount importance that activists and NGOs can have sustainable funding from foreign NGOs or foundations. However, the newly-made Law on the Management of Activities of Overseas Non-governmental Organizations, to a certain extent, has made such funding uncertain. According to the Law which took effect on 1st January 2017, overseas non-governmental organizations are not allowed to conduct activities or fund the entities or individuals in China to conduct activities without setting up a registered representative organization in China, or without filing the temporary activities in the state agencies in advance. Furthermore, there are also some requirements for overseas non-governmental organizations to set up their official offices and conduct activities in China. This Law is intended to strengthen the monitoring of overseas non-governmental organizations in China out of national security concerns. However, this law brings a lot of risks for overseas non-governmental organizations to set up branches or conduct funding activities. Although tobacco control generally is an area with low political sensitiveness, we can't exclude the possibility that the funding of foreign non-governmental organizations to some activists and NGOs in China will be negatively influenced.

---

[17] Li N Yang X, Director General of STMA say: It should avoid the tendency of change one—sidedly, an absolute and enlargement for tobacco control. Feb 27, 2017. http://money.163.com/14/1203/16/ACI73U1100253B0H.html.

Chapter 7
Monitoring Tobacco Use and Implementation of Tobacco Control Policies in China

Xia Wan, Jason Hsia, and Gonghuan Yang

Abstract The development and sustainment of a comprehensive tobacco-use surveillance system is critical to support its national plans, priorities, and programs, as
well as an obligation for the WHO FCTC's Parties. We discussed methodology used
in China' tobacco surveillance, including sample design, module and questionnaire,
along with the indicators and analysis methodology for policy performance assessment. China updated the surveillance data almost every 5 years with the similar
indicators; results from the five national adult surveys and 2014 youth survey provided the trend and distribution of tobacco use at national level. Prevalence of
tobacco use in China did not change a lot more than 10 years after WHO FCTC
came in force in 2005, decreasing 1% and hovering around 27%. The tobacco control policies implementation was very poor in China during this period: the average
score for the implementation of the five key policies of MPOWER assessment was
37.3 points based on 2010 GATS-China. The current system can't effectively monitor the tobacco industry and has trouble with data sharing and data use, therefore,
the surveillance system on tobacco is need to further improvement in China. In
addition, the regular funding is shortage and capacity for surveillance is still limited,
especially in local level.

Keywords Surveillance · Sample design · Module and questionnaires · Policy
performance assessment · Monitor tobacco industry · Data sharing · China

X. Wan (✉) · G. Yang
Institute of Basic Medical Science Chinese Academy of Medical Sciences, School of Basic
Medicine Peking Union Medical College, Beijing, China

J. Hsia
The U.S. Centers for Disease Control and Prevention,
Atlanta, GA, USA

© Springer Nature Singapore Pte Ltd. 2018   141
G. Yang (ed.), *Tobacco Control in China*,
https://doi.org/10.1007/978-981-10-8315-0_7

7.1 Introduction

A comprehensive tobacco surveillance and its evaluation should integrate all major elements of all tobacco control policies and programmes, which might support successful national tobacco control policies. Tobacco surveillance is a system which periodically monitors and reviews tobacco use, tobacco caused health and economic consequences, and implementation of tobacco control policies. The surveillance is designed to ensure to supply adequate information throughout the evaluation process. Outcomes of surveillance provide substantial evidences with the national and sub-national reports on implementation of tobacco control policies.

The development of a surveillance and evaluation system is an obligation for the Parties of WHO FCTC. Article 20 of WHO FCTC described the responsibility: "The Parties shall establish, as appropriate, programmes for national, regional and global surveillance of the magnitude, patterns, determinants and consequences of tobacco consumption and exposure to tobacco smoke. Towards this end, the Parties should integrate tobacco surveillance programmes into national, regional and global health surveillance programmes so that data are comparable and can be analyzed at the regional and international levels, as appropriate."

A strong national tobacco surveillance is essential for curbing tobacco epidemic successfully. Tobacco surveillance data offer necessary and timely benchmarks of implementation of WHO FCTC. Accurate and reliable measurement helps to understand existing problems and challenges we run into. Evidences from comprehensive surveillance and evaluation also informs government leaders and general population how the tobacco epidemic is harmful to individuals, families, communities and entire nation. The surveillance information also helps to allocate resources for tobacco control activities effectively. Through monitoring and evaluation, one can learn whether policies works effectively within a nation and across countries. Tobacco control strategy can then be further developed.

China carried out the national tobacco surveys in 1984, 1996, 2002, 2010, and 2015, respectively. The earlier surveys focused more on prevalence of tobacco use and the later ones were added implementation of tobacco control related to WHO FCTC besides of tobacco use. Tobacco surveillance realizes its goal by using the quantified indicators. China tobacco surveillance adopts indicators used in the global tobacco surveillance system. The global tobacco surveillance system uses indicators "(1) of tobacco use including prevalence of tobacco use; (2) impact of policy interventions including protect people from tobacco use, offer help to quit tobacco use, warm about the dangers of tobacco, enforce bans on tobacco advertising, promotion and sponsorship and raise taxes on tobacco; and (3) of tobacco industry marketing, promotion and lobbying".[1]

Effectively disseminating tobacco surveillance findings serves as evidence for governments or decision-makers to implement or enforce effective policies data

---

[1] World Health Organization. *WHO Report on the Global Tobacco Epidemic, 2008: the MPOWER package.* Geneva, World Health Organization, 2008.

from timely monitoring system are the most important information sources for advocating stronger policies.

WHO, the US Centers for Disease Control and Prevention (US CDC) and the Canadian Public Health Association (CPHA) began development of the Global Tobacco Surveillance System (GTSS) in 1998, which includes the collection of tobacco-specific data for both youths (13–15 years) and adults (15 years and older) through four surveys. At present, the Global Youth Tobacco Survey (GYTS) and the Global Adult Tobacco Survey (GATS) run very well.[2]

In addition, WHO conducts a variety of multi-risk factor surveys that contain sections on tobacco use and exposure, including the Global School Health Survey (GSHS)[3] and the WHO STEP wise Approach to Chronic Disease Risk Factor Surveillance (WHO STEPS).[4] The questionnaires designed in these survey rarely focuses on the implementation of tobacco control policies and tobacco industry marketing, promotion and lobbying, besides the use of tobacco.

In 2008, WHO provided six effective tobacco control policies for countering the epidemic based on WHO FCTC: Monitor tobacco use and prevention policies, Protect people from tobacco smoke, Offer help to quit tobacco use, Warn about the dangers of tobacco, Enforce bans on tobacco advertising, promotion and sponsorship and Raise taxes on tobacco, i.e. MPOWER policy package with the first capital letter of each policy.[5] MPOWER policy package gave countries a roadmap to implement WHO FCTC. In order to evaluate the status of the tobacco epidemic and the impact of WHO FCTC in every country, WHO issued a series of reports in 2008, 2009, 2011, 2013, 2015 and 2017 based on MPOWER strategies. The number of countries engaged in full scale monitoring of tobacco use increased from 46 (20%) in 2007 to 76 in 2016 (39%).[6]

China has updated and representative data on tobacco use. As the data obtained from different individual survey with different purposes, the country had a lot of challenges for making a standard national tobacco surveillance system, integrating tobacco surveillance programmes into national surveillance system, and using these results to serve tobacco control in China. In this chapter, we will discuss advantages and disadvantages of existing tobacco surveillance in China. Our ultimate goal is to progressively establish a national tobacco surveillance to monitor tobacco consumption, impact on policy, and related social, economic and health indicators. Additionally, these data should be comparable and accessible, as well as shareable at the regional and international levels.

---

[2] Tobacco Free Initiative, Survey, http://www.who.int/tobacco/surveillance/survey/en/.

[3] Non-communicable diseases and their risk factors, Global school-based student health survey (GSHS), http://www.who.int/ncds/surveillance/global-school-student-survey/en/.

[4] Non-communicable diseases and their risk factors, STEP wise approach to surveillance (STEPS), http://www.who.int/ncds/surveillance/steps/en/.

[5] World Health Organization. *WHO Report on the Global Tobacco Epidemic, 2008: The MPOWER Package.* Geneva, World Health Organization, 20.

[6] World Health Organization. *WHO Report on the Global Tobacco Epidemic, 2017: Monitoring tobacco use and prevention policies.* Geneva, World Health Organization, 2017.

7.2 Tobacco Surveillance in China

7.2.1 Tobacco Survey for Adult

The first national representative tobacco survey was traced back to the duration of China reforming and opening to the outside world. In order to learn the epidemic of tobacco use and its trend, in February 1979, the Ministry of Health (MOH), Ministry of Finance (MOF), Ministry of Agriculture, and Ministry of Light Industry jointly issued the notice *"Health education on smoking is harmful and control smoking"*,[7] pointing out that it urgently need to know the prevalence and trend of tobacco use in Chinese Population. In 1984, China conducted the first national epidemiological survey on tobacco use. The target population was people of 15 years and above. The survey collected sample of 519,600 people from all 29 provinces, municipalities, and autonomous regions. This survey reported the prevalence of current smoking was 61.0% among men and 7.5% among women, respectively; the prevalence of smoking cessation was 5%; and the prevalence of exposure to secondhand smoke (SHS) was 39.8%. All findings were published in the first manuscript of population-based smoking survey in China, "Smoking prevalence in Chinese aged 15 and above",[8] which have been served as baseline prevalence of smoking and related indicators in China.

From 1984 to 1995, China tobacco industry developed rapidly. However, monitoring tobacco use was quite limited to a few small scale tobacco surveys, e.g., survey in Minhang District of Shanghai.[9] There had been no national epidemiological surveys on tobacco use for that 10 years.

In 1997, the 10th World Conference on Tobacco or Health (WCTOH) held in Beijing brought opportunities of monitoring tobacco use back. In order to obtain updated smoking behavior information among Chinese population so as to effectively carry out tobacco control and prepare for the 10th WCTOH, MOH and National Patriotic Health Central Committee entrusted Chinese Association of Smoking or Health (rename Chinese Association of Tobacco Control, CATC) to launch a national tobacco survey in 1996. The implementing agency of the survey was the Chinese Academy of Preventive Medicine (CAPM) (later renamed to China Centers for Disease Control and Prevention, China CDC in 2002). County level Hygiene and Anti-Epidemic Prevention Station (rename local CDC) over all 30 provinces, municipalities and autonomous regions participated in the field work. This survey was conducted in 145 Disease Surveillance Points (DSPs), a representative sample of both rural and urban areas. The target population of the survey was people of 15–69 years old. A random sample of 1000 households were selected

---

[7] Central Patriotic Public health Campaign Committee, Ministry of Health of P. R. China, 1984 Compilation of national smoking sampling survey, People Health Press, 1988, Beijing.

[8] Wen XZ, Hong ZG, Chen DY, Smoking prevalence in Chinese aged 15 and above. Chin Med J (Engl). 1987 Nov;100(11):886–92.

[9] Gong YL, Koplan JP, Feng W, et al. Cigarette smoking in China. Prevalence, characteristics, and attitudes in Minhang District. JAMA. 1995 Oct 18;274(15):1232–4.

using a multistage cluster sampling from each DSP. The total sample was 123,930 people. The survey reported that prevalence of current smoking was 63% among men and 3.8% among women; the prevalence of smoking cessation was 9.4%; and the prevalence of exposure to secondhand smoke was 53.5%.[10] It showed that the prevalence of current smoke among men were increasing 2%, but the prevalence among women decreased from 7.5 to 3.8%, and quit rate had a little increase comparing to a dozen of years ago. The Minister of MOH, Dr. Chen Minzhang highly regarded the survey, "After careful evaluation, epidemiologists and statisticians from both China and the US Johns Hopkins University agreed that the survey design methodology was strict and rigorous, with high quality of the fieldwork of survey and data analysis. To the great extent, the evaluation reflected the scientific attitude and commitment of participants in the survey".[11]

In 2002, the Ministry of Science and Technology (MOST) funded China CDC to carry out a behavioral risk factor survey. Target population, sample design and tobacco related questions of 2002 survey were similar to the survey conducted in 1996 except for smaller sample size (16,407), about 1/8 of sample size in the 1996 survey. The 2002 survey included more behavior risk factors, which was similar to behavior risk factors surveillance of Health Promotion Programs in seven cities, such as Beijing, Shanghai, and so on (Health VII, *Project ID:* P003589).[12] The 2002 survey reported that the prevalence of current smoking was 57.4% among men and 2.6% among women, the prevalence of smoking cessation was 11.5%, and the prevalence of exposure to SHS was 51.9%.[13] The current smoking prevalence decreased, but not for the prevalence of exposure to SHS compared with the 1996 survey.

In 2010, China CDC, as the implementing agency, conducted the Global Adult Tobacco Survey, China (GATS-China). The survey was a component of the Global Adult Tobacco Survey using a standard tobacco indicators,[14] funded by the Bloomberg Initiative to Reduce Tobacco Use, and the Bill and Melinda Gates Foundation. GATS China used a randomly selected representative sample of 13,354 of 15 years or older people.[15] The survey reported that the prevalence of current smoking was 59.2% among men and 2.4% among women; the prevalence of smoking cessation was 16.9%, and the prevalence of exposure to SHS was 72.4%.

In 2015, funded by the National Health and Family Planning Commission (NHFPC), China CDC conducted the China Adult Tobacco Survey (CATS), using

---

[10]Yang GH, Fan LX, Samet J, et al. Smoking in China: findings of the 1996 National Prevalence Survey. JAMA. 1999 Oct 6; 282(13):1247–53.

[11]Chen MZ, Forward of 1996 National Prevention Survey of Smoking Pattern edited by CAPM, CASH, MOH and NPHCC, China Science and Technology Press, August,1997 Beijing.

[12]The World Bank, China: Disease Prevention Project, IMPLEMENTATION COMPLETION REPORT (TF-25197 IDA-27940 TF-52892), Report No: 30,613.

[13]Yang GH, Ma JM, Liu N, et al. Smoking and passive smoking in Chinese, 2002. *Chin J Epidemiol.* 2005, 26(2):77–83 [in Chinese].

[14]WHO TFI, Global adults tobacco survey (GATS), http://www.who.int/tobacco/surveillance/survey/gats/en/.

[15]China CDC, Global Adult Tobacco Survey: China 2010 Country Report, edited by Yang GH. China San Xia Press, Nov. 2011 Beijing.

the same core questionnaire as in the 2010 GATS China. However, a different sample design from 2010 GATS China was employed, selecting subsample from a predetermined 336 units used for a national health knowledge survey. The second and third sampling procedures were similar to 2010 GATS-China. The survey reported that prevalence of current smoking was 52.1% among men and 2.7% among women; prevalence of smoking cessation was 14.4%, and the prevalence of exposure to SHS in indoor workplaces was 54.4%.[16]

From 1996 to 2001, CAPM conducted a Behavioral Risk Factor Surveillance (BRFS) in seven cities: Beijing, Shanghai, Tianjin, Chengdu of Sichuan province, Liuzhou of Guangxi Province, Weihai of Shandong province, and Luoyang of Henan province as an element of Disease Prevention (Health VII, *Project ID:* P003589) with loan of the World Bank. The BRFS included some indicators related to tobacco use. Monitoring tobacco use over 6 years provided a dynamic trend for seven studied cities.

As the output of Health VII project, since 2004, China has set up a BRFS system using sample surveys. The system was comprehensive in topics and at national level. Its sample was selected from 161 disease surveillance points, where 42 DSPs were moved and 58 DSPs supplemented to DSPs randomly selected in 1990s to improve national representativeness. The system consists in a series of repeated cross sectional surveys of BRFS related to chronic non-communicable diseases for every 3 years, including tobacco use.[17] Some results of BRFS were similar as the results from national surveys, such as tobacco use, but some were different, like exposure of SHS.[18,19,20,21] In BRFS, the prevalence of exposure of SHS was under 40%.

7.2.2   Tobacco Survey for Youth

The earliest survey on smoking behavior of adolescent could be traced back to the survey of cigarette smoking among junior high school students in Beijing, China in 1988.[22]

---

[16] China CDC *China Adult Tobacco Survey Report, 2015. edited by Liang XF,* China (Beijing): People's Health Press. 2016 [in Chinese].

[17] Chronic Non-communicable Disease preventive Center of China CDC, Non-communicable disease and BRFS Surveillance, Newsletter, No. 4 special issue, 2010, http://ncncd.chinacdc.cn/cbw/mbzxtx/201203/P020120312586082266424.pdf.

[18] China CDC Analysis Report on BRFS related to Non-communicable Disease, 2004, Peking Union Medical College Press, 2009 Beijing.

[19] China CDC Analysis Report on BRFS related to Non-communicable Disease, 2007, People's Health Press, 2010 Beijing.

[20] China CDC Analysis Report on BRFS related to Non-communicable Disease, 2010 Military Medical Press, 2012 Beijing.

[21] China CDC Analysis Report on BRFS related to Non-communicable Disease, 2013 Military Medical Press, 2016 Beijing.

[22] Zhu BP, Liu M, Wang SQ, et al. Cigarette smoking among junior high school students in Beijing, China, 1988, Int J Epidemiol. 1992 Oct; 21(5):854–61.

The Global Youth Tobacco Survey (GYTS)[23] is a school-based survey that collects data from students aged 13 to 15 years using a standardized methodology for constructing the sample frame, selecting schools and classes, and processing data. In 1999, 43 countries successfully completed GYTS, and China was one of them.[24] Totally 10,978 students aged 13–15 in Chongqin, Guangdong, Shandong and Tianjin were covered. The highest percent of currently using any tobacco product was in the Chongqing (30.1%), and the lowest in Shandong (16.2%), 22.5% of respondents (32.5% of males and 13.0% of females) reported having ever tried smoking; 54.8% of them started to try smoking before the age of 12 years old.[25] In 2004, Tianjin, Shanghai, Zhuhai and Puyang attended the second GYTS.[26] Although China has carried out two rounds of GYTS, it couldn't represent the tobacco use status in Chinese adolescents because of a few primary sampling unit (PSU).

In addition, a population-based survey of children ages 11–20 years, both in and out of school was completed in 1998.[27] Since about 40% of Chinese youths aged 15–19 years have already left their schools, the survey covered 24,000 youths (students and non-students of middle school age) in 24 DSPs, including equal numbers of urban and rural children. The experimenting smoking prevalence was 47.8% for boys and 12.8% for girls. The prevalence of regular smoking among non-students was higher (8.3%) than that of students (5.2%).

In the year of 2004–2005, Institute of Child and Adolescent Health of Peking University was conducted in urban areas of 18 provinces, municipalities, and autonomous regions in China with the principle of voluntariness. The cities in each province were classified into three groups according to social—economic status, and one city from each group was selected as study field. A two-stage cluster sampling method was used in each city to produce a representative sample of students in junior middle school, senior middle school and college school. A self-administered questionnaire including seven module, such as dietary, physical activity, addiction behavior, et al., was completed by 213,353 students (male, 103,483; female, 109,770). This survey reported the prevalence of current smoking, for male (22.4%) and female (3.9%). However, it is hard to compare with the other study as different questionnaire and age of target population.

In 2013, NHFPC entrusted China CDC to carry out the first national youth tobacco survey in 336 counties (township or district of city), which is same point with 2015 CATS. The country was stratified by urban/rural at the PSU level. Then, probability proportional sampling (PPS) method was used to select PSUs. Then, schools were

---

[23] TFI, Global youth tobacco survey (GYTS), http://www.who.int/tobacco/surveillance/gyts/en/.

[24] The Global Youth Tobacco Survey Collaborative Group. Tobacco use among youth: a cross country comparison. *Tob Control.* 2002; 11: 252–70.

[25] Li AL, Huang YQ, Wang YL, et al. A preliminary Analysis on Smoking Behavior and its Psychosocial Factors among Junior High School Students in the Four Areas of China. *Chin Public Health.* 2001, 17(1): 75–7 [in Chinese].

[26] Warren CW, Jones NR, Peruga A, et al. Global Youth Tobacco Surveillance, 2000–2007. *CDC MMWR.* 2007, 56(20):1–21 (https://www.cdc.gov/mmwr/preview/mmwrhtml/ss5701a1.htm, access Feb 22nd, 2017).

[27] Yang GH, Ma JM, Samet JM, et al. Smoking among adolescents in China: 1998 survey findings. Int J Epidemiol. 2004 Oct; 33(5):1103–10. Epub 2004 Jun 24.

selected within each selected PSU with the same PPS method. Within each selected schools, one class was randomly selected. All the students in selected class participated the survey. The survey used the standard core questionnaire of GYTS and collected sample of 155,117 junior students aged 13–15 from 1020 middle school. The prevalence of current smoking was 6.9%; boy (11.2%) was higher than girl (2.2%); urban (4.8%) is lower than rural (7.8%). 19.9% junior students reported having ever tried smoking (30.1% of boy and 8.7% of girl); 82.3% of them started to try smoking before the age of 13 years old. 72.9% reported to exposure SHS at home, indoor or outdoor public places or public transportation. The survey was the first national level GYTS and also could represent the junior students at provincial level.

7.3 Characteristics and Change of Tobacco Surveillance in China

Reliable tobacco surveillance systems exist in many countries. For example, in the United States, the National Health Interview Survey (NHIS) since 1957 (https://www.cdc.gov/nchs/nhis/index.htm) and the Behavioral Risk Factor Surveillance System since 1984 (https://www.cdc.gov/brfss/) have been used to monitor tobacco use. However, those surveys contained only questions about tobacco use and smoking cessation instead of in depth policy related questions. To better understand impacts of tobacco control policy, the US CDC later on also conducted the National Adult Tobacco Survey (https://www.cdc.gov/tobacco/data_statistics/surveys/nats/index.htm) to improve the surveillance. In Thailand, for the same reason, the BRFS System, National Smoking and Alcohol Drinking Survey, and GATS Thailand have been used to monitor its tobacco use and implementation of tobacco control policy. While in China, because of large population and heavy burden of smoking, there have been a challenge of tobacco surveillance to meet the need of national and subnational tobacco control. In this section, we will discuss methodology used in China tobacco surveillance and aim to provide useful information for improving current tobacco surveillance.

7.3.1 Sample Design of Tobacco Surveys

In this section, we will discuss sample designs of adult tobacco surveys. As described in previous section, there were five national tobacco related surveys used to monitor tobacco use: 1984 National Tobacco Survey, 1996 National Smoking Prevalence Survey, 2002 National Behavioral Risk Factor Survey, 2010 GATS-China, and 2015 CATS. For the details of their sample design could be found in previous references.[28] Brief descriptions are as following.

---

[28] Hsia J, Yang G, Li Q, Xiao L, Yang Y, Asma S. Methodology of the global adult tobacco survey in China, 2010. Biomed Environ Sci. 2010. 23(6):445–50.

For 1984 National Tobacco Survey, the target population was non-institutionalized people of 15 years or older. The sample design was stratified into multistage cluster sampling. The strata were all city and rural areas of 29 provinces, autonomous regions and municipalities. The total sample size was 519,600. Overall response rate was 95%. The design effect for current smoking was estimated around 75.[29]

For 1996 National Smoking Prevalence Survey, the target population was non-institutionalized people of 15–69 years old. The sample design was stratified multi-stage cluster sampling. The strata were urban-rural and socioeconomic index (three groups in urban areas and four groups in rural areas). The PSUs were 145 counties, previously randomly selected as disease surveillance points.[30] The total sample size was 120,298. The Overall response rate was 94%. The design effect for current smoking was estimated around 42.[31,32]

For 2002 National Behavioral Risk Factor Survey, the sample design was the same as that used in the 1996 survey, including target population, sampling strategy, strata, and primary sampling units. The total sample size was 16,056. The design effect for current smoking was estimated around 6.5.[33]

For 2010 GATS-China, the target population was non-institutionalized people of 15 years or older. The sample design was stratified multistage cluster sampling. The strata were region (east, central, and west) and urban-rural. PSUs, 100 districts/counties, were randomly selected. The total sample size was 13,354. The Overall response rate was 96%. The design effect for current smoking was 3.7.

For 2015 CATS, the target population was the same as GATS, non-institutionalized people of 15 years or older. The sample design was multistage cluster sampling. However, strata and PSUs used in the survey were adopted from National Health Knowledge Survey, where 336 districts/countries were determined to assure about 10 districts/counties from each province, autonomous region, or municipality. The total sample size was 16,800. The overall response rate was 92.2%. The design effect for current smoking was 6.6.

It is worthy of noting that evolution of tobacco surveillance in China was rapid comparing to other health related surveys. China did not have its first fertility survey, conducted by the State Family Planning Commission until 1982, nor its first health survey, conducted by the MOH until 1993, both of which used nationally representative samples.

[29] Weng XZ, Hong ZG, Chen DY. Smoking prevalence in Chinese aged 15 and above. *Chin Med J (Engl)*. 1987;100(11):886–92.

[30] Yang GH, Zheng XW, Zeng G, et al., Selection of Disease Surveillance Points in second stage and its representative. Chinese J. Epidemio. Vol 13(4), 197–201, 1992.

[31] Chinese Academy of Preventive Medicine, Chinese Association of Smoking or Health, Dept. of Disease Control, Ministry of Health, P.R. China and Office of Committee of the National Patriotic Health Campaign. *1996 National Prevalence Survey of Smoking Pattern.* China (Beijing): China Science & Technology Press. 1997 [in Chinese].

[32] Yang GH, Fan LX, Samet J, et al. Smoking in China—Findings of the 1996 National Prevalence Survey. *JAMA.* 1999; 282(13): 1247–53.

[33] Yang GH ed. *Deaths and Their Risk Factors among Chinese Population.* China (Beijing): Peking Union Medical College Press. 2005 [in Chinese].

Characteristics of the development of tobacco surveillance design are significant. First, the sample size was getting smaller and smaller. At early time, survey planners believed that a large sample size was more important to reduce survey errors and costs of fieldwork were not a major concern because of government in-kind contributions and its administrative power. During 1980s and even 1990s the beliefs resulted in extremely large sample size in national surveys. However, survey errors are composed of not only sampling errors but also non-sampling errors. While a large sample size reduces sampling errors, it would unavoidably increase interviewers, field supervisors, large scale or multiple level of trainings, all of which would increase non-sampling errors. That survey planners gradually realized price of non-sampling errors plus survey costs increments might be reasons that the sample sizes of tobacco survey were getting smaller.

Second, one important concept in sample design is design effects, defined as 1 + rho (average number of units per PSU + 1),[34] where rho is an intra-class correlation for a studied variable and it is estimated usually around 0.05 for current smoking. Design effects can be thought as a scale to convert a sample size under simple random sampling design to that under current sample design. This is often referred as an effective sample size. Therefore, the larger design effects are, the less efficient a sample design is, comparing to the equivalent sample size under simple random sampling. It might be why tobacco survey designers more focused on reducing its sample size and increasing the number of PSUs, so as to reduce the average number of units per PSU. Those effects were shown from a fact that design effects were getting smaller in tobacco surveys.

Another interesting point was that 1996 and 2002 surveys used DSP as PSUs, while 2010 survey sampled PSU directly from a frame based on census data. Preliminary thoughts of developing DSPs was for the sake of management. DSP system is especially important to collect information continuously in highly populated country. A key question was then representative at DSP level. In constructing the DSPs, a socioeconomic indicator was developed by applying principle component analysis to county level census data, including gross domestic product (GDP), illiteracy under 12 years old, birth rate, age distribution under 14 years old and 65 years or older, total mortality, infant mortality. Counties grouped by the socioeconomic indicator were more homogeneous within a group. Then counties were randomly selected within each stratum, making a total of 145 DSPs. An advantage of this approach is that PSUs are representative and limitations are (1) census data are only available for every ten census years, and (2) China has different levels of economic development and the groups based on indicator would not be true a few years later. The other type of sample design selecting PSUs directly from externally stratified frame of census data would not run into this problem. In order to improve its efficiency, some controlled sampling approach, e.g., *cube sampling*, used in 2010 GATS could overcome the challenge.

Summary of tobacco survey design benefits for future designs. First, designing a surveillance or a repeated survey is different from designing one time cross sec-

---

[34] Kish, L. (1965) Survey Sampling, Wiley and Sons, New York.

tional survey. Second, some parameters used in sample size determination are worth of mentioning. Key variables for tobacco surveys are often current smoking for men and smoking cessation. A fair estimate is between 50 and 54% for prevalence of male current smoking and no more than 20% for prevalence of smoking cessation. Design effect is estimated between 3 and 4 for the key variables. Reasonably assume those parameters can assure sufficient sample size. Third, how allocate and randomly select a sample is more complicated than sample size determination per se. A number of PSUs should be carefully evaluated in order to assure realization of assumed design effect, where there is often a gap between planned design effects and implemented design effects in practice because of survey cost. Forth, tobacco surveillance is used for monitoring implementation of tobacco control policies. A comprehensive BRFS might not be able to include enough policy related questions. Tobacco surveys are still needed in this situation unless tobacco control policy questions can be piggybacked. Another direct application of tobacco surveillance is to estimate smoking attributable mortality. Linkage between tobacco surveillance, say tobacco surveys over 10 years and mortality system needs to be considered. Last, all discussion above did not take survey cost into account. In practice, cost plays an important role in designing tobacco surveillance.

So from these national surveys, we could see sampling survey plays a vital role in providing an adequate estimate of the magnitude of a disease and risk factors for China, especially the multi-stage stratified cluster sampling design. And a good design doesn't need too much sample size. Although China has more than 1.3 billion population, only 15,000 sample size could represent the whole country. The 1984 survey had interviewed more than 0.51 million population, however, it is not the strict national representativeness, just represented urban/rural. So the sampling design is very vital technique should be considered in the survey.

From repeated surveys, the variance for estimated difference for an interested variable exists. Take two repeated surveys as an example, the variance can be partitioned to three variation components of (1) between PSUs, (2) between selected individuals within PSUs, and (3) between the measurements from two times. The third component is what we want to detect. If the same interviewees in the first survey are interviewed in the second survey (repeated one), the first and the second components are zero, which is the best situation. If the repeated survey is totally independent from the first survey, the first and second components are largest. Since it is not feasible to locate the same participants in the first survey to be interviewed in the repeated survey, one compromise is to keep the same PSUs in the second survey (this is often manageable) and resample individuals (to overcome the difficulty to locate the same persons) from the PSUs previously selected in the first survey. In this case, the first component is zero but not the second component. However the total variation is between two extreme situations. Therefore, using the same PSUs in repeated surveys is common practice. From these five surveys, only the 1996 and 2002 surveys used the same PSUs. So the total variation between them was lower than other surveys.

Other surveys, such as 2002 Chinese Citizen Nutrition & Health Survey, 2003[35] and 2008.[36] China Health Service Survey, 2004,[37] 2007,[38] 2010 and 2013 National Chronic Disease Risk Factors Surveillance, included tobacco use information, but the smoking rates from these surveys were hard to assess the national smoking prevalence without strictly random sample and different definitions. Xiao, et al., compared the 2002 BRFSS survey with 2002 Chinese Citizen Nutrition & Health Survey and 2003 China Health Service Survey and found that only the estimated total number of cigarettes consumed from the 2002 BRFSS was very close to the tobacco industry's released data on cigarette production.[39] Therefore, these four national adult surveys, 2002 BRFSS and 2014 youth surveys provided important evidence for China's tobacco control policy.

7.3.2 Module and Questionnaires

It is essential to have high quality surveillance data for national, sub-national, and international tobacco control programmes[40] and many groups have sought to standardized definitions of smoking status for surveillance purposes.[41]

All of these five adult national surveys included the prevalence of tobacco use & secondhand smoke exposure (SHS), cessation, and knowledge, attitude & perceptions of tobacco harm. The GATS questionnaire, called Tobacco Questions for Surveys (TQS),[42] includes some indicators on tobacco policy, which was used in GATS-China 2010 and CATS 2015. Therefore, the 2010 and 2015 survey could

---

[35] Center for Health Statistics and Information, MOH. National *Research on Health Service—the Third National Health Service Survey*. China (Beijing): Peking Union Medical College Press. 2004 [in Chinese].

[36] Center for Health Statistics and Information, MOH. *National Research on Health Service—Report on the Fourth Family Health Survey*. China (Beijing): Peking Union Medical College Press. 2008 [in Chinese].

[37] Chinese Center for Disease Control and Prevention. *Report on Chronic Disease Risk Factor Surveillance in China 2004*. China (Beijing): Peking Union Medical College Press. 2009 [in Chinese].

[38] Chinese Center for Disease Control and Prevention. *Report on Chronic Disease Risk Factor Surveillance in China 2007*. China (Beijing): Peking Union Medical College Press 2010 [in Chinese].

[39] Xiao L, Yang J, Wan X, Yang G. What is the prevalence of smoking in China-comparison of three national tobacco surveys. *Chin J Epidemiol*. 2009, 30(1):30–3 [in Chinese].

[40] World Health Organization. *WHO Report on the Global Tobacco Epidemic, 2008: the MPOWER package*. Geneva, World Health Organization, 2008.

[41] Copley TT, Lovato C, O'Connor S, et al. *Indicators for monitoring tobacco control: a resource for decision-makers, evaluators and researchers*. Toronto, Ontario, Canada: Canadian Tobacco Control Research Initiative, 2006.

[42] TFI, Protocols and guidelines, core questionnaire with optional questions, 6_GATS_CoreQuestionnairewithOptionalQuestions_v2.1_FINAL_13June2014.pdf.

assess the SHS exposure policy implementation, which we will describe in the part "Impact of Policy Intervention" in detail.

Across these five adult national surveys, there are many differences among definitions of current smoking, including whether occasional or non-daily smokers are included and whether an explicit time frame is used, as well as the definition of SHS exposure.

7.3.2.1 Definition of Smoking

The definitions of current smokers and former smoker from WHO classifications for these five surveys were same. Current smoker means smoking tobacco products at the time of the survey while former smokers were not. However, the definition for ever smoker had some difference. In 1984, 2010 and 2015, ever smoker means a person who has ever smoked any tobacco in his/her lifetime. In 1996 and 2002, the definition for ever-smokers was persons who had ever smoked at least 100 cigarettes or 100 g tobacco.

Question about the origin of the 100 cigarette was motivated by the need for psychometric development and validity.[43] Bondy's research found that adding the 100 cigarette rule to either 30 day prevalence or self-report of every day or occasional smoking lowers prevalence estimates by 1–3 percentage points fairly consistently. In addition, among these data, the difference between the lowest and highest prevalence estimates, within each year, was not significant[44] (Fig. 7.1). And in 1996's survey, the two definitions for ever smoker with smoking 100 cigarette or smoking at least for 6 months were included, but there was just 1 percentage difference. In the later study, the measurement of prevalence of ever smoker has been given up, and the prevalence of tobacco use has been described with the current smoker and former smoker. Here we just use the two indicators to describe the trend of tobacco use in the past 30 years in China.

Experts recommended that indicators should include a single puff for experimentation but 100 cigarettes for "established smoking".[45] In GYTS and 2004–2005 BRFS, current cigarette smokers are defined as students who answered one or more days to the question *'During the past 30 days (one month), on how many days did you smoke cigarette?'*[46] Again, definitions used vary across studies.

[43] Pierce JP. Tobacco control factsheets: conducting a smoking prevalence survey. International Union Against Cancer. http://www.globalink.org/en/prevalence.shtml (accessed 11 June 2009).

[44] Bondy SJ, Victor JC, Diemert LM. Origin and use of the 100 cigarette criterion in tobacco surveys. *Tob Control.* 2009; 18:317–23.

[45] National Advisory Group on Monitoring and Evaluation. *Indicators for monitoring tobacco control: a resource for decision-makers, evaluators and researchers.* Toronto, Ontario, Canada: Canadian Tobacco Control Research Initiative (CTCRI), 2006.

[46] Warren CW, Lea V, Lee J, Jones NR, Asma S and Mckenna M. Change in tobacco use among 13–15 year olds between 1999 and 2008: findings from the Global Youth Tobacco Survey. *Global Health Promotion,* 2009; Suppl (2): 38–90.

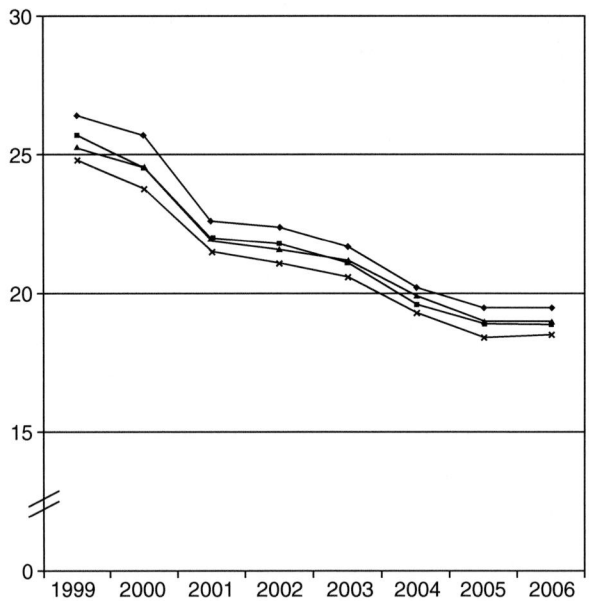

Fig. 7.1 Percentage of "current smokers" by varying definition of current smoking status. Canadians aged 15 and older in Canadian Tobacco Use Monitoring Surveys (1999–2006). (♦) 30 day prevalent smoker (one or more cigarettes in past 30 days) (19.5% in 2006); (■) 30 day prevalent smoker + 100 cigarette criterion (19.0% in 2006); (▲) self-reported "daily" or "occasional smoker" (18.9% in 2006); (×) self-reported "daily" or "occasional smoker" + 100 cigarette criterion (18.5% in 2006). Source: secondary data analysis, Statistics Canada. Estimates are population weighted. Pooled sample = 171,948. (Bondy SJ, Victor JC, Diemert LM. Origin and use of the 100 cigarette criterion in tobacco surveys. *Tob Control.* 2009;18:317–23)

7.3.2.2 Definition of SHS Exposure

From 1984 to 2010, four nationwide tobacco epidemiological questionnaire-based surveys showed an upward trend in exposure levels to SHS exposure for adults in China. However, as the definitions of exposure to SHS were different among those surveys, it is still in doubt whether or not the exposure levels to SHS increased. In 1984, the definition of exposure SHS was to inhale passively environmental tobacco smoke (ETS) *for more than 15 min every day*.[47] In 1996 and 2002 surveys, they had same definition which means to inhale ETS *for more than 15 min at least one day per typical week*.[48,49] In 2010 GATS and 2015 CATS survey, the definition was more restricted: to inhale ETS *for at least one day per typical week*. GATS-China 2010

---

[47] Weng XZ ed. *Report on the National Smoking Survey in 1984*. China (Beijing): People's Medical Publishing House. 1988 [in Chinese].

[48] Yang GH, Fan LX, Samet J, et al. Smoking in China: findings of the 1996 National Prevalence Survey. *JAMA*, 1999, 282(13): 1247–53.

[49] Yang GH, Ma JM, Liu N, Zhou LN. Smoking and Passive Smoking in Chinese, 2002. *Chin J Epidemiol.* 2005, 26(2): 77–83 [in Chinese].

kept the question to ask respondents about their overall exposure to SHS for any time in a day and at least one day in a typical week, but without at least 15 min per day limitation.[50] In China, most surveys including national chronic disease risk factors surveillance and local surveys[51,52,53,54,55,56] used the above three non-GATS definitions, which cause the incomparable of results from different survey.

Therefore it suggests that when we design the questionnaire, standard definitions must always be considered in order to time-trends or international comparisons.

7.4 Surveillance on Prevalence of Tobacco Use in China

7.4.1 The Extent of the Tobacco Epidemic

These five national adult surveys can provide the national representative picture of tobacco use.

Tobacco use prevalence among males remains at a very high level in China and the number of current smokers in China is over 300 million. Despite a very slight decline in the male smoking prevalence, it is still in a high plateau stage, more that 50%. China's current smoking prevalence among adult males was the second highest among the countries that completed the GATS survey in 2010. The female smoking prevalence always remains low level. Due to the elder women smoking prevalence declined, the female prevalence dropped from 7% in 1984 to 2.4% in 2015. By adjusted with the 2000 National Census Data, the standardized smoking rate among Chinese seems no change over the last decade or so. (See Table 7.1).

However, in terms of SHS, it is hard for us to describe the trend directly without standard definition and same questions. As we mentioned before, if we simply say SHS showed an upward trend from 1984 to 2010, based on the SHS prevalence in 1984

---

[50] Xiao L, Yang Y, Li Q, et al. Population-based survey of secondhand smoke exposure in China. *Biomed Environ Sci.* 2010, 23(6): 430–6.

[51] Yin P, Zhang M, Li Y, et al. Prevalence of COPD and its association with socioeconomic status in China: findings from China Chronic Disease Risk Factor Surveillance 2007. *BMC Public Health,* 2011, 11: 586.

[52] Meng X, Chen N, Yang H, et al. Smoking, Secondhand Smoking and Quit Survey for Residents in urban and rural areas of Guangxi Province. *Chin J Prev Chron Dis.* 2011, 19(2): 206–7 [in Chinese].

[53] Fang H, Zhang JL, He DD, et al. Smoking Prevalence Survey in Minhang District, Shanghai. *Health Education and Health Promotion.* 2009, (02): 33–5 [in Chinese].

[54] Chen ML, Zheng YL, Lv ZL, et al. Prevalence of smoking behavior among residents aged 15~69 in Shandong Province in 2007. *Chin J Disease Control and Prevention.* 2009, 13 (2): 163–6 [in Chinese].

[55] Wang CP, Wang JF, Xu XF, et al. The Epidemiology of Passive Smoking in Counties in China. *Med and Philosophy.* 2008. 29(5): 43–4 [in Chinese].

[56] Zhou HB, Ma QY, Peng J, et al. Analysis on Smoking, Quit Smoking, and Passive Smoking among Permanent Residents in Shenzhen. *Chin J Social Med.* 2011, 28(5): 329–33 [in Chinese].

Table 7.1 Current smoking prevalence among population aged 15–69 in different years (%)

Current smoking prevalence	1984	1996	2002	2010	2015
Male	61.0	63.0	57.4	54.0	53.0
Female	7.04	3.8	2.6	2.1	2.4
Urban (Male)		57.0	52.4	51.0	50.1
Rural (Male)		63.0	60.0	56.5	56.0
Machine Operator (Male)		67.4	56.3	67.0	55.0
Agriculture Worker (Male)		66.6	61.2	61.2	60.9
Leaders of Organization (Male)		58.5	54.2	54.2	51.6
Medical/Health Personnel (Male)		55.4	45.0	40.5	43.6
Teaching Staff (Male)		51.0	48.4	36.9	48.7
Total (Crude)	33.9	35.3	31.1	28.7	28.1
Total (Age-Standardized)[a]	36.0	33.7	28.5	27.9	27.1

[a]Age-standard prevalence was computed using China's 2010 census population structure

(39.75%), 1996 (53.48%), 2002 (52.9%) and 2010 (72.4%), it would be not right. After cross-walking adjustment, the true is the SHS prevalence was kept stable from 1996 to 2002 and the heavy SHS exposure (every day to SHS exposure) was still not change from 2002 to 2010, but the light SHS exposure (one day to SHS exposure per week) was increasing since there is no limit with at least 15 min. So, owing to the difference of definition of SHS exposure, these results are not comparable directly. Only after adjustment, it is valid to compare levels of SHS exposure in different periods.

The GATS-China 2010 could be compared across countries easily with the same standard questionnaire and procedure. Figure 7.2 showed that China was one of countries with highest exposure to SHS either at home or at the other indoor places, including workplace and public places among 14 GATS countries in 2010.[57]

As described in Sect. 7.2.2, it is hard to describe the trend of tobacco use for the youth because the target population and areas of these surveys is not the same.

7.4.2 Public Awareness of the Epidemic and Attitudes Towards Tobacco Control

The slogan "Smoking is harmful to your health" has been very familiar by the Chinese public. However, the knowledge about the specific health hazards caused by tobacco use and SHS exposure was very poor. Most people know that smoking could cause lung cancer, 77.5% in 2010 and 79.5% in 2015, respectively. But the percentages of those who were aware of stroke, myocardial infarction and erectile dis-function caused by smoking were very low, with only 31.0%, 42.6% and 19.7% respectively in 2015. Even for medical professionals, in 2015, only 52.5% of them

---

[57]Nazar GP, Lee JT, Arora M Socioeconomic Inequalities in Secondhand Smoke Exposure at Home and at Work in 15 Low- and Middle-Income Countries, *Nicotine & Tobacco Research*, 2016, 1230–1239.

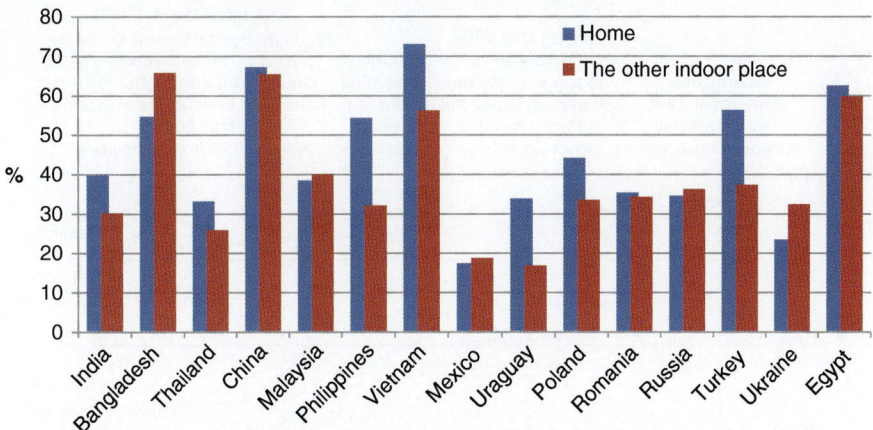

Fig. 7.2 Exposure to SHS at home and the other indoor places—15 GATS countries 2008–2011 (Authors made the figure based the literature) Reprint with permission from Nazar GP, Lee JT, Arora M Socioeconomic Inequalities in Secondhand Smoke Exposure at Home and at Work in 15 Low- and Middle-Income Countries, Nicotine & Tobacco Research, 2016, 1230–1239

knew about the health hazards from smoking caused by the above four diseases. Therefore, the results has shown that slogan "smoking is harmful to your health" do not enough to communicate the health risk of tobacco use or SHS exposure.

7.4.3 Tobacco Survey at Local Level

Although China doesn't have national smoke-free legislation, eighteen cities, including the national capital of Beijing, have enacted or amended sub-national smoke-free public places legislation, and some provinces have conducted many tobacco control programmes. So evidence from city-level in China is needed to tailor policies and tobacco control programmes.

The International Tobacco Control Policy Evaluation project (ITC) China Survey showed in seven cities, the percentage of smokers who noticed smoking in their indoor workplaces decreased from 2007 to 2012 because of different city-level smoke-free policy enforcement at wave 3 (Fig. 7.3).[58]

Some other projects also concerned and provided the results of tobacco use at provincial- or city-level, such as Epidemiology and Intervention Research for Tobacco Control in China project (EIRTC) (9R01TW007949-06), funded by National Institute of Health (NIH). In order to develop an approach for rapid assessment of tobacco control intervention at province and city of China, stratified random sampling was used to select five types of organizational and household

---

[58]World Health Organization Western Pacific Region and University of Waterloo, ITC project. Smoke-free policies in China: evidence of effectiveness and implications for action. Manila: World Health Organization Regional Office for the Western Pacific; 2015.

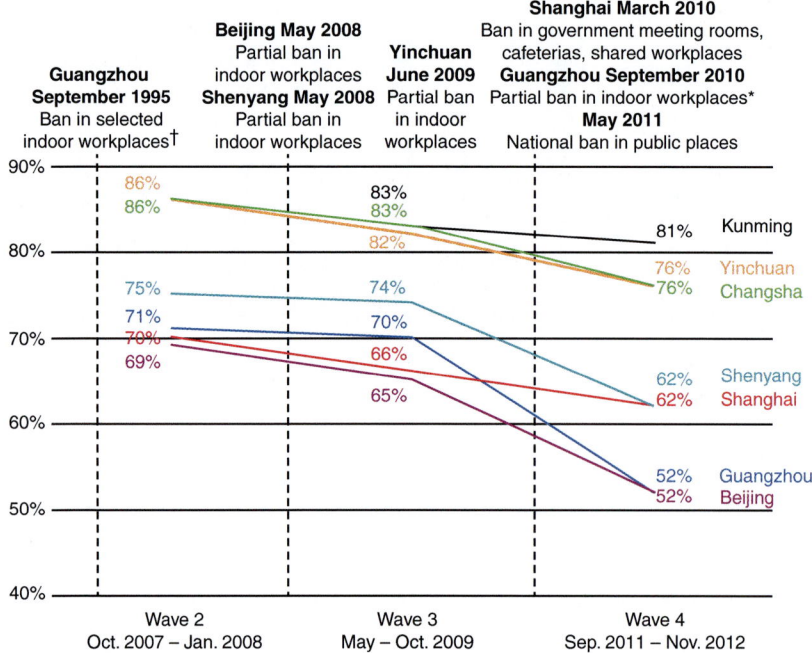

†Ban Included classrooms, meeting rooms and air-conditioned offices
* Ban Included offices, meeting rooms, cafeterias, elevators and corridors

Fig. 7.3 Percentage of smokers who noticed smoking in their indoor workplaces, by city, by wave. Source: Western Pacific Region of WHO and University of Waterloo, ITC project. Smoke-free policies in China: evidence of effectiveness and implications for action. Manila: World Health Organization Regional Office for the Western Pacific; 2015

respondents in two municipalities and five provinces in China (Shanghai and Tianjin, Heilongjiang, Henan, Guangdong, Zhejiang and Jiangxi, respectively). The results showed that in 2010, the prevalence of SHS in these seven locations ranged from 65.7% in Shanghai to 78.6% in Tianjin, and male smoking rates ranged from 35.5% in Shanghai to 45.2% in Zhejiang. Among them, Shanghai relatively implemented tobacco control policy better than other provinces. (See Fig. 7.4).[59]

In China, about 18 cities now have local legislation or regulation (either complete or partial) to protect people from second-hand smoke exposure, including Harbin,[60] Tianjin, Shanghai, Guangzhou, Qingdao, Lanzhou, Changchun, Tangshan, and Shenzhen and Beijing,[61] and so on. In order to evaluate the progress of imple-

---

[59] Wan X, Stillman F, Liu H, et al. Development of policy performance indicators to assess the implementation of protection from exposure to secondhand smoke in China. *Tob Control.* 2013; 22: Suppl 2: ii9–15.

[60] Public announcement (No. 11th) by the Standing Committee of 13th People's congress in Harbin: Rules to protect people from secondhand smoke exposure Sept 5, 2011. http://wenku.baidu.com/view/02c3b46eaf1ffc4ff f47ac04.html.

[61] No.8 Proclamation by Beijing municipal People's Congress standing committee: Beijing control smoking ordinance. http://210.75.193.155/rdzw/information/exchange/Laws.do?method=showInf oForWeb&id=2014321 (accessed Jan 25, 2015).

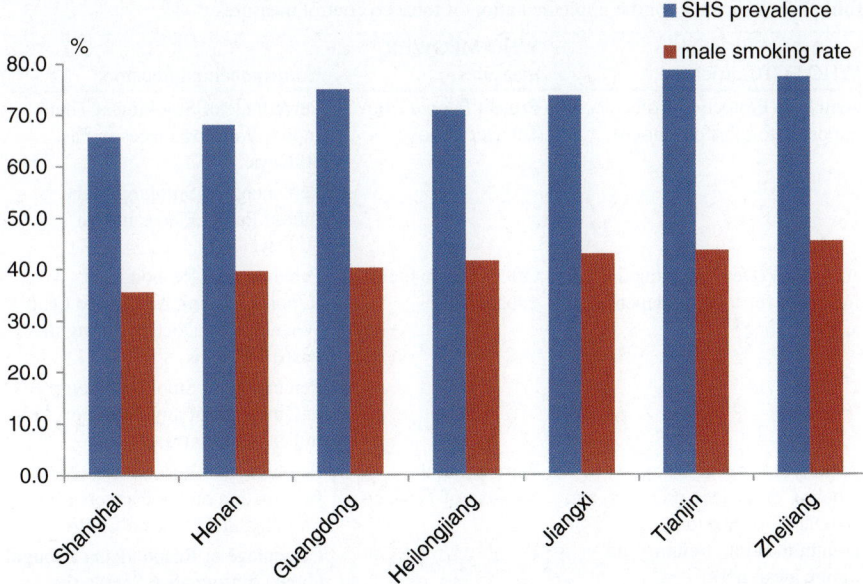

Fig. 7.4 Prevalence of SHS exposure and Male Smoking in Seven Province and municipality in 2010 (standardized)

mentation of tobacco control policy, short and long term impact of tobacco control programs and health outcome, and correlates of social and economic factors, there was an urgent need to set up city or province level tobacco surveillance system. China CDC, U.S. CDC and other international organization conducted China City Adult Tobacco Survey.[62] However, lots of work are yet to be done, including standardizing working protocol, creating measurable indicators, capacity of conducting surveys, as well as disseminating and using their local level surveillance results.

7.5 Surveillance Impact of Tobacco Control Policy in China

7.5.1 Policy Performance Indicators

Based on MPOWER policy package of WHO[63] and GATS 2010 questionnaire, Yang GH and her colleague developed a set of policy performance indicators (PPI), to assess the enforcement of the five key policies of WHO FCTC (Table 7.2).[64]

---

[62] China CDC, US CDC, WHO WPRO, et al., *2013–2014 China partial adult tobacco survey report*, Military Medical Press, 2012 Beijing, April, 2015.

[63] World Health Organization (WHO). *WHO Report on the Global Tobacco Epidemic, 2008: The MPOWER Package*. Geneva: WHO; 2008.

[64] Yang GH, Li Q, Wang CX, et al. Findings from 2010 Global Adult Tobacco Survey: Implementation of MPOWER Policy in China. *Biomed Environ Sci*. 2010, 23: 422–9.

Table 7.2 Indicators for the implementation of tobacco control measures

WHO FCTC articles	WHO MPOWER measures	Corresponding indicators
Article 8 (Protection from exposure to tobacco smoke)	Protect People from Tobacco Smoke	Percentage of Smoking at Their Indoor Working Places in Past 30 Days
		Percentage of Smoking in the Indoor Public Places in Past 30 Days
Article 14 (Demand reduction measures for tobacco dependence and cessation)	Offer Help to Quit Tobacco Use	Percentage of Respondents Reporting Being Advised to Quit When Seeing Doctors during the Past 12 Months
		Percentage of Smokers Attempted to Quit without any Cessation Aids in Past 12 Months
Article 11 (Packaging and labeling of tobacco products) and Article 12 (Education, communication, training and public awareness)	Warn about the Dangers of Tobacco	Percentage of Respondents Notices Information on the Dangers of Smoking and Tobacco Control
		Percentage of Respondents Thought about Quitting after Seeing the Health Warnings on Cigarette Packages
Article 13 (Tobacco Advertising, promotion and sponsorship)	Enforce Bans on Tobacco Adverting, Promotion and Sponsorship	Percentage of Respondents Noticed Tobacco Marketing during the Past 30 Days
		Percentage of Respondents Noticed Tobacco Marketing on TV programs during the Past 30 Days
Article 6 (Price and tax measure to reduce the demand for tobacco)	Raise Taxes on Tobacco	Maximum Expenditure to Buy a Pack of Cigarettes Paid by 50% Smokers
		Expenditure of 100 Packs of Cigarettes as a Percentage of 2009 GDP per Capita

Wan X, et al.[65] examined the relationship between components of the Strength of Tobacco Control (SOTC) index and the performance of tobacco control polices. The results has shown that the percentage of indoor workplaces with no smoking in past 30 days and the percentage of indoor public places with no smoking in past 30 days were correlated well with certain components of the SOTC.

ITC project also developed a model and a questionnaire to measure the behavioral and psychosocial impact of all of the demand reduction policies of the WHO FCTC by prospective cohort surveys. The project completed multi-wave surveys in

---

[65] Wan X, Stillman F, Liu H, et al. Development of policy performance indicators to assess the implementation of protection from exposure to secondhand smoke in China. *Tob Control*. 2013; 22: Suppl 2: ii9–15.

nine countries, including China.[66] For example, the project evaluated the progress of Article 11, packaging and labeling, including health warnings and the elimination of potentially misleading descriptors (such as, "light" or "mild").[67]

7.5.2   Assessment of Tobacco Control Policy Implementation

In 2011, when the FCTC became effective in China for 5 years, Yang et al. used 2010 China-GATS data to assess the implementation of five key tobacco control policies in China by using the above PPI. The results showed that the average score for the implementation of the 5 policies of MPOWER in China was 37.3 points, indicating tobacco control policies in China was poor and there was a large gaps from the WHO FCTC requirements.[68] This event was reported by many domestic and international media outlets, which pushed the 12th National Economic and Social Development 5 year plan, passed at the National People's Congress conference in 2011, and adopted a resolution calling for the "full implementation of banning smoking in public places".

2015 CATS found China has made some progress in some strategies of MPOWER. Unfortunately, only 6 indicators were available in 2015 survey. Four indicators were missing or different definition, including *"Percentage of Smoking in the Indoor Public Places in Past 30 Days"*, *"Percentage of Respondents Noticed Tobacco Marketing on TV programs during the Past 30 Days"*, *"Expenditure of 100 Packs of Cigarettes as a Percentage of last year' GDP per Capita"* and *"Percentage of Respondents Noticed Tobacco Marketing during the Past 30 Days"*. The progress of the three policies, that is P, E and R of MPOWER cannot be compared between in 2010 and in 2015, although the other three individual indicators showed there were some progress for other three policies. For example, "Percentage of Smoking at Their Indoor Working Places in Past 30 Days" dropped down from 63.3% in 2010 to 54.3% in 2015. The two indicators for offering quit help showed good progress: The percentage of smoker' received cessation advice from physician was average increased 20%, up to 58.2% and the percentage of seeking aid in attempting smokers was increasing in 2015. Unfortunately, there is not any progress of implement of "Warn about the Dangers of Tobacco". *"Percentage of Respondents Noticed Information on the Dangers of Smoking and Tobacco Control"* was from 59.8% in 2010 to 61.2% in 2015; *"Percentage of Respondents Thought about Quitting after*

[66]Fong GT, Cummings KM, Borland R, et al. The Conceptual Framework of the International Tobacco Control (ITC) Policy Evaluation Project. *Tob Control.* 2006; 15 (Suppl III): iii3–11.

[67]World Health Organization Western Pacific Region, University of Waterloo, ITC Project and Think Tank Research Center for Health Development. Tobacco health warnings in China: evidence of effectiveness and implications for action. Manila: World Health Organization Regional Office for the Western Pacific; 2014.

[68]Yang GH, Hu AG. *Tobacco control and China Future.* China: Beijing, Economic Daily Press. Jan. 2011 [in Chinese].

Seeing the Health Warnings on Cigarette Packages" was from 36.4% in 2010 to 37.9% in 2015.

In addition, ITC project affirmed that the lower effectiveness of text-only health warnings in China compared to pictorial health warnings in Malaysia.[69]

7.6   Monitor Tobacco Industry in China

In order to protect tobacco control policy from tobacco industry interference, alerting to any efforts by the tobacco industry to undermine or subvert tobacco control efforts, is a key requirement for full WHO FCTC implementation. Rooting out such interference of tobacco industry is firstly to know what tobacco industry have done, that is to monitor tobacco industry so as to be informed of activities of the tobacco industry that have a negative impact on tobacco control efforts, which is considered an important measure for implementation of the Article 5.3 guidelines. WHO report on *"Tobacco industry interference: A global brief"* in 2012[70] summarized the various forms of tobacco industry interference. 2012 theme report *"To disclose and resist the interference of tobacco industry in China"* by Think Tank[71] revealed how State Tobacco Monopoly Administration (STMA)/China National Tobacco Company (CNTC) interfered the tobacco control policies in detail. The cases of interference is described in most Chapters of this Book *"Tobacco Control in China"*. The seven strategies of STMA/CNTC interference are summarized in Chap. 3, including (1) Exaggerating the economic importance of the tobacco industry; (2) Manipulating and affecting the political and legislative process; (3) Funding of Scientists and Researches, generating "pseudo-science"; (4) Discrediting and distort proven scientific information; (5) Disseminate tobacco culture, against tobacco control; (6) Manipulating public opinion to improve the tobacco industry's social image and (7) Political intimidating tobacco control advocators. The routing roadmap, indicators and contents related will be set up based on these strategies of tobacco industry.

Based on the lessons learned over the past 10 years in tracking the tobacco industry, it is found that there are two difficulties although the activities of the tobacco industry generally could be identified. First, it is hard to trace all activities of tobacco industry because of too many activities. Second, some activities are not transparent.

---

[69] Tara Elton-Marshall, Steve Shaowei Xu, Geoffrey T Fong, et al. The lower effectiveness of text-only health warnings in China compared to pictorial health warnings in Malaysia Tob Control 2015;24:iv6–iv13.

[70] World Health Organization, Tobacco industry interference: A global brief, http://apps.who.int/iris/bitstream/10665/70894/1/WHO_NMH_TFI_12.1_eng.pdf.

[71] Think-Tank, Chinese Association of tobacco control, Chinese Preventive Medicine Association, The theme report of World No Tobacco Day in 2012: To disclose and resist the interference of tobacco industry in China. http://www.catcprc.org.cn/upload/file/2012-05/2012%E6%8E%A7%E7%83%9F%E6%8A%A5%E5%91%8A.pdf.

Once it is open to the public, it has already been determined and hard to be corrected.

Take the research on "Low tar low risk cigarette" of tobacco industry researcher Xie JP as an example, Xie won several awards of National Science Technology Award, and he also became the Academician of Chinese Academy of Engineering (CAE) with the pseudo scientific research, which became a scandal of Chinese scientific society. It is a key question why nobody pointed out that Xie' study is a pseudo scientific research during several scientific reviews? If any expert of reviewing group criticizes that the study of low tar low risk has been proved to be a pseudo science, the scientific awards could not be given Xie, and tobacco industry could not gain the success. Based on these lessons, we realized that we should monitor the Tobacco Industry effectively by doing the below things.

First, China tobacco control communities pay more attention to raise awareness of the related government departments and agencies about tobacco control, tobacco products' addictive nature characteristics and their harm to health, as well as tobacco industry' interference for tobacco control policies. Only raising their awareness, the staff will open their eyes to concern the intervention of the tobacco industry.

Second, where have the related information about the tobacco industry' interference come from? It is from media' reporting, from tobacco publication, website, such as official website of STMA, China Tobacco Journal, China Tobacco Society, Chinese Tobacco Science Network; and comprehensive tobacco network, including Chinese Tobacco Market, Oriental Tobacco, China Tobacco Online, as well as provincial tobacco company and tobacco enterprise. Recently, implementing tobacco control policies raised awareness of media reporters and volunteers about tobacco industry interference with tobacco control policies, especially about the social responsibility, tobacco advertising, promoting and sponsorship of tobacco industry, which resulted in that media closely monitored tobacco industry's interfering activities and informed the public.

Third, an important aspect of monitoring tobacco industry was to make tobacco industry transparent, requiring accurate tobacco industry activities' information provided by STMA. The Inter-Ministry Coordination and Steering Committee for Implementation of WHO FCTC should require the tobacco industry to regularly submit information on tobacco production, manufacture, marketing expenditures, revenues or any other activity, including lobbying, philanthropy and political contributions.

Besides routine monitor, it is necessary to set up monitoring themes around tobacco control events. For example, when amending the *Advertising Law*, the monitoring priority is what STMA to say and how they to lobby, and to whom to lobby to stop or weaken amending the *Advertising Law*.

It's necessary to set up a team to monitor tobacco industry. A non-governmental organization, Think-Tank Research Center for Health Development, has made important contributions in monitoring tobacco industry's interference. Since 2008, it has published a *Briefing Report on Tobacco Tracking* quarterly, which is the only one report so far for monitoring to monitor tobacco industry in China currently by monitoring tobacco industry website, publications & research, and tobacco advertising, sponsorship & promotion tip-offs by the public, mass media, CDC and other tobacco control organizations.[72]

Currently, there is still a big gap to monitor tobacco industry interference in China. The current monitoring tobacco industry is not systematic, even not timely. WHO suggested that establishing the tobacco industry monitoring centers or observatories address the needs of understanding tobacco industry current and future approaches. It is necessary to set up systematic monitoring tobacco industry on the existing basis.

7.7   Data Access, Sharing

WHO FCTC requires the Parties shall, subject to national law, promote and facilitate the exchange of publicly available scientific, technical, socioeconomic, commercial and legal information, as well as information regarding practices of the tobacco industry and cultivation of tobacco. So data should be made as widely and freely available as possible under the condition of safeguarding the privacy of research participants, and protecting confidential and proprietary data.

WHO established Global Health Observatory (GHO) data (http://www.who.int/gho/about/en/), which collects all country-level data on important NCD related risk factors for its member countries, which includes tobacco use information. The GHO database provides access to an interactive repository of health statistics. The US Centers for Disease Control and Prevention (CDC) also makes smoking & tobacco use survey data and documents for the public use, including questionnaires, survey manuals and datasets for state, national, and international tobacco related surveys. All the information is online (https://www.cdc.gov/tobacco/data_statistics/surveys/index.htm), where survey report and original dataset can be accessed easily.

China is a country of rich data, but the data haven't been put into deserved usage. Data are deposited in different institutions, but they are not shared with anyone outside the institutions. Not sharing data is serious waste of government resources. MOST pointed out that only data sharing among different institutions or different fields could benefit its potential values. Therefore, about in 2003, MOST started Science Data Sharing Program, including more than 6000 database covering most of research fields.[73] China CDC set up the Center for Public Health Data Sharing (CPHDS) (http://www.phseieneedata.cn). Since 2004, Public Health Data Sharing through CPHDS has provided data support to meet the national data sharing strategy requirement, to serve for scientific research and education, and to practice integrating some data sources, including some valuable data sources. These data include infectious diseases, non-communicable disease, vital registration data, behavioral

[72] Li JK. The Exploration of Tobacco Industry Tracking System and Practice. (http://www.docin.com/p-1170939266.html, accessed July 17, 2017).

[73] Fan X, Li XX, Zhang YJ, et al. Discussion on the Public Health Data Sharing Mechanism. Chinese Journal of Public Health Engineering. 2006, 5(2): 113–8.

risk factors and basic information, which covers the whole public health major fields. Tobacco use data embeds in the risk factors module, only with the 1996 National Smoking Prevalence Survey database, 2002 BRFSS survey database and some database for youth survey in 1998. The GATS-China 2010, supported by Bloomberg initiative, has already been shared in the US CDC website, but the CATS2015 haven't been shared now. In addition, other risk factors surveys including tobacco use conducted by China CDC have not been shared in the China CDC and CPHDS websites either.

Therefore, in order to meet the WHO FCTC requirement and realize the tobacco use data sharing, we call for regulation or law for data sharing and its enforcement. Meanwhile, advocacy and dissemination on the concept of data sharing are needed. Also the coverage and depth of data sharing should be expanded with standard data producing procedure. We should explore the new technology and train some high-level data mangers to improve the data sharing service.

7.8   Conclusion

China has conducted national tobacco use surveys in 1984, 1996, 2002, 2010 and 2015 among adults. Although the funding sources varied and the surveillance indicators were not 100% consistent over time, China has updated the surveillance data almost every 5 years with the similar indicators, which were comparable and could describe the trend of current smoking prevalence for Chinese population. The prevalence of tobacco use in Chinese adult did not change a lot over the last 10 years after WHO FCTC came in force in 2005, decreasing around 1%.

The evolution of tobacco surveillance in China was rapid comparing to other health related surveys. The five national adult surveys and 2014 youth surveys provided the trend and distribution of tobacco use at national level, with some information on tobacco control policies implementation provided by the last two surveys.

After China ratified WHO FCTC, it is particular important to monitor the policy implementation. In 2010, by using GATS-China data, the average scores for five policies, including the protect peoples from second-hand smoke, comprehensive banning tobacco advertisement promotion and sponsor, warn about the dangers of tobacco, support for smokers to quit, and increasing tobacco taxation and price was only 37.3 out of 100 points. The surveillance and assessment of implement of tobacco control policies evoked that the whole society pays attention to tobacco control, and the 12th National Economic and Social Development 5 year plan adopted a resolution calling for the "full implementation of banning smoking in public places". This is further illustrated the great impact on policy assessment and these indicators can be used to closely monitor and assess implementing tobacco control policy at national or local levels.

Second, in order to promote smoke-free public places' legislation and introduction of tobacco control programs at local level, there are great needs to conduct tobacco surveys, for both adults and youths, especially for assessment the impact of tobacco control policies and assessment of health impact at the local levels.

Third, at present situation, it is necessary to develop a comprehensive data platform to collect all kinds of monitoring data for tobacco control. The platform should include following indicators (1) tobacco use including prevalence of tobacco use and its health hazards; (2) impact on policy interventions including protecting people from tobacco smoke, offering help to quit tobacco use, warming about the dangers of tobacco, enforcing bans on tobacco advertising, promotion and sponsorship and raising taxes on tobacco; and (3) tobacco industry marketing, promotion and lobbying.

Last, although China conducted five national tobacco surveys, only 2015 survey was supported by the NHFPC through a regular funding. Since Chinese government has recognized the important role of tobacco control and approved WHO FCTC, MOF should allocate regular financial resources to support sustainable tobacco control monitoring and maintaining the operation of the integrated tobacco control monitoring system.

Chapter 8
Protecting China from Secondhand Tobacco Smoke

Quan Gan

Abstract The 1980s saw the burgeoning of local and national smoke-free laws to protect nonsmokers from the harms of tobacco smoke in China. Most of these early laws had loopholes in them in particular allowing designated smoking areas and enforcement was generally poor. More localities passed smoke-free laws in the 2000s following the guidelines of the FCTC and high compliance was achieved in several cities especially in Beijing and Shenzhen. Valuable lessons were learned in pushing for smoke-free initiatives with collective partnership and in ensuring effective implementation through mobilizing political leadership. The momentum generated from these successes failed to expand to the entire country when the first national comprehensive smoke-free law proposal was blocked by the tobacco monopoly. Interference from the tobacco monopoly in smoke-free policy making intensified after the successes in implementation in Beijing and Shenzhen. The power wrangling between tobacco control advocates and the tobacco monopoly in the smoke-free arena and beyond will likely continue both at national and at local level. The engagement of the tobacco monopoly in tobacco control policy making continues to be a major impediment in tobacco control in China. This serious conflict of interest needs to be addressed before any major development in tobacco control policy can be achieved.

Keywords Smoke-free law · SHS · Beijing · Shenzhen · China

Q. Gan
The International Union Against Tuberculosis and Lung Disease, Paris, France
e-mail: qgan@theunion.org

© Springer Nature Singapore Pte Ltd. 2018
G. Yang (ed.), *Tobacco Control in China*,
https://doi.org/10.1007/978-981-10-8315-0_8

8.1   Introduction

Exposure to secondhand smoke (SHS) is a risk factor for a host of diseases among nonsmokers.[1] According to the Global Adults Tobacco Survey in 2010, 72.4% of nonsmokers were regularly exposed to SHS in China.[2] Since the first research paper linking SHS exposure and lung cancer was published in 1981,[3] many studies provided additional evidence on the relationship between SHS exposure and diseases. The 2006 U.S. Surgeon General Report concluded that: (1) SHS causes premature death and disease in children and in adults who do not Smoke; (2) Children exposed to SHS are at an increased risk for sudden infant death syndrome, acute respiratory infections, ear problems, and more severe asthma. Smoking by parents causes respiratory symptoms and slows lung growth in their children; (3) Exposure of adults to SHS has immediate adverse effects on the cardiovascular system and causes coronary heart disease and lung cancer. With accumulating research evidence, policy makers and the public began to realize the need to ban smoking in public places to protect the health of nonsmokers from harms caused by SHS(see Footnote 1). Article 8 of the World Health Organization Framework Convention on Tobacco Control (WHO FCTC) requires that all parties should adopt policies to ban smoking in public places, workplaces, and public transport.[4] The guideline of Article 8 of WHO FCTC further specifies that "There is no safe level of exposure to tobacco smoke … Approaches other than 100% smoke-free environments, including ventilation, air filtration and the use of designated smoking areas … have repeatedly been shown to be ineffective," and that "all people should be protected from exposure to tobacco smoke." In addition, "legislation is necessary … Voluntary smoke-free policies have repeatedly been shown to be ineffective".[5]

8.2   The Pre-FCTC Era of Smoke Free Movement[6]

The late 1980s to1990s saw unprecedented political interest from the government of China in tobacco control.[7] The first legislative effort came when the State Council

---

[1] Office on S, Health. Publications and Reports of the Surgeon General. The Health Consequences of Involuntary Exposure to Tobacco Smoke: A Report of the Surgeon General. Atlanta (GA): Centers for Disease Control and Prevention (US), 2006.

[2] Yang GH, Li Q, Wang CX, et al. Findings from 2010 Global Adult Tobacco Survey: implementation of MPOWER policy in China. Biomedical and environmental sciences: BES 2010;**23**(6):422–9. https://doi.10.1016/s0895-3988(11)60002-0 [published Online First: Epub Date].

[3] Hirayama T. Non-smoking wives of heavy smokers have a higher risk of lung cancer: a study from Japan. British medical journal (Clinical research ed) 1981;**282**(6259):183–5

[4] World Health Organization. WHO Framework Convention on Tobacco Control. In: Organization WH, ed., 2003.

[5] WHO. WHO Framework Convention on Tobacco Control: guidelines for implementation Article 5.3; Article 8; Article 11; Article 13. In: WHO, ed., 2009.

[6] Order of the General Administration of civil aviation of China, Provisions on the prohibition of smoking in civil airports and civil aircraft, No. 71, Dec. 30, 1997, http://sqgk.caac.gov.cn/000014170/200612/t20061220_8557.htm.

[7] FCTC MoHLOoIo. 2007 China Tobacco Control Report, 2007.

adopted the Regulation on Hygiene Management in Public Places in 1987.[8] An implementation guideline of the regulation issued by the former Ministry of Health (MOH) a few years later in 1991[9] (later amended in 2011[10]) banned smoking in 13 types of public venues. In the same year, two other national laws containing smoke-free provisions were adopted. The China Tobacco Monopoly Law required that smoking be banned or restricted in public transport and public places[11] The China Youth Protection Law further banned smoking in venues for the youth such as schools and kindergartens.[12] In 1997, months before the 10th World Conference on Tobacco or Health opened in Beijing, China implemented another national policy that banned smoking in public transport and its waiting areas,[13] including in civil airports and civil aircraft.

Many localities also passed laws in the 1990s and early 2000s to ban smoking in public places. By October 2006, 154 sub-national jurisdictions had passed local ordinances to ban smoking in public places such as hospitals, schools, government offices, public transport and its waiting areas(see Footnote 7). All of these policies were partial bans and most did not require restaurants, bars, and entertainment venues to be completely smoke-free. Some policies did not require penalties and for those that did require, the amount was usually low (see Footnote 7). The focus of these laws was on educating the public to achieve self-enforcement rather than on strong enforcement to deter violations. Very few jurisdictions ever issued any penalties and compliance was usually poor. Despite of this, the momentum generated by these policies was enough to make the tobacco monopoly worried.[14]

A few years after the 10th World Conference on Tobacco or Health was held in Beijing, a joint project on interventions to reduce passive smoking was launched by Peking Union Medical College (PUMC) and Johns Hopkins University in 2003 under the support of the U.S. National Institute of Health Fogarty Center (Fogarty project). Carried out in three provinces in China—Jiangxi, Sichuan, and Henan, then expanded five provinces the project found increase in knowledge level to be linked with higher public support for smoke-free environment in rural areas. The project also identified policy analysis and policy development as a capacity gap at the local level and concluded that support from the national level was needed for local policy changes.[15] The collaborative mechanism between national support and local leadership for tobacco control policy change established by this project continued for many years into after FCTC was implemented in China in 2006.

---

[8] State Council. Regulation on Hygiene Management at Public Places, 1987.

[9] Ministry of Health. Implementation Guideline of Hygiene Management at Public Places, 1991.

[10] Ministry of Health. Implementation Guideline of Hygiene Management at Public Places, 2011.

[11] People's Congress. China Tobacco Monopoly Law, 1991.

[12] People's Congress. China Youth Protection Law, 1991.

[13] National Patriotic Health Campaign Committee, Ministry of Health, Ministry of Railways, et al. Regulation on Smoking Ban on Public Transportation and its Waiting Rooms, 1997.

[14] Muggli ME, Lee K, Gan Q, et al. "Efforts to Reprioritise the Agenda" in China: British American Tobacco's Efforts to Influence Public Policy on Secondhand Smoke in China. PLoS medicine 2008;5(12):1729–69. https://doi.10.1371/journal.pmed.0050251 [published Online First: Epub Date].

[15] Yang G. *The Establishment of Intervention Model and Process Evaluation of Forgarty Project*, 2010.

8.3   Smoke-Free Policies in Post-FCTC Era

8.3.1   Smoke-Free Healthcare Facilities Policy

China's ratification of WHO FCTC in 2005 and implementation in 2006 did not lead to immediate national tobacco control policy changes.[16] It was not until 2009 that the first major national policy was released.[17] The policy, issued by the former MOH, set the goal that half of the healthcare facilities in China should achieve smoke-free status by 2010 and all healthcare facilities by 2011. Behind this initiative was the important collective recognition within the former MOH that physicians and public health doctors should take the lead in controlling smoking. Starting from 2010, a nationwide annual inspection by the former MOH was carried out and performance was ranked by province as an incentive for implementation. Observation of smoking in hospitals decreased from 36.8% in 2010 to 26.9% in 2015,[18] but the goal of all healthcare facilities in China being smoke-free is still yet to be achieved. The former MOH was successful in exploiting administrative measures to pressure local governments in implementation of the policy, however, the policy lacks an enforcement mechanism and penalty measures, which undermined the outcome of compliance.

8.3.2   Smoke-Free Schools Policy

Following the Smoke-free Healthcare Facilities Policy in 2009, the Ministry of Education and the former MOH released a joint directive in 2010 calling for the establishment of smoke-free schools across the nation.[19] The guideline outlined in the directive banned indoor smoking in all schools as well as outdoor smoking on the premises of elementary and middle schools. The directive also lacks an enforcement mechanism and penalties for violations. Implementation was poor and the directive's reliance on self-compliance is reflected in the worrisome observation from the Global Youth Tobacco Survey in 2014, which found that more than half of the students still reported being exposed to SHS at school.[20]

---

[16]Yang G, Hu A. Tobacco Control and the Future of China, 2011.

[17]Ministry of Health. Decision on Smoking Ban across All Healthcare Systems in China in 2011, 2009.

[18]Nan Y, Xi Z, Yang Y, et al. [The 2015 China Adult Tobacco Survey: exposure to second-hand smoke among adults aged 15 and above and their support to policy on banning smoking in public places]. Zhonghua liu xing bing xue za zhi = Zhonghua liuxingbingxue zazhi 2016;**37**(6):810–5. https://doi.10.3760/cma.j.issn.0254-6450.2016.06.014 [published Online First: Epub Date].

[19]Ministry of Education. Recommendation by Ministry of Education and Ministry of Health on Further Strengthening Tobacco Control at Schools, 2010.

[20]Prevention CCfDCa. China Youth Tobacco Survey in 2014, 2014.

8.3.3 Joint Notice on Smoking Ban of Public Officials in Public Places

The smoke-free momentum took an important turn at the end of 2013 when the Joint Notice on Smoking Ban of Public Officials in Public Places was released (hereafter referred to as The Notice).[21] Political implications of The Notice are significant as it was released by two very influential political governing bodies in China—the Office of the Communist Party and the Office of State Council. The Notice prohibited public officials from smoking in public places. In an effort to curb corruption as much as controlling smoking, The Notice also banned the use of cigarettes in business meetings and events, as well as purchasing of cigarettes using government budget, which used to be commonplace. Many saw the release of The Notice as a milestone in tobacco control in China. Although The Notice only applied to public officials, the impact went beyond, largely due to the exemplary role of public officials in society. The Notice was issued in the midst of an anti-corruption campaign launched by the president. The anti-corruption campaign, which came with severe disciplinary measures and was highly effective, covered both corruption control as well as general misconducts by public officials including smoking. However, implementation of The Notice suffered as there have been few proactive actions to promote compliance. The main effort came from the Smoke-free Government Office Program launched by China CDC.[22] The program provides guidance for local governments to issue smoke-free government office policies. Beijing was the first to join and Shanghai and four other provinces followed. Two years after the release of The Notice, a national tobacco survey found that smoking in government office buildings decreased from 59.4% in 2010 to 38.1% in 2015 (see Footnote 18). Although much progress has been achieved since The Notice was issued in 2013, the level of political attention it received waned over time. Same as the Smoke-free Healthcare Facilities Policy and the Smoke-free Schools Directive, the Notice does not have an enforcement mechanism or requires penalties for violations.

8.3.4 Sub-national Smoke-Free Initiatives

The importance of international events in helping push for early city-level smoke-free laws should not be underestimated. Three of the four major city-level smoke-free policies that were adopted between 2008 and 2010 aimed to prepare for international events to be hosted by the cities. Beijing government issued a

---

[21] Office of Central Party, Council. OoS. Notice on Smoking Ban of Public Officials in Public Places, 2013.

[22] National Tobacco Control Office. Smokefree Government Experience Sharing Meeting Held in Qinhuangdao. 2016.

smoke-free policy in 2008 in anticipation of Beijing Olympic; Shanghai passed a smoke-free law in 2010 before the World Expo; and Guangzhou adopted a smoke-free law in 2010 ahead of the Asian Game.[23] All these policies allowed designated smoking rooms, which posed a serious challenge for enforcement (Beijing would close this loophole in 2015 and Shanghai in 2016). What needs to be highlighted in the Guangzhou law is that it banned smoking in offices of government officials for the first time in China. While an early draft allowed smoking in single occupancy offices in government buildings, the local NGO launched a successful media campaign and used public opinions to pressure the People's Congress to close this loophole.[24] This precedent was followed and the advocacy strategy was borrowed by many cities that would pass local smoke-free laws later.[25,26] After 1 year of implementation, the government of Guangzhou quickly realized that very few penalties were collected, mainly because the law required that enforcement officers warn first upon violation and penalty can only be issued if violation is not corrected. Such a requirement undermines the deterrent power of the law. The Guangzhou People's Congress passed an amendment in 2012 and granted enforcement officers the authority to issue penalty upon spotting violations.[27] This proved to be a valuable lesson learned for city-level smoke-free laws that would follow later.[28]

The adoption of WHO FCTC prompted unprecedented international attention to tobacco control (see Footnote 4). One of the changes with long-lasting impact was the donations made by high profile philanthropists including the then New York City Mayor Michael Bloomberg and the Microsoft founder Bill Gates. In 2006, Bloomberg started the "Bloomberg Initiative to Reduce Tobacco Use" and Gates joined in 2008. The two philanthropists made a joint announcement in 2008 pledging $500 million worth of financial commitment to international tobacco control.[29] China was among the countries supported by this initiative. The donation from Bloomberg and Gates proved critical in advancing local smoke-free laws as well as the subsequent national smoke-free law in China.

"Toward a Smoke-free China", the very first major smoke-free project undertaken in China after the WHO FCTC was implemented, was launched by China CDC, PUMC and John Hopkins University in 2007 under the support of the

---

[23] Smokefree Policies and Enforcement in China and around the World. 16th Tobacco Control Annual Conference in China; 2013.

[24] Chen J, Jiang X. Guangzhou: Officer are Reintroduced in Smoking Ban. *Nanfang Daily* 2010.

[25] Li Y. Beijing: Debate Around Whether Smoking Should be Banned in Single Occupancy Offices. *Xinhua News* 2014.

[26] Wang H. Shanghai Tobacco Control Regulation First Review: Smoking Ban in Single Occupancy Offices, How to Enforce? *Shangguan News* 2016.

[27] Anonymous. Guangzhou to Amend Tobacco Control Regulation, Penalties of 50 RMB without Warnings. *China Radio Network* 2012.

[28] Yang J. *Investigative Report on City Level Smoke-free Law Enforcement in China*: China Democratic Law Publisher, 2015.

[29] Bloomberg News. Michael Bloomberg is joining Microsoft co-founder Bill Gates in an effort to curb smoking in developing countries. 2008.

Bloomberg Philanthropies.[30] The initiative could be seen as a continuation of the National Institute of Health Fogarty Center project in 2003–2007. Similar design was adopted to promote public education and local legislation, change social norm of giving gift with cigarette, create smoke-free hospital, school and government building and set up social network of tobacco control at a much larger scale than the previous project. The project lasted for 2 years and spanned across 40 cities and townships in 20 provinces. Recognizing the importance of political commitment for policy change, support was sought from local governments, a model that was replicated by many similar projects later.

Following "Towards a Smoke-free China" was the launch of two major initiatives for local smoke-free policies that have gained tremendous momentum. The two initiatives were launched in parallel in 2010 under the support by Bloomberg Philanthropies and Bill and Melinda Gates Foundation. The Bloomberg initiative in particular signaled a clear direction from the outset toward passing smoke-free laws in major cities in China. This objective was built on the lesson learned from the Fogarty project in China and the United States and other developed countries that smoke-free policies can be more achievable at grass-root level, where interference from the tobacco industry is weaker compared to at the national level.[31] By first engaging these large and strategically important cities, the project would later expand to smaller cities and towns across the country. The focus on passing laws marked a significant shift from education and administrative policy oriented programs in the past. Administrative policies such as the Smoke-free Healthcare Facilities, Smoke-free Schools, and The Notice helped reduce SHS exposure, but the impact was limited as none of these policies require compulsory compliance and penalties for violations. The city-level smoke-free laws that would be passed in the next several years grant enforcement agencies the authority to issue penalties for violations, which would considerably boost law compliance. The clear focus on policy change marked the beginning of an era in China in which tobacco control professionals, most of whom were trained public health doctors, started to engage in policy advocacy efforts. And it also became clear soon that it was not a battle to be fought by public health professionals alone, a broad alliance of legal professionals, media experts, journalist, and economists needed to be built to achieve the goal.[32]

Seven cities were enrolled in the Bloomberg initiative kicked off by a joint partnership between China CDC and the International Union against Tuberculosis and Lung Disease.[33] All are major cities in China, and many are provincial capitals with multi-million populations. Following the lesson learned from the "Toward a Smoke-free China" project, endorsement from the highest leadership in the local govern-

[30]Yang G. *Toward a Smokefree China: Findings from Baseline Survey*. Beijing, China: Peking Union Medical College, 2008.

[31]National Cancer Institute. *State and Local Legislative Action To Reduce Tobacco Use. Smoking and Tobacco Control Monograph No. 11*. Bethesda, MD: U.S. Department of Health and Human Services, National Institutes of Health, National Cancer Institute, 2000.

[32]Wei M. 59 Legal Experts Formed Alliance to Push for Tobacco Control Laws. *New Beijing* 2010.

[33]Sina News. Promoting a Smokefree Environment Project Launched in Beijing. 2010.

ment was obtained. The initiatives adopted the model of close partnership between experts at the national level and local leadership to push for policy change.

In less than 2 years, Harbin became the first among the seven cities to pass a comprehensive smoke-free law in 2011. Tianjin followed a few months later. In the next 2 years Lanzhou and Shenzhen also passed comprehensive smoking bans (see Footnote 23). The game changer came in 2015 when Beijing passed a smoke-free law that banned smoking in all indoor public places, workplaces, and public transport.[34] Not the first city in the nation to pass a 100% smoking ban, but the implications were long-lasting because of Beijing's weight on the political map in China.

In parallel to the Bloomberg initiative, another 17 cities were enrolled by the Think-Tank Health and Development Research Center in 2010 and 2011, under an initiative supported by the Bill and Melinda Gates Foundation.[35,36] Although the initial focus of the initiative was not on city-level smoke-free policies, it did gradually shifted toward policy-oriented advocacy and four cities (Tangshan, Changchun, Anshan, and Qingdao) passed comprehensive smoke-free laws between 2012 and 2014.

Eighteen cities in total passed or amended local smoke-free laws between 2008 and 2016. These cities account for approximately 10% of the population in China (Fig. 8.1). Compared to the smoke-free laws passed in the 1990s, the smoke-free coverage in these laws is more comprehensive, including most indoor public places, workplaces, and public transport. Whether designated smoking rooms should be allowed was always at the center of debate when these policies were reviewed by the local legislatures and governments. In some cities e.g. Hangzhou, Guangzhou, and Tianjin, designated smoking rooms were allowed (see Footnote 23). In other cities e.g. Harbin, Lanzhou, and Shenzhen, a grace period during which smoking rooms were allowed was introduced to allow enforcement to ease into businesses where smoking occurs often e.g. restaurants, bars, and KTVs (see Footnote 23). In cities e.g. Changchun, Tangshan, and Beijing (2015), comprehensive bans in line with WHO FCTC Article 8 and its guidelines were passed. In general, local laws that allow designated smoking rooms tend to be passed earlier and those that ban smoking completely tend to be passed more recently.

Several cities failed to pass a smoke-free law. In Nanchang, Shenyang, and Chongqing, despite efforts to engage in local leaders, political consensus on the smoke-free law was never achieved. Most of the efforts to push for smoke-free laws in these cities took place before the Notice was released in 2013, at which time political environment was less favorable to tobacco control. Support for these cities from the former MOH was also not as strong—such support proved to be crucial later in Beijing and Shanghai. Nonetheless, the most important reason for failing to pass the smoke-free laws in these cities is the low awareness level among both the public and the government officials on the harms of SHS and the need for the law. Although an educational campaign was launched in each city before the legislative process was initiated, the intensity and length of the campaigns were inadequate to influence opinions of the public and political leaders.

---

[34] Jin K. "Beijing Tobacco Control" Applauded by WHO. 2015-11-25;002.

[35] Han J. Seven Cities in China Discussing "Smoke-free Policy" Plan. *Free Asia* 2010.

[36] Shan J. Smokefree Cities—Gates China Tobacco Control Project Launched. *China Daily* 2011.

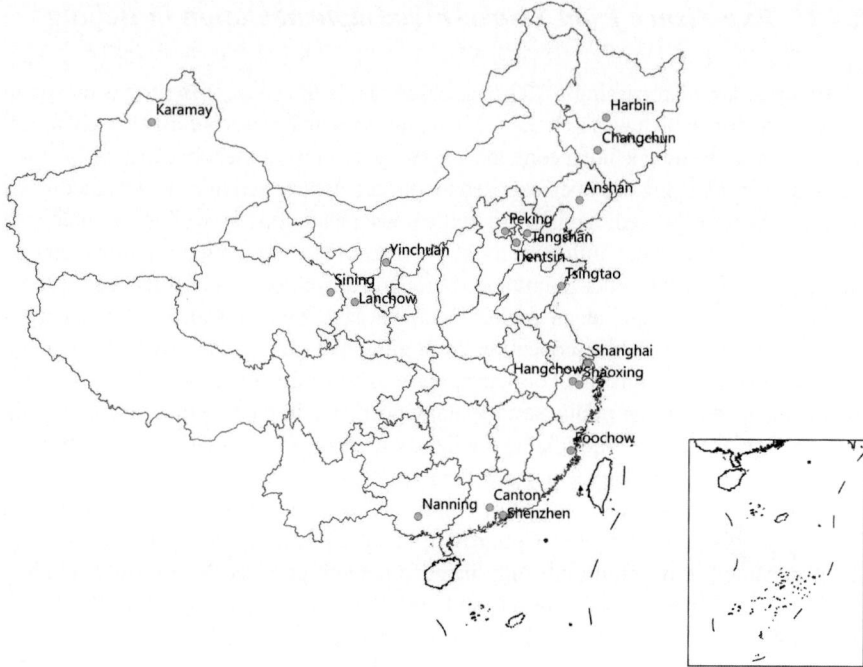

Fig. 8.1 Eighteen cities that have passed smoke-free laws since WHO FCTC was implemented in China in 2006

Probably due to the poor implementation of smoke-free laws passed in the 1990s, interference in policy making process of smoke-free law by the tobacco monopoly was not common before 2015. After the success in implementation from Beijing and Shenzhen, such interference from the tobacco monopoly in smoke-free policy making became more prominent at both sub-national and national levels.

8.4 Implementation of Sub-national Smoke-Free Laws

Quality of implementation varies across cities, with compliance generally being good in Beijing[37] and Shenzhen[38] and continuing to be a challenge in many other cities, particularly in office buildings, restaurants, internet cafes, and KTVs.[39,40]

---

[37] Xiao L, Jiang Y, Liu X, et al. Smoking reduced in urban restaurants: the effect of Beijing Smoking Control Regulation. Tobacco control 2017;**26**(e1):e75–e78. https://doi.10.1136/tobaccocontrol-2016-053026 [published Online First: Epub Date].

[38] Xiong J, Xie W, Yang Y, et al. Implementation of Shenzhen Special Economic Zone Tobacco Control Regulation. China Health Education 2016(05):400–03.

[39] Sun H. After 1 Year of Implementation of Beijing Smokefree Law, Fewer People Light up in Public Places. *Xinhua News* 2016.

[40] Lin Z. Shenzhen 2015 Tobacco Control Law Evaluation. *Shenzhen Evening News* 2016.

8.4.1   Experience from Smoke-Free Implementation in Beijing

More important than passing a 100% smoking ban is the success Beijing achieved in implementation, which was a challenge in many cities that passed similar laws before.[41] The success in Beijing is not a coincidence. Home to most of the tobacco control advocates in China, Beijing has been exposed to tobacco control activities and its media has been regularly sensitized, having fostered a conscious public as well as an interested leadership. International influence is also critical. The growing familiarity among Beijing residents with other countries where smoke-free is the norm has cultivated a desire to live in the same clean environment. Massive media resources were successfully mobilized for public education in Beijing before the law went into effect. Contribution from international organizations was considerable, covering social media, earned media and airing public service announcements in paid media. The leadership by local organizations in mobilizing media resources was particularly exemplary.

Political commitment for enforcement from the Beijing government was high. The commitment to put on an intensive enforcement effort came from top down. The local legislature (People's Congress) put a significant amount of pressure onto the government through monitoring the enforcement process. As a result, the presence of enforcement was ubiquitous and both business owners as well as the public were vigilant. Complaints directed to hotlines were addressed in a timely manner and enforcement officers were dispatched. While most other cities shared the enforcement duty among multiple agencies, Beijing granted the sole enforcement authority to the health inspection team, which has been proved to be effective. As a result, multi-agency coordination was of a much less challenge. Because of the high-level commitment within the Health Bureau, the health inspection team was fully mobilized and prioritized smoke-free inspection. The health inspection team also successfully used high profile cases to maximize the publicity of enforcement.[42] Because smoke-free is an additional enforcement duty for the health inspection agency in Beijing and the amount of work is significant, other enforcement duties were put aside temporarily to give way to smoke-free during the first several months of implementation. To enhance the efficiency and to ensure the sustainability of enforcement, Beijing Tobacco Control Association successfully mobilized the city's volunteers network to pinpoint violations and report to the enforcement agency.

8.4.2   Experience from Smoke-Free Implementation in Shenzhen

Shenzhen's proximity to Hong Kong exposes its residents to many aspects of life in Hong Kong including living in a smoke-free environment. Journalists in Shenzhen are more proactive than in other mainland cities and immediately embraced the

---

[41] Zhan C. Enforcement of Tobacco Control Law, Beijing in Action—Interview with Wang Benjin, Deputy Director of Beijing Health Inspection Institute. China Health Inspection Journal 2015(06):506–08.

[42] Fang F. Golden Leaf Center Fined for Tobacco Control Regulation Violation. *Beijing Daily* 2015.

prospect of a smoke-free city even when the law was still being reviewed at People's Congress. With the support from international NGOs, efforts by local government agencies in mobilizing local media resources were instrumental in raising public awareness.

The Shenzhen government is widely considered to be one of the most efficient among all cities in China. When the smoke-free law took effect in Shenzhen, public confidence about compliance was high. The enforcement agencies took the smoke-free law seriously and a vast number of violators were caught and fined. The local government collaborated with local TV network to broadcast enforcement visits and successfully maximized the publicity of the enforcement effort. One of the highlights of Shenzhen's implementation is that the local legislature established an effective monitoring mechanism to ensure enforcement was adequate to deter violations. Under this mechanism, not only the municipal legislature monitors the performance of the municipal level enforcement agencies, the district legislatures also monitor the district level enforcement agencies. While enforcement duties are mostly carried out by the agencies at the district level, this monitoring mechanism successfully ensures the functioning of the entire enforcement network. Implementation of the law has been a success in general except in internet cafes, where enforcement by the police has been sparse and compliance is low.

8.4.3 Smoke-Free Implementation in General

Many other cities face a more challenging situation when it comes to smoke-free law implementation than Beijing and Shenzhen. It has been shown in many countries around the world that hard-hitting messages are a more effective way of educating the public on tobacco control, however, the acceptance of the concept by local governments takes time, as hard-hitting messages are often deemed unorthodox. In addition, resources mobilized by cities to air PSAs can also be limited. Quite often the free or discounted air time is during off-peak hours.

The role played by journalists in social mobilization in these cities has also been limited due to general lack of interest in tobacco control from the government and its owned media despite trainings organized to equip journalists with the necessary tobacco control knowledge.

One of the most heatedly debated topic in smoke-free enforcement mechanism is the pros and cons of single agency vs. multi-agency enforcement approach. Most cities adopted a multi-agency approach. A coordination mechanism for enforcement has been established in all cities and is usually led by the health authority. In cities where there is consensus for the smoke-free law across enforcement agencies e.g. in Shenzhen, the coordination mechanism functions well. Whereas in cities such consensus is absent, the health authority is usually not equipped with the political influence to coordinate and mobilize the other government agencies. On the other hand, the single agency enforcement model would only need the commitment from the health department director, who is usually supportive of tobacco control. While the traditional remit of the health inspection agency only covers healthcare facilities, to expand its duty to other public places and workplaces does pose a challenge to the capacity of the agency and to the sustainability of the enforcement effort. Increasing the size of the health enforcement team is necessary to match the needed manpower for enforcing smoke-free law.

Facing with limited resources, most cities use the existing enforcement staff and an additional task of smoke-free enforcement is simply added to their duties. However, very often the enforcement teams in these cities are already overloaded with various duties and are reluctant to take on more tasks. An additional challenge is that many city governments are overstaffed and there is a perpetual push for downsizing, which often inevitably affects the already stretched enforcement teams. Only in very rare cases were the city governments able to increase the size of the inspection teams to match the additional workload from enforcing the smoke-free law.[43] When facing with limited enforcement resources, a stepwise approach with priorities set for each stage of enforcement might be a more efficient and effective way of implementation. Priorities of implementation in the initial stage include types of public places and workplaces where SHS level is high and the majority of the public spends most of the time every day, such as restaurants and office buildings. In the second stage of enforcement, resources can be shifted to public places and workplaces with high SHS exposure but less frequented by the general population, such as KTVs, internet cafes, and massage parlors. In the final stage of enforcement where compliance has been achieved in the majority of venues, enforcement should be focused on black spots.

While all of the cities have followed international best practice to require both individual smokers and business owners and managers to be responsible for violations, some city laws require enforcement officers to issue a warning upon violation and a penalty can only be issued if the violation is not corrected. In practice, most people would stop smoking after being warned by the enforcement officer and few penalties are collected. Although it is not the intention of the law to maximize the number of penalties, such requirement does considerably reduce the deterrence of the law. Guangzhou set the precedent by amending its law to give enforcement officers the authority to issue penalty upon violations without the need to issue a warning first. Both Beijing and Shenzhen followed this best practice. All cities with a smoke-free law should be encouraged to remove warning and grant enforcement officers the authority to issue penalty immediately upon violation.

Every enforcement agency has a hotline for the public to submit complaints. As a result, more than one complaint hotline exists in cities where the smoke-free law is enforced by multiple agencies. Some of these hotlines are not easily memorable and often poorly managed. A few cities e.g. Harbin, Shenzhen, Tianjin, and Shanghai took the initiative to integrate the complaint hotlines from each enforcement agency into one memorable line e.g. 12320 and 12345. The central hotline would relay the complaints to each enforcement agency and request feedback for each complaint. This setup allows for the central hotline to monitor the enforcement performance of each agency.

---

[43] Mei X. First Team of 36 Tobacco Control Inspectors in Guangzhou, monthly wages under 3000 RMB. *South China City News* 2015.

The past 5 years have witnessed both successes and challenges in enforcement and implementation of local smoke-free laws in China. Now is the time to promote the lessons learned from successful cases across all sub-national jurisdictions. The central government including NHFPC and China CDC and international organizations need to play an active role in promoting experience sharing through building an information network of cities and provinces where smoke-free laws are implemented or to be passed.

8.5   Smoke-Free Momentum: From Sub-national to National

Eighteen cities in China have passed smoke-free laws between 2008 and 2016, accounting for 10% of the population in the nation. Successes in implementing these smoke-free laws has also been achieved in Beijing and Shenzhen, generating good experiences for other cities to follow. The most recent success in smoke-free came from Shanghai, where a comprehensive smoke-free law was passed in late 2016.[44] Signs indicate that Shanghai is ready to meet the implementation challenges with intensive public educational campaigns and well-mobilized enforcement agencies. Guangzhou, a major city in South China that used to be a leader in smoke-free law a few years ago and now being the only city among the top four first tier cities not yet to have complete smoking ban, seems also ready to catch up. The local government and legislature of Guangzhou have expressed strong interest in amending its current smoke-free law and making it a total smoking ban. Many other cities such as Hangzhou and Xiamen as well as provinces like Guangdong and Yunnan have shown interest in making their jurisdictions smoke-free. A smoke-free ripple effect from Beijing, Shanghai, and Shenzhen has been created.

It was probably not a surprise to the tobacco monopoly that several cities that passed good smoke-free laws between 2010 and 2014 did not achieve full compliance as enforcement has been a challenge in the past. The success in implementation of the smoke-free law in Beijing and Shenzhen may have caught the tobacco monopoly off guard. And it was no surprise when the National Health Family Planning Commission (NHFPC, the former MOH) submitted the proposal for a national smoke-free law, the tobacco monopoly was determined to stop it.

Encouraged by the momentum generated at the sub-national level, NHFPC decided to take the initiative to call for a national smoke-free law. A draft law requiring100% smoke-free public places, workplaces, and public transport was developed in 2013 and was later endorsed by the NHFPC's leadership and submitted to the State Council for further review. The draft included many tobacco control measures besides smoke-free, such as ban of tobacco advertising, promotion, and sponsorship, pictorial warning on cigarette backs, and earmarked tobacco tax to fund tobacco control programs. The commitment from the senior political leadership of

---

[44] Wang X. Shanghai Passed New Tobacco Control Law, Smoking will be Banned in Public Places. *China Daily* 2016.

the government was clear and the legislative proposal quickly moved up to the top tier of the legislative plan, which made it a priority for the State Council in the year. The State Council consulted with several government agencies including the STMA for feedback and it became clear soon that the STMA had very different expectations of what should go into the law. Most of the measures in the proposal other than smoking ban e.g. graphic health warnings, tax raise, total ban on TAPS were requested to be removed by the STMA. Even with the smoking ban, the extent to which smoking should not be allowed was fiercely challenged by the STMA.[45] The STMA wanted designated smoking rooms and areas to be allowed with the argument that if the total ban could not be well implementated, the power of the law would be undermined. The NHFPC held the position that allowing designated smoking rooms would do no help in implementation and after all, China needs to comply with what is required under WHO FCTC, a treaty the country has ratified. The debate has been ongoing for over a year and it seems the difference in positions between the two sides is still too large to be resolved any time soon.

The delay in passing the national smoke-free law has had serious impact on progress in subnational smoke fee initiatives. Since the national smoke-free law initiative was launched by NHFPC in 2014, many subnational governments that were poised to pass local smoke-free laws expressed the unwillingness to proceed. If the local law passed became inconsistent with the national law passed later, then an amendment process would need to be initiated to make the local law congruent.

8.6 Conclusion

Among the many measures recommended by the WHO FCTC to control tobacco use, protecting nonsmokers from the harms of SHS is probably the measure where the most progress has been made in the past 10 years. Significant progress in policy making has been made at both national and sub-national levels. Enduring efforts to make healthcare facilities across the nation on smoke-free have made impressive headway. The Notice to require public officials not to smoke in public places was seen by many as the culmination of years of effort to push for political commitment.

Local smoke-free policies have been the initial tobacco control effort and the real momentum. The policies passed in the 1990s were generally weak, however, with the guidance of the WHO FCTC and the financial support from international philanthropies, those passed post the WHO FCTC were much stronger. Started with Beijing (2008), Guangzhou (2010 and amendment in 2012) and Shanghai (2010), and with the most recent successes in Beijing (2015), Shenzhen (2017), and Shanghai (amendment in 2017), around 10% of the population in China have been protected by the total 18 local smoke-free policies. Attesting to these changes, a

---

[45] Wen L. Tobacco Industry Behind National Smokefree Law Backlash. *Jinghua Times* 2016.

recent national survey found that fewer people were exposed to SHS in their daily lives in 2015 compared to 2010 (see Footnote 18).

Looking in hindsight, among the successes are also challenges in both passing smoke-free policies and implementation. China has made enormous progress in economic development in the past 30 years. Such economic growth comes with costs. The overriding priority on economic development can sometimes lead to deprioritization of public health policy. Such lack of political will coupled with limited resources for education and enforcement have made tobacco control efforts challenging particularly in less developed regions. In cities such as Beijing, Shanghai, and Shenzhen where, after years of fast economic growth, a middle-class majority has emerged. Citizens in these cities are paying more attention to physical health and spiritual well-beings. Such a change of mentality is reflected in the development agenda of the city government, which is more and more pro-health and economic growth is no longer the paramount priority. This has created an opportunity for tobacco control policies, particularly smoke-free, for which the local government and legislature have authority to enact. Such a viable political and social environment is even more critical to the success of implementation of smoke-free policies as high level of commitment across the government system and a supportive and collaborative public are both indispensable. At the national level, there is a growing consensus among both the public and political leadership that it is high time to change the direction of the development agenda toward benefiting the well-being of the citizens, among which health and environment are two prominent issues.

One of the highlights in the past 10 years of tobacco control in China is that several cities such as Beijing and Shenzhen have achieved good compliance in smoke-free law. Many lessons learned from these successful cases should be promoted to other sub-national jurisdictions. Before the law is passed, adequate effort should be dedicated toward educating both policy makers and the public. A supportive government would pave the road for enforcement and a collaborative public would alleviate the pressure from enforcement. Such education should last for longer than a few months and need to be a multi-facet effort. It has been proved that both the single agency and the multi-agency enforcement approach would do the job with a supportive government. However, if there is a lack of consensus among government agencies for the smoke-free law, the single agency approach might be more practical as the health agency can usually ensure that the enforcement be properly carried out. The challenge would be the health agency's limited capacity so resource input is needed. With limited enforcement resources, a stepwise approach can be taken to first tackle the types of venues with the highest exposure of SHS and frequented by the majority of the public. A common mistake made in many cities is that enforcement officers are required to issue a warning before a penalty is given to violators. This would significantly limit the deterrence of the law and should be avoided by granting enforcement officers the authority to issue penalties immediately upon violations. A uniform complaint hotline has proven to be much more efficient than each enforcement agency maintaining a separate line as the uniform hotline can function as a monitoring mechanism of the performance of the enforcement agencies.

Opposition from the tobacco monopoly will continue to be the main challenge in passing any tobacco control policies, particularly for policies at the national level such as the national smoke-free law. As an influential government agency, the STMA can wield power at the negotiation table against the NHFPC when it comes to discussing tobacco control policy making. The fact that WHO FCTC implementation in China is led by the Ministry of Industry and Information Technology, within which the tobacco monopoly is a key department, means that the industry interference in tobacco control policy making will continue until the structure is changed. The tobacco monopoly has grown more vigilant than ever due to the impact of recent tobacco control successes in smoke-free laws in Beijing and Shenzhen and tax raise in 2015. While continuing to push for tobacco control policy making, the community need to ponder upon an approach to addressing the issue of interference from the tobacco monopoly. This is a fundamental conflict of interest that needs to be resolved for further progress in tobacco control policy making to be made.

Chapter 9
Support for Smokers to Quit

Gonghuan Yang

Abstract In this chapter we review how to implement Article14 of WHO FCTC assisting smokers to quit tobacco use in China. In 2015, the currently smokers run up to 315 million, only 18% ever smokers gave up smoking, but proportion of taking action to quit (quitter and relapse maker) was increasing over 50%, which revealed the tremendous and increasing demand for smoking cessation in China. Chinese government has supported the popularization and establishment of cessation clinics and hotlines, introduced simple smoking cessation intervention techniques, updated guidance in cessation clinics and developed guidance cessation hotline although these strategies and measures are need to be further improved. However, why a few people visit the smoking cessation clinic in China with great demand for smoking cessation? The fundamental reasons are related to that Chinese government have not integrated tobacco dependence diagnosis, treatment and counseling into their health-care systems, especially into the primary medical service. Also the costs of quitting services and treatment are totally not covered with the medical insurance plan or by public funding or reimbursement schemes. Chinese government should adjust the current cessation strategy and take effective measures on the WHO recommendations approach of offering quit help, to promote cessation of smokers and adequate treatment for tobacco dependence.

Keywords Quit · Smoking cessation · Relapse · Tobacco dependence · Quitting service · China

G. Yang
Institute of Basic Medical Science Chinese Academy of Medical Sciences, School of Basic Medicine Peking Union Medical College, Beijing, China

© Springer Nature Singapore Pte Ltd. 2018
G. Yang (ed.), *Tobacco Control in China*,
https://doi.org/10.1007/978-981-10-8315-0_9

9.1   Introduction

1988 Surgeon General Report recognized that nicotine, the principal pharmacological agent of tobacco, is a powerfully addictive drug. ***"Cigarettes and other forms of tobacco are addictive", "Nicotine is the drug in tobacco that causes addiction", "The pharmacological and behavioral processes that determine tobacco addiction are similar to those that determine addiction to drugs such as heroin and cocaine"***.[1] The terms nicotine dependence and nicotine addiction were taken to be scientifically equivalent as they refer to a situation in which nicotine unreasonably controls behavior. Quitting tobacco is not easy as cigarettes and some other products containing tobacco are highly engineered so as to create and maintain dependence.

A lot of studies have reported the benefits of smoking cessation to reduce of mortality and morbidity risks. In general, former smokers live longer than continuing smokers.

The pathogenic mechanism has almost been illuminate, including how carcinogen, such as benzo[*a*]pyrene and tobacco-specific nitrosamines in cigarette smoke impair the immune system and cause the kind of cellular damage that leads to lung cancer and in carcinomas of the organs. Smoking cessation reduces the inhalation of these carcinogens, reducing the pathogenic processes leading to cancer.[2] In general, "after 10 years cessation, the risk of lung cancer falls to about half that of a smoker and the risk of cancer of the mouth, throat, esophagus, bladder, cervix, and pancreas also decreases."[3]

Smoking increases the risk of morbidity of cardiovascular disease including coronary heart disease, hypertensive heart disease, stroke and peripheral vascular diseases. The main components of cigarette smoke causing cardiovascular disease are oxidizing chemicals, nicotine, carbon monoxide, and particulate matter. These materials strengthen lipid peroxidation, arising chronic inflammation, speeding up endothelial dysfunction, oxidation of low-density lipoprotein, and platelet activation, then increasing thrombosis, and causing myocardial infarction, sudden death, and stroke, nephropathy, macro-vascular and micro-vascular complications, and so on. It is important that there is a non-liner dose response between exposure to tobacco smoke and cardiovascular risk.[4] That means the obvious increase of cardio-

---

[1] US Department of Health and Human Services. The health consequences of smoking. Nicotine addiction. A report of the Surgeon General. Washington, DC: US Government Printing Office; 1988.

[2] U.S. Department of Health and Human Services. *How Tobacco Smoke Causes Disease: The Biology and Behavioral Basis for Smoking-Attributable Disease: A Report of the Surgeon General.* Atlanta, GA: U.S. Department of Health and Human Services, Centers for Disease Control and Prevention, National Center for Chronic Disease Prevention and Health Promotion, Office on Smoking and Health, 2010. Chapter 5.

[3] World Health Organization, Fact sheet about health benefits of smoking cessation, http://www. who.int/tobacco/quitting/benefits/en/.

[4] U.S. Department of Health and Human Services. *How Tobacco Smoke Causes Disease: The Biology and Behavioral Basis for Smoking-Attributable Disease: A Report of the Surgeon General.* Atlanta, GA: U.S. Department of Health and Human Services, Centers for Disease Control and

vascular risk when smoking a few cigarettes per day or occasional cigarette smoking, and exposure SHS. The effect of smoking cessation on cardiovascular disease is immediate, i.e. "set up a pole and see its shadow—to get instant results": "After quitting within 20 min, smoker's heart rate and blood pressure drop", "after 12 hours, the carbon monoxide level in smoker's blood drops to normal", "after 2–12 weeks, smoker's circulation improves and their lung function increases".[5] With the extension of smoking cessation time, the risk of cardiovascular disease caused by smoking will gradually decrease. "After 1 year, the risk of coronary heart disease of quitter is about half that of a smoker's"; "after quitting 5 to 15 years, their stroke risk is reduced to that of a nonsmoker"; "after quitting 15 years, the risk of coronary heart disease is that of a nonsmoker's."[6] If people after having a heart attack, quit smoking, their chances of having another heart attack reduce 50%.

When the smokers inhale combustion of cigarette or the other tobacco products directly into their lungs, oxidative stress are triggered; these defenses are overwhelmed by the sustained inhalation of tobacco smoke. In addition, protease-antiprotease imbalance has been shown to increase destructive enzyme activity that reduces the lung's elasticity by damaging its structure and causing emphysema.[7] The structure damage seems not to be repaired, but "coughing and shortness of breath decrease after 1–9 months cessation."[8]

The other health benefits of cessation will not be described in details, such as women who quit before pregnancy or within the first 4 months reduce their risk of having a low birth weight baby, and so on. Although the different studies reported the different size of risk reduction time after cessation with different smoking histories and other components among the study populations, the health benefits of cessation have been consistently demonstrated. Smoking cessation at all ages reduces the risk of premature mortality has a lot of immediate and long-term health benefits with or without smoking-related diseases.[9] In general, benefits of cessation in comparison with those who continued, gain almost 10 years, 9 years, 6 years and 3 years of life expectancy at about 30, 40, 50 and 60 years old, separately.[10] So, helping

Prevention, National Center for Chronic Disease Prevention and Health Promotion, Office on Smoking and Health, 2010. Chapter 6.

[5] World Health Organization, Fact sheet about health benefits of smoking cessation, http://www.who.int/tobacco/quitting/benefits/en/.

[6] World Health Organization, Fact sheet about health benefits of smoking cessation, http://www.who.int/tobacco/quitting/benefits/en/.

[7] U.S. Department of Health and Human Services. *How Tobacco Smoke Causes Disease: The Biology and Behavioral Basis for Smoking-Attributable Disease: A Report of the Surgeon General.* Atlanta, GA: U.S. Department of Health and Human Services, Centers for Disease Control and Prevention, National Center for Chronic Disease Prevention and Health Promotion, Office on Smoking and Health, 2010. Chapter 7.

[8] World Health Organization, Fact sheet about health benefits of smoking cessation, http://www.who.int/tobacco/quitting/benefits/en/.

[9] US Department of Health and Human Services. The health benefits of smoking cessation. A Report of the Surgeon General. Washington, DC: US Government Printing Office; 1990.

[10] World Health Organization, Fact sheet about health benefits of smoking cessation, http://www.who.int/tobacco/quitting/benefits/en/.

current smokers to quit is effective strategy of reducing prevalence of tobacco use, preventing mortality and morbidity of chronic non-communicable diseases.

Before the 1980s the main treatment model for smoking cessation was based on psychological models of behavior modification and hence the treatment was also psychologically-based. Accepting that nicotine is powerfully addictive gave a new perspective to the tobacco use problem.[11] Recognizing that tobacco use is an addiction behavior and explains why people smoke despite the known health risks related to its use.

Withdrawal symptoms are a collection of signs and symptoms caused by abstinence or decrease in the use of a drug to which there has been physiological adaptation. Nicotine withdrawal symptoms are physiological. Their origins are found directly in altered central nervous system neurons.[12] Symptoms occur when nicotine concentration is decreased in smoker's blood. These nicotine withdrawal symptoms, even though they may be severe and incapacitating, are completely relieved within minutes of smoking just one cigarette. Research data suggest that withdrawal symptoms among adolescent smokers are similar to those found in adults with craving, irritability, frustration or anger, anxiety, difficulty concentrating, decreased heart rate, sleep disturbance and increased appetite or weight.[13]

As tobacco addiction is accord with all the characteristics of drug addiction to use repeatedly a substance and to withdrawal difficultly, WHO has classified tobacco dependence as a disorder in major international classifications of diseases with f17.2 of ICD-10 code. Helping to quit tobacco use is a complicated systematic programs with completeness. So *Demand reduction measures concerning tobacco dependence and cessation* is important **Article of WHO FCTC** and *Offer help to quit tobacco use* is important component of the MPOWER of six proven policies introduced by WHO. This chapter discusses how to implement Article14 of WHO FCTC, assisting smokers to quit tobacco use. What is to be successful and to be improved in the future in China.

9.2 Tremendous and Increasing Demand for Smoking Cessation in China

There are huge number of smokers in China. The prevalence of tobacco use in Chinese men is one of the highest in the world. Between 2010 and 2015, smoking prevalence of male aged 15 years was not obvious declined, 52.9% (50.6–55.2%) in 2010 and 52.1% (49.4–54.8%) in 2015, separately. Although the low prevalence in Chinese women, there are about 15 million current smokers. The actual number of

---

[11] Nicotine addiction in Britain. A report of the Tobacco Advisory Group of the Royal College of Physicians. 2000. Chapter 4 pp. 83–106.

[12] Sachs DPL. Tobacco dependence: patho-physiology and treatment. In *Pulmonary Rehabilitation: Guidelines for Success*. 4th edn. 2000. Edited by JE Hodgkin, GL Connors, & BR Cell.

[13] Rojas NL, Killen JD, Haydel KF, *et al.* Nicotine dependence among adolescent smokers. *Archives of Pediatric and Adolescent Medicine* 1998; 152:151–156.

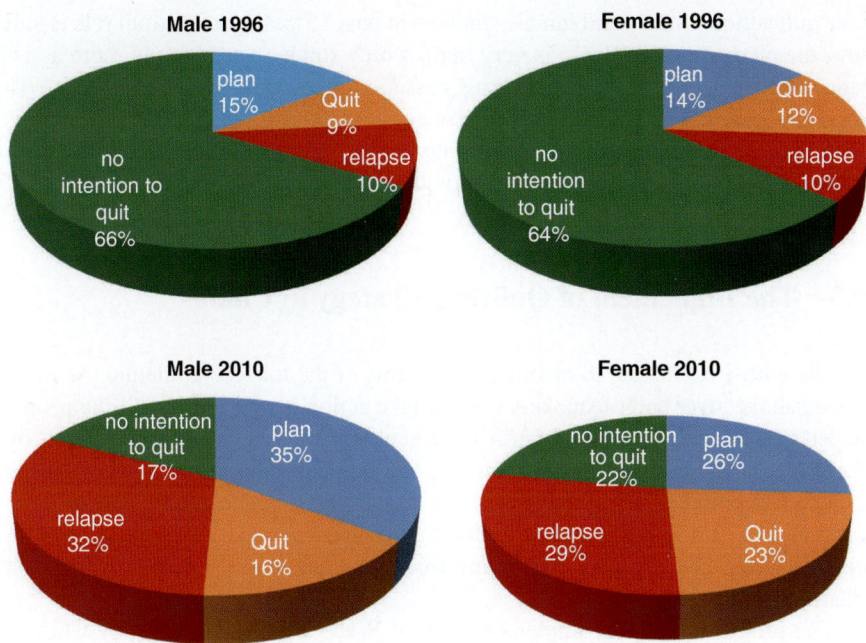

Fig. 9.1 Distribution of ever smokers at different stages by gender, 1996 and 2010

currently smokers run up to 316 million among more than 1.3 billion population in China in 2015.[14]

In addition, cessation attempt and qui rate of smokers have been slowly increasing in the past 20 years. Two-thirds of ever smokers do not intend to quit smoking in 1996, and this proportion has dropped to about 20% by 2010. Cessation attempt is the beginning of quitting smoking. The percentage of ever smokers who plan to quit increased from 15% in 1996 to 35% in 2010.The increasing percentage in male than that in female. Forty percent of ever smokers with cessation attempt express to quit in the next 12 months, 14% to quit in the next 1 month.[15]

Compared with other countries, very low proportion of ever smokers give up smoking, but the quit rates have slowly been increasing, from 4.1% in 1984, 9.4% in 1996, 11.5% in 2002, 16.9% in 2010 and 17.6% in 2005.

However, the proportion of relapse increased over 20%, from 10% in 1996 to 32% in 2010, which just is the reason of the low success quit rate in China. The quitter or relapse smoker are regards people who takes action to stop smoking. The proportion of taking action to quit was 20% in 1996, but increasing over 50% in 2010. Figure 9.1 indicates that it is successful to promote the cessation attempt and

[14] China CDC *China Adult Tobacco Survey Report.* China (Beijing), edited by Liang XF, People's Medical Publishing House. 2016 [in Chinese].

[15] China CDC, Global Adult Tobacco Survey (GATS), China 2010 Country Report, edited by Yang GH Chinese Sanxia Press, 2011, 11, Beijing.

take quit action of male and female smokers in past 15 years, but the quit rate is still low, the proportion of relapse is very high, which smokers need to get more assistance. A survey on demand for smoking cessation in six cities revealed that 15.67% residents actively asked health workers to get quitting service.[16] In summary, increasing Cessation attempt and quit rate, and the proportion of relapse in China indicate that there are huge room for providing the quitting service.

9.3 The Implement of Quitting Strategy in China

People who are addicted to nicotine are victims of the tobacco epidemic. As mentioned above, over half of smokers want or take action to quit in China. Like people dependent on any addictive drug, it is difficult for most tobacco users to quit by themselves. The basic treatment interventions can help tobacco users who want to quit. WHO pointed that three types of strategies should be included in any tobacco prevention effort: (1) tobacco cessation advice incorporated into primary healthcare services; (2) easily accessible and free quit lines; and (3) access to low-cost pharmacological therapy.[17]

The progress report of implementation of WHO FCTC submitted by Chinese government in 2616 said that Chinese government supported the popularization and establishment of cessation clinics and hotlines, introduced simple smoking cessation intervention techniques, updated guidance in cessation clinics and developed guidance cessation hotline.[18] Here the implementation of these measures is described in practice.

9.3.1 The Very Low Proportion of Smokers Visit the Cessation Clinic

The control of smoking is a priority for all health professionals, advice from healthcare practitioners can greatly increase abstinence rates.[19] The first smoking cessation clinic was set up in Swede in 1956. The smoking cessation clinic includes three part-time professionals (a physician, a nurse, a psychologist), operates with a few,

---

[16] Yang Y, Jiang Y, Yang XL, et al., Survey on Demand for Smoking Cessation in Six Cities, Chinese Journal of Health Education, September 2004, Vol. 20, No. 9, 773–6.

[17] WHO Report on the Global Tobacco Epidemic, 2008: The MPOWER package. Geneva, World Health Organization, 2008.

[18] FCTC, Implementation Database, China Mainland 2016 report, Submission Date: April, 26, 2016 http://apps.who.int/fctc/implementation/database/parties/China.

[19] Fiore MC. *Treating tobacco use and dependence: a public health service clinical practice guideline*. Rockville, MD, U.S. Department of Health and Human Services, press briefing, 27 June 2000 (http://www.surgeongeneral.gov/tobacco/mf062700.htm, accessed 16 December 2007).

cheap technical instruments and uses an simple and effective way to treat tobacco use and dependence. The smoking cessation clinic provides strengthen treatments to smokers with awareness to quit, ensuring a higher success rate, but also treats "difficult" patients. Any district authority can start a clinic because it is a "low resource-low budget" structure.[20] However, it is possible that running cost of smoking cessation clinics located in the senior hospital is increasing.

The first cessation clinic in China was set up at Beijing Chao Yang hospital (a municipal hospital) in 1996, and 22 hospitals have established a smoking cessation clinics later in Beijing. These cessation clinics generally have been set up in senior hospitals in Tianjin, Shanghai and so on after 2000. However, most smoking cessation clinics have been closed as no patients. For example, there were only 3 clinics, other 21 clinics were closed in Beijing. The final clinic of Tianjin were closed in 2004. With WHO FCTC came into force, China government strengthened tobacco control, many cities have set up a smoking cessation clinics, and the other cities are also actively preparing to set up clinics under the support of the government.[21] However, media reports in Beijing, Shanghai, Xi'an, Chongqing, Fuzhou, and Guangzhou mentioned that only 1–2 patients per week per hospital sought assistance in these cessation clinics. Based on a survey,[22] a total of 94 smoking cessation clinics were still in operation in 2014, in which 51% belonged to the department of respiratory diseases in senior hospitals. Averagely, there were 3.24 doctors or nurses in each clinic, and the average weekly clinic admission was 6.92 smokers in recent months. Since 2014, under the support of central government' finances, a new enthusiasm of setting up smoking cessation clinics in hospital started to run. As of December 2016, the smoking cessation clinics were set up in 256 hospitals, and helped about 15,000 smokers to quit. The program drive the development of smoking cessation clinics and improve the capacity of the medical staff' to providing quit consulting.[23]

How about the effect of quitting in these clinics? A face to face interview to 398 smokers visited in ten senior hospitals of Beijing indicated that 1 month average quit rate of these smokers was above 50% (the paper did not report how many smokers visit the clinics).[24] Among the smokers surveyed, 48% were aware of cessation clinics and 21.9% would go to clinics if they want to stop smoking. The smokers didn't choose clinics as they didn't believe tobacco dependence was a disease. 256 cessation clinic is obviously insufficient compared to half with cessation attempt among 300 million current smokers. However, there are 1 or 2 smokers averagely

[20] Nardini S. The smoking cessation clinic. Monaldi Arch Chest Dis. 2000 Dec;55(6):495–501.

[21] Wu X, Yang Y ad Jiang Y, Development and progress of smoking cessation clinic in China, Health Research, 38, 50–52, 2009.

[22] Wang LL, Shen Y, Jiang Y, et al, Survey on the current status of smoking cessation clinics in China, Chin J Epidemiol, September 2015, Vol. 36, No. 9 P 917–920.

[23] Chinese Association of Preventive Medicine, Research Report to promote tobacco control legislation (Inter report).

[24] Wang LL, Shen Y, JIang Y et al, Investigation and analysis on current status of smoking cessation clinics in China, Chin J Epidemiol, September 2015, Vol. 36, No. 9, 917–20.

per week each clinic.[25,26,27] Assessment from China CDC revealed that the average annual number of patients with smoking cessation in each clinic was less than 100 per year, about 6000–8000 smokers visited the cessation clinic nationwide during 2015–2016.[28]

9.3.2 Quit-Line Needs to Be Further Improving in China

The another important strategy is set up easily accessible and free quit lines, which comprise toll-free phone numbers and waivers of access charges for mobile phone users, as well as qualified staff who can provide quit service for long working time. Quit lines are inexpensive to operate, confidential and easily accessible for smokers with try to quit no matter where they live or what time they call. Quit lines can link to counseling services, and call people back and follow up their progress. Some quit lines have expanded into the Internet, providing more abundant free support materials. The first national smoking quit-line was set up in mainland China in 2004.[29] The national quit-line provides residents in mainland China with free telephone smoking cessation services. Of 8260 callers from December 1, 2009 to May 31, 2012, less than 10 callers average per day. The study included 1049 callers who gave basic information during the call.[30] Of the 1049 live-access callers, 90% counseled about smoking cessation methods or pharmacotherapy. Among the 908 callers identified, most were from Beijing, next from Guangdong Province. The number of incoming calls every month increased 2 times after May 2011, especially the calls steep increases about May 31, the World No Tobacco Day.

   12320 Health hotline was set up in 2005 and update in 2012 by NHFPC (Former Ministry of health).[31,32] The function of 12320 hotline includes consulting,

---

[25] A few people visit smoking cessation clinics in Guangzhou, only up to 7 per day http://www.deqing.gd.cn/zxbs/showNews.asp?ID=7820.

[26] Fujian province:Quit smoking clinic embarrassing: only 30 people visited to quit in six months, http://digi.dnkb.com.cn/dnkb/html/2010-06/01/content_116574.htm.

[27] Only hundreds people visit the smoking cessation clinics for two years in Shaanxi http://dszx.my399.com/html/2010-05/31/content_5702224.htm.

[28] Ma XH, Smoking addiction is a chronic disease, experts call for quitting service into the health insurance Chinese Business News, http://m.yicai.com/news/5227439.html.

[29] Xinhua Website, China's first smoking cessation hotline opened in Beijing Chaoyang Hospital, Capital online, May 26, 2004, http://www.bj.xinhuanet.com/bjpd_sdzx/2004-05/26/content_2205363.htm.

[30] Chen WL, Xiao D, Wang C, et al. Characteristics of Callers Accessing the Tobacco Cessation Quitline in Mainland China, Biomed Environ Sci, 2013; 26(8): 697–701.

[31] Ministry of Health, Notice of the Ministry of health on the opening of the "12320" national public health telephone ([2005] 486), http://www.nhfpc.gov.cn/zwgkzt/pzhgl1/200806/36749.shtml.

[32] Ministry of Health, Notice of the Ministry of health on Further Strengthening the construction of 12320 public health telephone ([2012] 14) http://www.gov.cn/zwgk/2012-03/14/content_2091665.htm.

complaining and reporting, suggestion, hospital reservation and telephone survey, and so on.[33] At present, 12320' service covered 28 provinces, municipalities and autonomous with more than one billion population in China. From 2009 to 2013, 5.71 million public calls were accepted, 3.69 million calls were for counseling. The number of calls were 2.27 million in 2013, which increased 75.13% compared with 2012. It is 12320 that really a good carrier for the smoking cessation Hotline, but there are no more information as quit line. For example, how about working time of 12320? How many call related to quit smoking? Have these operators been received any training course for advice service for smoking cessation? Are they eligible for smoking cessation counseling? Beijing 12320 calls back the smoker and provides counseling of smoking cessation in a systematic manner.[34] However, capacity for assistance to quit is need to further promote by providing systematic and professional training course and new online-mentors. The online services should supplement with new online-mentors. It is just beginning for quit hotline in China.

9.3.3 Accessibility and Affordability of Pharmaceutical Products for the Treatment of Tobacco Dependence

Nicotine is the principal addictive component in tobacco, it is the primary factor in continued and compulsive tobacco use, which is the basis for using nicotine replacement therapy to support cessation. Nicotine replacement therapy was developed in Sweden during the 1970s. Since then a range of delivery vehicles have been introduced, including nicotine chewing gum, transdermal patch, oral inhaler, nasal spray and sublingual tablet. In addition developed medications such as bupropion and varenicline have higher quit rates than a nicotine replacement medicine.[35] Nicotine replacement therapy is generally used as a non prescription drug, usually available over-the-counter, while other medications are often prescribed by doctor. At present, nicotine patch and nicotine chewing gum as non-prescription drugs, and Bupropion Hydrochloride Sustained Release Tablets and varenicline as prescription drugs have been approved to listing by China Food and Drug Administration (CFDA). However, these drugs are available only in a few large cities, such as Beijing, Shanghai and Guangzhou. The proportions of those using smoking cessation medications were very low, only 3.3%.[36] The proportion were higher in young smokers and those with high education levels.

---

[33] 12320 health hotline, http://www.12320.gov.cn/qg12320wz/index_en.shtml.

[34] Beijing Public Health and Family Planning Hotline, http://www.bj12320.org/News/kyindex?id=215.

[35] Jorenby, D.E., Leischow, S.J., Nides, M.A., Rennard, S.I., Johnston, J.A., Hughes, A.R., Smith, S., Muramoto, M.L., Daughton, D.M, Doan, K., Fiore, M.C., Baker, T.B. A controlled trial of sustained-release bupropion, a nicotine patch, or both for smoking cessation. *The New England Journal of Medicine* 340: 685–691, 1999.

[36] China CDC, Global Adult Tobacco Survey (GATS), China 2010 Country Report, San Xia Press, Beijing, 2012.

9.3.4   Not Enough Personalized Advices from Health Professionals About Quitting

All health-care workers should take the initiative to provide smoking cessation advice. It is the basic responsibility of health-care workers. Also, advice from health-care practitioners seem to have a significant impact on promoting smoker' quit attempt. The measure, as a basic cessation intervention, can magnify their effect predominantly on improving long-term success, to greatly increase cessation rates.[37] There is no extra-cost as health-care worker only give quit advice in their health service programs.

2010 Global Adults Tobacco Survey—China report[38] found that 40.8% were asked if they smoked and 33.9% received cessation advice among smokers who visited a health care provider during the previous 12 months, only 23.1% for women. The younger the smokers was, the lower the percentage received advise of smoking cessation, 26.6% for smokers aged 25–44, and 17.7% for smokers aged 15–24. The percentage of smoker' received cessation advice from physician was average increased 20%, up to 58.2% in 2015, especially for younger smokers, 51.3% for smokers aged 25–44, and 46.1% for smokers aged 15–24. But there is still a lot of room for development.

More information was provided by special survey. The survey on the capacity of providing smoking cessation services among 39,248 Chinese physicians in 96 sites of different levels hospitals (province, city, and county) of 31 provinces (autonomous region, municipality) and Xinjiang Production and Construction Corps was carried out during 2008.[39] The survey revealed that 45.2% physicians reported usually or often to ask patients about the smoking conditions, and 59.1% of the physicians always provide smoking cessation suggestion to the smoking patients, only 2.4% provided smoking cessation medication to patients. Actively providing smoking cessation advices was associated with areas, the level of hospital and department that the physician working at, as well as the gender, their education, smoking conditions and the knowledge about tobacco harms. The proportion of giving quit suggestion of health worker at county hospital was lowest, the higher from community health service center. In general, the physicians' consciousness of controlling smoking are still absent and the capabilities of providing smoking cessation services need to be further improved.

---

[37] WHO, *WHO Report on the Global Tobacco Epidemic, 2008: The MPOWER package.* Geneva, World Health Organization, 2008.

[38] China CDC, Global Adult Tobacco Survey: China 2010 Country Report, edited by Yang GH, China San Xia Press, Nov. 2011 Beijing.

[39] Wu X, Yang Y, Jiang Y, et al., Study on Abilities of Smoking Cessation Services and its Associated Factors among Chinese Physicians, Chin J Prev Contr Chron Dis, August 2010, Vol. 18, No. 4.

9.3.5 The Poor Capacity of Tobacco Control in Health Professionals

In China, awareness and capacity for tobacco control among health-care workers are very weak. At present, the current smoking rate of male health professionals is still up to 43%.[40] Over the past few years, the rate of male health worker is not any changed. Medical professional training only involve the most basic knowledge of the treatment of tobacco dependence, and many health professionals do not understand tobacco control as a part of their job. Recently, some training on tobacco dependence treatment incorporated into the curricula at the medically schools. Also training programmes on the diagnosis and treatment of tobacco dependence are carried out to improve the consulting capacity of offering help of quit in health worker.[41]

The National Medical Examination Center (NMEC) is an agency of the technical service responsible of organizing the National Medical Licensing Examination for all kinds of specialized professionals, compiling reference Book and database of examination questions, and so on. In 2013, the NMEC compiled the Book "*Medical Professional and Tobacco Control*",[42] and appointed the book a reference book for licensing examination. The action has great effect on improving medical staff's knowledge, awareness and attitude of tobacco control.

The study on assessment found that cessation consulting capacity of health worker is still very poor. A few health professionals received the training course on helping smokers to quit in 96 programs areas, 10.3% were trained to make cessation plan for patient, 6.6% trained on treatment the withdrawal symptoms of quitter, 4.2% were did on using cessation medicine. 68.6% of all health professionals had heard of smoking cessation medicine, only 2.4% used some medicine for patients, 1.0% used NRT, 0.6% used bupropion hydrochloride and varenicline in practice. In addition, 1.2% health professionals used Chinese herbal medicine or acupuncture to treat, although there is not enough evidence for Chinese medicine therapy.[43]

---

[40] China CDC, 2015 Chinese Adult Tobacco Survey Report, edited by Liang XF, People's Health Publishing House, Beijing, 2016.

[41] The national tobacco control training course and Initiative on cessation successfully held in Jiangxi, Yichun, sponsored by NHFPC, May 8, 2017. http://www.sohu.com/a/139146008_159234.

[42] National medical examination center, Medical Professional and Tobacco Control, People' Health Press, Beijing Jan.1, 2013.

[43] Wu X, Yang Y, Jiang Y, et al Study on Abilities of Smoking Cessation Services and its Associated Factors among Chinese Physicians, Chin J Prev Contr Chron Dis, August 2010, Vol. 18, No. 4, 346–9.

9.3.6   Clinical Practice Guideline for Treating Tobacco Use and Dependence Is Only a Technical Document

WHO Collaborating Centre for Tobacco Cessation and Respiratory Diseases Prevention, the Tobacco Control Office of China CDC et al. jointly compiled *"Chinese clinical guideline for smoking cessation, 2007"* to guide the health of science, effectively help smokers quit in 2007. *"Chinese clinical guideline for smoking cessation, 2015"*[44] was updated and published referring the new clinical evidence from the results of clinical trials in the field of international smoking cessation, combining the practice of smoking cessation intervention in China.

"*Chinese clinical guideline for smoking cessation, 2015*" clearly pointed that tobacco dependence is a chronic condition with f17.2 of ICD-10 code. The guideline describe that the diagnostic criteria, methodology and questionnaire (Fagerström test for nicotine dependence, FTND) of assessment of tobacco dependence severity, as well as and treatment procedures, the process of successful smoking cessation and smoking cessation drugs. 2015 guideline provided the measures for administrative support and management for smoking cessation intervention, smoke free policy, trailing and allocating the professional for quitting, as well as requirement of smoking cessation clinic, and so on.

Compared to the similar guidelines of the other countries, the guideline is only technical documents. It is essential that Chinese clinicians and health care delivery systems (including administrators, insures, and purchasers) have not institutionalized the consistent identification if offering help to quit tobacco smoke should be incorporated into primary medical care system, at least brief treatment (5 A or 5R) should be included the area of primary medical service or basic public health service. So, the Chinese clinical guideline for smoking cessation cannot mention the related policies to ensure treatment of every tobacco user seen in a health care setting.

9.4   The Great Demand for Quit and Fewer Visit the Cessation Clinic

Objectively, the demand for smoking cessation services among Chinese people is very large, at least over 50% current smokers with quitting attempt or relapse need to be support. However, smoking cessation clinics are rarely visited. How to explain this contradictory phenomenon? For the first reason depends on the awareness of the smokers. The smokers do not think smoking addiction as a disease and not intended to seek health care system assistance owing to not enough mass media communication. The second reason may is from supply without matching the quitter's demand, in other word, the smokers attempting to quit not to do enjoying the quitting service with economic or distance and so on. Taking Beijing as an example,

---

[44] **WHO Collaborating Centre for Tobacco Cessation and Respiratory Diseases Prevention**, the tobacco control office of China CDC et al., Chinese clinical guideline for smoking cessation, 2015.

there are 3.99 million smokers in Beijing,[45] 19.8% of smokers (about 800,000 smokers) want to seek assistance the health care service for smoking cessation,[46] but in fact, only 7722 people, less than 1%, go to the hospital to seek help to quit smoking. Obviously, the kind of smoking cessation clinic service does not match the demand of patients, the reasons are as follows.

9.4.1 Quitting Service Not Integrated into Primary Medical Service

Although In 2014, the NHFPC requires that there should be quitting doctor and hotline in smoke-free medical and health institutions at all levels and forms to provide at least brief advice on smoking cessation and a quitting service.[47] In fact, according to *"Outline of national health service system planning"* approved by State Council, the main responsibility of primary health care is to provide the basic public health services such as prevention, health care, health education, family planning and so on, and diagnosis and treatment services of common diseases, frequently occurring diseases, as well as rehabilitation and nursing of some diseases, referral services. List on preventive and treatment of chronic non-communicable diseases includes prevent hypertension, diabetes, cancer, not mentioned quitting service.[48] At present, requirement of quitting service only is from notice on creating free-smoke hospital issued by the Press and Publicity Department of NHFPC.

9.4.2 Quitting Services Without Support of the Medical Insurance Plan

A substantial body of research has revealed that tobacco dependence treatments reduce the general medical cost.[49,50,51] Smoking cessation treatment including from brief clinical advice to specialist delivered intensive programs are not only clini-

---

[45] Beijing Health Education, Findings of Adult Tobacco Survey in Beijing in 2016, Dec. 30, 2016, http://www.bjjkjy.org/html/report/17010340-1.htm.

[46] Yang Y, Jiang Y, Yang XL, et al., Survey on Demand for Smoking Cessation in Six Cities, Chinese Journal of Health Education , September 2004, Vol. 20 , No. 9, 773–6.

[47] The Health and Family Planning Commission. Notice on further strengthening tobacco control and implement WHO FCTC, Feb 7, 2014, No. 8 (2014). http://www.moh.gov.cn/xcs/s3581/201402/6b85ec0e36974e1384843b0b77dd609c.shtml (accessed Oct 7, 2014).

[48] General Office of State Council, *Outline of national health service system planning (2015-2020)*, No. (2015) 14 http://www.gov.cn/zhengce/content/2015-03/30/content_9560.htm.

[49] Fishman PA, Khan ZM, Thompson EE, Curry SJ. Health care costs among smokers, former smokers, and never smokers in an HMO. Health Serv Res. 2003;38(2):733–49.

[50] Fishman PA, Thompson EE, Merikle E, Curry SJ. Changes in health care costs before and after smoking cessation. Nicotine Tob Res. 2006;8(3):393–401.

[51] Martinson BC, O'Connor PJ, Pronk NP, Rolnick SJ. Smoking cessation attempts in relation to prior health care charges: the effect of antecedent smoking-related symptoms? Am J Health Promot. 2003;18(2):125–32.

cally effective but are also extremely cost-effective relative to other common disease prevention and medical treatment, such as the treatment of hypertension and hypercholesterolemia, and preventive screening intervention, such as periodic mammography.[52,53,54,55,56] 78% Parties of WHO FCTC covered the costs of services and treatment in primary health care fully or partially through public funding or reimbursement schemes.[57]

In China, medical reimbursement scope stipulated by provincial governments do not cover quit service and drug, as same as beauty and dental treatments, as they are been to no-disease treatment. In April 2012, the Minister of MOH, Chen Zhu has publicly said, "The smoking cessation counseling and drugs will gradually be included into the basic medical insurance plan, the related cessation medicine will be add to the National Essential Drug List (NEDL) through further medical reform".[58] It triggered a heated public debate. Opposite party deemed that smoking cessation drug cost for one patient was about 3000 RBM. The expenses of cessation medicines of more than 300 million smokers will squeeze originally not wealthy medical insurance funds. Although the representatives of NPC and Members of CPPCC proposed that smoking cessation treatment should be included as paid services in health insurance packages.[59] NHFPC still think that basic medical insurance fund is not enough, cannot pay the costs related to the smoking cessation services at present.[60]

The disease, including cancer, stroke, and coronary heart disease, as well as COPD, et al. related to tobacco use, have been included in health insurance packages in China. Every year, a large number of health insurance funds are spent in the treatment of these diseases related to tobacco use. A substantial body of research evidences and the other countries' experiences have revealed that tobacco dependence treatments are cost-effective and reduce the general medical cost. But there is

---

[52] Parrott S. Godfrey C. Raw M. West R. Mcneill A. for the Health Educational Authority. Guidance for commissioners on the effectiveness of smoking cessation interventions Thorax. 1998; 53 (5 suppl 2) s1–s38.

[53] Crogham IT, Offord KP, Evans RW, et al Cost-effectiveness of treating nicotine dependence; the Mayo Clinic experience, *Mayo Clin Proc* 1997;72:917–924.

[54] Commings SR, Rubin SM, Oster G. The cost-effectiveness of counseling smokers to quit. JAMA. 1989; 261: 75–79.

[55] Plans-Rubio P. Cost-effectiveness of cardiovascular prevention programs in Spain. *Int J Technol Assess Health Care.* 1998; 14: 320–330.

[56] Lightwood JM, Glantz SA. Short-term economic and health benefits of smoking cessation: myocardial infarction and stroke. Circulation. 1997; 96: 1089–1096.

[57] WHO FCTC, 2016 global progress report on implementation of the WHO Framework Convention on Tobacco Control.

[58] Chen Zhu: Smoking cessation drugs to be included in the basic medical insurance, http://www.northnews.cn/2012/0417/752930.shtml.

[59] 2017, Homepage of NPC & CPPCC, Feng Danlong, smoking cessation treatment be included in health insurance packages. http://forum.china.com.cn/thread-6435769-1-1.html.2017.

[60] NHFPC, Response on No. 0347 proposal of the third session of the 12th National Committee of the CPPCC (fiscal and financial category 070) 2012, 12, 12, http://www.moh.gov.cn/zwgkzt/taxx/201512/59ca798dda574fbca82e4c672b5328c6.shtml.

still a long way to go that smoking cessation treatment is included in health insurance packages owing to the complexity of China's health care system and a few study on the cost-effectiveness of help smokers to quit in China.

9.5 Summary and Recommendation

Smoking cessation is a complex process rather than a specific event. For individual, it is repeated process from having attempts to quit smoking, to totally giving up smoking for a long period of time. Reviewing smoking cessation status in 360 million smokers, the quitting proportion of ever smokers was less than 20% in the Chinese population, far behind many countries.

The analysis on Chinese smoking cessation interventions practice show that although government input funds to establish smoking cessation clinics and smoking cessation hotline, but smoking cessation services does not join to primary health care and routine care, smoking cessation clinic mainly located in the senior hospitals, and medical staff rarely get training course on quit smoking. By 2015, more than 40% health workers did not ask whether patients smoke, and a simple advice, and nobody almost visit the smoking cessation clinic in senior hospitals. All smoking cessation service, including simple 5A and 5R smoking cessation programs, and simple smoking cessation drugs are not covered by the health insurance system. In addition, implement of the other tobacco control policies is relatively poor. In such a situation, it is impossible to achieve good results in smoking cessation interventions. It is why are there so many people who want to quit smoking, but few people go to the smoking cessation clinic, few people use smoking cessation drugs. It is also possible to explain that the proportion of Chinese smokers who quit smoking is so high, and that relapse rate is so high and the percentage of successful smoking cessation is rare. China's current approach of offering quit help, from the decision-making ideas, many of the key points are contrary with WHO recommendations.

Based on requirement of Article 14 of WHO FCTC states that "each Party shall develop and disseminate appropriate, comprehensive and integrated guidelines based on scientific evidence and best practices, taking into account national circumstances and priorities, and shall take effective measures to promote cessation of tobacco use and adequate treatment for tobacco dependence", the following recommendations are made for China's strategic planning for smoking cessation.

Firstly, in order to provide quitting service for over 300 million smokers, the total existing health system and resources should be mobilized, all health workers should take care tobacco dependence. Including:

- Incorporate tobacco dependence and cessation into the core curriculum and continuing professional training of medical, dental, nursing, pharmacy and other relevant undergraduate and postgraduate courses and in licensing and certifying examinations. The national medical examination center provided a good example.

- Set and developed the national training standards, and training materials and curriculum;
- Stipulate and train health-care workers to give brief advice according to a simple formula. In 2014, the NHFPC has required medical and health institutions a tall levels to provide at least brief advice on smoking cessation and a quitting service,[61] 2015 survey showed the regulation needs to be further strengthen the implementation.
- Provide an appropriate train to workers and service providers in non health sector about tobacco cessation and tobacco dependence treatment skills.
- Promote smokers among health-care workers to quit, and offer support to them to quit if they need it.

Second, Clinical cessation services should be included into the basic medical care and public health services. Including:

- NHFPC and the government at all levels should integrate tobacco cessation into primary health care, development working process and assessment criteria.
- The smoking cessation clinics are set in the community health service center if possible so as to provide brief smoking cessation intervention program, such as 5A or 5R, give smoking cessation medication as needed.
- The regulating and expanding the established free smoking cessation hotline.
- The international experience has proved that smoking cessation services can reduce the total medical cost, but also the lack of Chinese research, China needs to further accumulate the new evidences.

The third, the effective smoking cessation treatment (drug and counseling) should be in the coverage of the medical insurance plan

- To complete the imbursement standard in detail of smoking cessation services (such as reimbursement for first smoking cessation services), and increasing insurance costs for smokers as appropriate.
- To allocate a certain percentage of the tobacco tax to support smoking cessation services.

To achieve the purpose, especially the first one, the NHFPC and Ministry of Education should associate with various medical professional societies, such as the Chinese Medical Association, Chinese Hospital Association, Chinese Medical Doctor Association, and so on, as well as the leadership of medical colleges and universities, to work together to amend the relevant policies and push implement. It is very important that administrators, insurers, and purchasers of health care delivery can also promote the treatment for tobacco use/nicotine dependence. Administrators can help ensure that institutional changes to promote cessation

---

[61] The Health and Family Planning Commission. Notice on further strengthening tobacco control and implement WHO FCTC, Feb 7, 2014, No.8 (2014). http://www.moh.gov.cn/xcs/s3581/20140 2/6b85ec0e36974e1384843b0b77dd609c.shtml (accessed March 7, 2017).

interventions are systematically and universally implemented. Insurers should make effective treatments a covered benefit, and purchasers should make tobacco use assessment, counseling, and treatment a contractual obligation. In addition, it is important to implement tobacco dependence treatment measures synergistically with other tobacco control measures.

Chapter 10
Tobacco Product Regulation and Tobacco Industry Interference

Hanbing Guo

Abstract China's Tobacco Monopoly Law grants the State Tobacco Monopoly Administration (STMA)/China National Tobacco Corporation (CNTC) power to devise and enact any and all regulations related to tobacco products. Rather than strengthening regulations on the contents of tobacco products, STMA/CNTC has instead launched the "low tar, low harm" campaign, despite the mountain of scientific evidence debunking the claim. As its profits swelled, STMA's chief scientist was rewarded with a prestigious academic title, causing strong public outcry. STMA/CNTC's other efforts in countering tobacco control measures include its forcing the partial adoption of the Guidelines on Articles 9 and 10 of FCTC, thwarting attempts to regulate its use of additives such as Chinese herbal medicines designed to enhance the attractiveness and palatability of tobacco products. STMA/ CNTC does not disclose to the public the contents and emissions of its tobacco products that are harmful to health, and its aggressive campaign of misinformation has caused widespread misperception among the public. Aside from traditional tobacco products, STMA has also been eying for novel products such as e-cigarettes, which are mass-produced in China but remain to be regulated. STMA has done little towards tobacco control and spent more energy maximizing the tobacco industry's profits. In compliance with FCTC Article 5.3, other relevant government agencies, instead of STMA, should be given the authority to regulate tobacco products in China. The international tobacco control community should also be vigilant against interference from the Chinese tobacco industry.

Keywords Regulation of the content of tobacco product · Regulation of tobacco product disclosure · Tobacco industry interference · Chinese style cigarettes · Tobacco Academician · China

H. Guo
International Union Against Tuberculosis and Lung Disease, Paris, France
e-mail: hguo@theunion.org

© Springer Nature Singapore Pte Ltd. 2018
G. Yang (ed.), *Tobacco Control in China*,
https://doi.org/10.1007/978-981-10-8315-0_10

10.1   Introduction

To date, no comprehensive tobacco control law at the national level has been passed in China. The *Law of People's Republic of China on Tobacco Monopoly* (Tobacco Monopoly Law) serves as the backbone for tobacco product regulation and was enacted to "exercise tobacco monopoly administration, organize the production and management of tobacco monopoly commodities in a planned way, improve the quality of tobacco products, safeguard consumers' interests and ensure the national revenue".[1] The Law was passed in 1991 and amended in 2015. It grants the State Tobacco Monopoly Administration (STMA) complete control over virtually all stages of the production, sales, import, export and distribution of tobacco products in China. STMA possesses regulatory powers over China National Tobacco Corporation (CNTC), but they are essentially the same organization: the head of STMA also happens to be the chief executive of CNTC, while the same headquarters in Beijing, the same organizational structure, and even the same website are shared between STMA and CNTC. Therefore this tobacco monopoly entity exists as both a government agency and a corporate enterprise.

Cigarette products in China are produced by the 17 tobacco manufacturers nationwide that are also responsible for developing new products. The products are then purchased by the 33 provincial-level commercial enterprises, known as exclusive "wholesalers" of cigarettes, which then distribute the products to the numerous retailers with monopoly licenses. Presently, each of the 17 manufacturers owns two to three cigarette brands and only produces those specific branded products. Consolidation of CNTC's factory base led the number of cigarette companies to decrease from 185 in 2001 to 30 in 2010, while the number of brands has dropped from 1183 to 90 in 2013.[2] The number of cigarette factories and brands was reduced based on CNTC's strategy to create economies of scale and to enhance CNTC's ability to compete in the international market by focusing production and investment on a limited number of carefully chosen brands.[3] Efficiency in production subsequently increased to a higher level than were possible before within the industry.[4]

As the main goal of the Tobacco Monopoly Law is to maintain the tobacco monopoly, it does not regulate the product in any significant way. To this day, Article 5 of the Tobacco Monopoly Law still states that "[t]he State shall strengthen the scientific research and technical development of tobacco monopoly commodities, so as to improve the quality of tobacco products and reduce the content of tar and other

---

[1] National People's Congress of the People's Republic of China. Law of the People's Republic of China on Tobacco Monopoly, 2015. <http://www.tobacco.gov.cn/html/27/2701/270101/4830381_n.html>.

[2] Tobacco Market, "Zhongguojuanyanpinpaishichangjingzhengfenxi [Analysis of Chinese cigarette brand market competition]." 2014. <http://www.etmoc.com/market/looklist.asp?id=31733>.

[3] Tobacco China. "Chinese tobacco consolidation will stub out 200 brands", 2004. <http://english.tobaccochina.net/english2012/englishnews_info_wh.aspx?id=13882>.

[4] Martin, Andrew. "The Chinese Government Is Getting Rich Selling Cigarettes." *Bloomberg Businessweek*. December 12, 2014. <https://www.bloomberg.com/news/articles/2014-12-12/the-chinese-government-is-getting-rich-selling-cigarettes>.

hazardous ingredients in such products", providing legal justification for the industry to manufacture and market inviting new tobacco products, such as flavored cigarettes and light/low yield cigarettes. The *Regulations for the Implementation of the Tobacco Monopoly Law* stipulates that the State should regulate the tar contents and the major additives in cigarettes and cigars and that "[t]obacco products manufacturers should not use harmful additives and colorants in violation of the related provisions by the State".[5] However, while the STMA has released a list of permissible additives,[6] there is no specification on additives that cannot be used. The tobacco industry's practice of adding flavoring agents and Chinese herbal medicines to tobacco products to increase their attractiveness are therefore perfectly within legal limits. Furthermore, STMA/CNTC has been actively obstructing the implementation of Articles 9 and 10 of the World Health Organization *Framework Convention on Tobacco Control* (FCTC), which concern the regulation and disclosure of the contents of tobacco products. This chapter reviews the status of the manufacture and marketing of tobacco products in China, which reflects the actual state of implementation of FCTC Articles 9 and 10.

10.2   The Battle Over "Low-Tar" Cigarettes

10.2.1   International Consensus on Low-Tar Cigarettes

Since the 1950s, the tobacco industry in the West has been promoting low-tar cigarettes as a healthier alternative to regular cigarettes. Companies designed and produced cigarettes with "light/low/mild" labels which would produce lower tar and nicotine levels when measured by a smoking machine.[7,8] Even though such measurements do not mimic how humans smoke, the companies deliberately used a smoking machine to measure tar and nicotine levels because machine measurements of tar and nicotine were drastically lower than how much smokers actually receive.[9] Companies labeled these cigarettes "potentially reduced-exposure products," and marketed them as safer than regular cigarettes (see Footnote 8).

---

[5] National People's Congress of the People's Republic of China. Regulation on the Implementation of the Law of the People's Republic of China on Tobacco Monopoly (2016 Revision). 2016. <://www.tobacco.gov.cn/html/27/2701/270101/4923724_n.html>.

[6] State Tobacco Monopoly Administration."Guojiayancaozhuanmaijuguanyuyinfayancaotianjiajixukeminglu de tongzhi (2011–278) [STMA Notice on list of permissible tobacco additives (2011-278)]", State Tobacco Monopoly Administration, 2011. <http://www.tobacco.gov.cn/html/27/2701/270111/765336_n.html>.

[7] United States National Cancer Institute. "Risks Associated with Smoking Cigarettes with Low Machine-Measured Yields of Tar and Nicotine". *Smoking and Tobacco Control Monograph 13*. Bethesda: U.S. Department of Health and Human Services, National Institutes of Health, National Cancer Institute, 2001.

[8] United States Institute of Medicine. *Clearing the Smoke: Assessing the Science Base for Tobacco Harm Prevention.* Washington: National Academy Press, 2001.

[9] Judge Kessler Final Opinion. United States v. Philip Morris., Civil Action Number 99-2496 (GK), 2006; <www.tobaccofreekids.org/reports/doj/FinalOpinion.pdf>.

However, extensive research on tar yields and health risks has shown that low-yield cigarettes are just as harmful to health as regular cigarettes (see Footnote 7).[10] As a result, in 2008, the United States Federal Trade Commission (FTC), which had developed the machine testing of cigarettes, recognized the failure of machine testing in providing accurate measurements and revoked their machine testing method.[11]

There is no strong scientific evidence to suggest that lowering tar levels made cigarettes safe, or that smoking low-tar cigarettes led to a decrease in the diseases caused by smoking cigarettes (see Footnote 8). For example, a large-scale 2010 study examined the risk of lung cancer in smokers of medium tar filter cigarettes compared with smokers of low-tar and very low-tar filter cigarettes in more than 900,000 participants over 6 years. Results show that the increase in lung cancer risk is similar in people who smoke medium-tar cigarettes (15–21 mg), low-tar cigarettes (8–14 mg), or very low-tar cigarettes (≤ 7 mg).[12] The evidence shows that irrespective of the changes in tar level over the last several decades, these filtered, low-tar, and "light" variations do not reduce overall disease risk among smokers (see Footnote 7).

Moreover, smoking low-tar cigarettes could lead to smoker compensation, as smokers of low-tar cigarettes tend to draw smoke more deeply into their lungs. A number of studies have revealed that the smoker compensation from smoking low-tar cigarettes could lead to more cases of adenocarcinoma of the lung, a type of malignant tumor affecting the very small airways of the lung that had previously been rare.[13,14,15]

In light of the strong scientific evidence, Article 11 of FCTC requires each of the 181 Parties including China to ensure that terms such as "light," "low-tar" and "mild" do not appear in tobacco product packaging and labeling in order to prevent marketing that is false, misleading, or deceptive.[16]

---

[10] U.S. Department of Health and Human Services. The health consequences of smoking—50 years of progress: A report of the Surgeon General. Atlanta, Georgia: U.S. Department of Health and Human Services, Centers for Disease Control and Prevention, National Center for Chronic Disease Prevention and Health Promotion, Office on Smoking and Health; 2014.

[11] Federal Trade Commission. Press Release: FTC rescinds guidance from 1966 on statements concerning tar and nicotine yields. FTC; 2008 <ftc.gov/opa/2008/11/cigarettetesting.shtm>.

[12] Harris JE, Thun MJ, Mondul AM, Calle EE. Cigarette tar yields in relation to mortality from lung cancer in the cancer prevention study II prospective cohort, 1982-8. *British Medical Journal* 2004;10;328(7431):72.

[13] Stellman SD, Muscat JE, Thompson S, Hoffmann D, Wynder EL. Risk of squamous cell carcinoma and ademocarcinoma of the lung in relation to lifetime filter cigarette smoking. *Cancer* 1997;80(3):382–8.

[14] Russo A, Crosignani P, Franceschi S, Berrino F. Changes in lung cancer histological types in varese cancer registry. *European Journal of Cancer* 1997;33(10):1643–47.

[15] Osann K. Epidemiology of lung cancer. *Current Opinions in Pulmonary Medicine.* 1998;4(4):198–204.

[16] World Health Organization. "Guidelines for implementation of Article 11 of the WHO FCTC", 2008. <http://www.who.int/entity/fctc/guidelines/article_11.pdf?ua=1>.

10.2.2   Fighting Against The Current: STMA's Push for "Harm Reduction" And Low-Tar Cigarettes

While the mountain of scientific evidence on the ineffectiveness of low-tar cigarettes to reduce harm has forced the tobacco industry in the West to shy away from marketing low-tar cigarettes, the situation is very different in China. Chinese cigarette manufacturers have decided to use the same tricks in the playbook and begun marketing low-tar cigarettes in an effort to appeal to consumers concerned about the negative health effects of smoking. Such efforts were even claimed by the industry as measures to implement FCTC in China.[17]

In the past two decades, STMA has launched a nationwide campaign to lower the machine-measured tar level of cigarettes produced in China. By 2002, the average tar content in cigarettes had already been lowered to 14.6 mg.[18] In 2003, STMA adopted the "China Cigarette Science and Technology Outline", making tar and harm reduction the main goal in their research work.[19] The Outline also recommends supplementing the funding of institutes like Zhengzhou Tobacco Research Institute, which later turned out outstanding work in producing low-tar cigarettes. A forum on low-tar and "low-hazard" cigarettes hosted by STMA the following year was attended by researchers from leading scientific institutions such as the Chinese Academy of Sciences, Chinese Academy of Agricultural Sciences, and University of Science and Technology of China.[20] Some mainstream researchers also collaborated with tobacco company researchers to work on tar reduction projects and published papers together to support the industry's "low tar, low harm" campaign.[21]

In 2006, STMA designated the development of "low tar, low harm" cigarettes as one of the priority areas in its "Tobacco Industry Mid- and Long-term Research and Development Plan (2006–2020)"[22] and ordered the phasing out of cigarettes with tar contents above 13 mg in the domestic market.[23] Further order from STMA

---

[17] Yang G. Marketing 'less harmful, low-tar' cigarettes is a key strategy of the industry to counter tobacco control in China. *Tob Control* 2014;23:167–172.

[18] Lei Z, Yang J, Chu G, et al. The past, present and future of cigarette tar reduction in china. *Cigarette Technologies* (In Chinese). 2003;5:29–31.

[19] State Tobacco Monopoly Administration. "China Cigarette Science and Technology Outline". 2003. <http://www.pkulaw.cn/fulltext_form.aspx?Gid=50388&Db=chl>.

[20] Hvistendahl M. Tobacco Scientist's Election Tars Academy's Image. *Science* 2012;335;153–154.

[21] Zhu MX, Yang ZH, Cao ZS, et al. Shennong cuiquyejiangdijuanyanweihaizuoyong de xibaoshengwuxuepingjia [Cellular evaluation of the effect of Shengnong Extract on reducing harm of tobacco], China Tobacco Society 2002 Annual Conference Proceedings. China Academic Journal Publishing House, 1994-2012, http://www.cnki.net.

[22] State Tobacco Monopoly Administration. "Tobacco Industry Mid- and Long-term Research and Development Plan (2006–2020)". 2006. <http://www.tobacco.gov.cn/history_filesystem/07zzcx/ltbj-1.htm>.

[23] Tobacco China Online. "Jianhaijiangjiao: kejichuangxinweizhichiweihuxiaofeizheliyi [Tar and harm reduction: technological innovation for consumer rights]", 2011. <http://www.tobaccochina.com/zt/2011Lowcoke/djnew04.html>.

stipulated that cigarettes with tar contents above 11 mg could no longer be sold after January 1, 2013.[24]

As STMA's tar reduction campaign went on, lower-yield cigarettes began to catch on among Chinese smokers. As a result, the development of "low tar, low harm" cigarettes to target health-conscious consumers became a core strategy for CNTC.[25] CNTC employed a number of tactics such as labeling tar levels on the pack and marketing so-called harm-reduction technologies. Labeling on cigarette packs used to include terms such as "light" or "mild," but since they are in blatant violation of Article 11 of FCTC, STMA came up with countermeasures by using blue or green colors to represent the same meanings. Zhongnanhai (中南海), one of the most famous cigarette brands in China, offers a slew of low-tar options ranging from 1 to 10 mg in tar content. The brand claims to use Chinese herbs and nanotechnology to reduce the harms of smoking.[26] Similarly, Changbaishan (长白山)'s reduced-harm products include both a low-tar series and cigarettes with ginseng, a plant seen as having medicinal qualities (see Footnote 23).

Following STMA's call to double the sale of "low-tar" cigarettes to 80 billion cigarettes in 2011, tobacco companies began to develop and manufacture low-tar cigarettes at a frantic pace. As of 2014, 35 brands marketed a low-tar series, of which 28 are major brands, meaning that all of the major brands in the Chinese tobacco market have a low-tar line.[27]

The invention of the low-tar cigarettes injected new life into the flaccid cigarette market. Cigarette sales in China had declined in the 1990s, but since the launch of the "low tar, low harm" campaign by STMA, low-tar cigarette sales grew rapidly. In China, sales of low-tar cigarettes, which can cost as much as three times the high-tar brands, increased by an average of 93% annually from 2008 to 2011, which dwarfs the 3.3% growth rate for all cigarettes sales.[28]

---

[24] State Tobacco Monopoly Administration. "Guojiayancaozhuanmaijuguanyutiaozhengjuanyanhe jiaoyouzuigaoxianliang de tongzhi (2012) 148 [STMA notice on promoting to improve risk of cigarettes by further reducing tar content (2012) 148]". 2012. <http://www.mofcom.gov.cn/aarticle/b/g/201206/20120608163450.html>.

[25] Jiang CK. Annual Meeting on Tobacco, 2010. <http://www.tobaccochina.com/news/China/highlight/20101/20101206213_392774.shtml>.

[26] Tobacco China Online. "Zhongnanhai: qiangtandijiaohunhexingjuanyanshichang [Zhongnanhai: expanding into the low-tar market]", 2004. <http://www.tobaccochina.com/zt/2004pandian/pinpai_con18.htm>.

[27] Tobacco China Online."2014 nian 1-5 yuefendijiaoyoujuanyanchanxiaoxingshi [Trend of Low tar cigarette manufacture and sales for Jan-May 2015]", 2014. <http://tobaccochina.com/news/China/data/20147/2014710145749_630521.shtml>.

[28] China National Tobacco Corporation."2011 nianquanguodijiaoyoujuanyanfazhanzhuangkuang [National development of low-tar cigarettes in 2011]", Eastern Tobacco, March 15, 2012. <http://www.eastobacco.com/dfycb/201203/t20120315_238958.html>.

10.2.3 Scientific Evidence Against Chinese Low-Tar Cigarettes

Most studies on Chinese low-tar and herbal cigarettes are sponsored by STMA/ CNTC or carried out by industry researchers.[29,30] The safety of cigarettes was evaluated only through basic chemical analysis of tobacco smoke collected using the aforementioned, already delegitimized US FTC method. Or in other cases, toxicological studies were only performed on animals, not humans, failing to use internationally recognized approaches to health risk evaluations.[31] None of these studies provided any evidence that low-tar cigarettes were actually less harmful to health and less addictive than regular cigarettes (see Footnote 17).

More encouragingly, independent research not supported by the tobacco industry has produced evidence that refutes the "low harm" claim. One study compared the levels of nicotine metabolites and tobacco smoke carcinogens present in the urine between low-tar and regular cigarette users in Shanghai, China. The results reaffirmed the findings from previous Western studies and found that people smoking cigarettes with lower machine-measured tar yields had similar levels of nicotine metabolites and carcinogens in their urine as those smoking regular cigarettes. More strikingly, even though smokers of low-tar cigarettes smoked fewer cigarettes per day, urine concentrations of tobacco-specific nitrosamines (a group of carcinogens) were in fact higher in smokers of lower tar than higher tar cigarettes.[32] Another study compared the levels of nicotine metabolites and carcinogens in urine samples between regular cigarette users and Chinese herbal cigarette users and also found no difference.[33]

A recent study compared the cigarette design in samples of Chinese cigarettes between 2009 and 2012, and found that rather than the change in levels of tar and nicotine as claimed by CNTC, the only cigarette design feature that significantly changed over time was ventilation. Given the substantial evidence that increasing filter ventilation does not reduce actual tobacco exposure and uptake, the use of ventilation to decrease tar, nicotine and carbon monoxide emissions can only create a false perception among smokers that "light/low" tar cigarettes are healthier. Unfortunately, as a result of CNTC's "low tar, low harm" campaign, Chinese

---

[29] Liu XZ. Pernicious effect on the tobacco control from harm reduction of cigarette by tobacco industry, F426.8;R193, 2009; China Center for Disease Control and Prevention. <http://cdmd.cnki.com.cn/Article/CDMD-84501-2009203572.htm>.

[30] Gan Q and Glantz SA. Relationship between the Chinese tobacco industry and academic institutions in China. *Tob Control* 2011; 20(1): 12–19.

[31] IOM (Institute of Medicine). 2012. *Scientific Standards for Studies on Modified Risk Tobacco Products.* Washington, DC: The National Academies Press.

[32] Gan Q, Lu W, Xu J, et al. Chinese 'low-tar' cigarettes do not deliver lower levels of nicotine and carcinogens. *Tobacco Control* 2010;19:374–379.

[33] Gan Q, Yang J, Benowitz NL, et al. Chinese 'herbal' cigarettes are as carcinogenic and addictive as regular cigarettes. *Cancer Epidemiol Biomarkers Prev* 2009;18:3497–501.

smokers that are increasingly aware of the harms of smoking may well fall into the marketing trap by switching to low-tar cigarettes rather than quitting.[34]

It is worth pointing out that even tobacco industry research has produced results that contradict their own "low harm" claim. A study conducted by an industry researcher indicated that the level of tar of cigarette smoke in each brand of cigarettes was not correlated with the levels of carcinogens, and that the levels of certain carcinogens such as benzo(a)pyrene and nitrosamine in some low-tar cigarettes were even higher than in regular cigarettes.[35]

While research done on Chinese cigarettes has been limited, the results are consistent with findings from the international scientific community: strategies to alter cigarettes by adding filters and Chinese herbal medicines and lowering tar content do not lower the amount of nicotine and carcinogens present in the human body after smoking.

10.2.4   *"The Killer Academician"*

Despite the abovementioned evidence demonstrating that low-tar cigarettes are not "low harm" cigarettes, STMA was keen on pushing forward the "low tar, low harm" narrative. The mastermind that provided the supposedly scientific justification and evidence for the false narrative is Xie Jianping, director of the Zhengzhou Tobacco Research Institute, an official research institute under STMA.

His major accomplishments include devising a hazard index of cigarette smoke using toxicological indicators[36] and adding Chinese medicine and reducing tar levels in tobacco products, arguing that those measures would render the products less harmful. According to his hazard index research, the hazard level of newly-produced cigarettes had been decreasing year after year.[37] The hazard index lent the "low tar, low harm" campaign the appearance of scientific legitimacy that STMA urgently needed. Based on this hazard index, STMA released a list of the seven most harmful chemicals that need to be reduced in cigarettes.[38]

---

[34] Schneller LM, Zwierzchowski BA, Caruso RV, et al. Changes in tar yields and cigarette design in samples of Chinese cigarettes, 2009 and 2012.*Tobacco Control* 2015;24Suppl 4:iv60–3.

[35] Du YM, Xia XZ, Wang YB. The smoke tar and safety of the cigarette. *Chin Tob Sci* 2002;(2):31–4.

[36] Ministry of Science and Technology of the People's Republic of China. "J-41juanyanweihaixingpingjiayukongzhitixijianliji qi yingying [Establishment and Application of A Cigarette Harm Evaluation and Control Framework]", 2010. <http://www.most.gov.cn/cxfw/kjjlcx/kjjl2010/201101/t20110117_84334.htm>.

[37] Wang CC. "Zhongshijuanyanjianhaixintansuo—xiezai 'juanyanweihaixingpingjiayukongzhitixijianliji qi yingying' xiangmuhuoguojiakexuejishujinbuerdengjiangzhiji [New exploration of harm reduction in Chinese-style cigarettes – in recognition of the project 'Establishment and Application of A Cigarette Harm Evaluation and Control Framework' winning Second Prize of National Science and Technology Progress Award]", *China Tobacco*, Feb 1, 2011. <http://www.echinatobacco.com/zhongguoyancao/2011-02/01/content_250361.htm>.

[38] Danny. "Qipilangchunyahuode 'jiankangyanwang' chenghao [Qipilang Chunya wins title of 'King of Healthy Tobacco']", June 29, 2013, <http://www.yanpk.com/article-216.html>.

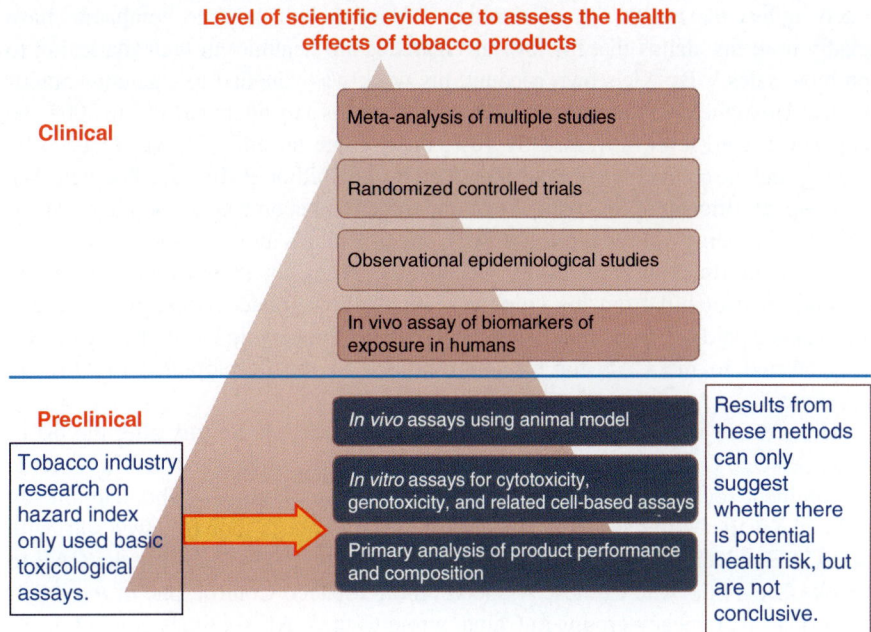

Fig. 10.1 Level of scientific evidence to assess the health effects of tobacco products (based on *Scientific Standards for Studies on Modified Risk Tobacco* Products (see Footnote 31))

The hazard index seemingly provided justification and evidence that the low tar cigarettes were indeed less hazardous, despite the fact that the index only assesses a mere seven chemicals, while at least 250 chemicals in cigarettes are harmful to health, including 69 that are known to cause cancer (see Footnote 10). In addition, the methods used to evaluate the hazard level in Xie's research only included acute toxicity test, *in vitro* cytotoxicity test, Ames test and micronucleus test.[39] Scientific consensus on methods for assessing the health impacts of tobacco products, however, require much stronger evidence which can only be obtained from population-based studies and clinical trials (see Fig. 10.1). Zheng Yuxin, an expert toxicologist with the Chinese Society of Toxicology, has publicly rebuked the validity of the tobacco industry research: results from primary toxicological assays (which contradict much stronger evidence from population-based studies) do not suggest that these modified tobacco products reduce harm to health.[40]

Xie himself has even conceded that current hazard assessment of tobacco products mainly focuses on the levels of a select few chemicals and harmful substances based only on some toxicological experiments and therefore cannot objectively and accu-

[39] Li X, Nie C, Xie JP, et al. *In vitro* Cytotoxicity Assay for Mainstream Cigarette Smoke with Whole Smoke Exposure System[J]. *Tobacco Science & Technology* 2012 (5): 44–47.

[40] Zheng, Yuxin. Speech at "Is 'low tar, low harm' science or scam?" Seminar. Jan 15, 2013. China Tobacco Control Resource Center. <http://www.tcalliance.org.cn/home/?action-viewthread-tid-22191>.

rately reflect the health risk of smoking.[41] Nevertheless, tobacco companies have gladly used his claims that his low-tar cigarettes are healthier in their marketing to promote sales.[42] By Xie's own account, his work was "applied to cigarettes brands such as Huanghelou, Furongwang and Hongtashan. As a result, from 2007 to 2009, the cigarette hazard level decreased by 10%, the average tar emission was reduced by 1.0 mg, and the cumulative revenue increased by 4.86 billion RMB" (see Footnote 41).

Despite criticism of his work, Xie campaigned to become an academician of the Chinese Academy of Engineering (CAE), one of China's most prestigious academic bodies, three times in 2007, 2009, and 2011. Each of his attempts was backed by official sponsorship from his employer, Zhengzhou Tobacco Research Institute. Persistence paid off, as he finally succeeded on his third try. In December 2011, Xie was elected to the CAE for his contributions to the development of "low-tar cigarettes".[43]

His election immediately sparked tremendous backlash. Shortly after the list of newly elected CAE academicians was released on December 8, 2011, Liu Zhifeng, a prominent social critic on the Chinese social media platform Weibo, had already dubbed Xie the "killer academician". More formal protests soon followed suit, with 103 CAE academicians writing a joint letter in May 2012 requesting the CAE to revoke Xie's title. The Chinese Association on Tobacco Control, one of the major anti-tobacco advocacy groups in China, wrote to the CAE six times voicing major objections: Xie's work on so-called harm reduction was no more than a marketing ploy used by the tobacco industry, hence he should be stripped of his title for the sake of scientific integrity. Then seven health associations demanded in a joint letter to the CAE in March 2013 that Xie's work be reevaluated and his membership be revoked (see Footnote 42).

While actions have yet to be taken to remove Xie's title, the CAE has relented a little under pressure and eliminated the Department of Tobacco Science and Engineering, which means the CAE would stop admitting members from the tobacco industry in the future (see Footnote 42). Another sign of progress is that Xie's election had at least generated strong public uproar. When Xie's mentor Zhu Zunquan was also elected to the CAE in 1997, becoming the first to represent the tobacco industry in the academic body, there was virtually no public objection (see Footnote 43). The change in public opinion mirrors increased public awareness of tobacco control. Unfortunately, these progresses seem minor in light of the fact that Xie has continued to use the prestige of his title as Academician to promote the "low tar, low harm" narrative for the tobacco industry. The "killer academician" incident is a major disgrace for China's scientific community.

---

[41] Wu, Yiqun. Speech at "Is 'low tar, low harm' science or scam?" Seminar. Jan 15, 2013. China Tobacco Control Resource Center. <http://www.tcalliance.org.cn/home/?action-viewthread-tid-22191>.

[42] "Fall of the killer academician". *Global Times*. March 27, 2013. <http://www.globaltimes.cn/content/771137.shtml>.

[43] Shan, Juan. "Tobacco scientist uproar flares". *China Daily*. December 16, 2011. <http://usa.chinadaily.com.cn/epaper/2011-12/16/content_14277674.htm>.

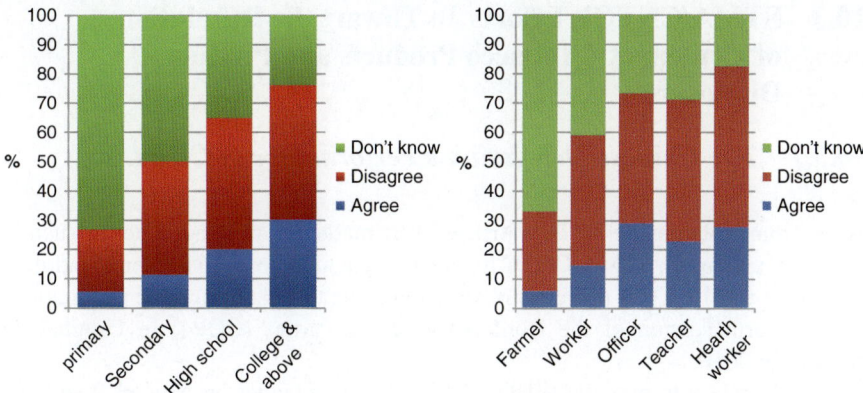

Fig. 10.2 Responses to "Do you agree that low tar cigarettes are as harmful as regular cigarettes?" by education level and occupation. Source: Yang GH Marketing 'less harmful, low-tar' cigarettes is a key strategy of the industry to counter tobacco control in China, Tobacco Control l 2014;23:167–172 Figure 3 and 4

10.2.5   Damage Done To Public Perception

Xie's work and the aggressive marketing campaign for low-tar cigarettes that followed had persisted in China for years, leading to long-term damage to public perception. Many were led to believe that "low tar" equaled "low harm". Concerning results from the 2010 Global Adult Tobacco Survey (GATS) and the 2013–2014 China City Adult Tobacco Survey both show that many Chinese adults falsely believed that low-tar cigarettes are less harmful than regular cigarettes.[44,45] The GATS survey revealed an especially alarming picture: only 14% of adults were aware that low tar cigarettes were as harmful to one's health as regular cigarettes, and the level of education of the individual did not seem to help. Adults with a college education or higher were more than twice as likely to have misconceptions about low-tar cigarettes as those with a primary school education or less. Medical professionals (57%) and teachers seemed most misled by the false marketing (Fig. 10.2).

It is likely that the well-educated segment, including medical professionals and teachers, has easier access to information (and misinformation) from marketing campaigns and tends to be more health-conscious, which unfortunately makes them more susceptible to the health benefit claims made by the tobacco industry. The tobacco industry's powerful propaganda highlights the importance for tobacco control advocates to combat the industry's campaign of misinformation.

[44] GATS China. Global Adult Tobacco Survey: China 2010 Country Report. 2010. <http://www.wpro.who.int/internet/files/chn/gats_china_report_en.pdf>.

[45] China CDC, Report of China City Adult Tobacco Survey 2013–14.2015.edited b Liang XF, supported by CDC Foundation, Atlanta, Georgia, USA.

10.3   STMA/CNTC's Efforts To Thwart the Regulation of Contents Of Tobacco Products and Product Disclosure

10.3.1   The Chinese Delegation's Performance at COP4

Aside from violating the FCTC's Article 11 by marketing misleading terms such as "low-tar" cigarettes, STMA/CNTC has also sought to oppose the implementation of Articles 9 and 10. Their power of obstruction came to light during the negotiations of the fourth session of the Conference of the Parties (COP4) in Uruguay in November 2010.

COP4 was set to pass the WHO FCTC draft "Guidelines on Articles 9 and 10" on the regulation of contents of tobacco products and product disclosure. Article 9 of the FCTC addresses testing and measuring the contents and emissions of tobacco products and for the regulation of these contents and emissions. Article 10 deals with measures that require manufacturers and importers of tobacco products to disclose to governmental authorities and the public information about the contents and emissions of tobacco products.[46] The Guidelines to the articles were drafted to assist Parties in meeting their obligations under the Articles. The Guidelines regulate the use of ingredients designed to increase the attractiveness of tobacco products through the addition of flavoring agents and ingredients that claim to be beneficial to health. The Guidelines aim to reduce the attractiveness, addictiveness and overall toxicity of tobacco products.[47]

Such measures made the tobacco industry uneasy. A campaign led by international tobacco industry groups sought to challenge the implementation of Articles 9 and 10.[48] The tobacco industry was heavily represented in several delegations at COP4, including China. China in particular boosted its number of representatives from the STMA in its delegation from two to six this time.[49] The debate during the negotiations was intense, splitting the countries into pro-industry and pro-tobacco control fractions. While in the minority, countries with industry representatives like China were steadfastly pro-industry and fought especially hard by deploying common industry tactics of "delay, dilute, and defeat". The Chinese delegation was also the first to reject the draft Guidelines.[50]

---

[46] World Health Organization. "Articles 9 and 10 WHO Framework Convention on Tobacco Control - Regulation of the contents and disclosures of tobacco products". <http://www.who.int/tobacco/industry/product_regulation/articles_9_10_fctc/en/>.

[47] World Health Organization. "WHO Framework Convention on Tobacco Control. Guidelines for Implementation", 2011. <http://whqlibdoc.who.int/publications/2011/9789241501316_eng.pdf>.

[48] Assunta M. Tobacco industry's ITGA fights FCTC implementation in the Uruguay negotiations. *Tob Control* 2012;21(6):563–8.

[49] World Health Organization. "List of Participants FCTC/COP/4/DIV/1 Rev.1", 2010. <http://apps.who.int/gb/fctc/PDF/cop4/COP4_DIV_Rev1.pdf>.

[50] Wu Yiqun. "2010 FCTC COP4".China Tobacco Control Resource Center. <http://www.360doc.com/content/11/0618/08/128196_127747684.shtml>.

A point of contention centered around the definitions of "attractiveness" and "palatability" mentioned in the Articles 9 and 10 draft Guidelines. Attractiveness was defined as "factors such as taste, smell and other sensory attributes, ease of use, flexibility of the dosing system, cost, reputation or image, assumed risks and benefits, and other characteristics of a product designed to stimulate use".[51] According to the draft Guidelines, ingredients intended to increase the palatability of cigarette products included sugars and sweeteners.

China and other pro-industry countries including the Philippines, Tanzania, and Zambia objected to the inclusion and definitions of the words "attractiveness" and "palatability".[52] The countries led by China contended that the definitions provided in the draft Guidelines were too vague for implementation and not backed by scientific evidence (see Footnote 50). China indicated that since the text as a whole had not been agreed upon, it would be premature to discuss it or approve the draft (see Footnote 52).

China's strong objection was rooted in its history of practices to enhance the attractiveness and palatability of tobacco products. It has long been the STMA's core strategy to counter the ratification of the FCTC by coming up with countermeasures such as attracting consumers with "high aroma, low tar, low harm" products.[53] The key to "high aroma" was to add flavoring agents to various products. The so-called "scientific advancements" in increasing tobacco's attractiveness and palatability have even drawn praise from the president of the Chinese Academy of Engineering.[54] Therefore unsurprisingly, China launched a ferocious attack at COP4.

The pro-industry objection only represented a small minority of the Parties, and the Chinese delegation even admitted that "[i]f the matter were put to a vote, obviously the majority would prevail" (see Footnote 52). But China insisted that FCTC measures are passed by consensus and not by vote. A compromise was eventually reached to label the Guidelines as "Partial" and adopt "Partial Guidelines to Articles 9 and 10". Furthermore, the text "[m]indful of the provisional nature of the guidelines and the need for periodical reassessment in light of the scientific evidence and country experience" was added to the preamble of the Guidelines (see Footnote 51), much to the satisfaction of the Chinese delegation.

---

[51] World Health Organization. "Glossary of Terms Used in the WHO FCTC and Its Instruments". <http://www.who.int/fctc/reporting/en_glossary_final.pdf>.

[52] World Health Organization. *Conference of the Parties to the WHO Framework Convention on Tobacco Control, Fourth Session*. Punta Del Este, Uruguay. 2010. Summary Records of Committees, Pg 43, FCTC/COP/4/REC/3. <http://apps.who.int/gb/fctc/PDF/cop4/FCTC_COP4_REC3-en.pdf>.

[53] Zhou RZ and Cheng YZ, eds., *Research on Counterproposals to WHO Framework Convention on Tobacco Control and Countermeasures to Address its Impacts on Chinese Tobacco*, Beijing, China: Economic Science Press, 2006.

[54] State Tobacco Monopoly Administration. "Zhongguogongchengyuanyuanzhang Zhou Ji kaocha Hubei Zhongyanhuangheloukejiyuan [President of Chinese Academy of Engineering Zhou Ji vists Hubei Tobacco's Huanghelou Science Park]". Aug 27, 2010. <http://www.tobacco.gov.cn/html/54/2821731_n.html>.

The COP4 negotiations present a sobering account of CNTC/STMA's power in joining forces with other international industry groups to influence the negotiations and defeat the adoption of FCTC Articles 9 and 10 Guidelines and Articles 17 and 18 progress report.

10.3.2 Regulation of the Contents and Emissions of Tobacco Products in China

According to the Partial Guidelines to Articles 9 and 10, the following in tobacco products should be regulated: (1) Ingredients used to increase palatability; (2) Ingredients that have coloring properties; (3) Ingredients used to create the impression that products have health benefits; and (4) Ingredients associated with energy and vitality.[55] STMA clearly stated in its "Tobacco Industry Mid- and Long-term Research and Development Plan (2006–2020)" that the industry "needs to reaffirm the development of Chinese-style cigarettes as an industry-wide goal and to strengthen technological innovation, market share, and brand value growth of Chinese-style cigarettes by highlighting their distinctive characteristics". Cigarettes with Chinese herbal medicines are an important component of "Chinese-style cigarettes". In fact, STMA/CNTC has heavily promoted the use of these additives.

The Chinese herbal additive "Shen Nong extract", which was synthesized by Xie Jianping, was one of the first medicinal additives used in Chinese cigarettes. Similarly, Jinsheng cigarettes included ginseng extract, and a Chinese herb called Hongjingtian was used in Huanghelou cigarettes. Although there is no scientific evidence demonstrating the health benefits of these herbal cigarettes, the tobacco industry's technical staff has worked tirelessly in the research and development of these so-called medicinal cigarettes and healthy cigarettes.[56]

Aside from producing cigarettes with additives used to create the impression that they have health benefits, the tobacco industry has also worked on adding flavoring agents to increase the palatability of cigarettes. On March 22, 2012, a research project nominated by STMA entitled "Chinese-Style Cigarettes in Theory and in Application" was shortlisted for the prestigious National Science and Technology Progress Award.[57] The project presented innovative methods to synthesize flavoring agents to enhance the palatability of cigarettes. The news was immediately met with criticism from tobacco control advocates, who stated that it was in violation of the

---

[55]World Health Organization. Partial guidelines for implementation of Articles 9 and 10 of the WHO Framework Convention on Tobacco Control. <http://www.who.int/fctc/guidelines/Decisions9and10.pdf>.

[56]Meng DL and Liu SH. The Development and Application of Herbal Medical Additions to Chinese Cigarettes. *Chinese Tobacco Science* 2006,(3): 19–21.

[57]"30 weiyuanshilianmingfanduizhongshijuanyanruweikejijiang [30 Academicians jointly oppose Chinese-style cigarettes being shortlisted for technology award]".*China Science Daily*. Apr 10, 2012. <http://news.sciencenet.cn/htmlnews/2012/4/262463.shtm>.

Implementation Guidelines to Articles 9 of FCTC. On April 10, 30 academicians from the Chinese Academy of Engineering jointly expressed in an open letter their opposition to the project being shortlisted for the award, pointing out that should the project win the award, not only would it be in violation the FCTC guidelines, but it would also be in violation of China's own *Scientific and Technological Advancement Law* and the *Regulations on National Scientific and Technological Recognitions*, which explicitly prohibit the development and application of research that is harmful to the public interest and to human health. Public rebuke from both tobacco control advocates and the scientific community eventually forced the project to be withdrawn from award consideration. But the fact that such a tobacco industry research project could even be considered for a prestigious award is a stark reminder that there is still a long way to go to fully implement Article 9 of FCTC in China.

10.3.3 Regulation of Tobacco Product Disclosures

Article 10 of FCTC requires manufacturers and importers of tobacco products to disclose to governmental authorities and the public information about the contents and emissions of tobacco products. Comprehensive evaluation of tobacco control policies in multiple countries shows that standardized reporting and disclosure by manufacturers about product design, contents, and emissions would enable regulators to effectively devise standards and regulation guidelines and evaluate the health effects of the products.[58]

Best practices in Brazil and Canada require manufacturers and importers to disclose the level of selected chemicals present in the mainstream and side-stream smoke of tobacco products and the whole product.[59] According to the Guidelines, laboratories used for testing should be independent laboratories that are not owned or controlled, directly or indirectly, by the tobacco industry, and only internationally recognized testing methods should be used.

In China, the public has no access to the information about tobacco products, except for the levels of tar, nicotine and carbon monoxide labeled on cigarette packs. No government agency other than STMA can obtain much information either, and since STMA is also a tobacco company, this act of self-disclosure cannot qualify as disclosing to government authorities. While the "China Tobacco Control Plan (2012–2015)", released in 2012, clearly states that one of its goals was "to establish and improve a system to regulate and disclose the contents of tobacco

---

[58] IARC Working Group on Methods for Evaluating Tobacco Control Policies, Methods for Evaluating Tobacco Control Policies, Tobacco Control Vol 12, International Agency for Research on Cancer, 2008, Lyon.

[59] Richter, AP. Best practices in implementation of Article 9 of the WHO FCTC Case study: Brazil and Canada. National Best Practices Series. WHO Framework Convention on Tobacco Control. 2015.

products",[60] there has hardly been any change in policies and regulations in the ensuing 5 years. On the other hand, the practice of adding flavoring agents and additives to boost the attractiveness of tobacco products in China remains rampant.

10.4 STMA's Plan for Expansion: e-Cigarette Regulation in China

Aside from the regulation of traditional tobacco products, STMA has also been eying for new products on the horizon. One such example is electronic cigarettes (e-cigarettes). Despite the rapid growth of China's e-cigarette industry, regulations on the manufacture, sale, and use of e-cigarettes in China remain absent. The regulation vacuum is very troubling, as access to and public use of e-cigarettes is unrestricted even to children, and manufacturing standards are extremely weak, allowing the market to be flooded with e-liquids of different flavors and with varying quantities of nicotine.[61] In China, e-cigarettes are readily available for purchase, particularly online.[62]

The tobacco industry in China would not miss the opportunity to tap into the profit potential of this novel product. Soon after the WHO issued recommendations for enhanced regulation over e-cigarettes in 2014, the Ministry of Industry and Information Technology, STMA/CNTC's parent agency, organized a conference in the e-cigarette manufacturing hub of Shenzhen, China. The purpose of the conference was not to address the WHO's concerns over e-cigarettes but to devise strategies to help the Chinese tobacco industry cash in on the $3-billion global e-cigarette market.[63]

It is no wonder that the Chinese tobacco industry lusts over the e-cigarette market, as China makes at least 80% of the e-cigarettes in the world (see Footnote 62). With greater public awareness of the harms of smoking and stronger government policies and laws on tobacco control, the industry needed to maintain their profit growth by investing in substitutes for traditional cigarettes. E-cigarettes were the perfect candidate. STMA's official document indicates that their goal is for a certain percentage of their sales to be from novel tobacco products, which include e-cigarettes. In 2015, the chief executive of STMA/CNTC Ling Chengxing delivered

---

[60]Ministry of Industry and Information Technology of the People's Republic of China. "China Tobacco Control Plan (2012-2015)", 2012. <http://www.miit.gov.cn/n1146295/n1146562/n1146650/c3074390/part/3074391.pdf>.

[61]Barboza, David. "China's E-Cigarette Boom Lacks Oversight for Safety". *New York Times*. Dec. 13, 2014; <http://www.nytimes.com/2014/12/14/business/international/chinas-ecigarette-boom-lacks-oversight-for-safety-.html>.

[62]Shan, Juan. "E-cigarette controls considered for safety". *China Daily*. January 7, 2015. <http://www.chinadaily.com.cn/china/2015-01/07/content_19255939.htm>.

[63]Shan, Juan. "Promotion of e-cigarettes should stop". *China Daily*. September 3, 2014. <http://europe.chinadaily.com.cn/opinion/2014-09/03/content_18537764_2.htm>.

an official report that called for the research and development of novel tobacco products such as e-cigarettes.[64]

STMA subsidiaries quickly heeded the call, and their performances did not disappoint. Zhengzhou Tobacco Research Institute, of which Xie Jianping, the aforementioned "killer academician" is the director, had already received a patent for "a type of smokeless electronic cigarette" in as early as 2008 (see Footnote 62). Then in July 2016, STMA issued a press release announcing that Yunnan Tobacco, a subsidiary of CNTC, had successfully manufactured e-cigarettes independently.[65] In September 2016, provincial tobacco company Hunan Tobacco revealed that they had received a total of 187 patents for inventions of novel tobacco products including e-cigarettes.[66]

STMA's research institutions have also published papers drumming up support for the STMA to regulate e-cigarette products. Li Baojiang, a prominent tobacco researcher with the Economic Research Institute of STMA, has argued for e-cigarettes to be regulated as tobacco products in China, as he claims that there is insufficient evidence for e-cigarettes to be labeled as medical/cessation device, while they are very similar to traditional cigarettes both in terms of appearance and of harm to health. Li argues that because STMA already has a mature and comprehensive production and distribution system, STMA should also have authority over the regulation of e-cigarettes.[67] Recently, a paper by the Zhengzhou Tobacco Research Institute compared and summarized the regulations and standards currently implemented by other countries and hoped that the paper would serve as reference for STMA to devise relevant regulations and standards.[68]

From a legal standpoint, e-cigarette regulation does not fall under the jurisdiction of STMA because the tobacco products as defined under the current Tobacco Monopoly Law do not include e-cigarettes. To revise such a national code, STMA would have to provide legal justifications and to draft revisions. In lieu of the complicated process to revise the law, STMA could also lobby for the Supreme People's Court and Supreme People's Procuratorate to issue a new judicial interpretation of

---

[64] E-cigarette Online. "Ling Chengxing: gaoduzhongshidianziyandengxinxingyancaozhipinyanfa [Ling Chengxing: highly value the research and development of novel tobacco products including e-cigarettes]", 2015. <http://news.yanyue.cn/?viewnews-13521>.

[65] Yunnao Tobacco Inc. "Yunnan zhongyanzizhuzuzhuang de shouzhidianziyanxiaxian [Yunnan Tobacco's first independently assembled e-cigarette comes off assembly line]", 2016. <http://www.fjycw.com/News/201607/20160704505417.shtml>.

[66] Tang, Aiping and Liang, Fen. "Hunan yancaochuangxinzhengxianchengguofengshuo [Hunan Tobacco's fruitful innovation]". *Hunan Daily*, Sept 27, 2016. <http://www.tobaccochina.com/qita/20169/201692615466_736996.shtml>.

[67] Li B, A global perspective on electronic cigarette's future development and related controversial and regulatory issues. *Acta Tabacaria Sinica* 2014;20; 2;101–0.

[68] Fan M, Zhao L, Cui H, Guo J, Liu S, Chen L, Liu H. Current situation of electronic cigarette regulation and development of legislation in various countries. *Acta Tabacaria Sinica* 2016;22;6;126–132.

the law.[69] News of a pending judicial interpretation of the Tobacco Monopoly Law was indeed reported by the media in 2013,[70] however no such interpretation has been issued as of 2017.

Extending STMA's regulatory control to e-cigarettes presents a troubling prospect. The STMA's current regulation of tobacco products has been far from satisfactory. As evident in this chapter, the STMA has rarely made efforts towards tobacco control, rather spending more energy actively thwarting tobacco control efforts. Extending this weak tobacco control regime to e-cigarettes should be of grave concern to all tobacco control advocates.

10.5   Concluding Remarks

After the FCTC was ratified in China, the State Council approved the creation of an inter-ministerial tobacco control steering committee in 2008, headed by the Ministry of Industry and Information Technology. STMA is also a member of the committee and responsible for the implementation of Articles 9, 10, and 11 of the FCTC, but it has clearly failed to carry out its responsibilities. Under the Tobacco Monopoly Law, STMA is given power to devise and enact any and all regulations related to tobacco products in China. Because of the duality of STMA/CNTC as the same organization, the entanglement of government supervision and corporate management of production and operation impedes STMA from effectively performing its duty in regulating tobacco products, while enabling it to actively suppress tobacco control measures.

Currently, the main issue surrounding the regulation of tobacco products in China is that the regulator in charge of assessing the harm of tobacco products also happens to be the manufacturer. Unsurprisingly, such a serious conflict of interest has led to the creation of a deeply flawed tobacco smoke hazard index and evaluation framework that completely disregards the need for stronger evidence from population-based research and the fact that existing population-based research thoroughly invalidates STMA/CNTC's tobacco hazard evaluation. Nonetheless, STMA/CNTC has used the hazard index to heavily promote the marketing and sales of "low tar, low harm" cigarettes, even though it is in direct violation of the FCTC to market tobacco products as such. This campaign of misinformation has also led more smokers that are concerned about their health to choose these "low harm" products rather than to quit smoking, consequently causing more people to be exposed to the harms of tobacco.

---

[69] Feldman EA and Chai Yue, "E-Cigarette Regulation in China: The Road Ahead. University of Pennsylvania Law School". Penn Law: Legal Scholarship Repository. 2016.

[70] Jiang, Fenfen. "Niandi Guojia Youwang Chutai Yancao Zhuanmai Sifa Jieshi Han Dianzi Yan [Tobacco Monopoly Law Judicial Interpretation Hopefully To Be Issued by the End of the Year, Which Would Include Electronic Cigarettes]". *Jinling Evening News*, Dec. 4, 2013. <http://js.people.com.cn/html/2013/12/04/272979.html>.

Tobacco products are highly addictive and toxic. The tobacco industry's practice of adding flavoring agents and other enticing additives such as Chinese herbal medicines to tobacco products has only one goal: to attract more people to become addicted to tobacco products. The FCTC requirements on the regulation and disclosure of the contents of tobacco products are effective measures to protect people from the harms of tobacco. But in China, the tobacco industry's "innovation" in developing Chinese-style herbal cigarettes was nearly awarded one of the most prestigious awards in science and technology. Although the research project was eventually withdrawn from award consideration, there are no regulations preventing the tobacco industry from putting these additives in tobacco products, so the practice is still rampant. To strengthen compliance with FCTC, the government should issue restrictions on ingredients that increase the attractiveness and palatability of tobacco products.

FCTC Article 5.3 clearly mandates the need to stop the involvement of tobacco companies in public health policies as one of the most critical tobacco control measures: "In setting and implementing their public health policies with respect to tobacco control, Parties shall act to protect these policies from commercial and other vested interests of the tobacco industry in accordance with national law".[71] STMA cannot continue to act as both the player and the referee in the tobacco industry. Considering that the regulation of novel tobacco products including e-cigarettes remains absent, discussions around that topic could serve as a good starting point to advocate for the transfer of regulatory powers of tobacco products and of the tobacco industry to government agencies that do not have such a glaring conflict of interest with the tobacco industry. To effectively implement the FCTC, the State Food and Drug Administration (SFDA), rather than STMA, should be given the power to regulate all tobacco products by: devising regulatory standards on the contents of tobacco products; instituting the independent laboratory analysis of ingredients of tobacco products and the routine and standardized reporting of product inspection results by tobacco manufacturers; and creating a tobacco product disclosure system and making public all relevant information regarding the contents and emissions of tobacco products. The review and approval for new tobacco products should also be handled by SFDA.

The international tobacco control community should be vigilant against China's state-owned tobacco enterprise. Representatives of China's tobacco industry cannot be allowed to participate in the WHO Tobacco Laboratory Network and the working group of Articles 9 and 10 of FCTC. Only by overcoming tobacco industry interference will China be able to establish a strong and comprehensive regulatory framework to ensure that the contents of tobacco products will be effectively regulated and made known to the public.

---

[71] World Health Organization. "Article 5.3 of WHO Framework Convention on Tobacco Control". <http://www.who.int/fctc/protocol/guidelines/adopted/article_5_3/en/index.html>.

Chapter 11
Health Warnings of Cigarette Package in China

Yiqun Wu and Gonghuan Yang

Abstract Article 11 has formed the basis for international action to communicate the health risks of tobacco use, and requires each Party to implement within 3 years after ratifying the treaty. *The Regulations on Cigarette Packaging and Labeling in the Territories of the People's Republic of China (the Labeling Regulation)* jointly issued and updated by STMA and GAQSIQ in 2008, 2011 and 2016, are the reproduction of STMA' *Research on Counterproposals and Countermeasures* against WHO FCTC. This is a typical case of national public power servicing for the interests of tobacco industry. The cigarette package display and assessment study strongly suggested that the Chinese text-only health warnings on cigarette packages are very low effective. By 2016, 105 Parties adopted the graphic warnings on cigarette packaging, covering 58% of the world's population. China is obviously behind.

To promote implement the Article 11 of WHO FCTC, tobacco control community called for the pictorial warning on the cigarette package by means of research or investigation report, letter of appeal, and so on. The representatives of NPC and members of CPPCC continually submitted their proposals. Tobacco control community carried out the itinerant exhibition of the Pictorial Health Warning from various countries and the others health education activities. However, so far, there has been no sign of improvement as the STMA/CNTC was in charge of implementation of the critical policy. The top priority of tobacco control should ask STMA leave the Steering Committee so as to effective implement Article 11 of WHO FCTC.

Keywords Health warnings · Article 11 of WHO FCTC · Tobacco industry
Tobacco control · China

Y. Wu (✉)
ThinkTank Research Center for Health Development, Beijing, China

G. Yang
The Institute of Basic Medical Science Chinese Academy of Medical Sciences,
School of Basic Medicine Peking Union Medical College, Beijing, China

© Springer Nature Singapore Pte Ltd. 2018   221
G. Yang (ed.), *Tobacco Control in China*,
https://doi.org/10.1007/978-981-10-8315-0_11

11.1 Introduction

Globally, many people don't understand, misunderstand or underestimate the risks for disease and premature death due to tobacco use and SHS exposure.[1] In order to change the current status, to achieve the objectives of the Convention and its protocols and to ensure successful implementation of its provisions, Article 4 of the WHO Framework Convention of Tobacco Control (WHO FCTC) ask Parties to inform every person the health consequences, addictive nature and hazards of mortality owing to tobacco use and SHS exposure. Well-designed health warnings and messages on tobacco product packages have been shown to be a cost-effective means to increase public awareness of the health hazards of tobacco use and to be effective in reducing tobacco consumption.[2] Effective health warnings and messages and other tobacco product packaging and labeling measures are key components of a comprehensive, integrated approach to tobacco control. Article 11 (tobacco packaging and labeling) of WHO FCTC stipulates that each Party shall have the obligation to achieve the global standards of health warnings. The third session of the Conference of the Parties (COP3) approved the guideline for implementation of Article 11.

Article 11 put forward a strong, clear and legally obligatory standards for health warning labels on tobacco packaging. These standards are supported by a lot of sufficient and strong evidences that health warnings encourage tobacco users to quit and help keep young people stay away from tobacco. Article 11 has formed the basis for international action to communicate the health risks of tobacco, and requires all Parties to implement compliant warning labels on all tobacco products sold or otherwise distributed within their jurisdictions within 3 years after entry into force of the treaty for that Party.

Article 11 requires that health warning labels on tobacco package (1) be approved by the competent national authority; (2) should cover 50% or more of the principal pack display areas, but should be no less than 30%; (3) be large, clear, visible and legible; (4) not use misleading terms like "light" and "mild"; (5) be rotated periodically to remain fresh and novel to consumers; (6) display information on relevant constituents and emissions of tobacco products as defined by national authorities; (7) appear in the principal language(s) of the country.

COP3 was held on November 17–22, 2008 in Durban, South Africa. Although Chinese representatives held opposing views,[3] *Guideline for implementation of*

---

[1] Hammond D et al. Effectiveness of cigarette warning labels in informing smokers about the risks of smoking: findings from the International Tobacco Control (ITC) Four Country Survey. *Tobacco Control*, 2006, 15(Suppl. 3):iii19–iii25.

[2] Thrasher JF et al. Smokers' reactions to cigarette package warnings with graphic imagery and with only text: a comparison between Mexico and Canada. *Salud Pública de México*, 2007, 49 (Suppl. 2):S233–S240.

[3] WHO FCTC, RECORDS OF COMMITTEES REPORTS OF COMMITTEES,THIRD SESSION DURBAN, SOUTH AFRICA, 17–22 NOVEMBER 2008, P25, http://apps.who.int/gb/fctc/PDF/cop3/FCTC_COP3_REC3-en.pdf.

Article 11 on Tobacco Control PACKAGING AND LABELLING OF TOBACCO PRODUCTS finally unanimously was adopted by COP3. The purpose of the Article 11 guidelines is to assist Parties in meeting their WHO FCTC obligations and to suggest means by which Parties can increase the effectiveness of their packaging and labeling measures. In order to increase the effectiveness of health warning, Parties should consider warnings on tobacco products that are at the top of the front and back of each package, cover more than 50% of the principal display areas, and are as large as possible. Parties should provide health warning text and messages in bold print using an easily legible font size to enhance visibility with full-color pictures, and two or more sets of rotating warnings with a range of messages, and elicit unfavorable emotions and personalize the warning and messages; and provide advice on cessation and sources for cessation help. It is important that Guideline has developed the effective packaging and labeling restrictions. The guidelines specifically recommend that figures for emission yields not be included on tobacco packages in order to avoid misleading a cigarette is less harmful than another one. WHO recommends that parties use plain generic packaging, limiting the use of logos, brand images and promotional information, and displaying the brand names and product names with a standard color and font style.[4]

In order to promote international cooperation, the COP requested that TFI, in collaboration with the WHO FCTC Convention Secretariat, has established such a database to facilitate sharing of pictorial health warnings and messages among countries and Parties.[5]

The Canadian Cancer Society compiled 5 waves International Status Reports on Cigarette Packaging Health Warnings, and have made an excellent evaluation on implementing of Article 11 of the COP in the World. The report in fifth edition pointed out that there has been tremendous progress internationally in implementing package health warnings, and that many countries have expanded the area of health warnings and increased warning size, more countries have used pictorial warnings, and many countries have completed two, three, four or even more rounds of warnings rotation. It is an irresistible trend to increase the area of graphic health warning, and more and more countries have responded to WHO call: "Get ready for plain packaging".[6]

WHO FCTC was approved by the 17th session of the Standing Committee of the 10th National People's Congress and entry into force in China from 9 January 2006. End of January, 2018 "the Convention" has been in force in China for 12 years. Although the tobacco control circle has been committed to promoting effective health warning, especially pictorial warning placed on the cigarette packages in line with the Convention since 10 years ago, so far, the domestic health warning in cigarette package still do not meet the requirements of "the Convention". In this chapter,

[4] WHO FCTC Guidelines for implementation Article 11, P53.
[5] The health warnings database is freely accessible to the public at: http://www.who.int/tobacco/healthwarningsdatabase/en/index.html.
[6] WHO World No Tobacco Day 2016: Get ready for plain packaging, http://www.who.int/campaigns/no-tobacco-day/2016/event/en.

the fight over the past more than 10 years between tobacco control and tobacco industry to promote the effective implementation of Article 11 of the Convention on the tobacco packaging and labeling has been reviewed in detail.

11.2   Article 11 of Convention: The Strong Resistance of Tobacco Industry and the Weak Performance of Chinese Government

11.2.1   Resistance of Chinese Tobacco Industry to Article 11 of WHO FCTC

In the early period of WHO FCTC negotiations, the State Tobacco Monopoly Agency (STMA) approved a research project on Counterproposals to *the WHO FCTC* and countermeasures to address its impacts on the Chinese tobacco industry (hereafter referenced as *Research on Counterproposals and Countermeasures*),[7] which was published in 2008. The preface clearly explained why to make all efforts against pictorial health warning on the cigarettes packages: "At present, transfer consumption of high-grade expensive cigarette accounted for a large share of total cigarettes consumption. If the cigarettes package is greatly changed (on requirement of Article 11 of the Convention), transfer consumption of the high-grade cigarettes would be rapidly come down or withdrawn from Market, the price of the high-grade cigarettes, as the main source of tobacco industry' gain, would be dropped, and the tobacco industry's profits would be substantially declined".[8] The authors of *Research on Counterproposals and Countermeasures* also pointed out that "It is necessary to pay high important attention on large and striking health warning on the cigarettes package. It is the cigarettes with large and striking health warning that would be hard to be accepted by consumers, as these cigarettes are traditionally essential goods for holidays, parties, celebrations, weddings and other special occasions, which directly affect the tobacco industry' profits".

The study was praised by STMA as a series of coping strategies against WHO FCTC.[9] In order to oppose the implement of Article 11 of the Convention, the research report provided: "The format of packaging warning should be accord with

---

[7] Zhou RZ, Cheng YZ, eds. *Research on Counterproposal to the WHO Framework Convention on Tobacco Control and Address its Impact on the Chinese Tobacco Industry.* Beijing, China: Economic Science Press, 2006:1–3.

[8] Jiang CK. Preamble one: advance research to meet the requirement of decision-making. In: Zhou RZ, Cheng YZ, eds. *Research on Counterproposal to the WHO Framework Convention on Tobacco Control and Address its Impact on the Chinese Tobacco Industry.* Beijing, China: Economic Science Press, 2006 P35.

[9] Department of Science and Education. STMA. No. 06. Summary table of project winning award for science and technology of CNTC, 2008. http://www. tobaccoinfo.com.cn/images/zhxx/szgdgg/Uploadpdf/2009/20090330.doc (accessed 31 Jan 2017).

Chinese traditional cultural values and mass consumption psychology". "China should only perform the minimum requirements of Article 11 within 3 years, that is not less than the visible part of the 30%". "Do not take the pictorial health warning, do not take warning with black frame and white background, and keep color of warning consistent with the original packaging color. The position of warning can be placed flexibly". "The State competent authority should be STMA".

11.2.2   The Regulations on Cigarette Packaging and Labeling in China

On April 2, 2008, the STMA and the General Administration of Quality Supervision, Inspection and Quarantine (GAQSIQ), as a member of the Inter-Ministry Coordination and Steering Committee for Implementation of WHO FCTC (the Steering Committee), jointly released *the Regulations on Cigarette Packaging and Labeling in the Territories of the People's Republic of China (the Labeling Regulation)*.[10] They said that the Labeling regulation was made out based on related requirements of WHO FCTC, Product Quality Law of the People's Republic of China and Law of the People's Republic of China on Tobacco Monopoly. The Labeling Regulation took effect in January 2009 and applied to all domestically produced cigarettes and all foreign imported tobacco products.[11]

Item 3 of the Labeling regulation ask that the health warning messages on the cigarette packaging should be printed in standard Chinese and English. There are two sets of health warning messages:

Group 1 SMOKING IS HARMFUL TO YOUR HEALTH QUIT SMOKING REDUCES HEALTH RISK
Group 2 SMOKING IS HARMFUL TO YOUR HEALTH QUIT SMOKING EARLY IS GOOD FOR YOUR HEALTH

Item 3 of *the labeling Regulation* sets out the two health warnings that will be rotated on Chinese tobacco packages for domestic use, which are similar the old one "smoking is harmful to your health" used before 2008. Also the authorities illustrate their dual components: a warning that smoking is harmful, and encouragement to quit early and thus reduce the risk of those harms eventuating. Item 4 of *the labeling Regulation* requires the warnings to be rotated, while Item 5 notes where they should appear (front and back of packs and cartons) and stipulates that the warning must

---

[10] STMA. GAQSIQ, the domestic regulations on cigarette packaging and labeling in the territories of the People's Republic of China, April 16, 2008. http://www.tobaccochina.com/law/nation/wu/20084/20084153948_297463.shtml (accessed Oct 7, 2014).

[11] STMA. QAQSIQ, the domestic regulations on cigarette packaging and labeling in the territories of the People's Republic of China, April 16, 2008. http://www.tobaccochina.com/law/nation/wu/20084/20084153948_297463.shtml (accessed Oct 7, 2014).

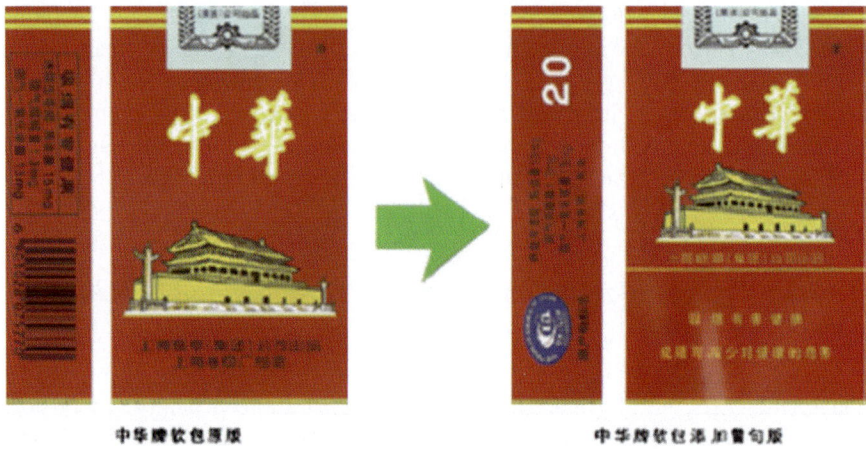

中华牌软包原版   中华牌软包添加警句版

Fig. 11.1 Old style (prior to October 2008) and new style (post October 2008) health warnings on cigarette packages in China

cover at least 30% of the pack or carton surface.[12] Reviewing carefully, the Labeling Regulation is totally different with key requirements of Article 11 of the WHO FCTC.[13,14]

First, the WHO FCTC requires health warnings at least to cover 30% of the display area. However, the Chinese regulations only require a line to mark 30% of the display area, while the warning text itself covers substantially less than 30% of the display area, the font was very small, only 2 mm high. Although the warnings now feature on the front of the pack rather than the side, as was the case previously, the warnings remain less prominent and impactful (Fig. 11.1).

Second, the two sets of information words (as mentioned above), do not provide any specific information on the health risk caused by smoking, such as "Smoking cause lung cancer", "Maternal smoking can endanger the health of the fetus" and so on, which generally adopted by the other countries. Communicating only very general risk information means the content of the Chinese warnings fails to meet WHO FCTC requirements to describe the harmful effects of tobacco use. It is impossible to promote smokers' the knowledge and awareness on hazards of tobacco use with the Chinese warnings. Several studies have concluded that, while smokers report they know the health hazards of tobacco, few truly appreciate the specific harm

---

[12] The State Tobacco Monopoly Administration and the General Administration of Quality Supervision, Inspection and Quarantine. The Regulations on Cigarette Packaging and Labeling in the Territories of the People's Republic of China. http://www.etmoc.com/look/lawlist.asp?id¼41832 (accessed 4 April 2017).

[13] Yang GH. Analysis on the gap between WHO framework convention on tobacco control and China's domestic policy. Chin J Health Policy, 3(2) March, 2009, 1–9.

[14] China CDC, Office of Tobacco Control. 2009 China Tobacco Control Report. Beijing: May, 2009.

tobacco can cause.[15] For instance, based on 2010 GATS-China report, 81.8% of adults knew that smoking is harmful for health, but 77.5%, 27.3% and 38.7% of respondents were aware that smoking cause lung cancer, stroke and heart attack, respectively. The percentage of those who were aware that smoking could cause the three diseases (stroke, heart disease and lung cancer) was only 23.2%.[16] That is, while most smokers may understand at a general level that smoking poses health risks, fewer can truly identify those risks, and far fewer believe that these risks will come to themselves.

Third, the general messages featured in the warnings have already become saturated among the public in China,[17] they need the knowledge on the specific health risk of smoking. Pictorial warnings may play an important role in promoting more detailed knowledge and understanding of smoking's risks.[18] Evidence suggests pictorial health warnings are more informative and have stronger effects on cessation than text only warnings.[19,20] Furthermore, FCTC Article 11 guidelines point out that health warnings containing text and pictures are more effective than purely text warnings,[21] and an important way for young people and people with lower literacy to obtain information.[22]

The fourth, half the messages of the Chinese warning were in English, a language most Chinese smokers do not understand. A survey shows that 73.2% adult Chinese smokers cannot translate 'Smoking is harmful to your health' correctly, and 89.9% of smokers cannot translate 'Quitting smoking early is good for your health' correctly.[23] Note "half the messages in English" obviously violated the requirement of Article 11 of WHO FCTC "warnings must be the main language", which intentionally not to play a warning role.

The fifth, item 5 of *the labeling Regulation* allows warnings to use the similar background color as the main pack surface, thus the messages are not visually

[15] Chapman S, Liberman J. Ensuring smokers are adequately informed: Reflections on consumer rights, manufacturer responsibility, and policy implications. Tob Control 2005;14:8e13.

[16] China CDC, *Global Adults Tobacco Survey (GATS), China 2010 Country Report*, edited by Yang GH, China San Xia Press, Beijing, 2011.

[17] Yang GH, ed. Baseline Survey Report of "Towards a Smoke-Free China" Beijing: Peking Union Medical College Press, 2008.

[18] Cunningham R. Gruesome photos on cigarette packages reduce tobacco use. Bull World Health Organ 2009;87:569.

[19] World Health Organization. Call for Pictorial Warnings on Tobacco Packs. Geneva: World Health Organization, 2009.

[20] Hammond D, Fong GT, McDonald PW, et al. Graphic Canadian cigarette warning labels and adverse outcomes: evidence from Canadian smokers. Am J Public Health 2004;94:1442e5.

[21] World Health Organization. Guidelines for Implementation of Article 11 of the WHO Framework Convention on Tobacco Control (Packaging and Labelling of Tobacco Products). Geneva, Switzerland: World Health Organization, 2008.

[22] WHO Report on the Global Tobacco Epidemic, 2008: The MPOWER package. Geneva, Switzerland: World Health Organization, 2008.

[23] Jiang Y, Fong GT, Li Q. Effectiveness evaluation of health warnings on cigarette packs in China, 2008. Chin J Health Educ 2009;25:411e13.

attractive. Integration of the poor warnings with the beautiful package and highlight the brand greatly reduces the effective of warning, and thus reduces the likelihood that smokers will notice, consider or act on the health messages provided. Item 8 of *the Labeling regulation* ask to label tar, nicotine and carbon monoxide on cigarette packages with more than 2 mm high, leading people to believe that so-called light cigarettes are less harmful than regular cigarettes.

The Chinese health warning did not meet WHO FCTC requirements, but very match the requirement of STMA, which were fully expressed in *Research on Counterproposals and Countermeasures*: "*The health warning should not be scaremongering*", "*The area of health warning do not over one third*", and "*The format of health warning cannot take the form of a black box warning, black and white, color should be the best warning with the original packaging color uniform*".[24]

In August 2011, CNTC issued a document on strengthening the health warning and adjusting labeling cigarette packaging.[25] However, adjusted health warnings in cigarette package still keep the general health warning, did not provide health warning on specific health risk of smoking, did not using the pictorial warnings. It has been changed to increase the size of text health warning to 4 mm high in cigarette package and to 6.5 mm high in cigarette bar, to cancel English warnings, and to quantify the value of chromatism between text warning and background.

In September 2016, the STMA and the GAQSIQ again jointly updated *the Labeling Regulations*. The updated regulation added the third set text health warning, total three sets of text health warning for rotation:

Group 1 SMOKING IS HARMFUL TO YOUR HEALTH QUIT SMOKING REDUCES HEALTH RISK
Group 2 SMOKING IS HARMFUL TO YOUR HEALTH QUIT SMOKING EARLY IS GOOD FOR YOUR HEALTH
Group 3 TO DISSUADE TEENAGERS FROM SMOKING, AND PROHABIT SMOKING OF STUDENT IN THE PRIMARY AND MIDDLE SCHOOLS

The size of the adjusted text health warning increases to 4.5 mm high in cigarette package and to 7 mm high in cigarette bar, the health warning cover 35% of the display area, and the value of chromatism between text warning and background also increases. However, these added health warning still do not provide information about the specific harms caused by smoking, and is not pictorial warning.

Overall, the domestic *the Labeling Regulation* fail to comply with Article 11 of WHO FCTC. Although there were two times modification in 2011 and 2016, the regulation stipulates that the size of health warning is increasing from 2 to 4 mm high, then to 4.5 mm high in cigarette package, the cover areas of health warning is

[24] Zhou RZ, Cheng YZ. Research on Countering Tactics for WHO Framework Convention on Tobacco Control and Impact from Tobacco in China. Beijing, China: Economic Science Press, 2006.

[25] **CNTC Notice on further strengthen cigarette packaging health warning, Office of CNTC 2011, No. 141, August 2011,** http://www.tobacco.gov.cn/html/49/3829706_n.html.

increasing from 30 to 35%, there is not substantial change on health warning as they do not provide information of the specific health hazards of tobacco use without pictorial warning. The figures for emission yields still are not limited on tobacco packages. Also the cigarette package is still beautiful and glitter.

11.2.3 2012–2015 National Tobacco Control Action Plan and Health Warning of Cigarette Package

Owing to the tobacco industry's interference, it was not until 6 years after the entry into force of the Convention, in China, that the first "Tobacco Control Plan (2012–2015)" (abbreviated to the "Plan") was issued by the Steering Committee in December, 2012 (the formulation lasted two and a half years). During the long process of making plan, it was the fierce controversial and the most intense argue to be issue on health warning on the cigarette package. Unfortunately, the STMA/CNTC was still dominant to make policy on health warning of cigarette package under support of MIIT.

"Continuously strengthen cigarette package labeling and health warning" in the "Plan" includes three points: (1) to strengthen cigarette package labeling management, comprehensively evaluate the outcome from implementing the Regulations on Cigarette Package Labeling in the Territories of the People's Republic of China, and further improve cigarette package labeling; (2) To improve the content and form of health warning and (3) to promote the authority and effectiveness of health warnings. According to the requirements for "large, clear, visible and legible" of Article 11 of WHO FCTC, "Plan" will ensure improving warning effect on health hazards of tobacco use by enlarging size, fonts and color contrast, etc. Also the health warning will gradually include the relevant information such as cessation service hotline to provide cessation counseling and assistance.[26]

At first glance, "Plan" seems actively to improve health warnings on cigarette packs, but the "Plan" actually avoids talking about requirement of Article 11 of the WHO FCTC and its Implementation Guidelines. In fact, "Plan" does not mention when to add the warnings of the specific health hazards, when to use graphic warnings, and how to prohibit misunderstanding information on cigarette packages. The concrete embodiment of Plan was update *the Labeling Regulation* in 2016, which still violated the requirement of Article 11 of WHO FCTC. We have analyzed it in the previous section. So experts criticized that the Plan was controlled by the tobacco industry; The Plan has not been intend to implement and only a perfunctory product for dealing with or deceiving the international and domestic tobacco control community.

---

[26] Ministry of Industry and Information Technology of the People's Republic of China. China Tobacco Control Plan, 2012–2015. Issued by Dec 22, 2012. http://www.miit.gov.cn/n11293472/n11293832/n12843926/n13917012/15071046.html (accessed Oct 7, 2016).

11.3 Health Warning of Cigarette Package in China and the Other Countries and Regions

11.3.1 Evolution of Health Warnings on Chinese Cigarette Package

As shown before, *the Labeling Regulation* was adjusted twice in 2011 and 2016 after issued in 2008. Taking "*the Zhong Nan Hai*" cigarette package as a example, we observed the change of health warning on the cigarettes package from 2008 to 2016 (Fig. 11.2). As you can see in Fig. 11.2, the health warning in English on the cigarette package was taken off in 2011 and 2016 version, the size of health warning is larger; however, the content of the health warning has not any changed, still do not any specify the health consequences of smoking. Also notice of the tar content "8 mg" or "5 mg" with white and light blue color on the package misdirect the customer that it is low tar and less harmful than other cigarettes. Based on the GATS China 2010, one-third of respondents believed that low-tar cigarettes were less harmful to health than regular cigarettes. Furthermore, 55% of health-care professionals and 48% of teachers believed that low-tar cigarettes were less harmful than regular cigarettes.[27] The misunderstanding is obviously related to the erroneous message on the cigarette package.

The cigarette packs in the domestic market of China after 2016 are shown in Fig. 11.3. These cigarette packages are still beautiful, the health warnings on package do not provide any messages about the various specific health hazards of smoking without the pictorial warning. It is 12 years From the WHO FCTC was in force in China, and it is 8 years from *the Labeling Regulation* firstly issued in China, there is not any substantial change on health warning. China government has said that they have fulfilled the Article 11 of WHO FCTC, it is true?

11.3.2 The Health Warning of the Other Countries and Regions

In the past more than 10 years, China has not made any substantive progress, but there has been tremendous progress internationally in implementing package health warnings, and so on. There is also enormous international momentum for implementation of plain packaging in order to deal with counterproposal of tobacco industry.

Except China, the cigarette package health warnings of all rest countries provided information of specific health hazards of smoking. Although Japan as same as China that is poor implement of Article 11: there is no pictorial warning, warning language

---

[27] Chinese Center for Disease Control and Prevention. Global Adults Tobacco Survey (GATS) China 2010 Country Report. 2011. http://www.who.int/tobacco/surveillance/survey/gats/en_gats_china_report.pdf?ua=1.

Fig. 11.2   Health warning on the cigarette package in China, 2008–2016
Source: The pictures is provided by Li JK

area accounts for only 30% of the display areas of package, its health warning in cigarette package also pointed out the specific health hazards, including more than ten health warnings: "**Smoking is a cause of lung cancer. According to epidemiological estimates, smokers are about two to four times more likely than nonsmokers to die of lung cancer**", "**Smoking increases risk of myocardial infarction. According to epidemiological estimates, smokers are about 1.7 times more likely than non-smokers to die of a heart attack**" and so on. On the back of cigarette packages: "Smoking during pregnancy is a cause of preterm delivery and impaired fetal growth. According to epidemiological estimates, pregnant women who smoke have almost double the risk of low birth weight and three times the risk of premature birth than pregnant women who do not smoke", and so on.[28]

---

[28] The Ministry of Health home page at www.mhlw.go.jp/topics/tobacco/main.html.

Fig. 11.3 Health warning on the cigarette package in China by brand, 2016
Source: The picture is provided by Li JK

The average area has 94 countries/jurisdictions placed in front and back of the cigarette health warnings reached 50% and above, of which 50 countries reached 60% and above.

By the end of 2016, there has been a tremendous progress in implement of Article 11 of the Convention. Totally, 94 countries and regions have stipulate the health warnings covering at least 50% of the principal display areas of the cigarettes package, of which 50 countries reached 60% and over. The covering areas of health pictorial warning of Nepal and Vanuatu have reached 90% of the package front and back.[29] Canada was the first country to implement pictorial warnings in 2001. By the end of 2016, 105 countries or regions had pictorial warnings, covering 58% of the world's population.[30] Hong Kong, Macao and Taiwan have implemented the pictorial warnings. For example, under Hong Kong Law, Chapter 371B *Smoking (Public Health) (Notices) Order*,[31] packaging with 20 and over cigarettes or cigars must lay the graphics depicting different health problems caused by smoking and covering 50% and over areas. The warnings are to be published in both official languages, Traditional Chinese and English. Warning begins with the phrase 'HONG KONG SAR GOVERNMENT WARNING' and then followed by one of the seven health warning, such as "Smoking Causes Lung Cancer", "Smoking May Cause Impotence", "Smoking Can Accelerate Aging of Skin" and so on. In Macau, Law on cigarette labeling issued in 2012, started to implementation in 2013. The Law stipulated that the health warnings must cover

---

[29] WHO FCTC, 2016 global progress report on implementation of the WHO Framework Convention on Tobacco Control. P31.

[30] Canada Cancer Society, Cigarette Package Health Warning International Status Report, September, 2016, fifth edition.

[31] Hong Kong Law, Chap 371B *Smoking (Public Health) (Notices) Order* https://www.elegislation. gov.hk/hk/cap371B!zh-Hant-HK@2014-12-05T00:00:00?severity=warn&OS=Windows%20 7&BRV=45.0&BR=Chrome&BRV_S=false&C_S=true&BR_S=false&OS_S=true&JS_S=true.

more than 50% of the front and the back of the package. The text of the warning appears in Chinese on one side of the package and Portuguese on the other. Rotation schedule and Six pictorial warnings, such as "Smoking cause oral cancer", are used on tobacco packages. Also the Law prohibit misleading information such as "light" and "mild" on packages display area.[32]

In all the rest neighboring countries of China, Nepal, India, Thailand, Laos, Burma, Vietnam, South Korea and Mongolia, Russia, Kazakhstan, Kyrgyzstan, Tajikistan and other countries, other than in Japan, their Laws have required using pictorial warning to indicate the health hazards of smoking and second-hand smoke.[33] Of the five countries that make up the BRICS. Brazil (in 2001), India (in 2009) and the Russian Federation (2013) have implemented pictorial warnings, covered from 50% to 85% areas of cigarette package. South Africa has taken steps towards requiring pictorial warning labels as an amendment to the Tobacco Products Control Act that came into force August 2009 to require pictorial warning labels.[34] Only in the mainland of China, the health warning on cigarette packs has been not reached the most basic indicators of Article 11 of the WHO FCTC, and no any sign of action on pictorial health warning.

In order to effectively curb the industry's use of the package as a promotional vehicle and deceptive means, increase the effectiveness of package warnings and reduce the attractiveness of tobacco products, the plain packaging is recommended for consideration by international guidelines under the WHO FCTC. In World No Tobacco Day on May 31, 2016, WHO announced a Moves: Get ready for plain packaging.[35] Plain packaging of tobacco products restricts or prohibits the use of logos, colours, brand images and promotional information on packaging other than brand and product names displayed in a standard colour and font style. Plain packaging is supported by extensive evidence.[36] Australia's world precedent setting plain packaging had full implementation at the retail level as of December 1, 2012. The United Kingdom and France implemented at the manufacturer level May 20, 2016, and Hungary will implement in 2018. There are 14 countries where plain packaging is in process or under formal consideration.[37]

It is the growing worldwide trend: Larger, pictorial health warnings and plain packaging, but China has not any substantial progress. So there are growing gaps between China and the all rest countries on health warning in the cigarette package.

---

[32] global.tobaccofreekids.org, Macau Warnings, 2013 http://global.tobaccofreekids.org/files/pdfs/en/WL_country_Macau_en.pdf.

[33] Tobacco Free Kids, Pictorial Health Warning Labels by Country/Jurisdiction by WHO Region, http://global.tobaccofreekids.org/en/solutions/international_issues/warning_labels/#pictorial.

[34] Saloojee Y, Ucko P, Drope J. South Africa. In: Drope J (Ed.) Tobacco control in Africa—people, politics and policies. London: Anthem Press; 2011:227–245.

[35] World Health Organization, "World No Tobacco Day: Get ready for plain packaging. Plain packaging of tobacco products to reduce demand, to save lives" May 31, 2016.

[36] David Hammond, "Standardized Packaging of Tobacco Products: Evidence Review. Prepared on behalf of the Irish Department of Health" March 2014.

[37] Canada Cancer society, CIGARETTE PACKAGE HEALTH WARNINGS, International Status Report, Fifth Edition, October, 2016.

11.4 Assessment of Health Warning on the Package Labeling in China

The Chinese government has always maintained *the Labelling Regulations* as the largest action in fulfilling the Convention.[38] However, many studies have demonstrated the low effectiveness of the current text warnings in China.

11.4.1 Assessment of Effect of the Chinese Text-Only Health Warning

In 2009, an International Tobacco Control Policy Evaluation Project (ITC) experimental study was conducted in 2008 with a sample of 1169 adult smokers, adult non-smokers and youth across four cities in China (Beijing, Kunming, Shanghai and Yinchuan). The respondents were ask to review and rank 10 health warning created on Chinese pack, including two Chinese Text-only warning located in front and back of case in 2008 and in side of case before 2008; four set of pictorial-and-text warning and text-only warning (translated Chinese) from Canada (Lung cancer), Singapore (Oral disease), Hong Kong (gangrene) and the European Union (Obstruction of artery) based on their receiving effectiveness to quit or not start smoking. The results were remarkably consistent across male and female adult smokers, adult non-smokers and youth in all four cities. The both of text-only Chinese warnings in 2008 and before 2008 were much less effective, ranked at the bottom, the ninth and tenth, respectively. All four pictorial-and-text health warnings were rated and ranked highest, and other text-only version of above the four pictorial warnings were rated in the middle[39] (see Fig. 11.4). The study concluded that picture warnings are rated as much more effective than the same warnings without pictures. The revised health warnings in China, introduced in October 2008, are only slightly more effective than the old one before 2008 and far less effective than even text warnings from other countries as without the specific health problem.

11.4.2 Study on Behavioral Impacts of Health Warning

The ITC China Survey, a prospective longitudinal study, were conducted to collect data from smokers and non-smokers aged 18 and over in seven cities with face-to face interview in China since 2006. ITC surveys include a broad set of

---

[38] STMA, Implement WHO FCTC, Strengthen measure, Execute effectively: Read and explain *the Regulations on Cigarette Packaging and Labeling in the Territories of the People's Republic of China*. http://www.tobacco.gov.cn/html/27/2703/4942826_n.html.

[39] Fong GT, Hammond D, Jiang Y, Li Q, et al. Perceptions of tobacco health warnings in China compared with picture and text-only health warnings from other countries: an experimental study. Tob Control. 2010;19(Suppl. 2):69–77.

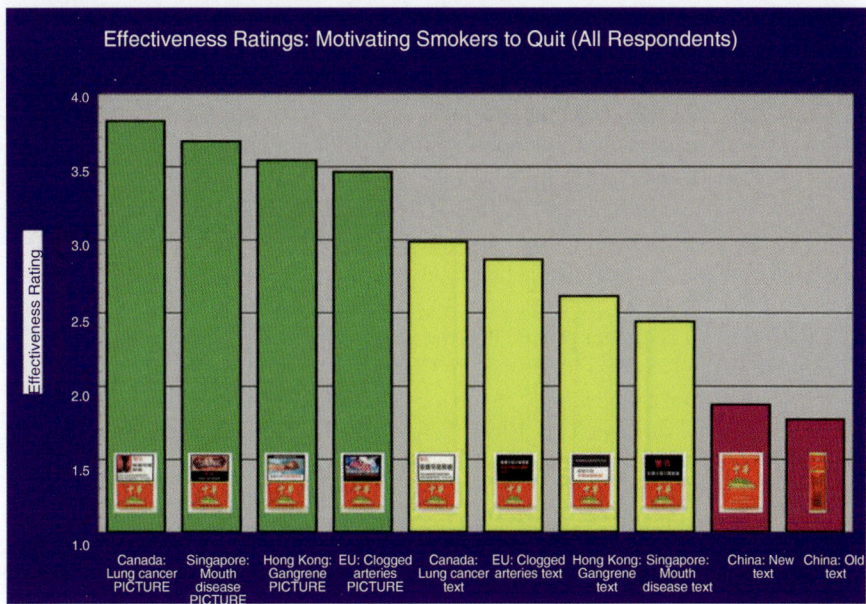

Fig. 11.4 Mean effectiveness ratings of each health warning: "How effective would each label be in motivating smokers to quit?" (All Respondents)
Asterisk (The figure is quoted from Fig. 11.3 of Perceptions of tobacco health warnings in China compared with picture and text-only health warnings from other countries: an experimental study—reference 39)

questions to assess health warning label effectiveness. Among these questions, it is related to some behaviors, such as *"To what extent, if at all, do the warning labels make you think about the health risks of smoking?"*, *"To what extent, if at all, do the warning labels on cigarette packs make you more likely to quit smoking?"* and *"In the last month, have the warning labels stopped you from having a cigarette when you were about to smoke one?"* ITC data show that on all measures of warning effectiveness that have been used to evaluate health warnings across the more than 20 ITC countries, the Chinese health warnings are much less effective in communicating the health hazards of tobacco use. Based on the Wave 3 China Survey of ITC findings, only 7% of all smokers said that the current health warnings made them think about the health risks of smoking "a lot", 22% said that labels have stopped them from smoking at least once, and 5.2% smokers stated that warnings made them want to quit smoking "a lot". The results are similar with that in the Wave 2, which means that The 2008 text-only warning labels introduced in China do not improve people' behavior, especially smokers' quitting awareness and attempt. Also 2008 text-only warning labels do not arouse strong emotional responses.[40]

[40] 2014 World Health Organization Western Pacific Region, University of Waterloo, ITC Project and Think Tank Research Center for Health Development. Tobacco health warnings in China: evidence of effectiveness and implications for action. Manila: World Health Organization Regional Office for the Western Pacific; 2014.

The report also pointed out that obvious differences of amending warning effective between China and Malaysia. In January 2009, Malaysia implemented pictorial warnings on 40% of the front and 60% of the back of the pack in line with Article 11 Guidelines. So, the percentage of male smokers who said the revised pictorial health warning made them think about quitting smoking increased from 6 to 20%, the percentage of male smokers who gave up a cigarette at least once in the last month due to the warning labels increased from 23% to 56%. Just described at previous, China has amended the health warning at cigarette package in 2008, the study found the both percentage change before and after revision were very small: from 3 to 5% in thinking about quitting, from 15 to 20% on giving up a cigarette at least once in China.[41] It is further proved that the amended text-only health warning at the cigarette package is almost ineffective in China.

"Forward a smoke-free China", a tobacco control project in 40 cities/counties of 20 provinces was supported by Bloomberg Grant in 2008. In order to assess the effects of the amended health warnings on Chinese cigarette packets accordingly to *the Labeling Regulation*, the project surveyed 16,000 people by stratified, multistage cluster-sampling in project areas in 2008, by comparing with the pictorial warning in the other countries. The investigator showed the pictures of pictorial health warning from other countries and Chinese text-only warning to respondent, then ask three questions: *"Do you know the health hazards of smoking?"*, *"Do you intend to quit?"*, and *"Would you like to use cigarettes as gifts?"*.[42] The results showed that more than 90% of smokers aware of the health risks of tobacco, and increased the likelihood of them quitting, in addition, 90% said they would no longer use cigarettes with the pack as a gift when they review the pictorial warning from the other countries. Also respondents believed that this kind of cigarette package would greatly change the adverse social norm and restrain corruption using cigarette as gifts and buying cigarettes with public fund. By comparison, 70% of people expressed that they did not understand the health risk of tobacco use, and didn't want to quit from Chinese health warning; they also expressed it was acceptable to use cigarettes with Chinese cigarette packs as gifts after to look at China' cigarette pack with the health warning.[43]

The Global Adult Tobacco Survey (GATS) is a cross-sectional survey of tobacco use among adults carried out by individual countries in collaboration with the U.S. Centers for Disease Control and Prevention and the World Health Organization. From December 2009 through March 2010, the Chinese Center for Disease Control and Prevention conducted the GATS China; all non-institutionalized persons 15 years of age or older ("adults") who resided in China at the time of the survey were considered eligible to participate. Through the stratified, multistage

---

[41] Fong GT, Xiao L, Jiang Y, Li Q, Li L, Yong H. The effectiveness of health warnings in China: Longitudinal findings from the ITC China Survey. Poster presented at the 10th APACT Meeting. August 19-21, 2013. Makuhari Messe, Chiba, Japan.

[42] Wan X, Ma S, Yang G, et al. Conflict of interest and FCTC implementation in China, Tob. Control. 2012 Jul: 21 (4); 412-5.

[43] Tobacco Control Office, China CDC, 2009 report of tobacco control in China: pictorial warning: reveal the truth of tobacco use, March, 2009.

cluster-sampling design 15,000 adults of 100 counties or districts in China were selected to carry out the investigation, and 13,354 participants were actually completed to review. In the questionnaire, there are two questions related to effect of the health warning in cigarette package: "*In the LAST 30 days, did you notice any health warning on cigarette packages?*", If YES, "*In the LAST 30 days, have warning labels on cigarettes packages led you to think about quitting?*".

The GATS results showed that 86.7% of current smokers noticed a warning label on a cigarette package introduced after 2008 but 63.6% of those did not consider quitting. The percentage were similar in different population by age, gender, education level and occupation.[44] 2015 Adult Tobacco Survey with similar sampling procedure and indicators on the health warning, totally interviewed 16,800 respondents in 336 units. The results revealed that 62.1% smokers do not think about quitting when they noticed the health warning in cigarette package revised in 2011.[45] There are not difference of the results of 2010 and 2015 adults tobacco survey. The evidences strongly suggested that the health warnings on Chinese cigarette packages introduced in 2008 and revised in 2011 both are very low effective. The text-only health warnings without special health hazards of tobacco use do not increase quitting attempt, do not play a sufficient warning and education role. Multiple evidences indicated that the text-only warnings without the specific health hazards of tobacco use on cigarette packages introduced in 2008 and revised in 2011 were not effective in increasing behaviors associated with quitting and motivation to quit. The delay in implementing pictorial health warnings in China will lose a lost opportunity for improving people's knowledge and awareness of the health hazards of tobacco use, and for motivating smokers to quit so as to promote the health of Chinese.

11.5   To Promote Chinese Government to Implement the Article 11 of WHO FCTC

Undoubtedly, in the process of control tobacco in China from 2006 to now, the most controversial and most intense debate is how to implement Article 11 of WHO FCTC, what is the qualified health warnings. Tobacco control circle has fought to promote pictorial warning on the cigarette package for more than 10 years. The efforts are divided into two aspects. The first is the policy advocacy, which opposed the Labeling Regulation issued by STMA and GAQSIQ in 2008, and called for the pictorial warning on the cigarette package. The second is mass mobilization. Tobacco control experts worked with mass media to tell public how to communicate health hazards of tobacco use in the other countries so as to support the pictorial warning on cigarette package in China.

---

[44] China CDC, Global Adult Tobacco Survey (GATS) China 2010 Country Report, edited by Yang GH, China San Xia Press, Beijing, 2012.
[45] China CDC, Chinese Adult Tobacco Survey, 2015, edited by Liang XF, People's Health Xia Press, Beijing, 2016.

11.5.1 Policy Advocacy of the Pictorial Warning on the Cigarette Package

In 2008, when *the Labeling Regulation* was released jointly by STMA and the GAQSIQ, the tobacco control community vociferously and strongly opposed it. In September 2008, over 40 medical and public health experts declaimed **that** *the Labeling Regulation* **obviously violated the Convention,** and appealed the **MIIT and SAQSQI** to immediate stop the implementation of *the Labeling Regulation*, and reenact new one.[46] A detailed analysis has been made on the reason that *the Labeling Regulation* was a violation of the Article 11 of WHO FCTC in the second section of this chapter. From 2008 to 2016, many famous public experts, clinical medical scientists, jurisprudential scholars lettered jointly or separately to MIIT, State Council, even the top leader to state the benefits of pictorial warnings on cigarette packages with multiple scientific evidences, urge to change current status in China. However, there is no reply, no clear instruction to place the pictorial health warning on cigarette packages. It is very popular way to appeal changing policy with writing letter in China. Letter writers believe that the suggestions are benefit for country and people, also believe that the officers of the various levels governments can listen to the voice of the people so as to correct some wrong practices. This time, however, the experts were disappointed.

Tobacco control community published a series of reports to communicate the requirement of Article 11 of WHO FCTC, describe the difference of the Labeling Regulation with Article 11 of WHO FCTC, introduce the global progress of the health warning on the package, assess the useless of Chinese text-only health warning on the cigarette package based on above assessment studies. The other researching articles pointed out that Chinese government was kidnapped by interest groups of tobacco industry as the Labeling Regulation was based on *Research on Counterproposals and Countermeasures* of Tobacco Industry. All these research reports provided the robust evidences for policy advocacy.

At the same time, China CDC associated with the news media to edit the special issue for annual two sessions of NPC and CPPCC (Fig. 11.5), as well as Think-Tank and Chinese Association of Tobacco Control organized the seminars, to promote the representatives of NPC and CPPCC concern tobacco control in China, and promote the pictorially health warning of cigarette package.[47]

For past more than 10 years, representatives of NPC and members of CPPCC continually submitted their proposals, to promote effectively implement the Article

---

[46] Sun YM, The experts collectively lambasted the new Labeling regulations of the STMA, Chinese Tobacco Market, Tobacco Observation, Sept., 27, 2008, http://www.etmoc.com/look/looklist.asp?id=16192.

[47] XINHUA News Chinese experts suggested on the pictorial warning on the cigarette package to the representative of NPC and CPPCC, Feb. 20, 2009, http://news.xinhuanet.com/newscenter/2009-02/20/content_10858284.htm.

Fig. 11.5   Report related to implementation of Article 11 of WHO FCTC issued by Civil Society

11 of the *Convention*, "To place the pictorial warning on the cigarettes packages", and call for vigilance against the commercial and other vested interests of the tobacco industry, and account the certain tobacco companies, such as the "Zhongnanhai" cigarette factory, for using tobacco packaging to deceive and

mislead consumers.[48] Also Members of NPC and CPPCC constantly inquiry MIIT and STMA why not to do anything on pictorial health warning on cigarette package.[49] However, MIIT and STMA always responded regardless of all the evidences and facts that (1) China have satisfied the standard of Article 11 of the Convention, (2) only a few countries (in fact 105 countries) have a pictorial health warning, and (3) the pictorial health warning is contradictory of Chinese culture (fact is all the other countries and region, Hong Kong, Macau, Taiwan and Singapore have a pictorial warning except the mainland), so it is impossible to place the pictorial warning on the cigarette package in China.[50,51,52]

11.5.2   To Mobilize Public to Promote Pictorial Warning on Cigarette Package

In February, 2009, "Smoke-free Action, Vision China" was jointly initiated by the "Towards a smoke-free China" project, the Think Tank, Sohu public welfare channel, and other mass media in order to collect public opinion on Pictorial Health Warning on the cigarette package, and promote to amend the *Labeling Regulations*.[53] Totally, more than 1,400,000 Internet users voted to support the action in 2 weeks.[54] At the same time, the collection of the creative pictorial health warning was announced so as to promote participation and understand of civil society though communication of activities, mobilization and submissions of produce, selection and award.

Since 2011, The Think-Tank Research Center for Health Development, Chinese Academy of Medical Science, and China CDC has been jointly initiated an innovative campaign entitled "*I want to tell you because I love you—The pictorial warning on the cigarette package*". The objective of the campaign is promote people in China to understand the health hazards of smoking and SHS, as well as know what

---

[48] Blog of Zhi XY, The proposal of remind the Domestic Labeling Regulation as soon as possible. 2010, 2, 28, http://blog.sina.com.cn/s/blog_69a89dcb0101bv4d.html.

[49] Zhang Y, Representative of NPC called on the pictorial warning on the cigarette package, query MIIT omission. China Economic Times, March, 3, 2013. http://finance.sina.com.cn/chanjing/cyxw/20120313/133011577083.shtml.

[50] Tobacco Control Forum Discussion: former Head of MIIT Li Yizhong's "Views" on China's performance, http://www.catcprc.org.cn/BBS/showtopic-60800.aspx.

[51] Think Tank Research Center for Health Development, A civil society perspective 2002, Tobacco Control in China: Expose tobacco marketing scam.

[52] Legal Evening News, Depute Director of STMA: The pictorial warning on the cigarette package does not accord with the traditional culture. 2016,3,15,http://news.sina.com.cn/c/nd/2016-03-15/doc-ifxqhmve9218438.shtml.

[53] Initiative to solicit public opinion on *Pictorial Health Warning on the cigarette package in Smoke-free Action, Vision China*, http://www.nihe.org.cn/news.php?id=15550.

[54] Xin Hua internet, 1.27 million netizen support the pictorial warning on the cigarette package. http://www.bqpu.net/news/466847.

Fig. 11.6   The exhibition of pictorial warning labels from different countries or regions

happened about the health warning on the cigarette package in the other countries so as to promote the pictorial warning on cigarette package in China.[55]

The innovation of the campaign is to carry out the exhibition tour using the pictorial warning labels from various countries or regions. One of the exhibition boards is the pictorial warning from Malaysia: a picture of oral cancer with a ward "Smoking causes mouth cancer". Another board is combined from Mauritius and Canada: "Smoking causes lung cancer with picture of normal lung and smoker's lung", and lung cancer patient noted a word "this is what dying of lung cancer looks like". Third board is borrow from Hong Kong' pictorial warning on women with skin changes before and after smoking with a warning "Smoking can accelerate aging of skin" (Fig. 11.6). The display of the pictorial warning of cigarette package from different countries not only visually communicates the health hazards of smoking, enhances its reliability of the knowledge, but also lets public to think why the pictorial warning do not place in cigarettes package in China. Then more and more people hope that the similar pictorial warning are placed on the Chinese cigarettes package just as in the other countries.

11,002 visitor was enquired in 22 exhibition cities during the 2011–2012. The results revealed that 90% visitors improved their knowledge on health hazards of smoking and SHS exposure, as well as 85.5% visitors supported the pictorial warning on the cigarette package in China.[56] Another survey was carried out in Shanghai by Fudan University, including 2300 people. The results were shown that 76.7% of respondents supported the graphic warnings on the cigarette package, of which over 90% students and medical staff, and 79.1% of floating workers support the pictorial warning.[57] The campaign was a great success, the exhibition is still touring until 2017.

---

[55] I want to tell you because I love you—the introduction of pictorial warning labels on cigarette packages' campaign. Attachment 2. Think-Tank Research Center for Health Development; 23 June 2013.

[56] I want to tell you because I love you—the introduction of pictorial warning labels on cigarette packages' campaign. Attachment 2. Think-Tank Research Center for Health Development; 23 June 2013.

[57] Ge X, Wang J, Zheng PP et al. Impact assessment of cigarette package labels on health warning among community residents in Shanghai, Chin Health Edu. 29(9), 2013 Sept. 775-778.

11.5.3   Criticism from International Society

The Chinese tobacco industry has been criticized by the international society for its blatant abduction of the government and the boycott of the 11 article of the WHO FCTC.

On the 17 November 2008, the COP 3 of WHO FCTC was held in Durban, South Africa. China delegate **opposed the "the guidelines for implementation of Article 11".**[58] The Chinese delegation said "...... using the pictorial health warning, ... affected to cultural and national feelings. There are the famous mountains and rivers, beautiful scenery and historical sites on cigarettes packages of China. It would hurt the feelings of the Chinese people to place these ugly and horrible pictures on the elegant package".[59] China delegate became the butt of cruel jokes about their such absurd speaking. The Dirty Ashtray Award (See BOX) goes to China for attempting to make a mockery of Article 11 guidelines including preferring beautiful cigarette packages over the health of its citizens in COP3 of WHO FCTC in the November 19, 2008.[60] The multiple mass media reported that international society criticized China delegate to opposite Guideline for implementation of Article 11 of WHO FCTC with absurd remarks and neglect Chinese people's health.[61] There were a lot of comments and blame to Chinese government' attitude on the pictorial warning on cigarette package and people's health on Blog, Wechat and so on. Many experts believe that the related government departments should revise *the Labeling regulation* in the face of such sharp criticism and powerful pressure. However, in fact there is do not any change in China.

The Dirty Ashtray Award

It was set up by Framework Convention Alliance, an civil society working toward a world free from the devastating health, social, economic and environmental consequences of tobacco and tobacco use. The award is offered winners in performance to condemn poor tobacco control efforts by collective selection of the NGO global representative attending WHO FCTC Conference. It reflects the civil society's concern and power on the global tobacco control.

---

[58] CONFERENCE OF THE PARTIES TO THE WHO FRAMEWORK CONVENTION ON TOBACCO CONTROL THIRD SESSION DURBAN, SOUTH AFRICA, 17–22 NOVEMBER 2008, FCTC/COP/3/REC/3, P13.

[59] Wu YQ, WHO observer for the Third Conference of the Contracted Parties to the "Framework Convention on Tobacco Control", 2008, China Tobacco Control Resources center. http://www.tcrc.org.cn/html/zy/nljs/qtgj/2668.html.

[60] COP3 - the Conference Blog, Dirty Ashtray Award http://blogsofbainbridge.typepad.com/cop3/dirty_ashtray_award.

[61] Gu QJ China's Tobacco Control becomes a global negative example, International Herald Leader, Nov. 27, 2008, http://news.xinhuanet.com/herald/2008-11/27/content_10419853.htm.

11.6 Summary

This chapter focuses on the implementation of the Article 11 of WHO FCTC, including the related policies, displaying the current health warning, assessing the effect of text-only warning, and advocacy campaign of civil society in China.

The text-only health warning on the cigarette package in China totally do not satisfy the basic requirement of Article 11 of the Convention as (1) the text-only warning did not show clearly the specific health risk of tobacco use; (2) the quantitative statements about cigarette component and emissions, such as tar, nicotine and carbon monoxide figures, are still shown on tobacco product packaging and labeling, which imply that one brand is less harmful than another; (3) there is not any pictorial warning. As an important and effective, low cost tobacco control tool, the larger, pictorial health warnings, even plain packaging becomes a growing and unstoppable worldwide trend. Canada was the only one country to implement pictorial warnings in 2001, 105 countries/jurisdictions, including countries without Parties of WHO FCTC, had implemented pictorial warnings by end of 2015.[62] Except Chinese Mainland, Hong Kong, Macau, Taiwan and Singapore also do so. China has fallen far behind the rest of the World.

However, so far, there has been no sign of improvement. During the 2017 NPC Conference, Mr. Duan, representative of NPC, deputy director of STMA arbitrarily said that it is impossible to place the pictorial health warning on the cigarettes package as it does not conform Chinese cultural traditions; we (STMA) have not intend to do so. In addition, China has implemented WHO FCTC very well, do not violate the Convention.[63]

Over the past 10 years, the fight for promoting the pictorial warning on the cigarette package has gathered momentum, but still regret to say, so far, no substantial progress has been achieved. Why the most cost-effective intervention means cannot be implemented in China? It is the tobacco industry that is an implacable opponent of the measure in China. STMA estimated that the consumption of the high-grade cigarettes as gift would be rapidly come down or withdrawn from Market, if the cigarettes package is greatly changed on requirement of Article 11 of the Convention. Then the price of the high-grade cigarettes, as the main source of tobacco industry' gain, would be dropped, and the tobacco industry's profits would be substantially declined.

In the other countries, tobacco industry has also made every effort to oppose the implementation of the Article 11 of the Convention. For example, the tobacco industry has brought legal challenges against Australia and a few countries' the plain packaging. While some rulings are pending, the tobacco industry has lost all of its legal claims so far. In Australia, the government won a constitutional challenge

---

[62] Canada Cancer Society, Cigarette Package Health Warning International Status Report, September, 2016, fifth edition.

[63] Taking Health day by day, It is totally different of the packaging Labeling in China with that of the rest Countries worldwide. June, 16, 2016. http://www.jcbrand.cn/jiankang/12028512.html.

against its legislation. An international arbitration claim filed by Philip Morris alleged that Australia had breached a bilateral investment treaty with Hong Kong, but the tribunal threw the claim out for lack of jurisdiction.[64] In the United Kingdom, the tobacco companies lost a High Court action seeking to prevent the legislation there. In his ruling the judge was highly critical of the evidence put forward by the industry to support their claims that plain packaging would not work.[65]

Why the situation is totally different in China? The STMA/CNTC was dominant to make policy and implement on health warning of cigarette package; If someone suit tobacco industry, STMA/CNTC even prevented court filing, which were described in Chap. 6 of the Book. It is obviously impossible that tobacco industry own approves the pictorial warning on the cigarette package, which, to use a Chinese idiom, would be like asking a tiger for its skin.

Either labeling regulations issued in 2008, 2011 and 2016, or "Continuously strengthen cigarette package labeling and health warning" in the "*2012–2015 Tobacco Control Plan*", are the reproductions of *Research on Counterproposals and Countermeasures* against Article 11 of the Convention. This is a typical case of national public power to service for the interests of tobacco enterprises. During the process of implementation of WHO FCTC, STMA and GAQSIS totally ignore the national long-term interests of China and the people's health and well-being, put the tobacco industry's largest profit in the first place. So they have become representatives of the tobacco industry with abusing the public power to obstruct, delay, and oppose the implementation of the Convention in China.

In this context, the top priority of tobacco control community should oppose kidnap of public power with the interests of the tobacco industry, and ask STMA leave the Inter-Ministerial Coordination and Steering Committee for Implementation of WHO FCTC, as well as more widely mobilize the people, let more people call for graphic warning on cigarette case.

---

[64] Peter Martin, Australia versus Philip Morris. How we took on big tobacco and won http://www.smh.com.au/federal-politics/political-news/australia-versus-philip-morris-how-we-took-on-big-tobacco-and-won-20160517-gowwva.html.

[65] **Matthew L. Myers,** In Victory for Global Health, UK High Court Upholds Plain Tobacco Packaging Law—Innovative Strategy Spreads from Australia to Europe, *May 19, 2016.*

Chapter 12
Comprehensive Ban on Tobacco Advertising, Promotion and Sponsorship

Pinpin Zheng, Lin Xiao, Fan Wang, and Gonghuan Yang

Abstract Marketing and promotion increase tobacco sales by encouraging current smokers to smoke more and decreasing their motivation to quit. Marketing also encourages potential users, young people specifically to try cigarettes and become long-term customers. The key point of Article 13 of WHO FCTC is to undertake a comprehensive ban all tobacco advertising, promotion and sponsorship (TAPS) within 5 years after ratifying the treaty. The Chinese Advertising Law promulgated in 1994 were obvious deficiencies compared with WHO FCTC. However, tobacco industry has been impeding the revision of national laws to reserve room for TAPS. Eight types of prevalent tobacco advertising in China are summarized: disguised forms of tobacco advertising or promotion in media, outdoor cigarette advertising, the displays at the Point Of Sale, grand scale gathering for brand recommendation and product presentations, tobacco advertising at internet and new media, cigarette packaging as advertising and production and distribution of items that resemble cigarettes such as sweets and toys. The tobacco industry often participates in sponsorship such as education, scientific research, sports, music, cultural, social events and public education campaigns in the name of social responsibility. Over 100 Tobacco Hope primary schools is a typical case. Surveys in 2009–2015 showed extremely high exposure to TAPS among urban population, especially among teenagers. To promote comprehensive ban all forms of TAPS, a lot of public

P. Zheng (✉)
Fudan Health Communication Institute, Shanghai, China

L. Xiao
Chinese Center for Disease Control and Prevention, Beijing, China

F. Wang
Fudan Health Communication Institute, Shanghai, China

School of Public Health, Fudan University, Shanghai, China

G. Yang
The Institute of Basic Medical Science at Chinese Academy of Medical Sciences, Beijing, China

© Springer Nature Singapore Pte Ltd. 2018
G. Yang (ed.), *Tobacco Control in China*,
https://doi.org/10.1007/978-981-10-8315-0_12

245

health advocacy campaigns have been carried out over past 10 years. The amended Advertising Law and the other regulations have come into force successively, most form of TAPS have been banned up to 2015.

Keywords Tobacco advertising · TAPS · Article 13 of WHO FCTC · Advertising Law · Tobacco industry · Tobacco control · China

12.1   Introduction

The tobacco industry claims that its advertising and promotion efforts are not aimed to expand sales or attract new users, but only to reallocate market share among existing users.[1] This is not the truth. Marketing and promotion increase tobacco sales and therefore contribute towards killing more people by encouraging current smokers to smoke more and weakening their attempt to quit. Marketing also encourages potential users—and adolescents specifically—to try smoking and become long-term customers.[2] Tobacco advertising targeting adolescents and some specific demographic subgroups is really effective.[3]

The World Health Organization (WHO) pointed out that *"Tobacco addiction is a communicated diseases—communicated through advertising, sports, marketing and sponsorship. Tobacco advertising bans protect people, especially the young. Lured in large numbers by the glare and glamour of tobacco marketing that sells a deadly product as the taste of freedom and fashion, between 80,000 and 99,000 children and adolescents in the world take to tobacco every day."*[4]

Since studies show that the majority of smokers start before the age of 18, the main targets of tobacco industry's advertising, promotion and sponsorship are young people.

Every year, the tobacco industry spends billions of dollars on advertising, marketing and promotion globally. In the United States alone, the tobacco industry spent more than $12.47 billion in 2002 (or more than $34 million every day) in promoting tobacco products.[5] The disclosed industry documents reveal that the

---

[1] Saffer H. Tobacco advertising and promotion. In: Jha P, Chaloupka FJ, eds. *Tobacco control in developing countries*. Oxford, Oxford University Press, 2000: 215–236.

[2] Basil MD, Basil DZ, Schooler C. Cigarette advertising to counter New Year's resolutions. *Journal of Health Communication*, 2000, 5(2):161–174.

[3] Smee C et al. *Effect of tobacco advertising on tobacco consumption: a discussion document reviewing the evidence*. London, Economic and Operational Research Division, Department of Health, 1992.

[4] WHO Press Release, "European Union Directive Banning Tobacco Advertising Overturned: WHO Urges Concerted Response", 5 October 2000; http://www.who.int/inf-pr-2000/en/pr2000-64.html.

[5] U.S. Federal Trade Commission (FTC), *Cigarette Report for 2002*; http://www.ftc.gov/reports/cigarette/041022cigaretterpt.pdf.

companies have attentively examined the habits, desires and tastes of their potential customers and then based on the results, they developed products and marketing campaigns aiming at the target population.[6] Despite the denials of tobacco industry, the vast majority of peer-reviewed, independent studies have shown that tobacco advertising has led to increased consumption.[7,8,9] Tobacco advertising also has huge impact on the youth. Studies have confirmed that tobacco promotional activities are causally related to smoking initiation among adolescents. Research has also indicated that following the broadcasting of tobacco advertisements that appeal to young people, the prevalence of using those brands, and even the prevalence of tobacco use overall, increases.[10,11]

In 2000, a study covered 102 countries' data found that partial bans were ineffective in decreasing tobacco consumption and the rate of decline in smoking was much steeper in those countries with relatively comprehensive bans.[12] Both the World Health Organization and the World Bank projected that the tobacco consumption could decrease 7%, if the comprehensive banning is adopted globally[13] and they recommend that countries should prohibit all forms of tobacco advertising and promotion. Furthermore, "Tobacco advertising and promotion" and "tobacco sponsorship" include promotion not only of specific tobacco products but also of tobacco use in general; acts with a promotional aim as well as acts that have or likely have promotional effect; and both direct and indirect promotion.

Besides direct tobacco advertising and promotion, there are at least the several categories: various sales and/or distribution arrangements, such as a variety of the product recommendations, display at points of sale; disguised forms of advertising or promotion, such as placement of tobacco products or tobacco use in various media contents; *Brand Stretching and Brand Sharing, means* association of

---

[6] N. Hafez, P.M. Ling, "How Philip Morris Built Marlboro into a Global Brand for Young Adults: Implications for International Tobacco Control," *Tobacco Control*, Vol. 14 No. 4 (2005).

[7] C. Lovato et al., "Impact of tobacco advertising and promotion on increasing adolescent smoking behaviors," *Cochrane Database of Systematic Reviews*, Issue 3, 2004.

[8] M.T. Braverman and L.E. Aaro, "Adolescent Smoking and Exposure to Tobacco Marketing Under a Tobacco Advertising Ban: Findings From 2 Norwegian National Samples," *American Journal of Public Health*, 1 July 2004; 94(7): 1230–1238.

[9] Keeler, et al. "US National Tobacco Settlement: The Effects of Advertising and Price Changes on Cigarette Consumption," *Applied Economics*, 36: 1623–1629, 2004; U.K.

[10] R. Fielding, Y.Y. Chee et al., "Declines in tobacco brand recognition and ever-smoking rates among young children following restrictions on tobacco advertisements in Hong Kong," *Journal of Public Health*, March 2004, Vol. 26, No. 1.

[11] Pierce et al. "Does tobacco marketing undermine the influence of recommended parenting in discouraging adolescents from smoking?" *American Journal of Preventive Medicine*, 23, 73–81, 2002.

[12] Saffer, H., and Chaloupka, F. "The Effect of Tobacco Advertising Bans On Tobacco Consumption", *Journal of Health Economics*, vol. 19, 2000. http://www.uic.edu/~fjc/Presentations/Papers/W6958.pdf.

[13] World Bank, *Curbing the Epidemic: Governments and the Economics of Tobacco Control*, Tobacco Control 1999;8:196–201 http://tobaccocontrol.bmj.com/content/tobaccocontrol/8/2/196.full.pdf.

tobacco products with events or with other products in multiple ways; and marketing promoting by packaging and product design features and creating brand identity to attract consumers, as well as Production and distribution of goods such as sweets and toys or other products that resemble cigarettes or other tobacco products.[14]

It is essential to clarify that the definition of "tobacco sponsorship" based on the Guideline includes any form of contribution, financial or otherwise, to any event, activity or individual with the aim, effect or likely effect of promoting a tobacco product or tobacco use either directly or indirectly, no matter how or whether that contribution is publicized or acknowledged.

Tobacco companies always shaped themselves into a good corporate citizens by contributing to deserving causes or by promoting "socially responsible" so as to promote tobacco products and expand team of smokers. The most common sponsorship covers includes the following fields: education, scientific research, social public activities, sports, music and cultural and public education, and so on.

Article 13 of the WHO FCTC on advertising begins with the following statement: "Parties recognize that a comprehensive ban on advertising, promotion and sponsorship would reduce the consumption of tobacco products" and requires ratifying countries to undertake a comprehensive ban on tobacco advertising, promotion and sponsorship (TAPS) within 5 years after ratifying the treaty. In this chapter, we review the current status of tobacco advertising, promotion and sponsorship in China, as well as the battle between supporting and opposing comprehensive ban on tobacco advertising, promotion and sponsorship since the Convention took effect.[15]

12.2 The Effort of Banning on Tobacco Advertising, Promotion and Sponsorship (TAPS)

Article 13 of the WHO FCTC was a time-based provision requiring each Party undertake a comprehensive ban of all TAPS in 5 years after the FCTC coming into force. WHO FCTC came into force in China on Jan 9, 2006, but the Chinese Government did not start to revise the *Advertisements Law of the People's Republic of China* promulgated in 1995, until 2014, in which tobacco advertisement was prohibited in only five types of media (broadcast, films, television, newspapers, and periodicals) and four places (waiting rooms, cinemas and theatres, meeting halls, and sports sites and gyms).

---

[14]WHO Framework Convention on Tobacco Control: guidelines for implementation Article 13–2013 edition.

[15]WHO FCTC, Article 13 of WHO Framework Convention of tobacco control. P 11.

12.2.1 The Domestic Laws and Regulations Related to Ban on TAPS

In the early 1980s, the health hazards of tobacco use already drew some attention and campaigns of tobacco control gradually rose in China. The State Council issued the *Regulations on the Administration of Advertising in P. R. China* on December 1, 1987 to prohibit cigarette advertising in television, radio and newspaper for the first time.[16] In 1992, the State Administration for Industry and Commerce (SAIC) released the *Notification on Strictly Prohibiting Tobacco Advertising in Radio, Television, Newspaper and Periodicals.*[17] In 1994, the *Advertisement Law of the P. R. China* promulgated by the Standing Committee of NPC stipulated specifically that tobacco advertisement was prohibited in five types of media (broadcast, films, television, newspapers and periodicals) and four public places (waiting rooms, cinemas and theatres, meeting halls, and sports sites and gyms). Tobacco advertising must indicate "Smoking is harmful to health".[18] In 1995, the *Interim Management Regulation for Tobacco Advertisement* stipulated implementing methods in detail, and supplemented that the sponsorship advertising activities held in the name of tobacco enterprises or under the name and brand of cigarette trademarks should be subject to review and approval by Industry and Commerce authorities at or above the provincial level.[19]

Although these provisions was progressive at that time, there were obvious deficiencies of these law and regulations compared with WHO FCTC approved by NPC. First, starting point of legislation was not comprehensive ban on all tobacco advertising but partial, leaving space for tobacco advertising without awareness of the danger of tobacco advertising, promotion and sponsorship. Second, there were many loopholes in the articles of the law for lack of clear understanding of the tobacco industry marketing strategies, such as no specific definition of indirect advertising, therefore, some provisions were not operational. No definite constrain was put on sponsorship and promotion. So these national laws and regulations cannot effectively curb almost rampant tobacco advertising, promotion and sponsorship activities in China.

---

[16] State Council Regulation on supervision of advertising, Oct. 26, 1987 http://www.saic.gov.cn/zw/zcfg/xzfg/198710/t19871026_215566.html.

[17] State Administration for Industry & Commerce of P. R. China, Notice on Resolutely banning tobacco advertising using radio, television, newspapers, periodicals and publish. No. 251 (1992).

[18] Decree of the Chairman of the People's Republic of China, the Law of Advertising, No. 34, Oct. 27, 1994 http://www.people.com.cn/GB/168602/10231798.html.

[19] State Administration for Industry & Commerce of P. R. China, The temporal method on management of tobacco advertising, No. 69, Dec. 30, 1996.

12.2.2 Impede the Revision of National Laws to Reserve Room for TAPS

In the book *Research on Countering Tactics for WHO Framework Convention on Tobacco Control and Impact on Tobacco Industry in China* (hereafter referred to as *Research on Countering Tactics and Impact*),[20] a series of coping tactics against *Article 13* of the Convention are listed. First, STMA members tampered the spirit of Article 13 during translating English version of the Convention into Chinese Version; then STMA falsely declared that it was not necessary to amend the national laws or regulations as the original "*Advertising Law*" and national regulations on banning tobacco advertising already met the requirements of the Convention.

Article 13.2 of FCTC reads: "Each Party **shall**, in accordance with its constitution or constitutional principles, undertake a **comprehensive** ban of **all** tobacco advertising, promotion and sponsorship ... ". There was a heated debate about how to translate "**comprehensive**" inside the delegation negotiating WHO FCTC. "**Comprehensive**" means "including all or everything", "broad in scope" and "being the most comprehensive of its class". Also "**comprehensive**" in all other international laws are translated using the meaning "including all or everything". However, the members of STMA insisted on translation "wide-ranging, extensive", thus to keep or reserve room for tobacco advertising. STMA's opinion prevailed with regard to this translation. The members of STMA recognized that "comprehensive" ban on advertising was translated into "全面 (*quanmian*)" (all or everything) in the draft Chinese Convention provided by WHO, but experts of *Research on Countering Tactics and Impact* suggested to translate it into "广泛 (*guangfan*)" (extensive). This suggestion was finally adopted by the Chinese government delegation."[21] The mistaken translation of COMPREHENSIVE left some space for tobacco advertisement. Then, STMA asserted that it was not necessary to make any change of the *Advertising Law* promulgated in 1995 and the national provisions for implementation of banning tobacco advertising as they already met the requirements of the Convention. STMA falsely stated that even some local laws and regulations exceeded the requirements of the Convention.[22] As a result, in 10 years after the Convention came into force, China did not improve the related regulations prohibiting TAPS.

---

[20] Zhou RZ, Cheng YZ, eds. *Research on Counterproposal to the WHO Framework Convention on Tobacco Control and Address its Impact on the Chinese Tobacco Industry*. Beijing, China: Economic Science Press, 2006:1–3.

[21] Legal Evening News, *Research on Countering Tactics and Impact* confirm to distort meaning of comprehensive in WHO FCTC Chinese version, Tencent, Nov. 9, 2010, http://news.qq.com/a/20101109/001183.htm.

[22] Zhou RZ, Cheng YZ, eds. *Research on Counterproposal to the WHO Framework Convention on Tobacco Control and Address its Impact on the Chinese Tobacco Industry*. Beijing, China: Economic Science Press, 2006, P268, P353.

12.3 All Sorts of TAPS in China

The *Advertising Law* promulgated in 1994 has only banned tobacco advertisements in five types of media, including television, radio, film, newspapers and periodicals, and four public places in China. So there are some outdoor cigarette advertising after 5 years when WHO FCTC came to force. Furthermore the tobacco industry has maintained a visible marketing presence through indirect advertising, sponsorships and promotions. The current status of TAPS in China is reviewed briefly as following.

12.3.1 Tobacco Advertising and Promotion

12.3.1.1 Disguised Forms of Tobacco Advertising or Promotion in Media

Due to the prohibition of tobacco advertising in radio, film, television, newspapers and periodicals based on *Advertising Laws*, the tobacco industry used some phrases implicating greatness, elegance and culture as well as inspirational wording as slogan to market cigarette products. These slogans associate cigarettes with desirable image through cultural empathy to evade the health risk of smoking. There are numerous examples. "People are the peak of the high mountain (山高人为峰 *Shan GaoRen Wei Feng*)" means that you will be at a high mountain peak as long as you are willing to climb. The phrase with inspirational cultural connotation became *Hong Ta* cigarette' slogan. "唯有牡丹真国色Only peony is the true national beauty" from a poetry of famous poet Liu YX in Tang Dynasty is used as *Peony* cigarette' slogan. "Cranes dance on white sand (Baisha) and my heart soars" with an image of a famous sportsman running like wind is used in *Baisha cigarette'* advertising.[23] "爱我中华Loving my China" is *Zhonghua* (China)cigarette' slogan. A telephone survey conducted by Fudan University in 2010 showed that 39.4% of respondents immediately associated it with *Zhonghua* cigarette when they heard "Loving my China".[24]

In some cinema to graphic works, footage implicating cigarette brands often appear, and there exist large number of smoking scenes in TV productions. In fact, this is a common strategy to promote and introduce tobacco products. From 2007, Chinese Association on Tobacco Control (CATC) counted the annual number of smoking shots in popular Chinese television series. The statistics of the top 30 movies and top 20 TV plays in 2007 showed that 26 of the 30 films had smoking scenes. In the film with the largest number of smoking shots, overall the smoking scenes

---

[23] Xinhua Internet, Suspected illegal release of tobacco advertising, Liu X' Cranes dance on white sand was taken off. Nov. 3, 2004. http://news.xinhuanet.com/sports/2004-11/03/content_2171088. htm.

[24] Zheng P., Ge X., Qian H. et al. 'Zhonghua' tobacco advertisement in Shanghai: a descriptive study. Tob. Control 2014 Sep;23(5):389–94.

Fig. 12.1 Disguised forms of advertising or promotion of tobacco product in media. (**a**) Hongtashan Cigarette's Commercial *Shan GaoRen Wei Feng* on China Central Television. (**b**) "Cranes dance on white sand (Baisha) and my heart soars", a slogan of Baisha Group

lasted up to 8.24 min, accounting for 7.14% of the total film length, and there were 115 smoking shots in the film, i.e. one shot appeared every 1.03 min. Eighteen of 20 TV series showed tobacco shots, and one of the TV series had 295 smoking shots, with up to 11.35 smoking scenes per episode.[25] The statistical results for the 40 most popular films and 30 most popular TV series in 2009 showed that only nine films had no tobacco shot sand 77.5% of the films included smoking shots. In the 30 TV series, two TV series had no tobacco shots and 28 TV series with tobacco lens accounted for 93% of all TV series.[26] The survey also indicated that the average time of teenagers' exposure to tobacco shots were 92 min. The more exposure to smoking scenes, the higher degree of acceptance of smoking behavior is among young people (Fig. 12.1).[27]

There are product placement in various media showing content related to tobacco products and tobacco use. For example, in February 2009, there are footage on Zhonghua cigarettes lasting nearly10 s (about 6 s of close-up shot) on the CCTV News (*Xinwen Lianbo*) '*New Year Home Gift*' by the China Central television when a CCTV reporter was interviewing the passengers on the train before the Spring Festival (Fig. 12.2).[28]

The news not only presented the name of the tobacco product, trademark, packaging and decoration, but also explicitly advocated concepts such as 'Zhonghua cigarette is high-grade and politest, it is a great gift and we should support families'

---

[25] CATC, The meeting of mass media on initiating smoking-free video and cleaning screen hold in Beijing, July, 30 2009http://www.catcprc.org.cn/index.aspx?menuid=4&type=articleinfo&lanmuid=122&infoid=1763&language=cn.

[26] China Daily, Survey of CATC: Smoking was popularized in domestic film and television, Sept. 2, 2010 http://www.chinadaily.com.cn/dfpd/2010-09/02/content_11248485.htm.

[27] Dong ZL, Yang J. The behavior and attitude in adolescent have been impacted by smoking image in Movie and TV drama, J. Chinese School Health, 2010(05):634–636.

[28] The Think-Tank, Special issue of Tobacco tracking, Action review and analysis that We will never give up comprehensive banning on TAPS, Sept. 2, 2014 http://www.tcrc.org.cn/UploadFiles/2014-09/249/2014091509531229678.pdf.

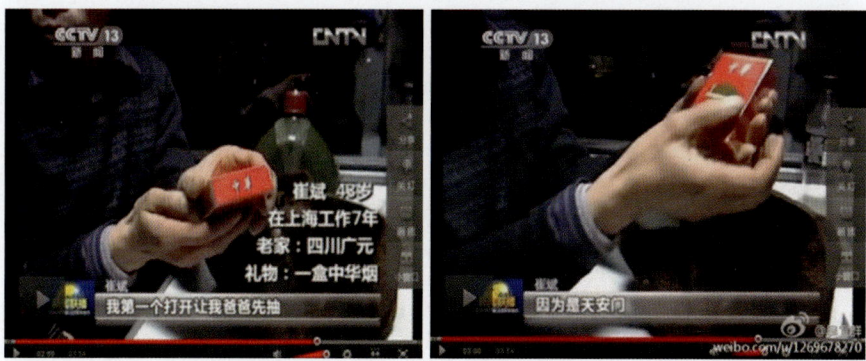

Fig. 12.2 Tobacco product placements in CCTV

Fig. 12.3 Outdoor advertising of cigarette. (**a**) Hongtashan brand Advertising. (**b**) Zhonghua cigarette adverting at Xibeiposight

smoking. Objectively speaking, this is obviously a promotion serving as tobacco advertising in general.

Another common strategy is promoting tobacco products through reporting tobacco corporations' events on newspapers. For instance, the Hong He, Hong Yun Centennial was covered by the Kunming City Daily with eight pages.[29]

12.3.1.2 Outdoor Cigarette Advertising

As the 1994 *Advertising Law of China* did not ban the outdoor tobacco advertising, billboards, light boxes, cigarettes display in and around local neighborhoods, moving advertisements painted on cars and sponsored shop signs are ubiquitous and dominate the landscape (Fig. 12.3).

---

[29] The Think-Tank, Who is marketing Death, 2013, P31, http://tcrc.org.cn/html/zy/cbw/ycggcx-hzz/2414.html.

12.3.1.3   Various Sales and/or Distribution Arrangements

Article 13 of the WHO FCTC and its Guidelines require a comprehensive ban of all TAPS, including tobacco product displays at the Point Of Sale (POS). Tobacco product displays undermine the effectiveness of tobacco control laws that ban TAPS and expose the population to tobacco industry marketing tactics, which intend to increase the sale and consumption of tobacco products. The following focuses on POS tobacco product display, which is called "Terminal Marketing" by China tobacco industry.

Tobacco marketing at the point of sale (POS) includes advertising, promotion (discounts, giveaways and display product), and product display at any location where tobacco products are sold. STMA has recognized that tobacco product display at the point of sale is an important measure for the tobacco industry to advertising its products long ago. Vice director of STMA said "Cigarette retailers are the tobacco industry's most important resource. We have a better marketing platform for product promotion and brand advertising if these resources are secured."[30] Since 2010, STMA has being developing a customer-targeted precise marketing system of cigarettes brands and setting up standardized demonstration points of cigarette sale. At the point of sale, meticulously designed exibits (samples) draw attention to the packegings by a variety of materials (such as acrylic), eye-catching illumination (such as backlit lightening) and color combinations. Prominent display is typically used to create an outstanding impression with posters and display cases to turn the stores into giant cigarette advertisements. Also there are a lot of direct cigarette advertising, product discount, misunderstanding communication on low tar cigarettes with low risk and free samples (Fig. 12.4). Adolescents are particularly vulnerable to pro-tobacco messages, and form positive attitude toward tobacco products and brands. POS marketing makes it harder for smokers to quit.

12.3.1.4   Product Recommendations

Product recommendation for different target groups includes various forms of promotion. Tobacco companies hold grand scale gathering for brand recommendation and product presentations. What's unique to China is, tobacco companies also invite government officials to visit or attend their marketing campaigns to advertise their own cigarette brands (Fig. 12.5). According to incomplete statistics, in 2010–2012, provincial and ministerial officials participated in up to 46 tobacco industry activities.[31]

---

[30] Entrepreneur, Tobacco retail terminal "new approach"—Discussion relationship between the retails and cigarette marketing system. 10, 31, 2011, http://www.cyzone.cn/a/20111031/217656. html.

[31] Think Tank, Who is marketing death? Tobacco tracking briefing, special issue, 2013 http://tcrc. org.cn/html/zy/cbw/ycggcxhzz/2414.html.

Fig. 12.4 Display and promotion at points of cigarette sale

Fig. 12.5 Cigarette product recommendation. (**a**) "Low hazard, novel technology", launch of Jinsheng cigarette. (**b**). A ceremony of Changchun Cigarette Factory

Social activities often combine advertising and marketing. Such activities and events were widely reported by the media, and therefore cigarette brands were constantly being promoted. For instance, in 2010, the Hope Project center of Beijing Youth Development Foundation and Beijing Cigarette Factory "Zhong Nan hai Love Found" co-sponsored a major event "2010 Zhong Nan Hai love action—blue fashion for love", which was subsequently relayed in Beijing and other five cities. In addition, on June 26, 2012, *Legal Daily* reported that China Tobacco Jiangxi Industry LLC opened "Golden Saint" black tiger theme park in Nanchang City Sports Park. The main events included master photo wall, advertisement collection

Fig. 12.6 Integration of tobacco advertising and marketing into social activities. (**a**) The first Zhong Nan Hai Parkour relay. (**b**) Jinsheng Black Tiger theme park

and distributing smoking and publicity materials. The sponsors also planned to carry out 100 similar events in other 11 prefecture-level cities and counties. The event included setting up five areas for brand feature publicity, new product display, new product experience and consumer activity area, and cigarette brand promotion activities such as publicity materials, new product display and smoking (Fig. 12.6).[32]

Another promotion strategy was face-to-face promotion. The main path was direct encourage of smoking behavior by giving out cigarettes to passers, smoking room construction, cigarette tasting, such as "Gold Saint" Grateful Cigarette Tasting, and so on. Especially in sports venues and government meeting sites, for example, representatives of the two conferences (NPC and CPPCC) of Wuzhou city in Guangxi province tasted Zhenlong cigarettes.[33]

12.3.1.5 Internet Advertising and New Media

As the age of new media comes, the number of Chinese micro-blog users exceeded 300 million, and the WeChat users are over 800 million. Because the internet tobacco advertising is a gray area and is not included in the corresponding ban, internet and new media have become one of the few advertising choices for tobacconists. The micro blog and WeChat platforms have become a new ground for tobacco culture communication and cigarette product promotion. The tobacco industry takes full advantage of new media and internet, which are tobacco marketing blind spots in legal system, and use websites, micro blog, WeChat and micro-films for marketing activities, For instance, through corporate website or introducing tobacco culture and knowledge to directly promote tobacco brands. In 2012, Fudan

---

[32] Legal Daily, Nanchang Tobacco advertising are on the TV and Newspaper, which are forbade by Article 18 of Advertising Law. Does it Jiangxi tobacco company know or see? 6,26,2012 http://www.legaldaily.com.cn/bm/content/2012-06/26/content_3660689.htm?node=20734.

[33] Think Tank, Who is marketing death? Tobacco tracking briefing, special issue, 2013 http://tcrc. org.cn/html/zy/cbw/ycggcxhzz/2414.html.

Fig. 12.7 Marketing of cigarette by new media. (**a**) Double Happiness Gold Group. (**b**) The celebrity smoking in the official Micro-Blog of Double Happiness

University investigated micro blogs of some tobacco companies and found that almost all of the tobacco companies have established their own micro-blogs named with their own brand name. In terms of tobacco communications, there are direct and indirect marketing strategies. Direct marketing strategy involves direct advertising of products, attracting more smokers by organizing events, and spreading tobacco culture to incite smoking behaviors. Indirect marketing strategy includes spreading philosophy of life, food and entertainment, working place management and so on. It may seem that marketing has nothing to do with tobacco, but in fact it makes tobacco closer to consumers, glorifies the tobacco industry and smoking behavior, and raises the social acceptance of tobacco use. For example, in the WeChat marketing of Shuangxi-Gold 1906, the hostess offer lighting up cigarette or celebrities smoke to promote cigarette acceptance (Fig. 12.7).[34]

12.3.1.6 Brand Expanding and Brand Sharing

Brand expanding and brand sharing associated tobacco products with events or other products in various ways and are a common form of tobacco product advertising. There are a lot of cases lending cigarette brands or logos to other entities in China, such as Hong Ta Shan Hotel, Hong Shuang Xi (Double Happiness) China Wedding Exposition, Zhonghua (China) cruise ship, Huang Jin Ye (Gold tobacco) jacket, Jiaozi (pander) baggage car and so on. Also cigarette brands and logos are artificially linked to other events. Tobacco companies' names, images and websites were found on rooftop signage and the windscreens of taxis in Kunming,[35] such as

---

[34] Xinhua News, Report: Chinaxiangcai and Terminal retail point should be the stress of tobacco marketing surveillance, June 1, 2015, http://news.xinhuanet.com/politics/2015-06/01/c_127862288.htm.

[35] Li, L. & Yong, H-H.(2009). Tobacco advertising on the street in Kunming, China. Tobacco Control 18: 63.

Fig. 12.8 Cigarette Brand Stretching and sharing

Hong Ta Sports Center in Kunming. These new marketing ventures are designed to keep promoting tobacco brand names even after tobacco advertising is banned (Fig. 12.8).

12.3.1.7 Cigarette Packaging as Advertising

Cigarette packages is an important part in tobacco industry's marketing strategy. At present, while more and more countries are implementing package health warning using disease images and plain packaging, Chinese cigarette packages still keep beautiful exterior. Appealing package design covers the name and logo of cigarette brand, color, picture and so on. This strategy is used to reinforce brand image, to minimize perceptions of risk, and to contribute to the smoker's identity and thus attract consumers. Places with political meaning such as "*Zhonghua* (China)", "*Zhongnanhai* (Sea Palaces)" and "*Remin Dahuitang* (Great Hall of the People)" became brands of cigarette, which undoubtedly increased public attention on these cigarette. *Hongtashan Gonghexinxi* (红塔山 恭贺新禧) uses red and golden as its base color with peony as the pattern on package, and therefore it is a typical example of popular festival and gift cigarettes. Some other brands use the name of beautiful sights in China with pictures, for example *Huanghelo* (黄鹤楼), or "Yellow Crane Tower," is named after a famous tower in China built in the first century, and *Huangguoshu* (黄果树), or "Yellow Fruit Tree," is named after Huangguoshu Waterfall, one of the largest waterfalls in East Asia. Some other images on cigarette brands are linked to totems in Chinese culture, including dragons on the *Red Golden Dragon* (Hongjinlong, 红金龙) and *Zhenlong* (真龙) and stone lions on *Shishi* (石狮) and *Xiongshi* (雄狮). The exterior of Nanjing "Twelve beauties of Jinling" cigarette packs is featured with a series of images of the beauties. In general, Chinese are hard to realize the health risk of smoking with these images of cigarettes packs (Fig. 12.9).

Fig. 12.9 Cigarette packaging as advertising

Fig. 12.10 Game machine
for taking cigarette

12.3.1.8   Production and Distribution of Items That Resemble Cigarettes Such as Sweets and Toys

To attract a new generation of tobacco users, the tobacco industry has devised many campaigns, such as claw crane for cigarette, tobacco placement in online games, and production and distribution of candy, toy and other products resembling cigarette and other tobacco products (Fig. 12.10).[36,37]

---

[36] Sohu TV grab the cigarette from the game machine with a dollar coin http://tv.sohu.com/20130131/n365229198.shtml.

[37] HC360, Game machine for grabbing cigarette, http://www.hc360.com/hots-dze/909196300.html.

12.3.2   Sponsorship and Corporate Social Responsibility

The tobacco industry often participates in social activities such as sponsorship in the name of social responsibility. Such participation may seem to be charitable activities, but in reality, it is disguised tobacco advertising and tobacco brand promotion intended to glorify the tobacco industry and attract more people to become smokers, especially young people. Results from monitoring tobacco promotion and sponsorship by the CATC in 2014 and 2015 showed that tobacco promotion was generally increasing and tobacco publicity was more often disguised in the form of sponsorship such as education fund and disaster management.[38] From January 1 to April 30, 2013, the media reported 149 tobacco sponsorship activities involving 22 provinces/municipalities. Wherein, there were nine government commendation activities, accounting for 6% of all activities. There were 123 welfare donation events, accounting for 82.6% (98 providing for people in poverty, difficulty and, disaster, accounting for 65.8%, 25 support for students in need, accounting for 16.8%). The total number of sponsoring social activities and social development were 26, accounting for 17.4%. Hong He Hong Yun Tobacco Company sponsored the five events with two million RMBs. In China, due to lack of legal restrictions, the tobacco industry's sponsorship activities involved a wider range than other countries, and funding education has led to an international scandal "Tobacco Hope Primary School". The following part will describe five aspects, namely education funding, scientific research funding, social welfare campaign sponsorship, sports and recreational activity sponsorship and public education.

12.3.2.1   Education Sponsorship of Tobacco Industry

According to incomplete investigation of CATC, there were over 100 Tobacco Hope primary schools, 17 tobacco Hope primary schools were founded during restoring after 2008 earthquake in Sichuan.[39] Hong Yun Hong He alone spent 55 million RMBs to set up "Hongyun Gardener Award" and "HongHe Scholarship" in 13 colleges of Yunnan, as well as "HongHe Hope primary schools" and "Hong Yun libraries" during 2008–2013. Hong Yun libraries were opened with funding in 600 schools all over the country.[40] Sponsorship of this type is so ubiquitous that it may only be controlled through institutional approach.

The donation of a tobacco enterprise often come along with certain conditions, such as name of the funded school, and name of the founded scholarship and events.

---

[38] Renmin networking, CTCA' Monitoring show: Tobacco Marketing disguised in program of student support and disaster relief. 4–15,2015, http://shipin.people.com.cn/n/2015/0417/c85914-26858847.html.

[39] Sohu News, 17 "hope" primary school were named "tobacco" in Sichuan disaster areas with that tobacco help you successful. 12,4, 2009 http://news.sohu.com/20091214/n268925079.shtml.

[40] Hongyun Honghe Group Ltd., 2013 report of implementing social responsibility http://csr.hyhhgroup.com/htmlnew/hyhhgy3/art15.html.

Fig. 12.11 Education Sponsorship of Tobacco Industry. Note: Images were taken from *Who is marketing death?*

As a result, primary school children are exposed to tobacco culture directly and made grateful to the tobacco enterprise, and therefore become potential smokers. This is an important strategy for tobacco companies to promote their products and build brand images. The tobacco industry has tied other public donations to their own platform to dilute the tobacco marketing attempts. For example, China Tobacco Zhejiang cooperated with 17 mainstream media and internet media in 16 different provinces and cities to organize "Passing love, building 'Liqun Sunshine' social welfare platform" campaign. Through this campaign, scholarship donation from the public had been made a tool of "Liqun Cigarette" propaganda. The scope of Liqun sunshine scholarship included 16 provinces and cities: Zhejiang, Shandong, Jiangsu, Guangdong, Hunan, Liaoning, Fujian, Hebei, Jiangxi, Sichuan, Shaanxi, Yunnan, Guizhou, Anhui, Gansu, Henan and so on. Tobacco industry appreciates this "Liqun sunshine" model, which has built a "Liqun" public welfare image among the public and has become one of most important impetus of 'Liqun' brand growth (Fig. 12.11).[41]

12.3.2.2   Scientific Research Sponsorship of Tobacco Industry

It is common in China that tobacco companies sponsor or cooperate with universities and other research institutions to carry out tobacco-related scientific research. Many universities and research institutions participated in study on

---

[41] Zi Y, Follow "Liqun sunshine" Public Model, China Tobacco Online 1, 30, 2010, http://www.tobaccochina.com/management/market/stratagem/20121/201211383957_499902.shtml.

Fig. 12.12 Social activity sponsorships of tobacco industry. (**a**) Launch of Gold Tobacco Mother Cellar, i.e. Gold Tobacco Foundation. (**b**) Hunan Tobacco donating Gold Tobacco Medical Charity Card

"Reduce Harm and Reduce Tar". The reason is that the tobacco industry needs researchers to develop so-called studies to weaken the medical evidence on health and tobacco, so as to mislead and deceive smokers. The most notorious case is the "Tobacco academicians".[42] Academy of Military Medical Science received funding from the tobacco industry and collaborated with tobacco companies' technical staff. Using the primary and conventional acute lethal toxicity indicators and the negative results from population based study, they intentionally reached false conclusions of "herbal cigarettes, low-tar cigarettes are less harmful for human health",[43] and the overall trend of China's cigarettes is becoming less harmful. These false evidences gained the National Science and Technology Award by cheating and the person in charge acquired Chinese Academic of Engineering Award. As a result, the National Science and Technology Award and the title of the academician have become a tool for tobacco companies to deceive the public, and "Low-tar and less harmful cigarette" have made a great achievement for tobacco marketing.[44]

12.3.2.3   Various Social Activity Sponsorships of Tobacco Industry

CNTC and Chinese Woman Development Fund jointly established the Gold Tobacco (Huangjing Ye) Foundation,[45] which has sponsored several poverty alleviation campaigns including "Gold Tobacco Mother Cellar", "Gold Tobacco Medical Charity Card" and "Gold Tobacco Ecological Fund", and so on (Fig. 12.12).[46,47]

---

[42] Hvistendahl M. Tobacco scientist's election tars academy's image. Science 2012;335:153–4.

[43] Hvistendahl M. Tobacco scientist's election tars academy's image. Science 2012;335:153–4.

[44] Yang GH, Marketing 'less harmful, low-tar' cigarettes is a key strategy of the industry to counter tobacco control in China, Tob Control 2014;23:167–172.

[45] Baike.com. Tobacco Foundation, http://www.baike.com/wiki/金叶基金.

[46] Health Daily News Center, helping the poor and the needy, alleviating losses incurred by natural disasters become a hot area of tobacco sponsorship. http://www.jkb.com.cn/news/industryNews/2015/0417/366829.html.

[47] STMA/CNTC, public welfare undertaking, http://www.tobacco.gov.cn/html/19/1901/82559904_n.html.

Fig. 12.13 Sponsor sports by tobacco industry

12.3.2.4 Sponsor Sports, Music, Cultural and Social Events of Tobacco Industry

Tobacco companies spend a lot of money sponsoring sports events, teams and athletes. Many sporting events sponsored by tobacco companies are broadcasted internationally and featured in leading newspapers and magazines globally. Sports sponsorship promotes the general social acceptability of tobacco use and creates misunderstanding about the relationship between athletic excellence and tobacco use. Formula One was once synonymous with the tobacco industry. In China, "Red River (Hong He)", as a famous cigarette brand in China, is a symbol of sports sponsoring by tobacco industry. In 1998, Hong He racing team was set up with sponsorship from Yunnan Hong He Industrial Co., Ltd. to attend China Rally Championship (CRC). Forms of sponsorship included featuring Hong He logos on CRC racecars and wear of driver. Although Grand Prix would end all tobacco sponsoring at the end of the 2006 season,[48] China tobacco industry continued to sponsor sport events, teams, and sportspeople with named cigarette brands, such as "Fairy Cup (Tongxian: a cigarette brand of Fujian tobacco industry)" championship tournament, Fairy Cup National Fitness games in Fujian province,[49] the Happy Days (HaoRiZhi as a cigarette brand of Shenzhen tobacco industry) marathon races,[50] and so on (Fig. 12.13).

Moreover, the tobacco industry is very active in various musical and cultural events, so as to win positive public opinion about the industry and to advertise their brands. There are hundreds of cigarette brands in China, and concerts and recreational shows named after these brands can be found everywhere, such as "King of

---

[48] Anon. F1 to ban cigarette ads. CNN. 22 November 2001. URL: http://europe.cnn.com/2001/WORLD/europe/11/22/fia.tobacco/.

[49] Xiamen Sports Bureau, 2016 11th "Tong Xian Cup" Bridge Championship in Xiamen is closed, 9, 27, 2016 http://www.xmsports.gov.cn/tyxw/201609/t20160927_1363930.htm.

[50] China News, Huizhou of Guangdong held HaoRiZi (Good Day) the Spring Festival long distance race. http://www.gd.chinanews.com/2011/2011-12-24/2/169645.shtml (accessed Oct 7, 2014).

Fig. 12.14 Sponsor cultural and social events by tobacco industry. (**a**) Transfer of the FeiTian image from Gansu Tobacco Industry to be carried by Shenzhou 7. (**b**) 2009 Jiaozi Cigarette Youth Leaders Awards Presentation

Confederate Rose (FuRong Wang as a cigarette brand)" symphony concert, "Wu Ye Shen" cultural touch program, which comprises a series of cultural events, such as "Da Hong Yin (Red Eagle)", "Hong Shuan Xi (Double Happiness)" Wedding Exposition, Jiaozi (panda) Concert, Jiaozi (panda) Model of the World Beauty Fashion Show,[51] and so on.

The tobacco industry actively sponsors large-scale social activities to gain political and public influence and discourse power in order to undermine tobacco control legislation. For example, Shanghai Tobacco Company sponsored the 2010 Shanghai World Expo (Shanghai municipal government has returned the fund). Another case is the election of Jiaozi (panda) cigarette youth leader. Youth idols, stars of film and television and the show business, figures of science and technology innovation and young scholars have been elected "Jiaozi Cigarette Youth Leaders". In fact, they were kidnapped for tobacco marketing. Address by the CEO of Sichuan Tobacco Company revealed the nature of this activity. "Thanks Southern People Weekly and friends from the press. This cooperation is an important measure to develop Jiao Zi brand cigarette".[52] When the "Shenzhou5" spacecraft lift off, Wu Ye Shen cigarette and Shenzhou 5 were tied together to promote the cigarette brand taking advantage of all the news on "Shenzhou 5". The "Shenzhou 7" spacecraft lift off with an image of FeiTian (the Flying Apsaras) symbolizing a cigarette brand of Gansu Tobacco Industry. When the public attention was drawn by the news on "Shengzhou7", the "FeiTian" cigarette also came into the public's sight (Fig. 12.14).[53]

[51] Daily S. "Jiao Zi" (Pander) Top model of the world, 2012—beautiful fashion show. http://special. scol.com.cn/12jzsjcm/ (accessed Nov. 16, 2017).

[52] Sina video entertainment, Address of Mr. Luo W, Chairman of Sichuan Tobacco Co. Ltd.12, 17, 2006, http://ent.sina.com.cn/s/2006-12-17/16001373165.html.

[53] Think Tank, Who is marketing death? Tobacco tracking briefing, special issue, 2013 http://tcrc. org.cn/html/zy/cbw/ycggcxhzz/2414.html.

Fig. 12.15 Public education campaigns of tobacco industry. Note: Picture from http://roll.sohu.com/20110804/n315478811.shtml

12.3.2.5   Public Education Campaigns of Tobacco Industry

The objective of public education campaigns by the tobacco industry, such as youth smoking prevention campaign, is encouraging young people to become smokers in the future by disguising replacement of concept in the process. In 2001, "Our Choice—the Sunflower Cup series of public welfare activities" was sponsors by STMA, Soong Ching Ling Foundation and British American Tobacco. The slogan of the Sunflowers Cup is "Smoking is an independent choice for adults",[54] which implies that smoking is a sign of maturity and young people can choose independently after growing up.[55] Another case is that Tobacco College of Henan Agricultural University organized students to communicate to public. "If hard to quit, smoke healthily" (Fig. 12.15).[56]

12.3.3   Promotion of Tobacco in General

"Tobacco advertising and promotion" and "tobacco sponsorship" include promotion not only of particular tobacco products but also of tobacco use in general. In 2002, while the WHO FCTC was being negotiated, the Tobacco Museum of China was opened, receiving 180 million RBMs ($21·7 million) from the Chinese tobacco industry to fund it.[57] The Tobacco Museum of China, the largest tobacco museum in

[54] General Office of STMA, Notice on strengthening publicity and education work on banning smoking among primary and middle school students, 5, 25, 2001. http://www.tobacco.gov.cn/history_filesystem/2007jzzxxsxy/xgwj-3.htm.

[55] Sunflower Cup Charity. Sunflower Cup. Beijing2011; Available from: http://www.sfy.cn/.

[56] China Network, "Red Heart to the Party" Volunteer Service Corpsinitiate health smoking, 8, 4, 2010. http://roll.sohu.com/20110804/n315478811.shtml.

[57] Varma S, Choi K, Koo M, Skinner H. China: tobacco museum's "smoky" health information. *Tob Control* 2005; **14**: 4–5.

the world, features smoking stories and images of great celebrities, leaders and famous people, to promote Chinese culture and civilization related to tobacco use, and their association with the tobacco industry.[58] The museum was granted various honorable titles such as patriotism education base, education base on popular science and excellent institution in promoting cultivating ideals and ethics among minors in Shanghai. It attracts a lot of visitor, especially young people. It is a typical case for promoting tobacco use in general.

All strategies and tricks of TAPS used by China tobacco industry have infiltrated virtually all media and transform all social activities as their marketing chance. These activities increased the social acceptability of tobacco and tobacco companies among people, especially young people. They will continue to develop new and innovative campaigns to create image of their products to keep old users and attract new users. Only comprehensive ban TAPS in all forms can effectively curb tobacco company's actions and reduce the consumption of tobacco products.

12.4   Assessing to Expose to TAPS Among Chinese

There are two ways to assess implementation of Article 13 of WHO FCTC: one is to review the implementation progress report submitted to the Secretariat of the Convention by each Party; another is to observe actual practice through surveys. The International Tobacco Control Policy Evaluation Project (the ITC Project) was the first international cohort study of tobacco use in order to evaluate the effect of national tobacco control related to WHO FCTC on social psychology and behaviors. Surveys of ITC project were carried out in seven cities: Beijing, Shanghai, Guangzhou, Shenyang, Changsha, Yinchuan and Kunming. The first three rounds of surveys covered 2006–2009.[59] Global Adult Tobacco Survey (GATS), Global Youth Tobacco Survey (GYTS) and 2015 Chinese Adult Tobacco Survey (see surveillance chapter in detail) monitored the actual prevalence of tobacco advertising, promotion and sponsorship in 2010 and 2015, respectively. Meanwhile, there were other surveys of TAPS covering specific areas in China. All these surveys evaluated exposure of Chinese population to TAPS from the public's point of view.

12.4.1   The Implementation Progress Report of Article 13 of WHO FCTC WHO

Global Progress Reports on the implementation of the WHO FCTC are an important information resources to assess the progress, challenges, needs and barriers of implementation of Convention. A series of progress reports show that Parties devote

---

[58] China Tobacco Museum. http://www.tobaccomuseum.com.cn/maincontrol?url=&linkType=AbstractCategory&id=8.

[59] The International Tobacco Control Policy Evaluation Project ITC China Project Report Findings from the wave 1 to 3 surveys: 2006–2009, China Times Economic Publishing House, Beijing, 2012, 12.

more attention to revise their laws and regulations concerning TAPS, specifically to prohibit indirect tobacco advertising. Parties' definitions of comprehensive ban on TAPS are different and do not always cover all of the essential measures required by the guidelines for implementation of Article 13. It is therefore more appropriate to analyze the media covered by each Party's ban to assess the progress made under the Article. 2016 global progress report on implementation of WHO FCTC list 10 types of TAPS: the main media banned, including the internet, tobacco sponsorship, product placement, smoking depiction in media,, cross-border tobacco advertisements (from other countries to China and *vice versa*), brand stretching, corporation in the name of the social responsibility of enterprises, display at points of sale, etc.[60] This is also the scale used by the secretariat of the Convention to assess the implementation of Article 13.

2014 and 2016 the Global Progress Reports showed that over two thirds of the Parties had introduced a comprehensive ban on TAPS. One hundred and twenty and 133 countries were included in the analyses in 2014 and 2016 progression reports, respectively. One hundred and ten countries considered their ban to be comprehensive and bans actually covered tobacco sponsorship of international events or activities. In 2016, 77 Parties banned displays of tobacco products at points of sale. Before 2015,China did not ban tobacco advertising in the above ten types with 2 point of 10 scores in 2014 progress report.[61] After the amended *Advertising Law* was came into force in September 1 2015,and have banned most form of tobacco advertising, but not ban general sponsorship, cooperation in the name of enterprise social responsibility, Brand stretching and/or sharing and display at points of sale.

12.4.2 Actual Practice of TAPS Observed by Surveys in China

TAPS is relatively more prevalent in major cities. Based on the ITC report, in third round survey, 39% of smokers from seven cities recalled that they noticed direct tobacco advertising in the last 6 months, including on television and billboards, in stores, newspapers and magazines, and in transport vehicles and stations despite bans on direct advertising on these media based on the *Advertising Law* issued in 1994, also including on posters, in discos and karaoke lounges, in restaurants and tea bars, around street vendors, at workplaces, on the radio and over the internet. In addition, around a quarter of smokers saw or heard about a sporting event or charity event related to either cigarette brands or tobacco companies in the last 6 months, including promotion in forms of free gifts or discount offers on other products when buying cigarettes, competitions linked to cigarettes, free samples of cigarettes, special price offers, and clothing or other items with a cigarettes brand name or logo.

---

[60] WHO FCTC 2016 global progress report on implementation of the WHO Fraction Convention of Tobacco Control, P 40.

[61] WHO FCTC, Annex 3 Current status of implementation of SUBSTANTIVE ARTICLES by the Parties, by income group in 2014 global progress report, P 81.

Over 80% respondents reported having seen people smoking in the entertainment media "often" or "once in a while" in the past 6 months.[62]

2010 GATS China[63] revealed that among all the adults surveyed, 19.6% had noticed tobacco advertisements and promotions in media and public places during the previous 30 days. More urban residents (24.2%) reported that they had seen tobacco advertisements or promotions as compared to the rural residents (15.7%). This proportion is much higher among young people, especially aged 15–24. The proportion among young urban men was 39.1%. About 7.4% of respondents noticed tobacco advertising on TV, and 4.3% and 4.1% from billboards and stores, respectively. 3.5% noticed the sports sponsorship.

2015 Chinese Adult Tobacco Survey[64] showed that 6.3% of the respondents saw tobacco advertisement in stores selling cigarettes and the proportion among male (7.5%) was slightly higher than female (5.1%). The rate of exposure to tobacco advertisement among the age group 15–24 (9.3%) was higher than the age group over 24 years old (4.7%). The rate in urban areas (7.9%) was significantly higher than the rural areas. In 5 years of time, the proportion of respondents who noticed any tobacco advertisement and promotion increased. Wherein, the proportion of those who had seen tobacco advertisement in stores selling cigarettes among the whole population rose from 4.8 to 6.3%.

Teenagers are more likely exposed to tobacco advertising than adults. A survey conducted among middle school students from Hangzhou, Taiyuan and Guiyang cities showed that 88.9% of students surveyed had noticed tobacco advertisements and promotions during the previous 30 days.[65] 2014 GYTS interviewed 155,117 junior students aged 13–15 from 3058 classes of 1020 middle schools in 336 sites through stratified random sampling. The results of the survey showed that 48.5% of junior students surveyed were exposed to advertising or promotion of tobacco through at least one medium. Boys were more likely exposed to advertising or sponsorship than girls. There were no difference between the urban students and the rural students. In addition, 4.6% students had items with tobacco brand logo and 3.6% of the students named their favorite tobacco brand advertising.[66]

A multi-center research was conducted through one-on-one interviews with urban and rural 5- and 6-year-olds from Brazil, China, India, Nigeria, Pakistan and Russia to explore their awareness and understanding of current health warning labels. In China, children were more familiar with the labels, and 86% of 5- and

---

[62] The International Tobacco Control Policy Evaluation Project, ITC China Project Report, China Modern Economic Publishing House, Beijing, 2012, 12.

[63] China CDC. Global Adults Tobacco Survey (GATS) China 2010 Country Report. 2011. China San Xia Press, Beijing, 2011, 11.

[64] China CDC.2015 National Adults Tobacco Survey in China. http://www.chinacdc.cn/zxdt/201512/t20151228_123960.htm.

[65] Xiao L. Jiang Y, Zhang YB, et al. Tobacco advertisement exposure of adolescent among three cities in China. Chin J Prev. Control Chronic Dis. 2011, 19(2):131–133. (in Chinese).

[66] Chinese Center for Disease Control and Prevention, 2014 Global Youth Tobacco Survey (GYTS) China Report, 2015 May.

6-year-olds could identify at least one cigarette brand logo in China and is much higher than other countries.[67]

Surveys during 2009–2015 showed extremely high exposure to TAPS among Chinese, which is coincident with the assessment of the implement of WHO FCTC Article 13 in China in 2014 via progress reports.

12.5   Campaign of Promoting Implement of Article 13 in China

On April 24, 2015, China approved the amendments to the *Advertising Law*. This amended *Advertising Law* came into effect on September 1, 2015.[68] The Amended Law imposed much stricter controls on advertising than before. It prohibited misleading or 'disguised' advertising and advertisement related to special medicine, health care food and tobacco products. In addition to increased power in regulating advertisements, heavier punishments will be exerted for violating the Amended Law.

Article 22 of the *Amended Advertising Law* prohibits publishing tobacco advertisements on mass media, in public places, on public means of transportation, or outdoors. Sending any form of tobacco advertisement to the minors is banned. It is also prohibited to publicize the name, trademark, packaging, decoration and other similar elements of tobacco products through advertisements on any other goods, services or public service advertisements. The notices issued by a tobacco product manufacturer or seller regarding its relocation, renaming, or recruitment, among others, shall not contain the name, trademark, packaging, decoration or other similar aspects of tobacco products.

Reviewing all campaigns, efforts and programs around comprehensively prohibiting all TAPS over past 10 years shows that public health advocacy played a key role in exploring political support for amending the *Advertising Law*.

Public health advocacy campaigns include the following aspects. First, tobacco control communities communicated the concepts of comprehensive ban on all forms of TAPS through Smoke-Free Day' theme activities and scientific research findings. Second, CATC and other NGOs jointed officials of the Departments of industrial and commercial to promote the effective implementation of current advertising law and regulation through smoke-free advertising city campaign. Third, the tobacco control community criticized some typical cases of TAPS so as to reveal the real nature of TAPS.

Over the past 10 years, such campaigns have added to their force one by one, and the support voice of comprehensively banning all TAPS has finally overwhelmed the voice of the tobacco industry. The following sections reviewed campaigns in the past 10 years in chronological order.

---

[67] Borzekowski DL, Cohen JE. Young children's perceptions of health warning labels on cigarette packages: a study in six countries. *Z Gesundhwiss* 2014; **22:** 175–85.

[68] NPC of P. R. China, Advertising Law of the People's Republic of China (2015), http://www.npc.gov.cn/npc/cwhhy/12jcwh/2015-04/25/content_1934594.htm.

12.5.1   2003–2007

12.5.1.1   Creating a Social Atmosphere Without TAPS

In 1994, the "Creating Tobacco Free Advertising City" campaign was launched with support from Professor Chen MZ, the Minister of Health. On February 21, 2003, the Ministry of Health (MOH) and the SAIC jointly issued the "*The measures for the implementation of the Tobacco Advertisement Free City Nationwide*" to revive the campaign.[69] Thanks to the promotion and cooperation of all sectors of society, many cities removed the outdoor tobacco billboards. In total 29 cities were awarded the "Tobacco Advertisement Free City" until 2007.[70] The campaign of banning TAPS have gradually drawn the public attention.

12.5.1.2   Monitor the Smoke Scene in Films and TVs, and Advocate Smoke-Free Film and TV

In 2003, China CDC monitored smoke scenes in eight TV series and ten movies.[71] Since 2007, CATC had monitored smoke scenes in popular films and TV shows for 6 years, and the results of the survey (see Sect. 12.2) were shocking. Tobacco control supporters appealed to the celebrities in the show business to consider children's health and prevent creating new generations of smokers. They also suggested that the celebrities do not smoke in the screen or advertise tobacco products so as to initiate "Smoke Free Film and Television". From 2007 to 2008, representatives in NPC and CPPCC proposed bills and proposals on "Restricting smoking scenes in films and TV series". The public health policy advocacy has begun.

12.5.1.3   Case Analysis: The Elimination of Marlboro Advertising in F1 Racing

F1 is the abbreviation for "Formula One". F1 is organized by the International Motor Sports Association and has become top of the annual series of racing competitions and the highest level racing competition in the world. Recently it has been amongst the "Three major sports event in the world" together with the Olympic Games and World Cup. The racing is an energetic, young and international game that is the one of most popular competition games among boys and young people. Since 1968, the sponsorship of tobacco companies has been an important source of

---

[69] MOH, SAIC, Notice on implementation measures to identify title of cities without Tobacco advertisement, Feb. 21, 2003. http://www.china.com.cn/chinese/PI-c/284543.htm.

[70] CATC, Summary on effort of tobacco control, 2007. Jan. 15, 2008. http://www.catcprc.org.cn/index.aspx?menuid=4&type=articleinfo&lanmuid=122&infoid=1837&language=cn.

[71] Zhao FM, WU GL, Duan LL, et al., Survey on smoke imagery of the recent film and TV shows in China, Chinese J. Public Health, 2004, 20(3): 372.

funding for F1. Tobacco companies use these sports to effectively reach the market and do marketing targeting youth. From 2004 to 2010, the F1 was held annually in Shanghai. In the 2004 F1 World Champion Chinese Grand Prix, F1 China Grand Prix Organizing Committee (CGPOC),General Administration of Sport of China (GASC), SAIC and China Automobile Association (FASC) proposed that the car body and racer clothing may display tobacco advertising. On February 13, 2004, more than 20 national and international experts in medical and culture field jointly released an open letter "Against tobacco advertising and sponsorship, calling on Smoke-free F1 race". Then, CTCA, China CDC and Think-Tank et al. also lettered to the Director General of SAIC and requested to supervise and manage the illegal activities. With the continuous efforts of all parties, the tobacco advertising was finally withdrawn from the F1 race. More than 75,000 entries related to "Shanghai Smoke-free F1 race" can be retrieved with Google Search. Obviously, this debate aroused people's concern about tobacco advertising and sponsorship issues in F1 race. In 2004, on the second session of the tenth CPPCC, professor Fang JQ and other members submitted proposal No. 2347, Limiting tobacco advertising in auto-race. The GASC actively replied that they will strictly follow the law and forbid all forms of tobacco advertising on the racing track and the press conference to ensure that the F1 World Championship, Chinese Grand Prix, will be a healthy international sporting event.[72]

12.5.2   2008–2012

12.5.2.1   Cultivating a Social Atmosphere Without TAPS

In 2010, the MOH and the Ministry of Education (MOE) requires hospitals and schools not to set up any form of tobacco advertising.[73] The National Patriotic Health Campaign Committee (NPHCC) revised and issued the guideline on the standard of national health city or district, and the methods of examination, supervision and management, and explicitly stipulated that "tobacco free advertising" is an important indicator of the health city.[74]

The tobacco control community promoted the comprehensive ban of all forms of TAPS with might and main at this stage, through various forms of reports, seminars and communication programs, so that the public understand the article 13 of FCTC, for instance, why it is important to have a comprehensive ban on all forms of

---

[72] SASC: To forbid all forms of tobacco advertising on F1 Shanghai playing areas http://news.xinhuanet.com/auto/2004-06/04/content_1508116.htm.

[73] MOE, MOH Opinions on further strengthening school tobacco control work, No.5 (2010), http://www.gov.cn/gzdt/2010-07/13/content_1653147.htm.

[74] National Committee of patriotic Health Campaign, Notice on the measures of the examination, nomination and supervision and administration for national health cities (2011)Health (10), http://www.moh.gov.cn/zwgkzt/pagws1/201101/50263.shtml.

TAPS. In addition, these activities helped people to see the rampant spread of TAPS in China. On the World No Tobacco Day of 2008 and 2010, the MOH launched nationwide campaigns with themes. "Protect the next generation by comprehensive ban on TAPS" and "Gender and tobacco with an emphasis on marketing targeting women", respectively. China CDC released tobacco control reports corresponding to themes described above in 2008 and 2010. The National Population and Family Planning Commission (NPFPC) also called for tobacco control campaign in each province with "The initiatives of eliminating TAPS", which was positively supported by each province. Shanghai successfully hold a smoke-free Expo after refunding the tobacco company, and subsequently, the smoke-free Asian Games and smoke-free UNIVERSIADE were also successfully held.

A series of reports of *2010 GATS China, Tobacco control and the future of China—a joint assessment report on tobacco use and tobacco control in China*[75] and the ITC China report (findings from rounds 1 to 3)[76] revealed the seriousness of TAPS in China. However, facing various of donations and sponsorship from the tobacco industry, many institutions still do not understand the true objective of tobacco industry. In this context, the School of Law, Tsinghua University carried out a simulate hearing on comprehensive ban of TAPS to guide public opinion. In fact, tobacco companies try to facilitate tobacco marketing with the name of "corporate social responsibility" and charitable sponsorship. The Think-Tank, China Cancer Foundation and other 45 commonweal organizations proposed "Protecting public health, actively fulfilling the FCTC and rejecting tobacco donations".[77]

12.5.2.2 Monitoring Smoking Scenes and Advocating Smoke Free Film and Television

In August 2010, the CATC released the results from monitoring the tobacco shots in 40 domestic films and 30 domestic TV shows (see Sect. 12.2). At the press conference, Feng YZ made a speech on behalf of 41 actors and actresses such as PuCX, Yang LX, etc., and call for "smoke-free films and TV shows", guiding the public, especially teenagers, away from tobacco.[78] In 2011, the CATC set up a "Dirty Ashtray Award", offered to those films and TV shows with a lot of smoking footages and tobacco advertising. The CATC hopes the "Dirty Ashtray Award" may promote smoke-free movies and TV shows. The film *Let the Bullets Fly* and TV

---

[75]Yang GH, Hu AG, *Tobacco Control and China' Furniture—The Chinese and Foreign Expertise Joint Assessment Report on Tobacco Use and Control in China*", Economic Time Press, Jan, 2011, Beijing.

[76]China CDC, University of Waterloo, ITC China Project Report Findings from the wave 1 to 3 surveys: 2006-2009.

[77]45 social organization Joint Initiative to reject tobacco sponsorship, China network, Sept. 26, 2010, http://news.xinmin.cn/rollnews/2010/09/26/6991800.html.

[78]Pu CX, et al. 41 actors and actresses advocacy Smoke-free films and TV programs, Xinhua Network, 7, 30, 2009. http://news.xinhuanet.com/health/2009-07/30/content_11798695.htm.

series *Red Cradle* won the first Dirty Ashtray Award in May 2011.[79] The second Dirty Ashtray Award was given to the film *Steel Piano* and the TV series *Iron Age* in 2012. In addition, movies *Close Enemies, Romance 33 Days* and TV shows *Things of Our Family* and other 12 movies and three TV series were awarded the "Smoke-free film and television series award".[80]

The public appeal received official response, the General Office of State Administration of Press, Publication, Radio, Film and Television of The People's Republic of China (the SAPPRFT) issued the notice on strict limiting smoking imagery in movies and TV series in 2011, which explicitly prohibited showing cigarette brands and displaying tobacco products, or any form of disguised tobacco advertising in movies and TV programs.

12.5.2.3   Case Analysis

During 2008–2012,with regarding to promoting comprehensive ban on all forms of TAPS, the most significant and spectacular aspect is the face-to-face confrontation between the tobacco control community and the tobacco industry. Here several typical cases are introduced.

Six Tobacco Enterprises Were Disqualified for China Charity Award

In 2008, the Ministry of Civil Affairs (MOCA) eventually revoked six tobacco enterprises' qualification for the China Charity Award. On November 26, 2008, the nominees of 140 "China Charity Award" enterprises were released on the MOCA website, including six tobacco companies.[81] Is the donation from the tobacco industry a "kindness" action or a marketing tactic? In 2008, the notorious donation was the "Smoking Hope Primary School" and the answer is very clear. Several tobacco control organizations and the director of the WHO Beijing office explicitly stated that it would be a serious violation of the Article 5.3 of WHO FCTC if the "China Charity Award" was given to any tobacco company. Finally, CNTC and other five tobacco companies failed to appear in the list of winners.

Shanghai World Expo Returned Tobacco Company Donations

On May 7, 2009, Shanghai Tobacco (Group) Company donated 200 million RMBs to the China Pavilion on the Shanghai World Expo. It was the largest sum since the launch of targeted donation in December 2007. But accepting donation of a

---

[79] BaiduPedia, Dirty Ashtray Award, http://baike.baidu.com/item/脏烟灰缸奖.

[80] TV series *Iron Age* was received Dirty Ashtray Award, Ban of the SAPPRFT is of no effect netease, 6, 30, 2012, http://ent.163.com/12/0630/08/85811GMH00032DGD.html.

[81] Publicity of MOCA, 2008 the nominees of "China Charity Award" enterprises, http://news.xinhuanet.com/politics/2008-11/26/content_10415537.htm.

tobacco company is a serious violation of the WHO FCTC and also a serious departure from the theme of the Shanghai World Expo, and would seriously damage China's international image as a responsible nation.[82] The CATC, Think-Tank, China CDC and more than 20 well-known medical and public health experts sent multiple letters to the Shanghai World Expo Organizing Committee and strongly urged the Committee to return tobacco enterprises' donations. This event caused a heated debate in the society. Many people did not understand and thought that donations, unlike sponsorship, did not involve marketing; therefore, accepting the tobacco enterprise' contributions did not violate the WHO FCTC.[83] In fact there is no difference between the donation with other sponsorship. The Shanghai World Expo Bureau stopped the donation contract with tobacco companies in July 2009 based on the idea and principal of World Expo and due to social pressure. The event communicated a clear message that tobacco and sports do not mix. Sports must not be used to spread messages that are associated with disease and death. The whole society needs to break the dependence of sport on tobacco and tobacco sponsorship.

Tobacco Hope School Renamed

In 2008, a 7.9-magnitude earthquake destroyed Sichuan province in west china, killing about 90,000 people, including thousands children trapped in shoddily built schools. With the public amid the despair, China's tobacco monopoly saw an opening for charity—and brand-building. CNTC and Sichuan Tobacco Company offered funding to rebuild these schools in distressed areas and named them following cigarette brands. The slogan "Talent Comes from Hard Work—Tobacco Helps You to Be Successful" was painted on the wall in the Sichuan Tobacco Hope Elementary Schools.[84] After this particular school became a flash point and was widely criticized, especially Think-Tank' administrative appeal, the slogan was removed and the school's name was changed by the Sichuan industrial and commercial bureau, and other 14 "tobacco schools" were cleaned up. But "tobacco schools" named after brands, such as "Jiaozi (panda) hope school", are not changed,[85] and a lot of schools across China are still sponsored by the tobacco industry (please see the Sect. 12.2 of the Chapter).

---

[82] Caixin, Shanghai World Expo Bureau stopped the 200 million RBM donation of Shanghai tobacco companies 7, 20, 2009 http://m.china.caixin.com/m/2009-07-20/100061250.html.

[83] Beijing Times, Shanghai World Expo returned tobacco company donation, 07, 23, 2009, http://gongyi.sina.com.cn/gyzx/2009-07-23/091811375.html.

[84] Eriksen M, Mackay J, Ross H. The Tobacco Atlas (Fourth Edition).American Cancer Society and World Lung Foundation. http://www.tobaccoatlas.org/.

[85] Beijing Morning Post, Sichuan "Johnson hope primary school" has not changed, 2013,05,31, http://shipin.people.com.cn/n/2013/0531/c85914-21684691.html.

Terminate Cigarette Brand Marketing of the "Zhong NanHai Love Action: Blue Fashion for Love"

On July 31, 2010, the Donation Center of Beijing Youth Development Foundation and Beijing Cigarette Factory "Zhong NanHai love funding" co-held the "2010 Zhong NanHai love action—blue fashion for love", a large-scale program sponsored by Zhong NanHai love funding. The program adapted one of adolescents' favorite sports form, "Parkour", selected ten "Parkour" winners from each of Beijing, Tianjin, Dalian, Qingdao and Shenzhen, and offered a prize of 1000 RBMs for each winner. The opening ceremony of Zhong NanHai Hope School will be held in Shangri-La of Yunnan as the finale of the program. "Each box of Zhong Nan Hai cigarette you consumed, is your offer of caring to the Hope project!" is printed on this product line's cigarette package.[86] The tobacco company employees cheered: "Let the 'blue fashion' blows up a blue storm, to make the "Zhong Nan Hai" more fashionable and healthier". Eventually, due to protest of the tobacco control community and the legal profession, the final show of the program had to be terminated. The Beijing Industrial and Commercial Bureau imposed an administrative penalty with 10,000 RBM fine as the program "Blue fashion for love" was in violation of the regulations on tobacco advertising and considered as illegal advertisement.[87]

Remove Honorary Titles of "Patriotism Education Base" and et al. of the China Tobacco Museum

China Tobacco Museum is neighboring Shanghai Cigarette Factory, was built with joint donation from the whole tobacco industry of China, and has become the largest tobacco museum in Asia. The Museum was granted "Patriotism education base", "Education base on popular science", "Excellent institution in promoting cultivating ideals and ethics among minors in Shanghai" and so on. It attracts many tourists, especially minors. According to a survey by the Fudan University, after visiting the Museum, the proportion of adolescent visitors who believed that smoking is very harmful to health decreased from 83.1 to 49.2%; and the proportion of those who were sure about their smoking quitting attempt dropped from 82.1 to 75%.[88] On August 21, 2012, the seminar "What message does tobacco museums communicate?" was held in Beijing. The truth of tobacco museums was revealed and analyzed in the meeting. Finally, experts requested to revoke these honorable titles, such as "Patriotism education base" and so on, and also required that the Museum

---

[86] Think-Tank, News Letter for Tobacco Control in China, Issue 4, August, 30, 2010. http://www.ghi-ctp.emory.edu/documents/TTHTCNewsletter_Issue04-8-10.pdf.

[87] Think-Tank, We will never give up—review and analyses of ban TAPS, Tobacco tracking Special issue. 9,12 2014 http://www.tcrc.org.cn/UploadFiles/2014-09/249/20140915095311229678.pdf.

[88] Wang F, Sun S, Yao X, et al. The Museum as a platform for tobacco promotion in China. Tobacco Control, 2016, 25(1):118.

should be closed and any wrong message should be removed to avoid misleading the Youth.[89,90] After coverage by the media, the museum event has aroused wide spread concerns by the public. Finally, all signs with various honorable titles on front wall of the Museum were removed on May 31 2014, World No Tobacco Day.

Remove Hongta Tobacco Billboard in Beijing Station

These was a huge billboard of Yunnan Hongta Group at the entrance on the south square of the Beijing West Railway Station. The billboard showed not only "Hongta Group", the enterprise name, but also the slogan of HongtaGroup, "People are the peak of the high mountain". The image resembling mountain was the symbol of HongtaGroup, which was consistent with the design of the Hongta cigarette pack. Words "Yunnan Hongta Group Co., Ltd. investment and development" were also printed on the billboard. The company is a wholly-owned subsidiary of Hongta Tobacco (Group) Co., Ltd. In accordance with Article 18 of the *Advertising Law* and Article 2 of the *Temporary measures for tobacco advertising management*, the billboard in Beijing West Railway Station was "a tobacco advertisement in disguised form shown at a place prohibited by the state". When complaint about the billboard was filed, both AICs in Beijing and Yunnan decided that this billboard was **not** advertising the Hongta Group corporate image rather than disguised tobacco advertising, and it was a normal corporate disseminating.[91] So the complaint was revoked. There are other similar failed cases, which show that the *Advertising Law* issued in 1995 is incompetent at banning such tobacco advertisements.

There are many cases of revealing and exposing the tobacco industry's marketing in the name of public welfare, which exposed the defects of the *Advertising Law*. These cases also informed the public that under the disguise of donation, the tobacco industry's marketing strategy is actually to influence young people to become new smokers in the future. However, it is impossible to eliminate TAPS if only relaying on reporting, exposing and punishing. For example, the qualification of the tobacco industry for the China Charity Award was revoked in 2008, however, tobacco companies such as the Hongta group and Guangdong Shuangxi were nominated the "Top ten outstanding enterprises of China corporate social responsibility list" again at the end of 2010. Therefore, revising the *Advertising Law* was placed on the agenda.

From 2008 to 2012, within 5 years, representatives in NPC and CPPCC continually submitted suggestions or proposals regarding the revision of the

---

[89] Think-Tank, Should end the negative orientation of tobacco museum News Letter for Tobacco Control in China, Issue 28, August, 30, 2012. http://www.ghi-ctp.emory.edu/documents/TTHTCNewsletter_Issue28-08-12.pdf.

[90] New Daily CATC required to cancel the title of patriotism education base of the museum Aug. 22, 2012 http://news.china.com/domestic/945/20120822/17386485.html.

[91] China Economic Times, Hongta group' disguised tobacco advertising is charged with violating WHO FCTC. 1, 10, 2011. http://news.qq.com/a/20110110/000236.htm.

Advertising Law, and there were also proposals on limiting smoking footages in movies and TV series, eliminating and prohibiting naming Hope Schools after the tobacco industry, and banning any form of sponsorship by tobacco companies.

12.5.3 2013–2016

12.5.3.1 Creating a Social Atmosphere of Free TAPS

In 2013, the NHFPC demanded each province to carry out health education of comprehensive banning TAPS based on the theme of World No Tobacco Day. At the same time, China CDC released "2013 China tobacco control report—comprehensive bans on tobacco advertising, promotion and sponsorship".[92] The report shows that "Tobacco advertising on the traditional media emerges in spite of repeated banning. The tobacco industry is constantly trying new promotional strategies using new media to circumvent advertising and promotion bans. The public awareness of tobacco advertising, promotion and sponsorship are extremely inadequate. Consumers should be alert to tactics adopted by tobacco companies to evade advertising and promotion bans." More than 6000 institutions, such as China CDC, Peking University Health Science Center, Chinese Academy of Sciences, Guangming Daily and so on, signed the commitment on "Rejecting Tobacco Advertising, Promotion and Sponsorship" to resist any form of sponsorship by tobacco companies in the name of the social responsibility, including scientific research funding, scholarship, and so on.[93]

Think-Tank released a report "Who is marketing death?",[94] which reviewed various types of the advertising, promotion and sponsorship of the tobacco industry in China. The report revealed how Chinese tobacco industry displays a variety of tricks, using all possible opportunities to carry out marketing.

From January 1 to April 30, 2013, the CATC launched a program "Take photo of tobacco advertising", which invited the public to observe various form of TAPS, take pictures and send them to website of CATC. 7346 people participated in the campaign, covering nearly four million fans in 15 provinces/municipalities.[95] The activities effectively mobilized the public to monitor TAPS. In 2014, the CATC continued this campaign. The Think-Tank also developed another program "Take photo of tobacco advertising when returning hometown", to encourage

---

[92] China CDC, 2013 China tobacco control report—comprehensive bans on tobacco advertising, promotion and sponsorship, http://www.chinacdc.cn/tzgg/201305/t20130531_81426.htm.

[93] Xinhua Network, More than 600 organizations promise to refuse TAPS. 5, 31, http://finance.qq.com/a/20130531/021167.htm.

[94] Think Tank, Who is marketing death? 2013, http://tcrc.org.cn/html/zy/cbw/ycggcxhzz/2414.html.

[95] CATC Take photo of tobacco advertising, 5, 29, 2013, http://www.catcprc.org.cn/index.aspx?menuid=4&type=articleinfo&lanmuid=122&infoid=4396&language=cn.

Fig. 12.16 Creating a social campaign of TAPS-Free

teachers and students to pay attention to tobacco advertising on local media during the Spring Festival holiday. These activities well mobilized the public to monitor tobacco advertising, promotion and sponsorship. There were also other new media campaigns, such as the "Tobacco advertising kills" program on micro-blog exceed six million reading within 2 weeks.

"*The tobacco control report in 2013*", "*Who is marketing death*" and "Take photo of tobacco advertising" bring the appeal of comprehensive ban TAPS to a climax (Fig. 12.16). The appeal has gradually formed a consensus in the whole society. The proposals on revising the *Advertising Law* of representatives in NPC and CPPCC also focused on the comprehensively banning all forms of tobacco advertising.

12.5.3.2 Promoting the Revision of the *Advertising Law* Regarding Comprehensive Ban on TAPS

The original *Advertisement Law* can no longer solve the recent problems in law enforcement. From 2013 to 2015, China launched there vision project of the *Advertising Law*. In addition, the newly issued *Interim Measures for the Administration of Internet Advertising* and the *Charity Law* also include provisions for tobacco advertising and sponsorship.

Back when the WHO FCTC was signed, the STMA, as a member of the ratifying work group, interfered translation of the Article 13 of the WHO FCTC into Chinese and changed "comprehensive (全面*quanmian*) bans on tobacco advertising, promotion and sponsorship" to "widely (广泛*guangfan*) bans on tobacco advertising, promotion and sponsorship", which subsequently impeded comprehensive ban on TAPS management in China. Should Chinese government leave some space for tobacco advertising? Comprehensive or widely ban is the focus of debate during the process of amending the *Advertising Law* (see Table 12.1).

Table 12.1 The process of revising the *Advertising Law*

Timeline	Process
2/28/14–3/24/14	The Legislative Affairs Office of the State Council collected public opinions on the draft amendment via the internet
06/04/14	The State Council held a standing meeting to discuss and approved the *People's Republic of China Advertising Law* (draft amendment)
08/25/14	The draft amendment was submitted to the tenth session of 12th Standing Committee of NPC for review
08/25/14–09/25/14	Seeking advice again
12/22/14	Reviewed again during the 12th session of the 12th Standing Committee of NPC
12/30/14–01/19/15	Seeking advice again
04/14/15	The revised draft was third reviewed at the 14th session of the 12 Standing Committee of NPC, and the new *Advertising Law* was approved and will come into force on September 1

The *Advertising Law* (Draft Amendment for Comment) and (Revised Draft)

From 2013 to 2014, SAIC drafted the *Advertising Law* of *People's Republic of China* (draft amendment for comment). From February 28 to March 24, 2014, the Legal Affairs Office of the State Council (LAOSC) posted the draft for comment on the internet asking for public opinions. Although the draft enriched ban on tobacco advertising, such as the medium, form and place, but essentially, it still reserved some place for tobacco advertising, and there was a considerable gap between the WHO FCTC and the revised draft.

The draft has received extensive responses. In less than 1 month time, many letters regarding revised amendments of the *Advertising Law* were sent to the LAOSC, hoping to have comprehensive ban on TAPS. In March 2014, the CATC organized a conversation between public health and legal experts with the officials of the SAIC and NHFPC. Experts analyzed current prevalence of Chinese TAPS and presented evidences that partial ban on tobacco advertising was ineffective. After the meeting, 68 well-known experts signed on a letter to the LAOSC and called for ban on all tobacco advertising. Then CATC, Think-Tank and China CDC also wrote a letter to the LAOSC. Some academic articles stated that the *Advertising Law* (draft for comment) could not fully prohibit tobacco advertising.[96] All appeals expressed the same meaning that it is no effective of partial banning tobacco advertising, it is impossible to keep room for tobacco advertising.

WHO expressed great concern on the revision of articles related to tobacco in the *Advertising Law*, congratulated the Government of China on its move to reinforce restrictions on tobacco advertising, and submit their suggestion on revision to

---

[96]Yang GH, Yang J, Huang JR et al. Comments and Revision Suggestion on banning tobacco advertisement items of the Advertisement Law revised Draft of People's Republic of China, Chinese Journal of Health Policy, June 2014, Vol.7 No.6 69–72.

the LAOSC. WHO supported reinforcement of the existing restrictions, but also kindly asked the LAOSC to consider further amendments that will ensure complete, enforceable ban on all TAPS in China. Comprehensive ban on tobacco advertising will significantly reduce the chances that Chinese children grow up to become smokers.[97]

On May 28, China CDC released *2014 China youth tobacco survey report*.[98] The report revealed that the prevalence of testing tobacco products was close to 20% among junior high school students, over 30% in male students; and 64% of these students is easy to obtain cigarettes from tobacco retail stores near the school, which is very serious. On June 5, The survey on the cigarette retail around the middle schools in four districts of Beijing revealed that there were the cigarettes retail store within 100 m near the middle school in over 80% of 128 schools.[99] On June 8,Think-Tank held a communication meeting on "Ban on all TAPS", and pointed out the shortcomings of the current Amendment Advertising Law (draft). "The *Advertising Law* should not leave aback door for tobacco advertising" as a clear appeal was disseminated by Media. After the meeting, 53 public health, medical and legal experts signed on a letter to the Sub-Committee of Legislative Affairs. The campaign give some pressure to legislative departments.

After the State Council submitted Advertising Law amendment to the National People's Congress (NPC), a new round of policy advocating started. Tobacco control group tried to persuade the members of NPC to add "Comprehensive prohibition of all TAPS" into the *Advertisement Law*. China CDC, CATC, Think-Tank and China University of Political Science and Law each wrote to the Sub-Committee of Legislative Affairs together with hundreds of experts. The Sub-Committee also felt the necessity to prudently handle tobacco advertising. In addition, a brochure on Comprehensive prohibition of all TAPS, was mailed to 12 vice-chairmen of the Standing Committee and 158 members of the NPC, to help them understand why the tobacco control community strongly insisted comprehensive banning all form of tobacco advertising.

In July 2014, the public health and tobacco control communities started a discussion topic about "tobacco advertising harms people" on micro-blog. Within 2 weeks, the hits exceeded six million, nearly 4000 people participated in the vote, and 96% of people were in favor of prohibiting all TAPS. These campaigns aggregated the strength of the society and public opinion, and effectively facilitate the process to revise tobacco advertising aspects in the *Advertising Law*.

---

[97] WHO: China needs comprehensive ban on tobacco advertising, promotion & sponsorship, http://www.wpro.who.int/china/mediacentre/releases/2014/20140328/en.

[98] China CDC, 2014 National Youth Tobacco Survey, May, 2014, http://www.nhfpc.gov.cn/ewebeditor/uploadfile/2014/05/20140528121514117.pdf.

[99] Think-Tank, Communication meeting on Don't let tobacco hurt teenagers' health. 6, 6, 2014. http://www.healthtt.org.cn/Item/Show.asp?m=1&d=2827.

The First Review on the *Advertising Law* (Draft Amendment)"

On August 21, 2014, 4 Days before the tenth session of the 12th Standing Committee of NPC reviewed (the first review) the *Advertising Law* (draft amendment), the Think-Tank held a communication meeting, "Review defects of the *Advertisement Law* from complaints on tobacco advertising". It is partial not comprehensive banning All tobacco advertising in 1996 *Advertising Law* that hard to ban the tobacco advertising.[100]

On August 25, 2014, the *Advertising Law* (draft amendment)" was submitted to the 12th session of the 12 Standing Committee of NPC. The Advertising Law (draft) was a great progress and had restricted tobacco advertising in the more media, more forms and more places, and expressly prohibits outdoor tobacco advertising. But the enumeration method was still adopted, leaving room for tobacco advertising. After the first review, articles of the draft were posted again for comments.

After the first review, a new round of campaign for policy promotion and advocacy had been launched. In September, several institutions jointly drafted the *Legislative principles of the Advertising Law*; a communication meeting, "Expectations on amending the *Advertising Law*" was held; in November a communication meeting was held to assess progress and regression of the *Advertising Law* and called for tobacco free films and TV shows, and put forward specific revision to the draft amendment to the *Advertising Law, which* draw attention from both media and the society.

The Second Review of the *Advertising Law* (Draft Amendment)

On December 22, 2014, the *Advertisement Law* amendment (draft)" move into the second review. The amendment (draft) after the second review has banned most tobacco advertising, only except that the tobacco advertisements in retail store. From December 30, 2014 to January 19, 2015, the second draft was solicited opinions from the general public in further.

Although the second draft was better than the first one, it still allowed tobacco advertising in "exclusive tobacco stores", i.e. the "sales terminal" called by tobacco industry, including tobacconist, the cigarettes retail shop in supermarkets, shopping malls, grocery stores, convenience stores, newsstands, etc. where public are free in and out. Some people thought that the revised version of *Advertising Law* on banning tobacco advertising was basically in line with the requirement of the WHO FCTC, but ignored that there were more than 5.4 million tobacco retail terminals, which were the base for tobacco industry to publish tobacco advertising, even deceptive advertisement.

---

[100]Think-Tank, We never give up—review and analysis on campaign of Banning TAPS. 2014, 9, 12.

It is key issues to expose the "hidden" loopholes of the "*Advertising Law*" (the second draft amendment) and let the committee members understand these deficiency of the version right before the third review. The key points of the advocacy are that Advertising Law should comprehensive ban all form of tobacco advertising, especially in the terminal sales.

Comprehensive or partial banning tobacco advertising, that is a question, which caused to discuss passionately. China CDC and CATC launched a micro-video "Comprehensive ban TAPS—to protect young people", to call for the public to support comprehensive ban TAPS. It received more than 100,000 clicks and helped creating the atmosphere of comprehensive ban on tobacco advertising.

The Think-Tank released report "Folk Perspective: 2014 China Tobacco Control Observations" and pointed out that the disaster would be come If tobacco advertising were allowed at 5.4 million selling points. And 55 experts jointly wrote to the Sub-Committee of Legislative Affairs, again call for not leaving space for tobacco advertising in the *Advertising Law*.

NPC representatives actively involved to revise make the *Advertising Law*. During the third review, many representatives supported that the *Advertising Law* should comprehensive ban all TAPS, not allow tobacco advertising in 5.4 million cigarette terminal sales.[101]

The Amendment to the *Advertising Law* Approved After the Third Review

On April 24, 2015, at the 14th session of the 12th Standing Committee of NPC, the amended *Advertising Law* was approved and implemented on September 1. The amended Advertising Law basically comprehensive ban on tobacco advertising. and closer to the requirement of Article 13 of WHO FCTC.

12.5.3.3 Interim Measures for the Administration of Internet Advertising

In order to regulate the internet advertising activities, the SAIC developed the *Interim Measures for the Administration of Internet Advertising* in accordance with the *Advertising Law* and other administrative regulations.[102] The Measures were promulgated on July 4, 2016 and came into effect on September 1, 2016. The Measures explicitly stated that "internet advertising" refers to commercial advertising that markets goods or services directly or indirectly through internet medias such websites, web pages, internet and other applications, e-mail, we-media, internet forums, instant messaging tools, software and other internet media resources, in the form of text, pictures, audio, video or others. According to the above provisions, currently common forms of internet advertising via micro-blog, WeChat, forums

---

[101] NPC, Representatives discussed passionately amendment of Advertising Law, suggested comprehensive banning tobacco advertising, 3, 12, 2015. http://www.npc.gov.cn/npc/xinwen/2015-03/12/content_1925071.htm.

[102] State Administration for Industry & Commerce of P. R. China, The temporal method on management of internet advertising, No. 87, July 4, 2016.

and mobile phone APP have been explicitly included in the regulatory scope. Advertising agencies, advertisers or advertising spokesmen are likely to be identified as internet advertisement publishers at the same time. Tobacco advertising through the internet was forbidden; therefore, any tobacco advertising appearing in circumstances above is illegal.

12.5.3.4 Amendment to the *Charity Law*

On March 9, 2016, the *Charity Law* was passed at the fourth session of the 12th NPC.[103] The *Charity Law* is an important law in the social field and the fundamental and comprehensive law of the charitable system. The "Charity activity" in this law is explicitly defined in the general principle: public interest activities voluntarily carried out by natural person, legal person and other organizations in the form of donating property or providing service or other means for helping the poor and the needy, assisting the elderly, orphans, diseased and disabled, providing the special care, alleviating losses incurred by natural disasters and other emergencies, promoting the development of educational, scientific, cultural, healthcare and sport causes, and protecting the environment, and other causes.

When the *Charity Law* was enacted in 2015, some experts, academics and tobacco control staff in the public health and legal fields suggested to prohibit any charitable donation and other campaigns by tobacco industry in the name of tobacco "corporate social responsibility" with the corresponding legal responsibility, in line with the WHO FCTC' principal. Any form of tobacco donation or sponsorship in the name of charity should be warned, forced to stop ongoing activity and fined. Finally Article 40, paragraph 2 of *Charity Law* has stipulated: "Any organization or individual shall use charitable donations to publicize tobacco products in violation of the law, and shall not use charitable donations or any other methods to publicize products and matters prohibited from being publicized by laws." It is a great progress. However, there are a lot of work to do. The whole society need to recognize that so-called donation of tobacco industry cannot be related to tobacco products publicity, e.g. "Golden Leaf Fund" and "Zhong NanHai Fund". Also it is needs to be further specified and detailed in the implementation guideline of the Law.

12.6 Closing Remarks

China' progress is impressive on the actions and progress of the comprehensive ban TAPS in the past 10 years in this Chapter. The *Advertising Law*, the *Interim Measures for the Administration of Internet Advertising* and the *Charity Law* related to ban TAPS have come into force successively.

---

[103] Decree of the Chairman of the People's Republic of China, the Charity Law of P. R. China, No.4 3, March 16, 2016.

There has been a decrease in smoking scenes in film and television programs. In 2015, among 30 domestic films, 22 films showed tobacco scenes, decreased 15% compared with that in 2007. Among the 22 films with tobacco scenes, there were on average 11.5 shots of tobacco in each movie, being half in 2007. Among 12 with tobacco shots of 30 domestic TV series, there were 225 tobacco shots in total, and the average 0.4 per episode, which was less than 10% of the number in 2007.[104]

It is necessary to promote the effective implementation of the new *Advertising Law*. The report "Folk Perspective: 2016 China Tobacco Control Observations"[105] and Report on tobacco advertising enforcement observation at the first anniversary of the New Advertising Law[106] revealed a lot of problems of banning tobacco advertising. The relevant legal explanations of the Advertising Law is absence. The law-executors had different understanding of the Article related to tobacco advertising, and implement very week. Internet medias were awash and flooded with tobacco advertising, such as Baidu, WeChat public platform and Sina micro-blog, and so on. Tobacco marketing via social media such as WeChat and micro-blog is the biggest concern.

All shows that China still has a long way to go regarding the implementation of Article 13 of the WHO FCTC, comprehensive ban TAPS.

---

[104] CATC: The smoking image significantly reduced in domestic film and TV, China News, May 17, 2016 http://www.chinanews.com/sh/2016/05-17/7873631.shtml.

[105] Think-Tank,Tobacco Control Observation 2016, by civil vision.

[106] Beijing Evening News, Is the internet not controlled by Law of tobacco control? Feb. 8, 2017 http://health.people.cn/n1/2017/0208/c14739-29065775.html.

Chapter 13
Tobacco Tax and Tobacco Economy in China

Rong Zheng

Abstract Tax and price policies are widely recognized to be one of the most effective means of influencing the demand for and thus the consumption of tobacco products. Consequently, implementation of Article 6 of the WHO Framework Convention on Tobacco Control (WHO FCTC) is an essential element of tobacco-control policies and thereby efforts to improve public health. It is well documented that increasing taxes on tobacco products can provide dual benefits of reducing the disease and death caused by tobacco use as well as generating income for government's revenues. However, the effectiveness of implementing tax and price policy depends on a few of key points of tax structure design and administration. China adopts a monopoly system for tobacco industry, the monopoly is extremely profitable and powerful to interfere with the tax policy applied in tobacco products and hence challenges the effectiveness and efficiency of implementing Article 6 in China. Nevertheless, the latest tobacco tax adjustment in 2015 proves that raising tobacco tax and price is a win-win strategy for the purpose of tobacco control. The 2015 tobacco tax adjustment increased government's revenue, decreased cigarette consumption, brought positive impact on public health. However, it's also notable that cigarette price is still extremely low and increasingly affordable over time; the tax as % of retail price is still far behind WHO recommended standard; the mixed tiered tax structure provides incentives for price manipulations to the extent that manufacturers can alter their pricing or production behavior to avoid higher tax liabilities. All these indicates China still has a long way on tobacco tax hiking, especially needs to focus on a few key issues such as reducing cigarette affordability, re-orienting excise tax structure towards specific in the medium-term, and towards a uniform system either mixed or specific in the long-term, as well as establishing a system that will earmark the tobacco tax revenue for public health services and sustainable development goals.

Keywords Tobacco tax · Tobacco industry · Tobacco control · China

R. Zheng
University of International Business and Economics, Beijing, China
e-mail: rosezheng@uibe.edu.cn

© Springer Nature Singapore Pte Ltd. 2018
G. Yang (ed.), *Tobacco Control in China*,
https://doi.org/10.1007/978-981-10-8315-0_13

13.1 Introduction

Smoking is a major obstacle to health and sustainable development in China. One million Chinese citizens die each year from smoking-attributable diseases, with this death toll set to double by 2030.[1,2] The treatment of diseases caused by smoking account for 3.4% of health expenditure in China, representing a substantial burden on health system resources especially as these expenditures are due to a preventable risk factor-smoking.[3] Furthermore, out-of-pocket medical expenditures associated with smoking impoverish tens-of-millions of Chinese households each year.[4] The Chinese Government's performance has been very slow, since WHO Framework Convention on Tobacco Control (WHO FCTC) came into force in China in Jan. 2006. Article 6 of the Convention obligates FCTC Parties to adopt pricing and taxation measures that reduce tobacco consumption.[5] Article 6 guidelines further recommend that Parties implement regular adjustment processes or procedures to make tobacco products less affordable over time, including periodic revaluation of tobacco tax levels that take into account price and income elasticity, inflation, and changes in household income.[6]

This chapter addresses economic aspects, particularly tobacco tax policy in China. Section 13.2 provides the key points of the implementation of article 6 of WHO FCTC; Sect. 13.3 describes China tobacco industry and tobacco market, cigarettes pricing mechanism and China's tobacco taxation system; Sect. 13.4 describes the studies on tobacco tax in China, the advocacy of promoting increasing tax of tobacco products, and assessment of cigarette excise tax adjustments in 2009 and 2015; Sect. 13.5 summarizes the barriers, challenges and policy recommendations of implementing tax and price policy for the purpose of tobacco control.

13.2 The Key Points of Implementing Article 6 of WHO FCTC

WHO FCTC marked a momentous achievement in the history of tobacco control when it entered into force in February 2005 after more than 3 years' negotiation. It has become one of the most rapidly embraced and measurably successful treaty in

[1] WHO global report: mortality attributable to tobacco. Geneva, World Health Organization, 2012.

[2] Peto R, Lopez AD. 2001. "Future worldwide health effect of current smoking patterns". In: Critical issues in global health, edited by Koop CE, Pearson CE, Schwarz MR. New York: Jossey-Bass.

[3] Sung HY, Wang L, Jin S, Hu TW, Jiang Y. 2006. "Economic burden of smoking in China". Tobacco Control 15:5–11.

[4] Liu YL, Rao KQ, Hu TW, Sun Q, Mao ZZ. 2006. "Cigarette smoking and poverty in China". Social Science & Medication 63: 2784–2790.

[5] World Health Organization. 2003. WHO Framework Convention on Tobacco Control. WHO, Geneva.

[6] Guidelines for implementation of Article 6 of the WHO FCTC. FCTC Secretariat: http://www.who.int/fctc/guidelines/adopted/Guidelines_article_6.pdf?ua=1.

united Nations history.[7] To ensure the compliance of FCTC, WHO released a set of six recommendations that make up the acronym MPOWER to help countries meet their WHO FCTC obligations. The acronym's last letter stands for "raising" taxes on tobacco. The WHO had defined its best-practice excise tax rate for this recommendation at a minimum of 70% of the consumer price of tobacco product.[8]

Price and tax measures has been widely recognized using as the most effective way to curb demand for tobacco products. Article 6 of the Convention states that, "price and tax measures are an effective and important means of reducing tobacco consumption by various segments of the population, in particular young person", which include:

- Implementing tax policies and, where appropriate, price policies, on tobacco products so as to contribute to the health objectives aimed at reducing tobacco consumption; and
- Prohibiting or restricting, as appropriate, sales to and/or importations by international travelers of tax- and duty-free tobacco products".[9]

To assist with implementation of Article 6, the guideline was adopted on 18 October 2014 further stresses:

- Determining tobacco taxation policies is a sovereign right of the Parties.
- Effective tobacco taxes significantly reduce tobacco consumption and prevalence.
- Effective tobacco taxes are an important source of revenue.
- Tobacco taxes are economically efficient and reduce health inequalities.
- Tobacco tax systems and administration should be efficient and effective.
- Tobacco tax policies should be protected from vested interests.[10]

Because of the complexity of the tax system and the other reasons, only 10% of the world's population lives in one of the thirty-three countries where the tax on a pack of cigarettes represented 75% of the pack's total cost.[11]

To make tax policy an effective measure for the purpose of curbing tobacco use requires a series of key points being well applied technically as well as politically. Technically, the tax structure needs to be well designed and well administered. Usually, a well designed tax structure ensures not only generating reliable revenue stream but also capacity of ensuring tax compliance. In addition, the complexity of

---

[7] World Health Organization. 2015. WHO report on the global tobacco epidemic, 2015: Raising taxes on tobacco. WHO, Geneva.

[8] World Health Organization. 2015. WHO report on the global tobacco epidemic, 2015: Raising taxes on tobacco. WHO, Geneva.

[9] World Health Organization. 2003. WHO Framework Convention on Tobacco Control. WHO, Geneva.

[10] World Health Organization. 2015. WHO report on the global tobacco epidemic, 2015: Raising taxes on tobacco. WHO, Geneva.

[11] World Health Organization. 2015. WHO report on the global tobacco epidemic, 2015: Raising taxes on tobacco. WHO, Geneva.

excise tax structure in many countries gives tobacco industry opportunities to keep tobacco tax at a low level. Besides, price and tax levels of tobacco product, affordability, and uses of tax revenue are need to be carefully deliberated by policy makers.

13.2.1 Tobacco Tax Structure Design and Administration

Choosing an appropriate tobacco tax structure for a country is paramount to a successful strategy for promoting both public health and public finance. Main aspects need to be carefully addressed for tobacco tax structure design include:

Tax types. Governments impose a variety of taxes on tobacco and tobacco products, including tobacco leaf at the agriculture segment, excise taxes, value added taxes (VAT), general sales taxes, duties on tobacco product imports or other special taxes. Of these, tobacco product excise taxes are most important for achieving the health objective of reduced tobacco consumption since these are the taxes that are uniquely applied to tobacco products and that raise the prices of these products relative to the prices of other goods and services.

Segments to impose excise taxes. Tobacco product excises are generally, but not always, applied early in the distribution chain (on importers/manufacturers or distributors). Most governments levy excise taxes and other taxes on tobacco products at import and production level. Given there are less importer/producers than wholesalers and retailers, it is easier to enforce tax compliance and reduce administrative costs at import and production level than at the wholesale and retail level.

Specific and ad valorem excise taxes. A specific excise tax is levied based on quantity (e.g., a fixed amount per cigarette or weight of tobacco), while an ad valorem excise is levied based on value (e.g., a percentage of the factory price or import price). Ad valorem tobacco excises are more difficult to administer, hence these increase opportunities for tax avoidance and evasion, and create greater gaps in prices between high and low-priced brands and thus to encourage switching down when tax increases. In contrast, greater reliance on specific excise taxes maximizes the impact of tobacco taxes on public health by reducing the gap in prices between premium and low-priced alternatives, thereby limiting opportunities for users to switch down in response to tax increases. Applying the same specific tax to all brands of a given tobacco product also sends the clear message that all brands are equally harmful. Global current trends point to a greater use of specific taxes, although mixed systems are also commonly used in different countries.

In 2014, there are 119 (92% of State providing report) WHO FCTC Parties levying some form of excise tax on tobacco products, ten countries, which do not have local cigarette production, apply only import duty on tobacco products. Most FCTC parties apply Value-added tax (VAT) or sales taxes on tobacco products, but VAT or

Table 13.1 FCTC Parties levying tax on cigarettes in 2014, by WHO region

WHO region	Excise tax						Import		Total
	Specific only	%	Ad valorem only	%	Both	%	Duty only	%	
Western Pacific	14	61	2	9	4	17	3	13	23
European	9	19	–	–	38	79	1	2	48
Americas	7	39	4	22	6	33	1	6	18
African	7	30	11	49	3	13	2	8	23
Eastern Mediterranean	2	16	3	25	5	42	2	17	12
South-East Asia	1	20	3	60	–	–	1	20	5
Overall	40	31	23	18	56	43	10	8	129

Resources: 2014 Global progress report on implementation of the WHO Framework Convention on Tobacco Control (World Health Organization. 2014. 2014 Global progress report on implementation of the WHO Framework Convention on Tobacco Control. WHO, Geneva)

sales taxes are not recognized as part of tobacco control policies since they are also imposed on all kinds of products with eh same tax rates. Therefor excise tax, which is imposed on tobacco and a few selected goods, is considered as part of tobacco control policy.[12] Information on the type of taxation applied to cigarettes, by region, is presented in Table 13.1.

The predominant type of cigarette taxation that the Parties impose vary in different regions. For example, the most-reported form of tax in the Parties of the African Region was ad valorem only; on the other hand, most Parties in the Western Pacific Region reported that they levy specific taxes only; Parties in the European Region (approximately 80% of the respondents) favored a combination of ad valorem and specific excise taxes.

Simplifying Tax Structure. Complex tax structures are difficult to administer, create opportunities for tax avoidance and evasion, and are less effective in achieving public health and revenue goals. A good candidate for a well-designed tax system is a simple and unified excise tax system with all tobacco products taxed at the same segment. Such a system would be an ideal system for tax authorities with respect to generating more revenues while reducing cigarette consumption.

Strong tax administration is a requisite for ensuring high compliance effectively and administering tax policies efficiently in the sense that administrative costs are low relative to revenue collected. Good tax administration requires strong technical capacity but also a well-designed tax. Tax administrative agencies should be aware of the market conditions and the factors affecting tobacco sales and hence their impact on the revenue stream. These factors should be taken into consideration when a tax policy is designed so that both public health and revenue objectives are achieved.

---

[12] World Health Organization. 2014. 2014 Global progress report on implementation of the WHO Framework Convention on Tobacco Control. WHO, Geneva.

13.2.2 Tax as % of Retail Price of Cigarettes

WHO recommends that tobacco tax as percentage of retail price of tobacco products should be over 75%. Based on *WHO Report on the Global Tobacco Epidemic, 2017*,[13] there were 32 Parties satisfied the standard in 2016, including 21 from high income countries, 10 from middle income countries and only 1 from low income countries. In addition, 70 countries' tobacco tax rates were between 50 and 75%, including China.[14] Thirty countries' tobacco tax rate was very low, less than 25%, even without a special tax imposing on tobacco products at all. It's important to promote the implement of increasing tobacco tax so as to keep pace with other policies because if the government does not impose a heavy tax on tobacco products, cigarettes would be affordable for most smokers, which would weaken the achievement from other measures.[15]

13.2.3 Cigarette Prices and Affordability

Overall, price and tax levels are higher in high-income countries than in middle-income countries and low-income countries. In 2015, the average price of a pack of cigarettes in high-income countries was $5.53, with excise and other taxes making up 64.8% of that figure. In low-income countries, the price of a pack cigarettes averaged $2.03, with excise and other taxes making up 45.8% of the price.[16]

In 2016, the weighted average price measured in purchasing power is PPP$7.19 for high-income countries, PPP$4.31 for middle-income countries, PPP$3.03 for low-income countries, and PPP$4.87 for global average.[17]

Comparing to price reported in 2012, in 2014, 86 countries (84%) reported an increase in nominal price, more than half of those reporting a growth in nominal price which is 20% higher. The price was stable in 13 countries and had declined in three countries (Bahamas, Bahrain and South Africa).[18] Table 13.2 presents lowest and highest cigarette prices in US dollars in 2014 by WHO region.

---

[13] World Health Organization. 2017. WHO Report on the Global Tobacco Epidemic, 2017,WHO, Geneva.

[14] World Health Organization. 2015. WHO report on the global tobacco epidemic, 2015: Raising taxes on tobacco. WHO, Geneva.

[15] World Health Organization. 2017. WHO Report on the Global Tobacco Epidemic, 2017, WHO, Geneva.

[16] World Health Organization. 2015. WHO report on the global tobacco epidemic, 2015: Raising taxes on tobacco. WHO, Geneva.

[17] World Health Organization. 2017. WHO Report on the Global Tobacco Epidemic, 2017, WHO, Geneva.

[18] World Health Organization. 2014. 2014 Global progress report on implementation of the WHO Framework Convention on Tobacco Control. WHO, Geneva.

Table 13.2 Prices for a pack of 20 cigarettes in 2014 (in US dollars), by WHO region

WHO region	Lowest (country)	Highest (country)	Ratio	Number of countries
Western Pacific	0.75	16.09	21.50	22
European	0.55	16.37	29.50	47
Americas	1.00	7.80	7.80	17
African	0.35	5.30	15.00	20
Eastern Mediterranean	0.77	2.40	3.20	10
South-East Asia	0.35	2.40	6.90	5
Western Pacific	0.75	16.09	21.50	22

Resources: 2014 Global progress report on implementation of the WHO Framework Convention on Tobacco Control (World Health Organization. 2014. 2014 Global progress report on implementation of the WHO Framework Convention on Tobacco Control. WHO, Geneva)

Policymakers need to pay attention to affordability of cigarettes over a reference of period because tobacco products become more affordable if price increases do not keep pace with increases in per capita income and consumer purchasing power over time.

13.2.4   Earmarking Tobacco Taxes for Health and Social Development Goals

It is increasingly common for Member States to allocate a proportion of tobacco tax revenues to social programs either through hard or soft earmarking practices. In 2014, WHO found that only 30 countries' tobacco taxes are for health purposes.[19] Examples from those countries include the following: in Bulgaria, according to Health Act, the state of excise taxes on tobacco products 1% tax to support projects in countries restrict smoking and drinking alcohol; in Costa Rica, a regulation adopted in 2012 offer funds to improve the allocation of tobacco consumption tax, including 60% for diagnosis, treatment and prevention of diseases associated with tobacco, and 20% will perform their functions of the ministry of health regulations, the rest will be used for alcohol and drug control programs and sports and recreational activities; in Jamaica, through the National Health Fund, 5% of a special consumption tax and 20% of a consumption tax on tobacco are used for public education and treatment of non-communicable diseases, including tobacco control; in Lao People's Democratic Republic, according to the Tobacco Control Fund Decree which was approved in May 2013, a special tax on local and imported cigarettes from 200 kip (about $0.02) in Laos is levied on health care and tobacco control activities; and in the Philippines, in 2012, the Sin Tax Law increases tobacco and alcohol taxes, and establishes that 85% of the extra income will be used to provide health insurance for low-income people; the remaining funds will be used

---

[19]World Health Organization. 2015. WHO report on the global tobacco epidemic, 2015: Raising taxes on tobacco. WHO, Geneva.

to fund health promotion programs and expand health infrastructure.[20] In Indonesia, a 10% surcharge on excise revenue from tobacco, with at least half of the amount collected being allocated to regional health programs.[21] In 2015, Bangladesh introduced a new Health Cess of 1% on the retail price of cigarettes. India has introduced a number of additional duties on tobacco products to help fund new initiatives, including the introduction of a Health Cess in 2005. The revenue from this cess goes into the Consolidated Fund, and spent to help meet the National Rural Health Mission (aimed at improving health infrastructure and strengthening rural health systems in India).[22] In 2001, India introduced a National Calamity Contingent Duty following an earthquake in the state of Gujarat. The tobacco tax revenue was transferred to a single fund maintained by the Central Government to help to provide disaster relief by transferring payments.[23]

These examples highlight a wide range of earmarking practices in developing countries, starting from the provision of small social sector allocations up to fully financing the scale-up of major initiatives such as health insurance in the Philippines.

13.3   China Tobacco Monopoly System and Tobacco Tax Structure

13.3.1   Management System of Tobacco Industry in China

China ranks No. 1 in both tobacco consumption and tobacco production. It produces and consumes one-third of the world's cigarettes.[24] China National Tobacco Company (CNTC) caters to its customer base of 316 million smokers,[25] who consume 2.3 trillion individual cigarettes in 2016.[26] In 2016, there are about 17 provincial cigarettes manufactories which produce 87 family brands of cigarettes with a total production of 47.1078 million boxes (50,000 individual pieces per box) cigarettes contributing 1079.5 billion RMB tobacco tax and profits, which accounts for

---

[20] World Health Organization. 2014. 2014 Global progress report on implementation of the WHO Framework Convention on Tobacco Control. WHO, Geneva.

[21] World Health Organization. 2016. Earmarked tobacco taxes: lessons learnt from nine countries. WHO, Geneva.

[22] SEARO World Health Organization. June 2011. "Innovative financing from tobacco taxation for health promotion". Report of the expert group meeting. SEARO WHO, New Delhi.

[23] World Health Organization. 2016. Earmarked tobacco taxes: lessons learnt from nine countries. WHO, Geneva.

[24] Hu TW, Mao ZZ, Shi J, Chen WD. 2008. Tobacco taxation and its potential impact in China. International Union Against Tuberculosis and Lung Disease, Paris.

[25] Chinese Center for Disease Control and Prevention. 2015. 2015 China Adult Tobacco Survey Report.

[26] Data calculated from the sales volume information provided by the 2017 National Tobacco Industry Conference. http://www.tobacco.gov.cn/history_filesystem/2017ycgzh/ldjh-1.html.

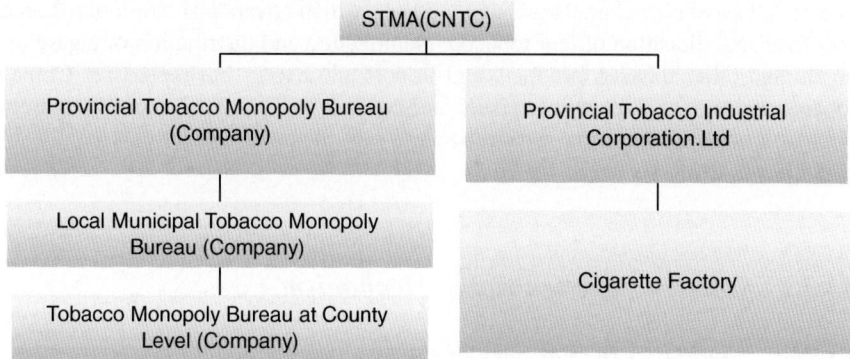

Fig. 13.1 China tobacco monopoly system. Note: Figure made by author based on China Tobacco Yearbook 2015 (China State Tobacco Monopoly Administration. China Tobacco Yearbook. Beijing: China Economic Publishing House)

6.8% of government's fiscal income.[27,28,29,30] Before 2015, both cigarette production and consumption had been steadily increasing, 2015 was the first year in the past two decades to see a convert of both cigarette production and consumption in China, and the declining trend kept in 2016.

China's tobacco industry adopts a system of unified leadership, vertical management and monopolized operation based on a series of laws and regulations which include: 'Rules on Tobacco Monopoly' issued by the State Council in September 1983; In 1984, the State Council agreed to change the Tobacco Monopoly Bureau of the Ministry of Light Industry into the State Tobacco Monopoly Administration (STMA) and merge into the China Tobacco Corporation, retaining two names: China Tobacco Company and the State Tobacco Monopoly Bureau. The so-called "one agency, two brands".[31] The 'Law of the People's Republic of China on Tobacco Monopoly' issued by the Standing Committee of the National People's Congress in June 1991; The 'Rules for Implementation of the Law of the People's Republic of China on Tobacco Monopoly' issued by the State Council in July 1997. The structure of the China's tobacco monopoly system is illustrated in Fig. 13.1.

The CNTC is a state-owned enterprise qualified as a legal person and authorized by the Chinese Government to act in the capacity of the state tobacco monopoly. According to the Law of the People's Republic of China (PRC) on Tobacco Monopoly promulgated by the Chinese Government, the CNTC is empowered to

---

[27] China State Tobacco Monopoly Administration. China Tobacco Yearbook. Beijing: China Economic Publishing House.

[28] Data sourced from the CEInet Statistics Database. http://db.cei.gov.cn/page/others.aspx.

[29] Data sourced from the 2017 National Tobacco Industry Conference. http://www.tobacco.gov.cn/history_filesystem/2017ycgzh/ldjh-1.html.

[30] Calculated by author with the data from the National Bureau of Statistics of China. http://www.stats.gov.cn/tjsj/zxfb/201702/t20170228_1467424.html.

[31] STMA, Chinese tobacco memorabilia. http://www.tobacco.gov.cn/html/10/1003/56860_n.html.

operate all aspects of China's tobacco industry, which covers plantation of tobacco, purchase and allocation of leaf tobacco, manufacture and distribution of cigarettes, cigars and other tobacco products and import and export businesses for China's tobacco industry. STMA directly sets and controls the retail price of all cigarette brands through its licensing system because only licensed retailer can legally sell cigarettes in China.

13.3.2 China Cigarette Pricing Mechanism

13.3.2.1 Cigarette Prices at Each Segment

Under the monopoly system, cigarette price structure in China consists of four prime categories, producer price, allocation price, wholesale price and retail price.

Producer price. Cigarette producer price is the price when cigarettes first enter into circulation which includes production costs, taxes and profits. Before June 2001, producer price is the tax base of cigarettes excise tax.

Allocation price. Under China's monopoly system, the STMA makes cigarette 'allocation plans' so that the price in the process is known as allocation price. The allocation price refers to the price which the tobacco producer offers to the wholesaler. The difference between producer price and allocation price is that producer price is an economic conception, while allocation price is peculiar to tax consideration. Allocation price only refers to producer price that has been approved by tax authority. Since 2001, allocation price has become the tax base for excise tax which has become an important factor in taxation consideration.

Wholesale price. Wholesale price is the price at which wholesalers offer cigarettes to retailers. In China, all of cigarette wholesalers belong to CNTC so that they are under direct leadership and management of STMA and CNTC.

Retail price. Retail price is the price at which retailers sell cigarettes to consumers, and it is the final price of tobacco products. Retailers are required to obtain cigarette sales permission from STMA/CNTC, but keeping themselves independent from STMA/CNTC.

Under the cigarette monopoly system, the profit margin plays a vital role in Chinese cigarette pricing mechanism. The allocation-wholesale profit margin (a) and wholesale-retail profit margin (b) are both set by STMA. Given the allocation price, STMA can control wholesale price and retail price with no difficulty as it wished by adjusting allocation-wholesale margin (a) and wholesale-retail margin (b).

Equation (13.1) demonstrates the pricing rationale where Pr is retail price, "A" represents allocation price (excise tax inclusive, VAT exclusive), a indicates the allocation-wholesale profit margin, b indicates the wholesale-retail profit margin, and Rtvat indicates the VAT rate.

$$Pr = A \times (1+a) \times (1+b) \times (1+Rtvat) \tag{13.1}$$

As addressed, retail price equals the allocation price plus the allocation-wholesale margin, wholesale-retail margin and VAT tax. In cigarette pricing process, A is excise tax inclusive, hence no excise tax appears in Eq. (13.1) and it is VAT exclusive. As we know, VAT is collected at all circulation segments, therefore, putting the one factor of (1 + Rtvat) at the end of the equation shall include all the VAT collected. Additionally, Tax C&E is collected along with excise tax and VAT which is included in the two margins and not showed in the equation.

13.3.2.2 Who Determines Cigarette Price?

Under the monopoly system, the STMA adopts the unified leadership and vertical monopoly administration and management to manage the tobacco industry, including cigarette price and market system. In the Law of the People's Republic of China on Tobacco Monopoly,[32] Article 17 states cigarette price development as following:

- *The department of tobacco monopoly administration under the State Council, together with the pricing authorities under the State Council, shall select cigarettes of certain brands as indicators on a grading basis.*
- *The prices of such indicators shall be set by the pricing authorities under the State Council together with the department of tobacco monopoly administration under the State Council.*
- *The prices of non-indicator cigarettes, of cigars and cut tobacco shall be fixed by the department of tobacco monopoly administration under the State Council or by the departments of tobacco monopoly administration of the provinces, autonomous regions and municipalities directly under the Central Government, as authorized by the department of tobacco monopoly administration under the State Council, and shall be submitted for the record to the pricing authorities under the State Council or to the pricing authorities under the people's governments of the relevant provinces, autonomous regions and municipalities directly under the Central Government.*

The Law of the People's Republic of China on Tobacco Monopoly was revised in 24 April 2015,[33] and Article 17 was deleted. There's no other laws or rules that mention the administration ownership of cigarette price.

In the light of tobacco monopoly law, both the STMA and the NDRC have the right to price cigarettes. But in fact, it is the tobacco industry (including cigarette factory, tobacco company, tobacco monopoly bureau and at last the STMA) who determines cigarette price in different fields.

---

[32] The Law of the People's Republic of China on Tobacco Monopoly. http://www.tobacco.gov.cn/html/27/2701/270101/765012_n.html.

[33] The Law of the People's Republic of China on Tobacco Monopoly revised in 24 April 2015: http://www.tobacco.gov.cn/html/27/2701/270101/4923721_n.html.

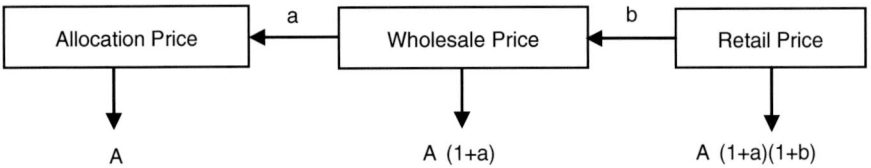

Fig. 13.2 Cigarette pricing mechanism in China

13.3.2.3 Cigarette Pricing Mechanism

Under the cigarette monopoly system, cigarette pricing mechanism is unique in China. According to Eq. (13.1), theoretically, cigarette retail price is set first, then push back to wholesale price and allocation price in accordance with wholesale-retail profit margin (b) and allocation-wholesale profit margin (a) respectively. The wholesale-retail profit margin (b) and allocation-wholesale profit margin (a) are both set by STMA, so once the retail price is determined, the wholesale price and allocation price are fixed accordingly as long as the two margins are strictly followed by tobacco companies. Likewise, given the allocation price, STMA can easily control wholesale price and retail price as it wished by adjusting allocation-wholesale margin (a) and wholesale-retail margin (b).

As mentioned, the retail price is equal to the allocation price plus allocation-wholesale margin, wholesale-retail margin and value-added tax. Among all the taxes discussed, only tobacco leaf tax, excise tax, VAT, and Construction and Education Tax are turnover tax which is directly related with cigarette price. Because tobacco leaf tax only amounts very little over the total tobacco tax, we do not consider it in this paper. In cigarette pricing process, A is excise tax inclusive, hence no excise tax appears in Eq. (13.1) and it is VAT exclusive. As we know, VAT is collected at all circulation segments, therefore, putting the one factor of (1 + Rtvat) at the end of the equation shall include all the VAT collected. Additionally, Tax C&E is collected along with excise tax and VAT which is included in the two margins and not showed in the equation. Other taxes discussed above are not involved in cigarette pricing mechanism and we do not address them in this paper. Figure 13.2 shows how cigarette prices are made at each segment and all the prices in the figure are VAT exclusive.

13.3.2.4 Cigarette Classification and Grading

For the purpose of cigarette pricing and management, all cigarettes are differentiated from Class I to Class V using allocation price as the standard of classification. Meanwhile, for tax purpose, cigarettes are also divided into Grade A and Grade B by differentiating their allocation prices. The two grades of cigarettes'ad valorem tax rates of excise tax are different. Table 13.3 shows cigarette classification from Class I to Class V and Grade A and Grade B since May, 2009.

Table 13.3 Cigarette classification and grading (since 2009)

Allocation price per pack (RMB)	Grade	Class
[10, +∞)	A	I
[7, 10)		II
[5, 7)	B	III
[3, 5)		
[1.65, 3)		IV
(0, 1.65)		V

Note: Table made by author based on China Tobacco Yearbook 2010 (China State Tobacco Monopoly Administration. China Tobacco Yearbook. Beijing: China Economic Publishing House)

13.3.3 China Tobacco Tax Structure

China's tobacco products are applied the following taxes: tobacco leaf tax, excise tax, value-added tax (VAT), urban maintenance and construction tax and extra charges of educational fee (C&E) (see Table 13.4). Among all of these, the tobacco leaf tax and excise tax are particularly targeted toward the tobacco industry. Cigarette excise tax ranks first in deciding the tax burden of tobacco products so that it has direct and important impacts on the tobacco industry.

13.3.4 Tax Revenue Generated from Tobacco Industry

CNTC contributed around 7% of the public revenue which has been ranked No. 1 among all the industries in China in the past two decades.[34] In 2016, CNTC's contributed 1000.6 billion RMB tax revenue and profit contribution which account to 6.8% of fiscal revenue.[35] Figure 13.3 illustrates tobacco tax and tobacco profit contribution as % of government's fiscal revenue between 2000 and 2016.

13.4 The Implementation of Article 6 in China

As WHO pointed out, tax and price policies are widely regarded as one of the most effective means of influencing demand and consumption of tobacco products. Therefore, Article 6 implemented by the WHO FCTC is necessary for tobacco

---

[34] Calculated by author with the longitudinal data on government revenue and State-owned capital gains collected by author.

[35] Calculated by author with the data from the 2017 National Tobacco Industry Conference report. http://www.tobacco.gov.cn/history_filesystem/2017ycgzh/index.html. and National Bureau of Statistics of China. http://www.stats.gov.cn/tjsj/zxfb/201702/t20170228_1467424.html.

Table 13.4 China tobacco tax structure (since May 2015)

Type of tax	Tax level	Tax base	Tax rate	Revenue beneficiary
Tobacco leaf tax	Agriculture	Value of tobacco leaf	20%	100% local government
Value-added tax at cigarette manufacture (VAT)	Produce wholesale and retail	Added value at each level	17%	75% central government
				25% local government[a]
Specific excise tax	Produce	Per pack	0.06 RMB	100% central government
	Wholesale		0.10 RMB	
Ad valorem excise tax	Produce, wholesale	Allocation price (without VAT)		
	≥70 RMB per carton		56%	
	<70 RMB per carton		36%	
	Wholesale		11%	
Urban maintenance and construction tax and extra charges of educational fee (C&E Tax)	Produce, wholesale, retail	Tax amount of VAT and excise tax	12%	100% local government

[a]Since 2016, VAT is distributed half and half between central and provincial governments
Note: Table made by author based on the tax legislation 2016 (The Chinese Institute of Certified Public Accounts. Taxation Laws. Beijing: China Economic Science Press)

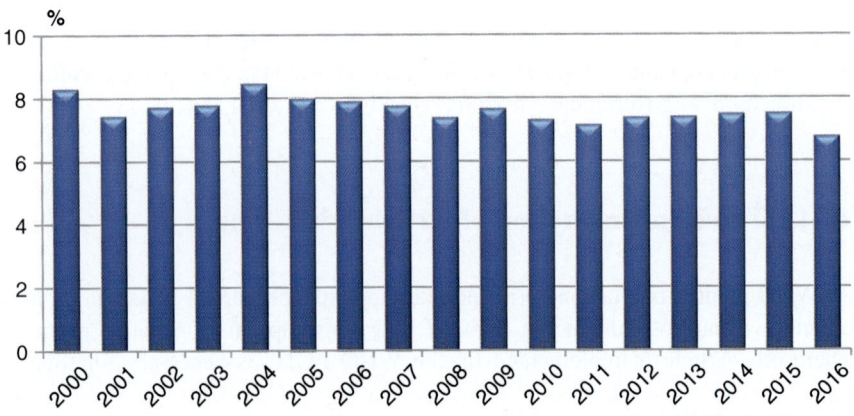

Fig. 13.3 The percentage of Tobacco tax and profit in total fiscal revenue (2000–2016). Note: Data collected and reproduced from the annual National Tobacco Industry Conference of each year and National Bureau of Statistics of China of each year (The link of 2017 National Tobacco Industry Conference. http://www.tobacco.gov.cn/history_filesystem/2017ycgzh/index.html. The other years' conference reports can also be searched on the Internet) (National Bureau of Statistics of China. http://data.stats.gov.cn/)

control and improving public health. Tobacco taxes should be regarded as part of a comprehensive tobacco-control strategy in accordance with other articles of the WHO FCTC.[36]

WHO FCTC has been came into force in China on January 9, 2006, the Chinese government has been prudent to take decisive action to increase tobacco tax and price since the tobacco industry trumpeted "the potential negative impact of tax increases on economic and social stability".

13.4.1 The Studies on Tobacco Tax in China

The policy advocates of increasing tobacco tax in China started since late 1990's. In view of the possible impact of increasing tobacco tax on China's economy, a lot of scientific research has been carried out. Hu et at (1997), and Zheng (2009) draw upon the experiences of foreign countries in implementing tobacco taxation to provide lessons for the Chinese government on the feasibility of raising additional taxes on cigarettes.[37,38]

Hu et al. (2002) analyzed the effects of cigarette tax on cigarette consumption and the Chinese economy, the empirical economic analysis and tax simulation results clearly indicate that increasing the tobacco tax in China is the most cost-effective instrument for tobacco control.[39,40] Mao et al. (2005) estimates demand of different income groups for cigarettes and impact of increasing tax on smokers, concluding that increasing tobacco tax will result in decreasing more cigarette consumption of lower income groups than higher groups, bearing more taxation of higher income groups than lower income groups, therefore tobacco taxation is not regressive.[41,42]

During this period, WHO started collaboration with China Ministry of Finance on tobacco tax policy, WHO TaXSiM model was adapted to China tobacco tax structure and market structure. The WHO TaXSiM China model has been used as a

---

[36] Guidelines for implementation of Article 6 of the WHO FCTC. FCTC Secretariat: http://www.who.int/fctc/guidelines/adopted/Guidelines_article_6.pdf?ua=1.

[37] Hu T. Cigarette taxation in China: lessons from international experiences. Tobacco Control 1997; 6:136–140.

[38] Rong Zheng, (2009) "The effects of tobacco taxation on global tobacco control and its prospect in China", Taxation Research Journal, 2009, No. 10. (In Chinese).

[39] Hu TW, Mao Z. Effects of cigarette tax on cigarette consumption and the Chinese economy. Tobacco Control 2002; 11:105–108.

[40] Hu T, Mao Z, Shi J, et al. The role of taxation in tobacco control and its potential economic impact in China. Tobacco Control 2010; 19:58–64.

[41] Mao Z, Hu TW, Yang GH. Demand of different income groups for cigarettes and impact of increasing tax on smokers (in Chinese). Chinese Journal of Evidence-Based Medicine 2005; 5:291e5.

[42] Mao Z, Hu TW, Yang GH. New evaluating of the demand for cigarettes from Chinese residents (in Chinese). Chinese J Health Econ 2005; 24:45e7.

tool for policy adjustment projecting scenarios of different schemes and assessing impacts of tax adjustment.

In 2009, Chinese government increased cigarette excise tax for the first time since ratifying WHO FCTC. However, the tax increase didn't lead to cigarette price increase, which means CNTC decreased its profit to deal with the increased tax, it also indicates that Chinese government's first attempt of using tax policy to decrease tobacco use failed. Hu et al. (2010) analyzed the potential impact of 2009 tax increase on tobacco control in China, projected the revenue and health impact if Chinese government would pass along the increased tax to the retail price.[43] Gao et al. (2011) disclosed cigarette pricing mechanism in China to explains why the 2009 tax increase doesn't link to cigarette retail prices.[44]

In 2015, China launched its second tobacco excise tax adjustment since 2005. Zheng et al. (2016) assessed the impact of 2015 tax adjustment on government's revenue, public health, and cigarettes market structure, making conclusion that raising tobacco tax and price is a win-win strategy by increasing government's revenue while decreasing cigarette consumption.[45,46] Zheng et al. (2017) investigates the affordability of cigarettes in China between 2001 and 2016, cigarettes have become more affordable because the income increase outpaces the price increase, and the cheap brands cigarettes have a higher level of affordability than other price categories. These findings confirm that for tax increases to reduce the number of smokers and deaths in China, policy makers need to review the potential effects of rising income and prices with a focus on reducing cigarette affordability.[47]

13.4.2 Cigarette Tax Adjustment in 2009

In May 2009, Chinese government promulgated Taxation Legislation No. 84 "The Notice Regarding Adjustment to Tobacco Product Excise Tax Policy" which became effective on May 1, 2009.The new policy increases the cigarette producers' excise tax rate and also allows the government to collect an additional 5% ad valorem excise tax from the wholesale segment. The government asserted that the tax adjustment aims at increasing government revenue from tobacco products and at the same

---

[43] Hu T, Mao Z, Shi J. Recent tobacco tax rate adjustment and its potential impact on tobacco control in China. Tobacco Control 2010; 19:80–82.

[44] Song Gao, Rong Zheng, Teh-wei Hu. "Can increases in the cigarette tax rate be linked to cigarette retail prices? Solving mysteries related to the cigarette pricing mechanism in China". Tob Control 2011.

[45] Zheng R, Wang Y, Hu X, "Tobacco tax, theory, system design and policy application", Financial Minds, Volume 1, Issue 6, November 2016, Pages 5–30.

[46] Hu T-wei, Zhang X, Zheng R, "China has raised the tax on cigarettes: what's next?" Tobacco Control(SSCI)2015, Volume 25, Issue 6.

[47] Zheng R, Wang Y, Hu X, Marquez, P V.2017. Cigarette affordability in China : 2001-2016. Tobacco taxation. Washington, D.C. : World Bank Group. http://documents.worldbank.org/curated/en/130301492424519317/Cigarette-affordability-in-China-2001-2016.

Table 13.5 Cigarette classification and tax rate

Allocation price per pack	Grade		Class		Specific tax per pack	Excise tax rate		Wholesale (Rtwh)
						Producer (Rt)		
Year	2008	2009	2008	2009	2008~2009	2008	2009	2009
[10, +∞)	A	A	I	I	0.06 RMB	45%	56%	5%
[7, 10)			II	II	0.06 RMB	45%	56%	5%
[5, 7)		B		III	0.06 RMB	45%	36%	5%
[3, 5)	B		III		0.06 RMB	30%	36%	5%
[1.65, 3)			IV	IV	0.06 RMB	30%	36%	5%
(0, 1.65)			V	V	0.06 RMB	30%	36%	5%

Note: Table made by author based on the information provided by the China Tobacco Yearbook and Taxation legislation (China State Tobacco Monopoly Administration. China Tobacco Yearbook. Beijing: China Economic Publishing House) (The Chinese Institute of Certified Public Accounts. Taxation Laws. Beijing: China Economic Science Press)

time, improving the tobacco tax structure and to meet WHO FCTC requirements of using tax or price-related policies for tobacco control purposes. However, the real reason behind this legislation is to seek additional tax revenue due to the China's economic decline in early 2009. In any case, the tax adjustment in May was still believed to be the start of using price tools for tobacco control in China.

The tax adjustment in 2009 mainly includes: (1) Grade A cigarettes' excise tax rates are increased from 45 to 56%and Grade B cigarettes excise tax rates are increased from 30 to 36% for, and Cigar's excise tax rate increased from 25 to 36% at producer level[48]; (2) 5% of ad valorem excise tax is applied additionally at cigarette wholesale segment; (3) the specific tax remains the same as 0.06 Yuan per pack; (4) the standard for grade A cigarettes and grade B cigarettes was adjusted with cigarettes costing more than 7 Yuan per pack (20 cigarettes) A grade, while those with allocation prices less than 7 Yuan were grade B. This standard was 5 YUAN before the tax adjustment. Accordingly, the classification standards for cigarette classes II and III are also changed.[49] Table 13.5 categorizes all cigarettes into six groups in terms of their allocation prices and the changes of cigarette Grades and Classes.

Along with the enactment of the tax adjustment, the STMA document No. 180 (2009) "Notice of adjusting cigarettes allocation price" which also came into force on May 1, 2009. It announced that, (1) cigarette wholesale prices keep as same nationwide as before the tax adjustments[50]; and (2) allocation-wholesale gross profit margin is re-regulated for each cigarette class. a09 is the adjusted allocation-

[48] Cigar is excluded from our calculation due to its very small market share in China.

[49] The document No.220(2009) whose name is "The Notice Regarding Adjustment to Cigarette Classification Standard" issued by the state tobacco monopoly administration.

[50] In fact, however, the STMA starts to control the retail price of premium cigarette products that their retail price cannot exceed 1000 Yuan per pack, which makes the overall cigarette retail price drops a little bit.

302 R. Zheng

Table 13.6 Cigarette profit margins

| Allocation price per pack | | Allocation wholesale margin | | | | Wholesale retail margin (b) (%) |
| | | Margin after May 2009 (a09) (%) | | Margin before May 2009 | | |
				Regulated (a08′) (%)	Actual (a08) (%)	
[10, +∞)	[14.6, +∞)	34	31.5[a]	40	47	15
	[10, 14.6)	29				
[7, 10)		25		40	43	15
[5, 7)		25		40	43	15
[3, 5)		25		30	38	10
[1.65, 3)		20		30	28	10
(0, 1.65)		15		30	18	10

[a]31.5% is the estimated average wholesale gross profit margin for Class I
Table made by author based on the information provided by the China Tobacco Yearbook (China State Tobacco Monopoly Administration. China Tobacco Yearbook. Beijing: China Economic Publishing House). Margin was calculated by author using TaXSiM China model (WHO TaXSiM is designed to describe the current market and tax situation for domestically consumed cigarettes within a particular country or tax jurisdiction, and then to forecast the impact of tax changes on final consumer prices, annual consumption volumes, and tax revenues for the Government. The WHO TaXSiM China model was jointly developed by WHO PND/TCE, the Tax Policy Department of the Chinese Ministry of Finance, and the WHO Collaborating Center on Tobacco and Economics, based in Beijing, China)

wholesale profit margin in 2009, a08′ indicates the regulated allocation-wholesale margin in 2008 by STMA and a08 tells the actual allocation-wholesale margin in 2008. b shows the wholesale-retail profit margin in both 2008 and 2009, which is not changed in the new tax policy.

As mentioned earlier, profit margin, which has been regulated by the STMA, plays a very important role in determining prices at different segments. Before the tax adjustment, the allocation-wholesale profit margin was no greater than 40% for Grade A cigarettes and no greater than 30% for Grade B cigarettes on average. However, this rule was not strictly followed by tobacco companies. The actual profit margin before tax adjustment is shown in the second to last column in Table 13.6. After the tax adjustment in 2009, the STMA started to require that the tobacco companies strictly follow the profit margins.[51] The wholesale-retail profit margins are stable both before and after the tax adjustment because they are comparable to other industry profit margins and are decided by the market.

In China, the tax base (allocation price) for excise tax is excise tax inclusive while VAT exclusive, so the increase of the excise tax rate makes the excise tax base (allocation price) increase as well. Therefore, the cigarette allocation prices increase by 2.6% averagely after the tax adjustment.[52]

A significant feature of the new policy is that the increased tax was neither transferred to the wholesale price nor to the retail price in 2009. As mentioned,

[51] Source: Notice of Adjusting Cigarettes Allocation Price (2009, No. 180) by State Tobacco Monopoly Administration.

[52] This is inner information from the STMA and the Ministry of Finance (MOF) which is not released publicly.

the STMA controls cigarette wholesale price and retail price through the two profit margins (a and b). Thus, when the STMA reduces the allocation-wholesale margin (a) to maintain the wholesale and retail prices as well as before, the increased tax is actually paid by the tobacco industry's profits. In essence, we might say that the new policy is a profit tax adjustment rather than an excise tax adjustment.

The 2009 tax adjustment does not increase cigarette retail prices, but increases government revenue by 58.987 billion Yuan, therefore transferring the tobacco industry's profit to government tax revenue.[53] The goal of the new cigarette excise tax policy is to increase the central government's tax revenue to make up for the financial revenue decrease due to the economic recession. This outcome implies that the increased tax does not affect the actual cigarette retail price, meaning that the excise tax mechanism as a tool to control tobacco use doesn't succeed in China. However, although the 2009 tobacco tax adjustment did not influence cigarette retail price. It was expected that the Chinese government may make further adjustment in terms of tobacco tax in the near future and consequently, to increase tax revenue and decrease cigarettes consumption.

13.4.3 Cigarette Tax Adjustment in 2015

In May 2015, the Chinese government has again adjusted the consumption tax on cigarettes. The tax adjustment in 2015 mainly includes: (1) Excise tax rate at the wholesale segment is increased from 5 to 11%; (2) An additional specific tax of 0.1 RMB (0.015 USD) per pack (with 20 sticks) is applied at the wholesale level (see Table 13.7).[54]

Table 13.7 2015 Cigarette excise tax adjustment

		Before adjustment	After adjustment
At produce price level	Specific excise tax (per pack)	0.06 RMB	0.06 RMB
	Ad valorem tax		
	≥7 RMB	56%	56%
	<7 RMB	36%	36%
At wholesale price level	Specific excise tax (per pack)	0	0.10 RMB
	Ad valorem tax	5%	11%

Note: Table made by author based on the information provided by the China Tobacco Yearbook and Taxation legislation (China State Tobacco Monopoly Administration. China Tobacco Yearbook. Beijing: China Economic Publishing House) (The Chinese Institute of Certified Public Accounts. Taxation Laws. Beijing: China Economic Science Press)

---

[53] The increased government revenue was calculated by author based on the information provided by the China Tobacco Yearbook.

[54] The Chinese government issued Taxation Legislation No. 60 "The Notice Regarding Adjustment to Tobacco Product Excise Tax Policy" which became effective on May 10, 2015. http://www.chinatax.gov.cn/n810341/n810755/c1601367/content.html.

This time around, the tax increase coincided with STMA's announcement that the wholesale price of all cigarettes brands should increase by 6%, the price regulation has been strictly obeyed by all provincial STMA branches. Furthermore, at the retail level, STMA circulated an internal retail price guidance among all provincial branches, in the meanwhile, STMA allows provincial branches to adjust retail prices based on local market with the requirement of retail margin no less than 10%.[55] This latest tax reform (both the May 2015 tax increase and STMA's pricing announcement) will therefore impact on the final cigarette price that consumers pay.

13.4.3.1   Impact on Price

The weighted average retail price (nominal price) (Fig. 13.4) increased from 11.61 RMB per pack in 2014 to 12.81 RMB per pack in 2015 by 10.29%, it continued to increase by 2.19% to 13.09 RMB per pack in 2016 due to the market structure transform, the market share of low price categories has been shrinking, while the middle and premium categories market share continues to expand. But, from a global view, China's weighted average cigarette price is still cheap, which is below average per pack Figs. 13.4 and 13.5 display Cigarette nominal weighted average retail price and Cigarette real weighted average retail price during 2001–2016. It is needed to mention that the price of each pack is the average price for all cigarettes at different categories. After cigarettes tax adjustment in 2009, the weighted average price of each pack cigarette was increasing owing to the increasing share of cigarette with higher price. In fact, the price of cigarette at each category was not change.

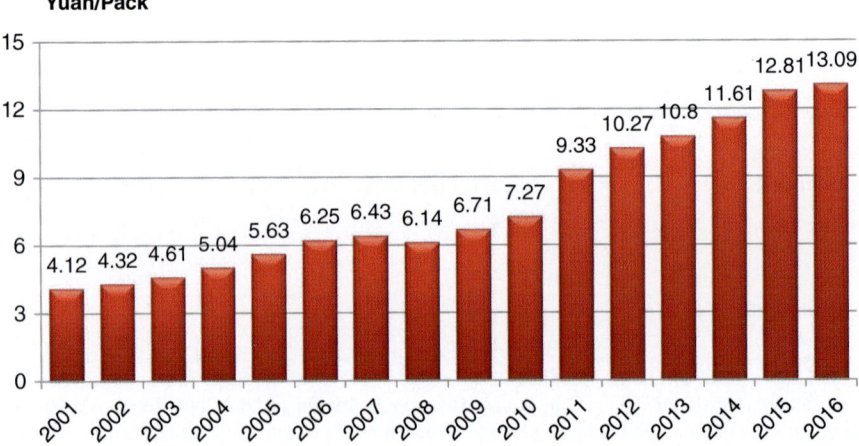

Fig. 13.4 Cigarette nominal weighted average retail price (2001–2016). Note: Nominal weighted average cigarette price for each year is calculated by author using the WHO TaXSiM China model

---

[55] Sourced from http://www.tobacco.gov.cn/html/35/3505/350503/4826212_n.html.

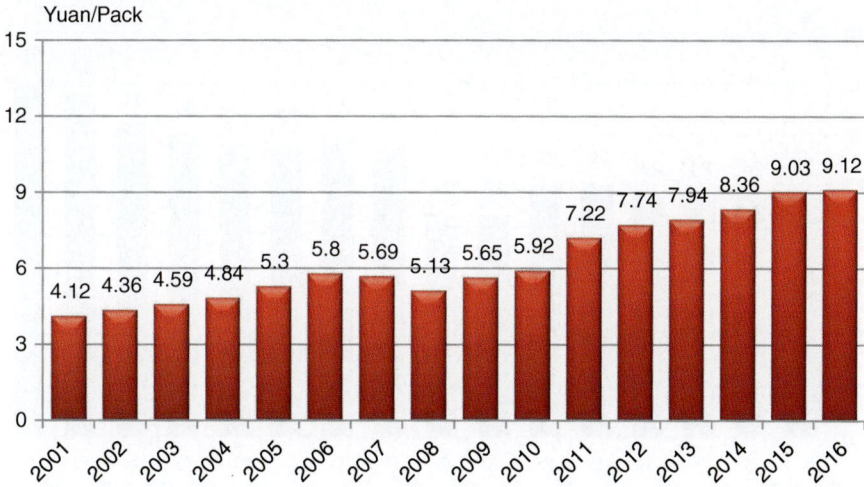

Fig. 13.5 Cigarette real weighted average retail price (2001–2016). Note: Real weighted average cigarette price for each year is calculated using the nominal weighted average price and Inflation rate (Based on CPI, Base year: 2001). Data of CPI was collected from National Bureau of Statistics of China (National Bureau of Statistics of China. http://data.stats.gov.cn/easyquery.htm?cn=C01)

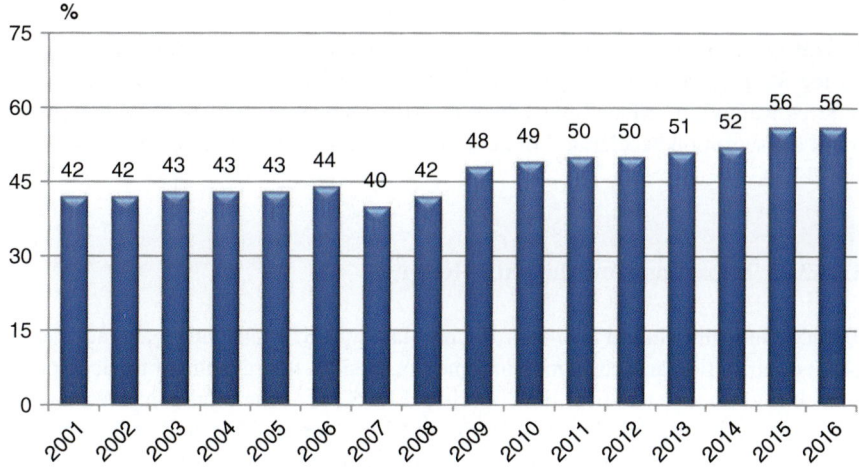

Fig. 13.6 Tax as % of retail price (2001–2016). Note: Calculated by the author using the WHO TaXSiM China model

13.4.3.2 Impact on Tax Incidence

The weighted tax share as % of retail price has been increased by 4%, from 52% in 2014 to 56% in 2015.And in 2016, the tax as % of retail price stayed around 56%, (see Fig. 13.6) which is still lower than WHO recommended standard of 75%.

The weighted excise tax share as % of retail price has been increased by 3%, from 31% in 2014 to 34% in 2015 (Fig. 13.7) which is also lower than WHO recommended standard of 70%.

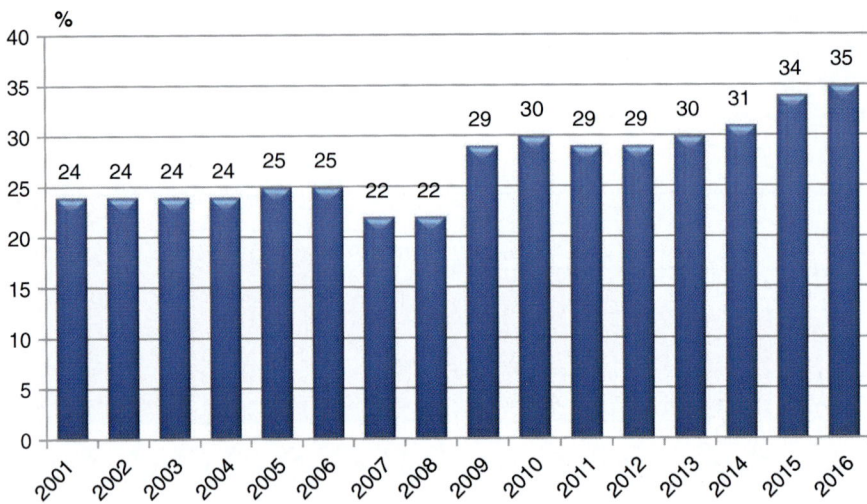

Fig. 13.7 Excise as % of retail price (2001–2016). Note: Calculated by author using the WHO TaXSiM China model

13.4.3.3 Impact on Consumption

It is the first time since 2001 that the volume of cigarette sales decreased, as approved by the State Tobacco Monopoly Administration (STMA) announcement that cigarette consumption reduced by 2.36% in 2015 compared to 2014. The downward trend consumption accelerated in 2016, decreased by 5.6% compared to 2015 (see Fig. 13.8).

13.4.3.4 Impact on Government's Revenue

Tobacco industry should turn over the regulated profit contribution and additional profit contribution and enterprise income tax, besides tax revenue of tobacco products. Based on the statistical data published by STMA, the total contributed revenue of the tobacco industry was 1095.0 billion Yuan in 2015 and 1000.6 billion Yuan in 2016. Compared with the total revenue in 2014, the total revenues in 2015 and in 2016 increased by 20%, and 9%, separately.[56] The annual change by sub-item of total revenue is list in Table 13.8. The tax revenue from tobacco products were 840.4 billion RMB (129.29 billion USD) in 2015 and 841.67 billion RMB (129.49 billion USD) in 2016 separately, which increased 9% compared with that in 2014.

---

[56] Zheng R, Wang Y, Hu X. 2016. "Tobacco tax: theory, tax design and policy practice". Finance Minds 1(6): 5–30.

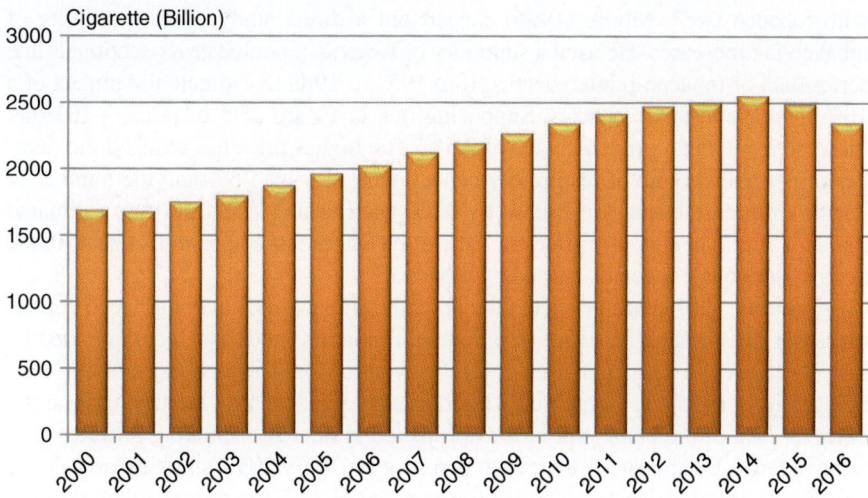

Fig. 13.8 Cigarette sales volume (2000–2016). Note: Data collected and reproduced from the China Tobacco Year book and annual National Tobacco Industry Conference (China State Tobacco Monopoly Administration. China Tobacco Yearbook. Beijing: China Economic Publishing House) (2017 National Tobacco Industry Conference. http://www.tobacco.gov.cn/history_filesystem/2017ycgzh/ldjh-1.html)

Table 13.8 The annual change of total tax revenue to government by sub-items

	Tobacco tax (VAT, excise, C&E)	Total profit contribution	Tax and profit contribution to government
	Billion RMB	Billion RMB	Billion RMB
2014	769.82	86.235	911.0
2015	840.4	191.0	1095.0
Annual △%	9.17%	121.49%	20.20%
2016	841.67	118.17	1000.6
Annual △%	0.15%	−38.13%	−8.62%

Source: China Tobacco Yearbook (China State Tobacco Monopoly Administration. China Tobacco Yearbook. Beijing: China Economic Publishing House)

13.4.3.5 Impact on Public Health

There are some studies directly assess the impact of tobacco tax and price about the health consequences of tobacco use, but nothing in China. As long as tobacco consumption and smoking can be reduced by increasing tobacco tax and price, then it is a virtual certainty to decrease the incidence of disease and mortality associated with tobacco use.[57] Moore (1996) carried out a direct study of the mortality of tobacco tax increases. He used a summary of American pooled cross-sectional time series data of tobacco-related deaths from 1954 to 1988 to estimate the impact of a 10% increase in tobacco taxes. Supposing that taxes are 25% of price, a 10% tax increase results in a price increase of 2.5%. The higher price has reduced the number of people who die of respiratory cancer each year by 1.5% and the number of deaths from cardiovascular disease by 0.5% each year.[58] Warner (1986) estimated that an 8% rise in cigarette prices in the United States would prevent some 450,000 deaths, or about 3% deaths caused by tobacco.[59]

Levy et al. (2014) has projected the potential impact in China of tobacco control measures on smoking by using a computer simulation model, as recommended by the World Health Organization Frame Convention on Tobacco Control (FCTC), being fully carried out. Compared with the status quo-scenario, increasing cigarette taxes to 75% of the blanket price was projected to decrease smoking prevalence in relative terms by almost 10% for both sexes by 2015. By 2050, smoking prevalence presented a relative decrease of 13% for men and of 12% for women in the taxation simulation. By the year 2050, about 134,000 lives and 1,644,000 life years would be gained annually with a 75% tax. Summing up the years 2015–2050, approximately 3.5 million deaths would be avoided (3,333,000 for men and 143,000 for women) and 44,315,000 life years gained (42,882,000 for men and 1,433,000 for women) thanks to the tax policy.[60]

If increasing the revenue of tobacco product continuously carried out, the consumption will continue to decrease, the quit ration of smokers will increase, the attempt smoking rate in adolescent will decrease, the prevalence of current smoking and the smoking number will cut down, so that the morbidity and mortality attributed tobacco use would naturally be declined. However, it is too short from increasing tax revenue of tobacco product in 2015, the direct impact of increasing tax revenue has not completely appeared, and the are many unanticipated subsequent factors, the impact on public health related to cigarette tax adjustment in 2015 need to be observed in further.

---

[57] U.S. National Cancer Institute and World Health Organization. The economics of tobacco and tobacco control. National Cancer Institute Tobacco Control Monograph 21. NIH Publication No. 16-CA-8029A. Bethesda, MD: U.S. Department of Health and Human Services, National Institutes of Health, National Cancer Institute; and Geneva, CH: World Health Organization; 2016.

[58] Moore MJ. Death and tobacco taxes. Rand J Econ. 1996;27(2):415–28. doi: https://doi.org/10.2307/2555934.

[59] Warner, K.E. (1986). Smoking and health implications of a change in the federal cigarette excise tax. JAMA, 255(8), 1028–32.

[60] David Levy, Ricardo L Rodríguez-Buño, Teh-Wei Hu, and Andrew E Moran. The potential effects of tobacco control in China: projections from the China Sim-Smoke simulation model. BMJ. 2014; 348: g1134.

13.5   Conclusion

It has been well documented that raising tobacco taxes is a 'win-win' policy by reducing the disease and death attributable to tobacco use, as well as generating additional revenue for government revenue. China's 2015 tobacco tax reform provides another practical demonstration of these dual benefits. However, it's also notable that cigarette price is still extremely low and increasingly affordable over time, the tax as % of retail price is still far behind WHO recommended standard. The differential mixture of both ad valorem and specific excises offers incentives for price manipulations to the extent that manufacturers can change their pricing or production behavior in order to avoid higher tax burden. Cigarettes have become more affordable in China, decrease in affordability 50% between 2008 and 2014 before 2015 tax adjustment. All these indicates China still has a long way on tobacco tax hiking, especially needs to focus on a few key issues including: regularly increasing tax and price to reduce cigarette affordability, reorienting excise tax structure towards specific in the medium-term, and towards a uniform system either mixed or specific in the long-term, and earmarking tobacco tax for health programs and sustainable development goals.

In 2015, United Nations achieved the "Addis Ababa Action Agenda" as part of the Sustainable Development Goals (SDGs). Clause 32 of the Addis Ababa Action Agenda urged countries to apply price and tax measures on tobacco as an effective and important means to reduce tobacco consumption and health care costs, and in the meanwhile to genera tea revenue stream for financing development projects.[61] Under the new SDG era, countries will need to pursue a broader, more coherent policy agenda beyond simply industrial development. Accordingly, China released its new Healthy China 2030 strategy which sets a target for policy-makers to reduce the adult rate of smoking in China by 7.7% in absolute terms from 27.7% in 2015 to 20% by 2030. There is little doubt that further increases in tobacco taxation will be necessary to achieve this target.

---

[61] UN. *Transforming our World: the 2030 Agenda for Sustainable Development*. New York, United National General Assembly; 2015.

Chapter 14
Conclusions and Recommendations

Gonghuan Yang

Abstract This book provides lots of information on tobacco control in China. China made the progress on tobacco control in the last 10 years, but there are a large gap from requirement of WHO FCTC and China and fell behind among 181 Parties of WHO FCTC. There are four factors affecting tobacco control in China: (1) Tobacco industry grabbed the partial leading power on tobacco control in China. (2) The development ideology of GDP first restricted the Chinese governor's understanding on the significant of tobacco control; (3) Evaluating the performance of Government officials based on GDP. (4) Political and financial resources have restricted the momentum of tobacco control campaign in China. In order to achieve the *Healthy China 2030*, China should focus on eight key issues: (1) To understand tobacco control from China's long term target and Sustainable development goals: Targets 3.4 (Tobacco control reduces premature mortality from non-communicable diseases.) and 3A ("strengthen the implementation of the WHO FCTC into assessment of all level government performance; (2) To adjust the Steering Committee, removing the obstruction of tobacco control; (3) To adopt a strong, comprehensive national smoke-free law urgently to ensure 100% smoke-free in indoor public and working places; (4) To regularly issue the national plan of tobacco control, and regularly increase tax and price of tobacco product, as well as include helping quit program into the primary health care and medical insurance; (5) To strength public education and place the pictorial warning on the cigarette package; (6) To regularly monitor, evaluate and report progress of tobacco control policy implement, especially the comprehensively banning TAPS and increasing tax and price of tobacco product; (7) To strengthen capacity building and ensure financial support of tobacco control. (8) To expand the coalition of tobacco control and promote nationwide tobacco control. Fortunately, in 2018, National People's Congress approved the State Council's report on Institutional Reform, and the function of tobacco control has finally shifted from the Ministry of Industry Information to the National Health

G. Yang
Institute of Basic Medical Science Chinese Academy of Medical Sciences,
School of Basic Medicine Peking Union Medical College, Beijing, China

© Springer Nature Singapore Pte Ltd. 2018
G. Yang (ed.), *Tobacco Control in China*,
https://doi.org/10.1007/978-981-10-8315-0_14

Commission. The National Health Commission should take the golden opportunity
to reset up an effective the Steering Committee and to remove the interference of
tobacco industry.

Keywords Tobacco control · Sustainable development · Tobacco industry · China

As a summary, *"Tobacco Control in China"* describes the tobacco control in China
from three aspects, the first two chapters addressed China's attitude toward and
position in the negotiations of WHO FCTC, and the scientific studies on the harm of
tobacco use and impact on Chinese health, explaining reasons that tobacco control
is an important issue and priority in China. The 3–4 chapters discuss the political
and social environment of tobacco control in China, the main body of tobacco control and the power of anti-tobacco control, as well as assistance of the international
community. Chapters 5–7 described infrastructures of tobacco control in China,
including capacity building, public education, legal action and surveillance as well
as program evaluation.

Chapters 8–13 talked about challenges and future actions of main strategies of
tobacco control, including protecting people from tobacco smoke, support in smoking
cessation, health warning labels on cigarette packages, tobacco product regulation and
tobacco industry interference, comprehensive banning all forms on tobacco advertising, and promotion and sponsorship and tobacco tax and tobacco economy. Since the
entry into force of the Convention, progress to strengthen tobacco control has been
weak during 2006–2010 and accelerated next 5 years, making breakthrough in 2015.

It is useful to review the development of tobacco control measures as understand
the deep factors of the institutional, cultural and political systems to influence
tobacco control so as to make difference of effectively promoting tobacco control in
China.

14.1 The Current Situation of Tobacco Control in China

China has made the difference on tobacco control in past 10 years, but there are
large gapes with WHO FCTC and dropped behind among 181 Parties.

In 2011, 5 years after ratification of WHO FCTC in China, China's implementation of WHO FCTC was far from the requirements of the international norm. China
CDC assessed the enforcement of the MPOWER policy package[1] proposed by
WHO: (1) Protecting people from tobacco smoke; (2) Offering a help to quit smoke
use; (3) Warning about the dangers of tobacco; (4) Banning tobacco advertising,
promotion, and sponsorship; and (5) Raising taxes and price of tobacco products.

---

[1] *WHO Report on the Global Tobacco Epidemic, 2008: The MPOWER package.* Geneva, World
Health Organization, 2008.

The assessment was completed with ten quantitative indicators developed on the principles of the WHO FCTC. Using data of GATS China 2010, Yang and Hu published *"Tobacco Control and China' Furniture—The Chinese and Foreign Expertise Joint Assessment Report on Tobacco Use and Control in China"* (*Tobacco Control and China' Furniture*)[2] in January, 2011. This report explored the relationship between China's tobacco epidemic, its health consequences and the socioeconomic development in China. All evidences indicated that the performance of tobacco control efforts and WHO FCTC implementation in China were very poor, and there was a significant gap from the WHO FCTC requirements. With detailed and robust data, the report convincingly documented key points: smoking prevalence in male was among the highest in the world, the tobacco epidemic is the leading factor to increase morbidity and mortality from the main chronic diseases, smoking has become the 'Top Killer' of the Chinese population. The tobacco industry has been the largest 'health hazard' industry. Although the industry remains as a 'major taxpayer' currently, it causes enormous social costs and overall poses a loss rather than a benefit to China. The report also pointed out that effect of tobacco control in China is weak, and the performance of actual tobacco control is very poor only with 37.3 points out of 100 possible points during 5 years of the entry into force of the Convention, which related to Chinese tobacco industry interference.

China's ranking was among the lowest 20% of countries for the implementation of WHO FCTC.[3] This ranking did not commensurate with its social and economic development status. Professor *Yang GH and Hu AG* frankly and straightforwardly pointed out the problems and criticized the ineffective implementation of WHO FCTC in China, which was reported by Chinese Central Television Station (CCTV), the Xinhua News agency and many other media. Based on statistics from the Public Communication center of Renmin University of China, the total number of media reporting this report was 4227, average reprint 9.7 times per original report with title "Implement of WHO FCTC: 37.3 point of 100 point", and "China break appointment" and so on. It was indicate that the poor implementation of WHO FCTC in China has been extensively concerned.[4] The report has played an important role in policy advocacy. In March, 2011, "Comprehensive promote banning smoking in Public Places" has been in the Outline of Twelfth Five Year Plan of national economy and social development (2011–2015).

From 2011 to 2015, China accelerated implementation of the international treaty, especially on protection non-smoker from SHS, comprehensive ban on TAPS and raising tax and price of tobacco product recommended by WHO FCTC, as described

---

[2] Yang GH, Hu AG, *Tobacco Control and China' Furniture—The Chinese and Foreign Expertise Joint Assessment Report on Tobacco Use and Control in China*", Economic Time Press, Jan, 2011, Beijing.

[3] Yang GH, et al. Findings from 2010 Global Adult Tobacco Survey: implementation of MPOWER policy in China. Biomed Environ Sci. 2010 Dec; 23(6):422–9.

[4] Public Communication center of Renmin University of China, Special report on 5th annual public opinion monitoring on WHO HCTC, Jan. 2011.

in Chapters 8, 12 and 13. Meantime, unfulfilled gaps to the requirement of WHO FCTC was also described in Chapters 9, 10 and 11.

The most successful implementation of WHO FCTC in the past 10 years was protecting nonsmokers from the harms of SHS in China. Because of the campaigns on smoke-free in the hospital, school, government building and the enterprises, and so on, knowledge health hazards from SHS, public awareness of health power has increased in general population. The National Health and Family Planning Commission (NHFPC), the Ministry of education (MOE), and over 20 metropolitan cities have enacted policies to ban smoking in indoor public places and workplaces. The prevalence of SHS exposure at home and in public place were 64.3 and 60.6% in 2010,[5] separately; but the rates have been down 46.7 and 54.3% in 2015,[6] separately. In 2014 the national legislation has been submitted to the Legislative Affairs Office of the State Council, though it was put on ice for more than 3 years owing to pullback of STMA.[7]

The second, success of tobacco control in China was to promote the implementation of the Article 13 of WHO FCTC. Chapter 12 described curbing almost rampant TAPS activities and eradicating industry's block, finally successfully promoting to publish of the *Advertising Law* with the banning most forms of TAPS in China. As this chapter shows, the cases, such as, tampering Chinese version of Article 13 of WHO FCTC by STMA, "Tobacco Hope School" sponsored by CNTC provoked outrage from public. After the arduous struggle, the new "*Advertising Law Emendation*", "*Internet advertising management Interim Measures*" and "*Charity Law*" and other laws and regulations have been introduced. It is still a great challenge to effectively implement *Advertising Law*, especially banning tobacco sponsorship, advertising at the retail shop and internet.

The third, successful implementation of WHO FCTC in China was raising taxes and raising prices for tobacco products. The author addressed assessment of cigarette excise tax adjustments in 2009 and 2015 and the related barriers and challenges from the Chinese tobacco industry in Chapter 13.

In brief, Chinese government increased cigarettes' excise tax rates of the different grades cigarettes, added 5% of ad valorem excise tax at cigarette wholesale segment, and adjusted the classification standards of cigarettes in May 2009. The 2009 tax adjustment increased the government revenue by 58.987 billion Yuan, but the STMA controls cigarette wholesale price and retail price through the two profit margins. During the actual implementation, the allocation price of cigarettes increased slightly, with an average up 2.6%, which did not produce obvious public health benefit. The 2015 cigarette tax increase coincided with STMA's announcement that the wholesale price of all cigarettes brands should increase by 6%. Furthermore, the STMA allowed its provincial branches to set retail prices with retail margins of at least 10%. Tax rate

[5] China CDC Global Adult Tobacco Survey (GATS) China 2010 Country Report, edited by Yang GH, China San Xia Press, 2011 Nov.

[6] China CDC, 2015 report of tobacco survey for adults in China, edited by Liang XF http://www.tcrc.org.cn/UploadFiles/2016-03/318/201603231215175500.pdf.

[7] The Paper News, Director of STMA said: It should be avoided the absolutization and expansion of tobacco control, Dec. 3, 2014. http://www.thepaper.cn/newsDetail_forward_1282818.

increased from 52% in 2014 to 56% in 2015. STMA announced that cigarette consumption decreased by 2.36% in 2015 and 5.6% in 2016 compared to the previous year. The author reported the impact of the recent tobacco tax increase on cigarette consumption and government revenues. It is need to further study on smoking behavior and population health related to 2015 tax increase.

The study on Relative Change in Affordability of Cigarettes, 1996–2006[8] pointed out that taking into account both inflation and purchasing power, cigarettes have become more than twice as affordable in China since 1990. So, what change on affordable how did China's cigarette affordability change between 2006 and 2016? It is necessary to continue observation of affordability of cigarettes. Also it is need more evidences to support the declining cigarettes consumption. So, it is impossible to reasonably estimate the impact of tax increases on the health of the Chinese population and providing evidences for policy making. In general, there are a lot of things need to do in the future, including to simplify tobacco taxation systems, and regularly increase a specific excise tax on tobacco products so as to prevent smoker from high- to low-priced brands and address continually inflation and the affordability of cigarettes, as well as promote the use of increasing revenues to improve medical health, helping smoker' quit and the other tobacco control. Continuing surveillance is very useful for the next round of tobacco tax policy adjustment.

A weak implementation of WHO FCTC was Article 14, to help quit smoking is relative poor. There are huge room for providing the quitting service owing to the increasing cessation attempt, quit rate and the proportion of relapse among more than 300 million smokers in China, which does not match the very low proportion of smokers visit the cessation clinic with the high demand. Chapter 9 reviewed quitting strategies in China and explained the reasons that the very low proportion of smokers visit the cessation clinic: (1) most cessation clinics were only in tertiary hospitals; (2) smoking cessation services are not integrated into the primary medical service; (3) smoking cessation services are not included in the medical insurance plan. NHFPC and provincial HFPC need to change policy to meet the requirement of the Article 14 and guideline of WHO FCTC.

The poorest implementation was of the Articles 9, 10 and 11 of WHO FCTC in China, which STMA is responsible for. Also to promote the implement of these Articles become the Game focus between tobacco control community and tobacco industry.

Chapter 10 *"Tobacco product regulation and tobacco industry interference"* described how STMA/CNTC blatantly curbed the implementation of Article 9 and 10 of WHO FCTC. STMA/CNTC was struggling to thwart the Guidelines on Articles 9, 10 and 11 of WHO FCTC at COP4 and COP3, and launched the "low tar, low harm" campaign, heavily promoted the use of the additives with a various Chinese herbal medicines to enhance the attractiveness and palatability of tobacco products in China. Meanwhile, STMA/CNTC does not disclose to the public the

---

[8] Blecher E, van Walbeek C. An Analysis of Cigarette Affordability. Paris: International Union Against Tuberculosis and Lung Disease; 2008.

contents and emissions of its tobacco products that are harmful to health, and its aggressive campaign of misinformation has caused widespread misperception among the public.

Chapter 11 described in detail the implementation of the Article 11 of WHO FCTC in China. STMA/GAQSIQ totally ignored the requirements of the Article 11 of the Convention and its implementation guideline, made the health warning policy according on STMA' *Research on Counterproposals and Countermeasures against WHO FCTC*. The text-health warning on the cigarette package in China did not meet basic requirement of Article 11 of the Convention completely. These cases have revealed how the State Public Power served the interests of Tobacco Enterprises. By 2016, 105 Parties adopted the graphic warnings on cigarette packaging, covering 58% of the world's population. It is clear that China fell behind. However, up to now, STMA still justified that it was impossible to place the pictorial health warning on the cigarettes package. The right of execution of implementation of Article 9, 10 and 11 of the Convention is in the hand of STMA/CNTC. It is impossible to let STMA/CNTC volunteered to implementation of Convention, which was similar to ask a tiger for its skin. No progress of implementation of Convention is inevitable.

14.2   The Influencing Factors on Tobacco Control Process in China

14.2.1   Tobacco Industry Grabbed the Partial Leading Power on Tobacco Control

The main resistance of tobacco control in China is the partial leading power of tobacco control taken by tobacco industry. This book described how the STMA/CNTC became a member of the Inter-Ministry Coordination and Steering Committee for Implementation of WHO FCTC, which was a combination of government function and enterprise operation, unlike tobacco industries in other countries. The Chapter 3 of the book described that the STMA and CNTC are an organization of both government and the enterprise. The STMA/CNTC attended the negotiation of WHO FCTC and a series of Convention of Parties as a member of Chinese government delegation, and opposed the related Articles of WHO FCTC and related implementation guideline, played the destructive role that other tobacco industry cannot do, which are described in several chapters of this book. As a government department, STMA/CNTC connects with other national and local governmental agencies to hinder tobacco control policy. A typical case is that *The Labeling Regulation* was jointly issued by STMA and GAQSIQ in name of implementation of WHO FCTC. Especially under the background of China corruption, tobacco companies can easily achieve their goal through money to trade benefit (权钱交易 Quan Qian Jiao Yi). These dirty practices hindered effective tobacco control at both central level and local levels. The destructive effect of these stakeholders on tobacco control cannot be underestimated. Fortunately, in 2018, National People's Congress approved the State Council's report on Institutional Reform, and the function of tobacco control has finally shifted from the Ministry of Industry Information to the National Health Commission. The National Health Commission should take the golden opportunity to reset up an effective the Steering Committee and to remove the interference of tobacco industry.

14.2.2   The Development Ideology of GDP First Restricted the Chinese Governor's Understanding and Action of Tobacco Control

As the State Council approved the STMA/CNTC as member of Inter-Ministry Coordination and Steering Committee, STMA/CNTC had a chance and power to resist implement of WHO FCTC. The approval of the State Council may imply to seek a balance between tobacco control and tobacco economy.

Over the past 20 years, "tobacco control" has become a hot topic in China. The idea of tobacco control was firstly introduced into China by the medical elite and international experts, and setting up Chinese Association of Tobacco Control became as an Hallmark Event. The conclusive scientific evidences have confirmed the health hazards of tobacco use to public health. The studies in China quantitatively estimated the disease burden of tobacco use to the Chinese. The Chapter 2 "Tobacco Epidemic and Health Risk in the Chinese Population" reviewed in detail scientific evidences about epidemic of tobacco use and health hazards in Chinese population. China is the world's largest tobacco producer, consumer and manufacturer; over 50% of male adults (people aged 15 years and older) are current smokers, the current smoking rate has not been declined since 2002. It was repeatedly proven that over one million premature deaths annually induced by tobacco use, this will grow to two million annually by 2030, and three million annually by 2050 without action to drastically reduce smoking rates. Tobacco use is a major driver in the rapid increase of non-communicable diseases, the biggest public health problem and health security issue in China. The key issue is that the research conclusion repeatedly communicated almost 20 years since the first research report was published in 1998, but the conclusion has not really accepted by policy maker as evidences of making policy. It may be related to the attitude of Chinese government: tobacco control or tobacco economy.

Since its initiation of the reform and open door policy in 1979, China began to show the image of a responsible great country, aspiring to exert its influence all over the World. However, as a country with a large state-owned tobacco production and consumption, the Chinese government worried that decline in tobacco consumption would hurt China's economy, not ready to take substantive control measures for tobacco control. So it is a balance strategy that let the STMA to join tobacco control as a brakes, and to ensure the implementation of tobacco control measures will not affect China's tobacco economy. In the past 10 years, it was very difficult to carry out tobacco control because of the tobacco industry's strategies. However, China, after all, has ratified the Convention and became a Party of WHO FCTC in 2006, and China have made a progress on tobacco control in recent years. We hope that China will eventually implement the responsibilities and obligations of tobacco control in accordance with international norms. Meanwhile, it is very clear that tobacco control would become the priority as long as the Chinese government has changed the development ideology.

14.2.3 Evaluating the Performance of Governors based on GDP Weakened Tobacco Control

Over the 30 years, under the guidance of ideology that "development is hard truth and nothing is more important than economic development",[9] the economy has rapidly grown in China. The only ideology guiding China's development in decades is the money-centered "*GDPism*". China's GDP is used as the only yardstick for economic performance by China's government, also as the indicators for performance check of government officials' promotion.

In 2015, the tobacco industry contributed ¥1.1 trillion (US$ 170 billion) to the central Government. In 2014, the industry's contribution accounted for 6.49% of total state revenues.[10] In some provinces where tobacco growing is a major component of the provincial economy, such as Yunnan, the proportion of state revenue that comes from the tobacco industry is much higher.[11] It was then difficult for Chinese government to put tobacco control prior to tobacco revenue even though there are considerable evidences that tobacco is hurting China' economic development and Chinese health.

The Chinese authorities proposed a new approach toward green development in the 12th Five Year Plan of national economy and social development (2011–2015) as past and current economic growth patterns caused the catastrophic environmental risks and health risks. However, China's "economic growth first" model is entrenched in the ideology, institutions and performance evaluation. In fact, so far, the authority has not really put tobacco control as a priority of national development, still adopted a GDP-first approach to tobacco control.

Changing the ideology of "GDP first" will be not something that happens overnight. There are a lot of issues to be changed, including related institutions, working style, assessment indicators and standards, as well as social opinions.

---

[9] "Bearing Development First in Mind forever", China CCTV, http://www.cctv.com/news/china/20050427/100018.shtml. Accessed Jan 3, 2012.

[10] Tobacco sector contributes more to China's revenue. Xinhua. 15 January 2016 (http://www.chinadaily.com.cn/bizchina/2016-01/15/content_23109622.htm, accessed 5 February 2016).

[11] Hu TW. Tobacco control policy analysis in China: economics and health. Hackensack, NJ: World Scientific; 2008.

14.2.4   Political and Financial Resources Restricted the Momentum of Tobacco Control Campaign in China

Tobacco control campaign in China has involved various social communities: public health professional, legal experts and lawyers, journalists, social celebrities, and domestic and foreign non-governmental organizations (NGOs). These groups have been the primary driving forces advocating effectively implementation of WHO FCTC. Unlike the other public health campaigns such as TB prevention and immunization, tobacco control campaigns were not only arranged by government departments, but also actively promoted by these experts, scholars and professionals. NGOs in tobacco control play an irreplaceable role. Especially, when government agencies were weak in tobacco control, the advocacy role of NGOs was very effective in changing the situation, as described in detail in each chapter of this book.

Meanwhile, the media actively worked together with tobacco control community and jointly promoted implementation of WHO FCTC. During the process, media began to shift in focus from individual behavioral change to participate in policy change, such as promote national and local legislation on comprehensive banning smoking in indoor public and working places, comprehensive banning advertising, promotion and sponsorship of tobacco product when revising Advising Law, promote pictorial warning on cigarette package and raise tax and price of cigarettes, and so on. If the bottom-up social movement and media advocacy were restricted, tobacco control movement would not have been today's situation in China. Promoting the development of non-governmental organizations and the supervision of the media would further promote tobacco control and bring more well-being to the Chinese people.

STMA made the political intimidating to tobacco control advocators. They accused that the international organization and foreign foundation supporting tobacco control in China to spread political democracy of the West and to convey the western values in name of tobacco control.[12]

Another major problem affecting tobacco control was the shortage of resources from Chinese government, which put only a small amount of fund for routine tobacco use surveillance and related health education. In fact, almost all tobacco control campaign carried out by NGOs, professional agencies, even government agencies were supported by international foundation. Such supports were used by STMA attacking public figures of tobacco control as the International Fund's assistance to tobacco control in China has effectively promoted the tobacco control campaign in China. All of these were described in details in Chapter 4.

In 2017 Ministry of Finance and Ministry of Civil Affairs issued a notice to support the development of NGO.[13] It is need to observe if to support tobacco control of

---

[12] Shi D, A number of the contentious issues and suggestions on tobacco control in China, The Major Report of Chinese Academy of Social Science (Inter reference), No.24 Feb. 23, 2012 (Secret 3 Months).

[13] Ministry of finance, Ministry of Civil Affairs, Guidance of supporting development of social organization though purchasing social service Finance (2016) No. 54, http://www.ngocn.net/column/2017-02-08-390795038dd57fa0.html.

NGO. Without financial support from government, tobacco control could not go far in China.

14.3 Recommendation for Future Tobacco Control

14.3.1 To Understand Relationship Between Comprehensive Tobacco Control and China' Future and to Include Tobacco Control in the Government Performance Assessment

In December 2013, the General Office of the Central Committee of the Communist Party of China (CPC) and the General Office of the State Council issued a joint notice on promoting smoke-free public places, requiring Government leaders and officials at all levels to take the lead in banning smoking in all public places.[14] The policy pointed out that the leading cadres should take the lead in ensuring existing smoke-free laws, effectively enforcing the laws, promoting awareness of the harms of smoking and importance of tobacco control, and ban smoking and cigarettes from all official activities at all levels of Party and Government. This document was significant not only because of its content, but also because of representation of strong commitments from China's political leadership to tobacco control. It is more helpful that State leaders should fully express their political will and commitment to comprehensive tobacco control.

In August 2016, President Xi Jinping has put emphasis on people's health at the strategic priority, making the need to include health in all policies an official government policy at National Health Conference.[15] "Healthy people in all policies" is government's best political commitment as it focuses on the people's life and health. Government agencies at all levels need to recognize the relationship between tobacco control and the future of China. Tobacco control is not simple measure of public health but an important part of innovative economic development and strategy of sustainable development, as well as key indicators of Health China 2030. At the seventh session of Conference of Parties of WHO FCTC, Parties committed achieving SDG Targets 3.4 (Tobacco control reduces premature mortality from NCDs.) and 3A ("strengthen the implementation of the WHO FCTC in all coun-

---

[14] Xinhua network. The circular from General Office of the Communist Party of China Central Committee and the General Office of the State Council, to prohibit Party and government officials from smoking in public in order to set an example for all to follow 29 Dec 2013, Beijing. http://news.xinhuanet.com/politics/2013-12/29/c_118753701.htm.

[15] Xi Jinping' important speech at the National Health Conference has been received with undiluted enthusiasm, People's Daily, Aug. 22, 2016 http://cpc.people.com.cn/n1/2016/0822/c64387-28653423.html.

tries, as appropriate").[16,17] It was pointed out that tobacco control was related to a number of Sustainable Development Goals and targets. Chinese government should include implementation of WHO FCTC (the SDG Targets 3.4 and 3A) as one of assessment indicators on government performance.

14.3.2   To Eliminate the Obstruction of Tobacco Control in the Tobacco Control Steering Committee

The book details the actions of the Steering Committee, led by the MIIT over the past 10 years, and makes it clear that the Steering Committee has failed to undertake its responsibilities on tobacco control. To fully carry out implementation of WHO FCTC, in accordance with the current institutional reform plan of the State Council: (1) the Steering Committee should be re-set as following: National Health Committee takes the lead and MOF and MFA take the depute head. The members of the New Steering Committee may be included Ministry of Education, Ministry of Justice, Ministry of Transport, Ministry of culture and Tourism, General Administration of Customs, State General Administration of Market Supervision and Management, and State General Administration of Radio and Television. The new Steering Committee has to strengthen the construction of the enforcement mechanism and make clear the responsibility of every member ministry and binding mechanism. (3) The new Steering Committee is in charge of formulation of the national tobacco control plan, determines the overall objectives and specific quantitative binding indicators, and supervises the implementation. (4) STMA should be removed from having any responsibility for tobacco control policy, and monitored by the Committee. By March 2018, the 13th National people's Congress (NPC) had reviewed the reform plan of the State Council, which proposed the establishment of the National Health Commission. The responsibility of implementation of WHO FCTC is entrusted to this department from MIIT, which will be an opportunity to eliminate tobacco enterprises' intervention to tobacco control.

---

[16] Sustainable Development Goal 3: ensure healthy lives and promote well-being for all at all ages. In: Sustainable development knowledge platform [website]. New York: United Nations; 2017 (https://sustainabledevelopment.un.org/sdg3, accessed 25 June 2017).

[17] Decision: contribution of the Conference of the Parties to achieving the non-communicable disease global target on the reduction of tobacco use. Geneva: Conference of the Parties to the WHO Framework Convention on Tobacco Control, Seventh Session; 2016 (FCTC/COP7(27); http://www.who.int/fctc/cop/cop7/FCTC_COP7(27)_EN.pdf, accessed 25 June2017).

14.3.3 The National Smoke-Free Law Should Be Adopted as Soon as Possible

The adoption of a strong, comprehensive national smoke-free law is a crucial step for tobacco control in China so as to ensure 100% smoke-free in indoor public and working places. The time has come for a strong national law, fully compliant with Article 8 of the WHO FCTC based on the success of Beijing and other cities covered one tenth of population in China. The State Council's 2014 draft of national smoke-free regulations has been delayed for more than 3 years owing to pullback by STMA. The government should be adopted and implemented in full, without exemptions or loopholes, and without any further delay.

14.3.4 To Regularly Issue the National Plan of Tobacco Control

By the end of 2017 when this book is completed, China has not published it tobacco control plan for 2016–2020, and the goals of National Plan of Tobacco Control 2012–2015 (Smoking prevalence in adolescent from 11.5% in 2010 to below 8.5%, and smoking prevalence in adults from 28.1% to below 25%) have not reached either. The Steering Committee have not provided any reasons and not been held accountable. Accordingly, China should formulate and issue the periodical national plan of tobacco control 2016–2020 as soon as possible on implement a comprehensive package of tobacco demand-reduction measures. There was no progress introduction of graphic warnings on the harms of tobacco use covering at least 50% of tobacco packages and tobacco product regulation since the last national plan started. The progress of expanding support for current smokers to quit -including the quit service into primary health service and national health insurance schemes was slow. So was continuing to increase the tax and price of tobacco products; a comprehensive ban on TAPS on the Advertising Law efficient since September 2015. Scaled-up roll-out of sustained mass media campaigns on the dangers of tobacco use was under expectation.

14.3.5 To Strength Public Education and Place the Pictorial Warning on the Cigarette Package

The tobacco control campaign should more closely work with those departments related to public education, such as CCP Publicity Department, The Ministry of Education, the State Administration of Radio, Film and Television, and, so on. These departments should be more actively involve or support the tobacco control campaigns in their general public education. A top priority of the campaign should be to target doctors and other health professionals as well as medical students effectively. Second, tobacco control should focus on the most cost-benefit public education measures, having pictorial warning labels on the cigarette packages. Obstacle coming from STMA should be removed since STMA is against having the pictorial warning on the cigarette package in China.

14.3.6 To Regularly Monitor, Evaluate and Report Progress of Tobacco Control Policy Implement

A set of effective indicators has been developed to measure and assess the progress of implementation of tobacco control policies based of tobacco use surveillance. Goals of tobacco control and the indicators used to measure tobacco control must be integrated into index of social and economic development plans and regular progress report including progress on increasing tax and price of tobacco product, and comprehensive banning TAPS.

14.3.7 To Strengthen Capacity Building and Ensure Financial Support of Tobacco Control

For sustainability of tobacco control, China should strengthen capacity building, built the mechanism of special fund of tobacco control, and increase routing financial investment. It is also necessary to encourage social finds to support tobacco control. On the basis of raising the tax rate and price of tobacco products, the part of the increasing revenue should be reinvested in primary medical service and public health, especially tobacco control.

14.3.8 To Build the Coalition of Tobacco Control

China's tobacco control campaign has effectively promoted legislation on tobacco control, but it also need to be expanded to more social organizations such as Party school at national and provincial levels, the Central Culture Office, the All China Women's Federation, the Chinese Communist Youth League, the All-China Federation of Trade Unions, and the large enterprise groups except tobacco industry. In contract, tobacco company/factories often considers adolescent, women, industrial workers, and PLA these important groups as their target groups. Building a strong coalition with these important constituencies will likely make a big difference in the battle against the tobacco epidemic.

The WHO FCTC is a powerful weapon to deal with the global tobacco epidemic. Unprecedented progress of the Convention in most Parties shows that the battle against the tobacco epidemic will be winnable. If China cannot response the challenge of tobacco epidemic, it is hard to really achieve the green and sustainable development in the future.